If You Never Quit,

You'll Never Fail!

If You Never Quit, You'll Never Fail!

Memoir of a Young Entrepreneur

By Jeff Bowling

Library of Congress Control Number: 2007923645

ISBN: 978-0-9790237-0-5

Editor: Michael Sion

Page Design: www.meshcreative.com

Published by: Bowling Ventures, LLC.

Printer: Sheridan Books, Chelsea, Michigan

Published in the United States of America

CONTENTS

CONTENTS

CONTENTS

For all the dreamers who never quit.

And for all the naysayers who motivate the dreamers.

ACKNOWLEDGMENTS

Sometimes the people who have helped you go the furthest are not the ones who get the most credit. This is for them.

My mom has always been my biggest supporter. If she would have listened to the doctors and quit, I would have never been. She trusted her heart and sacrificed everything for me. No matter what I did or got myself into, she was there. Without her guidance, I may have slipped by the roadside. Mom, I am proud of all the sacrifices you made to better my life. You had to be the mother and father. I know you gave up a few dreams. I hope now I can help you pursue them.

I met a man who forever changed my life, Al Havelka. He flowed with compassion, strength and honesty. I was only graced with his presence for a few years until he passed away. Not a day goes by that I don't hear his voice or see him in his son. Al — Bruce and I are doing well. I hope we have honored you and made you proud. We love you and have missed you every day since you left.

My mom always said that in life, if you can truly count your friends on one hand, you are lucky. I am truly blessed because I have a few like this.

Back in 1984 I meet a skinny shy kid in school named Bruce Havelka. He played hockey with us and was into hunting and fishing. We also played soccer together. He is my best friend and brother for life. We have experienced the good and the bad together. Bruce, you taught me not only to hunt but the appreciation of the hunt taught to you by your father. You gave me a place to sleep when I had none. You allowed me into your family and shared your spot at the table. I will always be here for you as you have been for me. I am proud of the man you have become and know that you have made your mother and father happy.

I'd just got out of the Army when I met John McClain. John, Bruce, and I hit it off instantly. Since then, Bruce and I accepted John as our brother. I want to thank you, John, for giving me a place to live and supporting me. You and your family have made a lasting impact in my life. I am proud of you for having compassion and helping others who are less fortunate.

I had no idea that I would meet my future wife on a blind date. If I did not take the chance, I never would have the completion in my life that I have now. My wife, Tanya, is as strong as they come. She is a phenomenal mother, wife and friend. She stole a piece of my heart when we first met and has never given it back. I have never met a woman whom I was so passionate about and in love with. Tanya, I count my lucky stars every day that I wake up next to you. I am honored to spend the rest of my life with you. You made a good choice in a husband, and a friend. I will prove it to you every day for the rest of our lives.

Last but not least, I need to thank my original partner in crime. One who has never left the team but made it difficult to be on at times, especially when she was a teenager. I am talking about the girl who taught me to burp, my sister, Jennifer. Since I was born she has been around telling me what to do (literally). Jennifer, I love you very much. I am also very proud of you whether you hear it enough or not. I have not forgotten that I still owe you a trip to Hawaii for introducing me to my wife. Whenever you are ready to collect, I am ready to go.

AUTHOR'S NOTE

The title, *If You Never Quit, You'll Never Fail!*, comes from a phrase I coined as a child. The power of perseverance was a lesson driven home to me a number of times — but never more amazingly than when I was 12, staying with some friends of my mother — in Lake Havasu, Arizona.

Mom was raising my sister and me as a single parent. She had friends in Arizona who had recreation toys I'd never seen before: jet skis. Since I loved speed — whether on my bicycle or skateboard — I just had to get out on the water and zoom around on one of those babies.

So there I was one morning, kneeling on the platform of a jet ski, tingling with excitement. These crafts were fairly new on the market; they weren't popular yet. They were a mystery, including how to get them started. I got the engine going and puttering. I rose from my knees and began raising the handle pole. But before I could reach a standing position and press the thumb throttle to give it gas, I fell off.

I pulled myself out of the water and back onto my knees on the platform. I tried standing again. This time, the engine died.

It became a cruel joke! Again and again I gingerly started the engine and carefully tried to stand and get the jet ski to take off. But either I'd end up in the water — or the engine would sputter and quit.

It was maddening!

I soon grew tired and frustrated. More than that, I was furious. The machine was vibrating under me as if mocking me, daring me to spring it into action. After a couple more failures, I was ready to give up and swim away, leaving the damn thing bobbing in the water. I was exasperated and exhausted.

Then a desperate thought:

Screw it, I'm going to give this thing full throttle and just hang on by the seat of my pants and see what happens.

I pushed up from my knees and lifted the pole. I pressed the throttle hard, gunning the engine. Instantly, the ski balanced out. It lurched forward, shooting up out of the water. I gripped the handles to hold on. The machine was alive and rumbling under my bare feet. Euphoria!

At that moment, the mechanics became clear. You have to give it gas so the ski will plane.

After that day, you couldn't get me off a jet ski. It became one of my great passions. Today I own five. Had I quit that day when I was 12, I never would have had this exhilarating hobby. Or absorbed an essential truth about life:

So many people quit at the start of something, when the going is rough. Or even when they're on the verge of success, but don't know it! If only they would stick it out just a little longer . . . and give their quest an extra spurt of energy. They'd make it!

MY MAIN REASON FOR writing this book — the story of my life so far — is to pass on the enduring lessons I've learned, particularly those that apply to business. I'm especially interested in inspiring fellow entrepreneurs or would-be entrepreneurs. That's why I've added the subtitle: *Memoir of a Young Entrepreneur.*

If I can empower kindred spirits, I will consider writing this book time well spent. And the biggest lesson I wish to convey to readers is to keep on pushing toward your goals, instead of doing what most people end up doing — giving in to failure.

I could have quit pursuing my own goals many times in my life. But I didn't. Today, my corporate biography identifies me as president and CEO of TELXAR Corporation — a premier information-technology firm that specializes in services for security-conscious corporations and individuals. We have clients worldwide. And TELXAR is only in its early stages. I'm still building the company into what I hope will be a global powerhouse.

But TELXAR wasn't my first business. It was my fourth. And it never would have gotten going, much less survived, had I not practiced what I preach: If you never quit, you'll never fail!

I REALIZE IT'S NOT typical for a 35-year-old to be writing an autobiography. When a business executive authors a book describing his life and career, he's either retired or has reached a professional pinnacle from which he can look down upon the road traveled, to share his wisdom with readers hungry for the keys to success. Think of Donald Trump, Richard Branson or the late Sam Walton. Titans of industry. World famous. Wealthy, powerful and visionary.

I, in contrast, am still fully absorbed in all the aspects of running and building my young company, with many more years lying ahead for TELXAR to attain its potential of earnings, market share and size.

But a big part of what makes this autobiography so different from the others is precisely that it is written by someone still very much in the trenches, fighting the daily battles, campaigning toward ultimate victory in the business world. Just like many of you readers.

In my book I describe situations that other young entrepreneurs will be able to relate to and identify with. My defeats and victories, prodigious plays and moronic missteps should prove valuable from that perspective. The decision making I undertook, the secrets I discovered — I share them in the following chapters. I'm hoping they will prove instructive and helpful.

I STARTED THIS AUTHOR'S note with an example to underscore the rule: If you never quit, you'll never fail! Let me add a corollary:

Never fear failure.

You don't succeed in the business world — or life — without experiencing setbacks. You don't learn without defeats.

In this world — when it comes to running your own business — your race, ethnicity, gender, education level, wealth or family connections ultimately don't matter. What matters is having a good idea, an unwavering focus — and the energy and commitment to stick with your enterprise through the ups and downs.

To never quit.

When readers see the challenges I faced in my childhood, they should realize they have few if any real excuses not to take the plunge themselves in pursuing their own dreams.

Bluntly put, I hope this book pushes readers to get off their butts and get going! Take a chance on creating the life you want.

Be tenacious.

Give it full throttle — and see what happens.

CHAPTER ONE: Escapes

Mom tells a story of when I was just past a year old. I was a happy, energetic infant who loved rocking, bouncing and jumping in my crib. One day, as she was leaving the house, I came walking into the living room holding a bar from the crib. I'd made my escape. I followed her into the yard, climbed into my wading pool and splashed around, mimicking swimming, grinning ear to ear.

And that was the pattern that was set: I was always exploring, getting in the middle of things, pushing the envelope.

That probably explains my first memory.

I'm 2, standing in a yard that is immense, like a park. I'm helping a gray-haired lady: "Gramsie," Mom's grandmother. Gramsie is swinging a golf club — *whish, click* — practicing her driving. I'm teeing up the balls for her, being a big boy.

Gramsie smacks a ball. I grab another from the bucket and set it carefully on the tee. These little dimpled balls are like eggs, only harder and perfectly round. She swings again. I tee up another ball.

I turn away to look at something. I hear the *whish*. I pick up a ball from the bucket and move forward. *Something is wrong.* A ball already is on the tee. I turn to look at Gramsie . . .

Wham!

The next thing I remember is Mom, blood soaking her white T-shirt, cradling my head against her blue-jean cutoffs as she drives me to the emergency room at Kaiser Hospital in Fontana, California. It's a 20-minute drive from Gramsie's home in Colton in San Bernardino County, east of Los Angeles.

Mom presses a cloth against my left eye as she steers with her other hand, so the blood won't gush so quickly. Blindness is spreading over the eye as I stare out the window at the palm trees racing past. The blindness is from the blood.

Mom carries me into the hospital. We both are frightened. I'm admitted right away. A doctor and nurse wrap me up in something they call a "mummy bag." Then they tell Mom to leave the room. They say I'll do better with her waiting outside. They push her out.

The doctor is rough. I'm not used to men. He and the nurse keep me from moving my head as he stitches up my face with a needle.

"This isn't that bad," he says.

"Don't be a sissy," the nurse says.

The needle scrapes against the bone. The sound vibrates. Somewhere out in the hospital I hear a child hollering that he's hurt.

Mom tells me later the screams were mine. They'd sounded like a wounded animal.

The doctor tells her how lucky I am.

"If the golf club had hit an eighth of an inch closer to his eye, he would have lost it . . ."

I SAID I WASN'T used to men when I was little. That's because my father wasn't around. He's a complete blank in my earliest memories.

Andy Bowling, so I'm told, had made up his mind while Mom was carrying me that he didn't want to be a husband or father anymore. He and Mom had married young. She'd been in her late teens, he in his early twenties. He was an enlisted man in the Air Force — I don't know what rank, just like I know little else about his past — and had just returned from a tour of duty in Vietnam when Mom got pregnant with me. It worried her. Since giving birth to my sister, Jennifer, a couple years before, Mom had suffered three miscarriages.

Andy Bowling was transferred from Hawaii to Travis Air Force Base in Northern California. Mom sought extra attention from the medical staff at Travis. She saw an obstetrician every two weeks. She, Andy and Jennifer were on vacation in Southern California when Mom started bleeding. A physician told her that her body was aborting the fetus. He advised her to go to nearby Norton AFB for a "procedure." Fortunately for me, Mom got a second opinion. This doctor gave her an injection "to hold things," ordered Mom to bed rest and said to not lift anything heavier than a gallon container of milk.

Mom was green with nausea much of the time. At six months she went through false labor. Then Andy Bowling dropped a bombshell: He said he couldn't take it anymore. Marriage was too difficult.

Mom made it to term without his support. She went into labor on a late-winter Friday evening while taking a walk with my sister and a neighbor. Andy Bowling drove Mom to the hospital at Travis. Forty-five minutes after she was prepped in the labor room, I came into the world, at 12:07 a.m.,

Feb. 12, 1972, healthy and strong, with all my fingers and toes. Andy Bowling was still completing the admitting paperwork while I drew my first breaths outside the womb.

He and Mom officially separated when I was 2. The divorce was final by the time I was 4. I've seen the man only a handful of times since.

I can say that the most he ever left me was his Irish surname.

CHAPTER TWO: You Ain't Poor if You Don't Know It

What Andy Bowling left Mom was the burden of raising two children by herself with slim opportunity to earn a decent wage.

It wasn't a very promising start in this world for me. But if you have to be poor in life, it's best it happens at the front end, when you're not aware of your situation.

Mom was determined to give her children the best life possible. She was a fighter. And a looker. The pinup queen of the 1970s was Farrah Fawcett, with her feathered blond locks and slender figure in a red, one-piece swimsuit. Mom bore a fair resemblance to Farrah.

As a young woman, Karen Wilkinson had no problem drawing attention from the guys in San Bernardino, California, where she grew up. She'd matured quickly in more ways than one. She'd raised her younger sister and brother since her own mother — my grandmother, whom we called Nana — was a divorced, working single mother before that was common, back in the 1950s. Nana was hardheaded; but the man she'd married, Herschel Wilkinson, was a piece of work himself (as I would find out years later, after we moved in with him). Grandpa Herschel was a brawling, drinking, womanizing cowboy out of California by way of the Oklahoma Dust Bowl: a man with an eighth-grade education who ended up using a combination of brains, balls and bullsh*t to make himself a success in business. By the time I got to know him, he owned whiskey joints in Reno, Nevada. Before that, he'd managed country musicians in Las Vegas, customized recreational vehicles, and even learned the jewelry trade.

Grandpa Herschel had never been around to be a father to his children, and so my Mom, the oldest of three, had gotten plenty of on-the-job parenting experience. Then she'd met Andy Bowling while visiting friends at Norton Air Force Base, where he was stationed. Andy was a tall, broad-shouldered, red-haired, brooding Irishman.

In America in the early 1970s, being a young, single mother still wasn't usual. To make it even tougher, when Mom and Andy separated, she was very ill and eventually required surgery. For practically a year she was too sick to get a job.

It was back to San Bernardino that Mom moved my sister and me. Nana, my Aunt Denise and Uncle Mark still lived there. Nana or Aunt Denise could help watch Jennifer and me during the day. "San Berdoo" seemed the logical place to go.

THE FIRST HOME I remember was the small apartment that Mom moved the three of us into. It was a comfortable place: a second-story, two-bedroom apartment.

I didn't know it, but where we had moved to was low-income housing. The neighborhood was a mix of races. We weren't allowed to play outside after sunset, but Jennifer and I didn't understand the concept of "poor." We had nothing to compare it to. That's why we didn't think it anything out of the ordinary if Mom didn't put much dinner on her plate so that there was more for Jennifer and me. Sometimes when the regular milk was low, we mixed up powdered milk. We figured it was normal that to get a drink of milk you had to stir powder and water in a glass.

Jennifer, being older, was sort of bossy. She had blond hair with bangs and a wedge cut in back. I had blond curly hair and a gap in my front teeth. She told me I was goofy looking. We shared a bedroom. I was in the top bunk. We also shared a wooden toy box. The box was an heirloom, passed down from a great-grandparent. It had originally been a luggage rack bolted onto a Model T Ford. Mom had painted the box yellow and lined it with quilted material.

Jennifer had her dolls and other girl toys in the box. My favorite toy was my Evel Knievel Motorcycle. I felt a special connection to it. The real-life Evel Knievel was a stunt rider. He jumped buses and river gorges. He was crazy. He didn't care about wiping out. He always survived. So did my Evel Knievel toy, which I sent off on stunt after stunt in my bedroom or the living room.

The Evel Knievel Motorcycle was a plastic action figure in a white motorcycle suit and helmet, sitting on a miniature motorcycle that was launched from a pad. I cranked the starter on the power launcher, and the rear wheel spun; I lowered the wheel and the cycle took off. Sometimes I flipped a handle on the rear seat and the bike popped wheelies. Sometimes I bent the arms up and put him upside-down on the bike to ride it in a handstand.

There usually was a big accident at the end. Evel Knievel could be thrown far off the bike — landing behind the sofa, smacking against a wall. I loved making him go as fast and wild as possible. I loved speed.

I loved pretending it was *me* on that motorcycle.

MY UNCLE MARK REALLY was a biker. He'd roar up on his Harley Davidson now and then, the engine chugging. Uncle Mark blew in and out of our lives. He seemed somewhere between a teenager and an adult. He smelled like mechanic's grease and fumes. He pretended he didn't like kids.

"Uncle Mark, I love you," I'd say.

"Well, I don't like *you.*"

Uncle Mark had a tattoo of Snoopy. I thought that was cool. Someone tough, like him, having Charlie Brown's beagle on his arm.

Uncle Mark drove a delivery truck for a produce company. Once in a while he'd swing by the apartment and Jennifer and I would climb in the truck and take cartons of fresh strawberries and heads of lettuce — whatever we wanted.

"Now get lost," he'd say.

Sometimes, Uncle Mark would show up with a longhaired woman. Usually, it was a different one every time. Uncle Mark always had women around him. He used to hang out with members of the pro drag-racing crews; he also helped build dragsters for top professionals. And he ran with members of the Hell's Angels. There was a large Angels chapter in San Berdoo. But Uncle Mark wasn't a member; he was a loner, a roamer, a real free-flowin' guy. Think of the Peter Fonda character in the 1969 movie *Easy Rider.* That's the kind of guy Uncle Mark was.

But I didn't grasp any of that at my tender age. Mine was the innocent world of the small child oblivious to adult matters. I didn't know that I was very short for my age. I didn't know that Mom, Jennifer and I were "disadvantaged." I didn't know that we lived in a poor neighborhood that today qualifies as a "ghetto." I didn't know that Nana, who was stern and unsmiling, could have given Mom money to make our lives easier, but never did, because she was from the tough-love school.

What I did know was that life was happy in the Bowling apartment. We seemed to have everything we needed. But there were always a few things I really wanted that we couldn't afford. Like one of those Huffy bicycles I saw kids riding on TV commercials. Man, how I longed for a Huffy!

I was Evel Knievel without wheels.

CHAPTER THREE: Threat of Pills; Bicycle Thrills

On the first day of kindergarten, at Newmark Elementary School on North Third Avenue, I was wearing a new yellow shirt with a white motorcycle on it, and blue Levi's. We pulled up to the curb in Mom's old blue Volkswagen Beetle and I put on my little backpack with the motorcycle motif.

I liked my teacher, Ms. Williams. She was very tall, extremely kind and patient. But class time was weird. It felt really, really slow. The kids seemed backward. In the restroom, there was pee on the toilet seats and floor. These kids hadn't gotten this simple act down yet. And that wasn't all. The surprises those first few days came one after another.

Mom always read to Jennifer and me, even when we were very small, sitting us on her lap with a book spread open. I knew the alphabet but the other kids with me in kindergarten were still learning the days of the week, how to count to 10, their colors. *How could they not know their colors?*

I also couldn't figure out how they could sit still for such long periods of time as Ms. Williams patiently explained lessons or talked about something or other. It was all so slow! My mind wandered. I fidgeted. I'd talk to my neighbors. I'd get up from my chair and walk around.

Ms. Williams didn't like that. She told me I was "disruptive." She'd send me to the chair in the corner. But I couldn't help myself.

Finally, she suggested to Mom that I be tested by the school district. The test revealed I was somewhat above the norm in intelligence. This partly explained why it was difficult for me to settle down in class. I was bored. But I was no candidate to be pushed up a grade. I was very small for my age, and still learning how to socialize.

The problem, it was decided, was that I was hyperactive. A counselor suggested I be put on Ritalin. As I sat next to Mom in the man's office, I could see she wasn't happy.

"What they want to do, Jeff, is put you on a drug."

"What's a drug?"

"It's pills. They want me to give you pills."

Taking pills to make me act differently didn't seem right to me.

As we drove home, Mom said, "We're going to find a natural way to help you."

She scheduled a "conference" with Ms. Williams. After school, Mom sat with my teacher at the front desk. I sat in my regular seat.

"What foods is Jeff eating?" Ms. Williams asked.

I lost interest in their discussion. My mind wandered. They talked for a long time.

"Jeff," Mom said, "come on up and sit with us." I did.

"We're going to make some changes to slow you down and help you focus more."

From now on, Mom explained, I couldn't have candy. That sounded bad to me! But I knew how serious the situation was. I didn't protest.

I also couldn't eat anything containing red or blue food coloring. I couldn't use toothpaste, either. That part sounded good.

"I don't have to brush anymore?"

Jennifer would be jealous.

"No," Mom said, "I'm going to make you a special kind of toothpaste."

That special kind of toothpaste turned out to be baking soda and salt. I couldn't have anything sweet anymore, except for fruit or sugarless gum.

Mom said there was another change I had to make if I wanted to remain in school without taking pills: I had to work harder on focusing on one thing at a time instead of having my attention wander.

I told her I'd do it. I wanted to avoid having to take pills. It sounded horrible. Focusing would be easier.

With that motivation, I figured out my own method of handling my roaming mind. Whenever I was sent to the chair in the corner, I'd purposely occupy myself with one of the easy-reading books from the shelf — memorizing lines ("See Spot run"), training myself to concentrate, working to block everything else out but the task at hand.

I got better at it. My focus improved. The subject of "pills" went away.

MOM GOT BETTER AFTER surgery. She took nursing classes and got hired at Loma Linda Hospital. There, she met a plastic surgeon who took her on as an assistant for his practice. It was an even better job. We now had cartons of fresh milk in the refrigerator all the time.

That December, the plastic surgeon gave Mom a bonus. When Nana brought us home one evening after baby-sitting us, Mom blindfolded my sister and me outside the door. Then she led us inside. The lights were off to make it even darker.

"What do you smell?" she asked. We could smell the pine scent of the Christmas tree. We held our hands in front of us and tried to head toward it. I stumbled around the room until I finally felt the pine needles. I was there.

Mom flipped on the lights. She told us to take off the blindfolds. We decorated the tree.

On Christmas Day there was a big surprise under the tree: a box containing a black Huffy bicycle. Nana and my Aunt Denise probably had chipped in so Mom could afford it. I didn't think about that, though. The only thought I had at that moment was to get on that sucker and ride it.

Aunt Denise's boyfriend, Jim, showed up and helped Mom put the bike together. But it was way too large for me. I couldn't straddle it and also have my feet reach the ground. It was all I could do to get them on the pedals, with Mom holding the bike to keep it from tilting. I understood that the large size was by design, so that Mom wouldn't have to buy me another bike until this one had gotten too small. But I wasn't about to let its size keep me off it.

I wrestled the bike down the stairs and out to the street. It was heavy, solid, shiny. It felt like magic. I stood up on the curb, holding the handlebars, pushed off on one leg and swung the other over the bar as I hopped onto the seat. I felt powerful for an instant — then the bike toppled over.

The crash didn't hurt. I was excited. I pulled myself up, and then the bike, and was back at the curb for another try.

I finally managed to push a pedal down and sustain forward momentum. Now I was coasting, the wheels turning. Then I was pushing a pedal back to brake. Mom came out to help me, and I got the pedals working, and then I was steering.

By the next day I was zipping around. The major problem was dismounting. I had to be fast enough, after braking to a stop, to hop free from the seat before the bike collapsed.

I was up to the challenge. I knew I had the daredevil in me. Pretty soon, the other kids in the neighborhood knew it, too.

Before long I was the kid on the block who was always being dared, because the other kids knew I couldn't resist. They'd set up wood ramps on the sidewalk then come to my door because they knew Jeff was a willing stuntman. So was Cory, a girl my age who lived in the apartment below me. She and I were the guinea pigs.

Cory was a tomboy. She wore as many Band-aids as us boys. She and I played together a lot, not even aware of the difference in our sexes. Cory had wanted a bicycle as badly as I had. She wanted to skateboard and roller-skate as badly as I did. We'd see the other kids on the block doing these things. We couldn't wait until we were old enough, or until our parents could buy us skates.

But now Cory, like me, had gotten a bike. And, like me, she quickly fell in love with catching air. She'd hit those ramps as hard as I would. We were partners in crime. There was something about us that was more reckless than the other kids. Something inside of us. If we wrecked on our bikes, then the other kids knew they needed to make the ramp lower.

The other kids had things we didn't. They had grip attachments on their handlebars that ran on a battery and could make a kick-start or motorcycle sound when you pushed the buttons. Cory's mother and mine couldn't afford stuff like that. But one day, Cory said to me, "I know how to make that sound." She fixed a playing card in the spokes of her bike. The mad flapping did the trick. I copied her.

Whenever Cory or I were called out to take a test run on a new ramp, we weren't even thinking about the outcome — whether we'd land safely. We just wanted to experience the jump, the thrill in the stomach and throat. Catching air was all we wanted to do. It was worth the scrapes and bruises from a wipeout.

I felt like I was that Evel Knievel action figure on the stunt motorcycle.

IT WAS IN FIRST grade that I discovered ways I was different from most other kids.

The first thing was that all the other kids were writing with their right hands. So I decided I was using the wrong hand. It felt funny holding a pencil in my right hand, but I forced myself to do it. If they could do it, I could do it. After a while it didn't feel funny anymore.

The second thing I discovered was that my sister and I didn't have all the nice things most of the other kids did, without even knowing how lucky they were.

The first week of lunchtime, I was shocked to see my classmates open their metal pails and take out things I'd never seen: Twinkies, Ho Hos, Ding Dongs, in shiny wrappers. These kids also had real meat in their sandwiches. When

Mom didn't have lunchmeat, she'd spread a light coat of butter and sprinkle a touch of sugar on bread to make our sandwiches.

Some of the kids let me sample little pieces of their Hostess goodies. By now I'd pretty much lost my taste for sweets. I didn't like the white filling, the soft sweet cake, the chocolate coating. I knew I wasn't missing anything. Potato chips, though — would've been nice to have a little bag of those in my lunchbox. Or the soup the others had in their thermoses. I'd thought thermoses were just for carrying your drink in. I had water in mine.

Most of the kids had dogs or cats at home — and sometimes both. We had no pets at our apartment. The other kids had new clothes. Mom ironed patches over the holes in my jeans. I didn't mind the patches. What I minded was that my pants were hand-me-downs from my sister.

I had an inkling, now, that we weren't as well off as other families. But it didn't bother me much. It wasn't like we never had nice items show up in our lives. There was that Huffy bicycle I'd gotten for Christmas, oversized as it was.

A third thing I discovered that made me different was that I liked dressing up as a businessman.

Mom had bought me a three-piece, maroon leisure suit to wear to church or special occasions, such as Aunt Denise's wedding. Some of my classmates were in the Cub Scouts and wore their uniforms to school on Tuesdays or Wednesdays. I decided that Friday would be my day to come to school in my "spiffy clothes." Uncle Jim, who by now had married Aunt Denise, had given me an old briefcase he didn't use anymore. That completed my outfit.

At first the other students were confused by my suit and briefcase. But they got used to it. They understood that on Friday, that's how Jeff came to school. They liked it. It became a class custom.

There is no easy explanation for why I wanted to be a businessman. I must have just been born with a predisposition, the way a natural athlete will pick up a ball or a natural musician will gravitate to a guitar. Often there is no accounting for any outside influence.

CHAPTER FOUR: Evil around Every Corner

Mom was going out on dates on the weekends. These guys dressed up: maybe a brown-leather jacket with a triangular collar, a colorful shirt with several buttons undone at the top, and a puka-shell necklace. They looked spiffy.

One Saturday afternoon, Mom told us we were going for a drive. "I want you to meet someone."

We got into the VW and drove out to the Highland area. Mom said we were going to meet "Fritz," and that he was very nice. I hadn't heard her mention that name before. I didn't make much of it. I figured he was just another of her friends.

Mom drove like she knew the way. We ended up in a nice neighborhood. She turned onto a street that was next to the drive-in movie theater and pulled up to the curb.

The house was set back from the street. A long driveway led down to it. There was a smaller guesthouse closer to the street and between it and the main house was a giant open court of concrete. Down at the end of the driveway, in the garage, two men were working under the hood of a car.

"There's Fritz," Mom said.

One of the men moved away from the engine and waved at us. He walked up the driveway. He was wearing a white T-shirt and blue jeans. As he got close, I saw his face was round and fleshy. He had sandy blond hair cut in a bowl and parted down the middle. He was obviously just some friend of Mom, not a boyfriend. He wasn't good-looking like the men who'd shown up to take her out on dates. He didn't look like much.

"Let's get out," Mom said.

She introduced us. We shook hands.

"I'm going to run a few errands," Mom said. "You hang out here."

That was unexpected. Jennifer and I watched her drive off.

Fritz stared at us for a long moment. It was awkward. He seemed like he wasn't used to children.

Then he piped up: "Hey, do you guys know what a pool table is?"

We shook our heads.

I had a fleeting image of a swim pool with a table in it.

"Follow me."

We followed Fritz through the garage, past the other man standing at the Corvette with the hood propped open, and into the house. Fritz led us into a big room. In the middle sat a large rectangular table with a green felt top. Hard, shiny little balls were scattered around it. They were different colors and had numbers.

Fritz reached onto the table and rolled a ball off the cushioned bank.

"Just use your hands to smack the balls around into the holes," he said. "But don't climb on the table or anything, and don't use the cues." He pointed at some long brown sticks on a rack on the wall.

"Can I trust you guys?"

We nodded.

"OK, I'm going to trust you. I'm going to be out in the garage."

He smiled for a second. And then he left.

Jennifer and I messed around with the pool balls. They were hard and cold. We couldn't see very high over the table, but it was fun rolling the balls against each other — *click, roll* — and seeing if we could knock them into the holes along the banks. It was harder than it looked. We took turns.

Something across the room caught my eye. An enormous wooden globe rested on a stand. I went over and gave it a spin. It was heavy. It rotated slowly. Then I realized it was meant to be opened. I ran my hands over it and figured out how to swing the halves apart on hinges. Inside were bottles and glasses on red felt. The globe had turned into a little bar. That was pretty cool.

Mom's friend had an interesting house.

By the time she returned, we were tired of the pool table. We went outside. Fritz and the other man were still working in the garage.

Mom spoke to him a few moments. Then we followed her to the car. We waved goodbye.

"See ya later," he called out. He ducked back over the engine.

We drove away.

"Did you have fun playing pool?" Mom asked.

We said we did.

"What do you think about Fritz?"

We looked at each other and shrugged.

A FEW WEEKS LATER, Mom announced she had some "exciting news." She and Fritz were getting married. We'd be moving out of the apartment and into his place. Jennifer and I would each have our very own bedroom. We'd make new friends.

My sister and I were dumbstruck. But there wasn't much time for the shock to settle in. We had to start packing.

Mom brought home large cardboard boxes and we wrapped the dishes in old newspaper and stashed our clothes and books and just about everything else in the boxes.

"Why are we moving?" I asked Jennifer.

"Mom fell in love."

"I thought she loved *us*."

"She does. It's different with a man."

Jennifer was older and understood things I didn't. Or pretended to.

The day the moving van came and parked on the curb below our apartment, I took my last bike ride around the complex. I said goodbye to Cory downstairs. I said I'd come back to visit. But I knew we'd be living too far away.

I rode past the Dumpsters and the swim pool area and the parking lots — all the familiar sites. It felt funny thinking that this would be my last time there. It didn't seem real.

For the hundredth time I thought, *Maybe Mom will change her mind.*

I spotted something out of place on a roof of one of the apartments. Some green plants were sitting up there. I pedaled up to the building and parked my bike. I climbed up the bricks on the wall and pulled myself onto the roof.

The plants had long slender, pointed leaves. I grabbed a planter's pot and eased myself down. I rode back to our apartment, cradling the pot carefully.

"Mom, I got us a plant for our new place."

She held it up and studied it. The two movers started laughing.

"Where'd you find that?" one asked.

Mom didn't look happy. "Do you know what that is?" she asked.

"Yeah, I know what that is," he said.

"You need to take that right back to where you found it!" Mom said to me. "We wouldn't want that kind of plant at our home."

I took it back to the roof of the building. It had seemed like a nice, healthy plant to me.

Adults were hard to figure out.

THE WEDDING WAS IN a park-like garden. There were lily pads with frogs. Jennifer was the flower girl. I was the ring bearer. We wore our spiffy clothes.

The ceremony took forever, in front of a bunch of strangers. Some of our family was there, too. Nana, Aunt Denise, Uncle Jim, Uncle Mark and one of his girlfriends.

Finally she and Fritz kissed and the ceremony was over.

AT FIRST, AFTER WE moved into Fritz's place, I wondered if he and I would hang out together, maybe throw a ball around. That's what dads did — even step-dads. I kept waiting for him to say something, or to knock on my bedroom door, holding a football or Frisbee. I had a bit of anticipation.

But each day went by and nothing happened. He didn't mention a word about hanging out together. Then I considered that maybe it was taking him some time getting used to Jennifer and me, just like we were getting used to all the attention he was getting from Mom. He still seemed uncomfortable around us. He didn't ask us to call him "dad." We called him by his name, and he called us by our names.

It was still summer vacation from school, and Fritz wasn't around the house that often. He was either at work at the Air Force base, or he was off somewhere, or he was out in the garage working on his cars. Maybe we'd see him in the morning at breakfast, or we'd see him when we ate dinner.

Fritz was a few years older than Mom. He was an enlisted man in the Air Force. He did something with "supplies." He had a bit of money saved. That's why he could afford a nice house, and a couple Corvettes, a Chevrolet truck and a couple motorcycles, too. Mom occasionally drove one of the Corvettes. We had plenty of food in the refrigerator, including real milk.

After the apartment, the house was awesome. There was so much space. We had a back yard — a place to play around in by ourselves. There was that big open concrete court between the house and guesthouse that was just the perfect place to roller-skate or skateboard. I'd never seen so much concrete in my life, outside of a playground.

But the funny thing was, the house didn't really feel like our home yet. The first week I'd wake up in the morning and take a few moments to remember where I was. But even after that wore off, it still didn't seem like home. One of the reasons was because Jennifer and I couldn't really move around the place and relax in it. We weren't allowed to use the cue sticks on the pool table. Fritz told us he didn't really want us to touch the pool game. We weren't allowed to move the furniture in the house. We weren't allowed to make any messes. We had to clean up after ourselves. We had to keep the place as neat as if we were at someone else's house.

Mom told us that's what Fritz was used to, and that's what he expected of us.

"His parents were from Germany," she said. "The house he grew up in, in New York, was like a museum. He couldn't touch anything. So that's why he's so particular about how he lives in this house. We have to respect the house. We must do everything we can to be neat.

"You can do that for me, can't you?"

I NOTICED THAT MOM seemed to be having as much trouble getting used to the new situation as us. She didn't seem any happier than when we were living in the apartment. She didn't seem any happier being around Fritz than she'd been before he'd come into the picture. She seemed kind of blah.

I began wondering why we'd moved out of the apartment into this place. I decided there must be something about Fritz that was special but which I had missed. I tried to figure it out.

His face was kind of boring. He still wasn't friendly to Jennifer and me. He still hadn't played catch with me. He wasn't fun. All in all, he kind of seemed like a dork. But I considered that maybe that's what grown men are, once you got to know them inside their homes.

After dinner the four of us would go into the living room and watch TV. One of our regular shows was *The Gong Show*. Fritz would crack up at stuff that wasn't even funny. "The Unknown Comic" would make an appearance once in a while. He had a plain brown bag over his head with a face drawn on it with black marker. He told corny jokes. But whatever the Unknown Comic said or did, Fritz would bust up in a high-pitched, hyena-like giggle.

We'd watch *Sanford and Son* and he'd chuckle hard at stuff when the laugh track wasn't even going. I didn't catch what it was that set him off.

I gave up trying to figure him out.

WHEN WE LIVED IN the apartment, Mom and I had gone jogging in the early mornings. But now she was too busy taking care of Fritz's place: shopping, washing and ironing clothes, vacuuming, dusting, mopping, doing the dishes, cooking. She was a housewife. Plus she still had her job with the plastic surgeon.

Early in the morning, Fritz would have breakfast, then leave the house in his uniform for Norton AFB. Sometimes he was on call on the weekend. One Saturday, he surprised me by taking me with him to work.

The base was like another world. We passed through a guard gate. Everyone was in uniform and wore short hair. Everything was neat and orderly. It reminded me of a giant school campus. Or maybe what a prison was like. The barracks had an overpowering antiseptic smell, like a hospital. The bathrooms were called "latrines."

Fritz looked perfectly at home in this place. I began to understand why he liked everything orderly at his house. It was what he was used to.

Not long after that, Fritz brought home two matching dressers. One was for Jennifer's room and one was for mine. I heard Mom arguing with him about stealing them. It turned out he'd snatched them off a delivery truck that was unloading furniture at the base. Later, Fritz painted over the serial numbers on the backs of the dressers.

I wondered why, if he had money, he would steal dressers. He not only owned the house and those classic cars and motorcycles but also the guesthouse in front, which he rented out for money.

The man was just odd. He hardly talked to Jennifer or me, except to yell at us to pick up our clothes and get our toys out of the living room. He wasn't really mean, though. It was more like he was kind of just tolerating us.

Then he surprised me again. He bought me a little Honda ATC three-wheeler.

I was excited!

Fritz took me outside to show me about the motorcycle.

"This is the brake," he said. "This is the gas. You pull this to do that. You press on this. Here you go."

He left me alone with it. He didn't have time to teach me to ride it.

Didn't matter. I was Evel Knievel. I could figure it out. I'd get this thing going fast in no time.

Soon I was puttering around the concrete court. It was so much more fun than a bicycle. I got more comfortable opening up the throttle. I got better at making turns. I could do this. I couldn't wait to get up to speed to start catching air.

I loved the smell of the gas. I loved the mechanical workings, and their power. I loved the loud whine the engine made. It blended in with the noises on our block. It was quite a block. There was action on it from time to time. There were muscular men, sometimes bearded, in sleeveless black leather jackets and sunglasses and bandanas, chugging up and down the street on choppers, going to or from a house at the other end of the street. Their motorcycles were loud, like Uncle Mark's. They filled the air with distorted sounds of miniature explosions that could be heard from far away.

Jennifer told me these bikers were "Hell's Angels." I didn't know what those were. I just figured they were like my Uncle Mark — riding motorcycles, drinking beer, hanging out with half-naked women at that house up the block, where loud music played.

"Stay away from there," Mom said.

I WAS STILL ATTENDING Newmark Elementary. Mom drove Jennifer and me back and forth. But I started making friends in my new neighborhood, too. There was a boy my age on the block whose name was Patrick. He had black curly hair. We rode bikes together. He was fascinated by my ATC.

"Let's take your motorcycle into the field."

There was a dirt field across the road that had plenty of berms. I was confident, although I wasn't that good on the motorcycle yet. But Patrick was pretty much my best friend.

"Get on behind me," I said.

He climbed on and we puttered out to the curb, across the street, and into the field. It was bumpy. I went slowly, then faster. I cranked the throttle and we went over a berm and caught air, our stomachs falling. We landed and bounced hard on the seat.

We yelled.

I felt free. We could be as loud as we liked out here.

We stayed out until dinnertime.

Patrick liked playing at my house. The house at the end of the block where the bikers hung out with their choppers was a Hell's Angels clubhouse, and Patrick's parents didn't want him hanging out at that end of the block, either. But the two of us would get a charge seeing the bikers fly down the street. We'd hear an engine approaching and we'd haul ass outside to watch. But the bikers never had anything to do with us. They left us alone.

There were a lot of kids on the block, and we'd ride our bikes around together. But we'd clear to the side of the street when a motorcycle came by.

I stopped thinking so much about the old apartment.

LIKE I SAID, FRITZ was a car nut. He was such a motorhead that he took us to hotrod shows up in Orange County. At one of these shows I saw actor Erik Estrada, who played "Ponch," one of the motorcycle-riding California state patrolmen in the TV show *CHiPS*. He was standing there with two women: a brunette and a blonde, each in a short skirt. I walked up to him and got my photo taken as he signed an autograph. I was wearing a Caterpillar cap. I still have that photo.

An even bigger highlight was the time when we were at Ontario Motor Speedway. We met Shirley Muldowney. She autographed a T-shirt for me. I already knew about the racing circuit, and Shirley Muldowney was my favorite drag racer. She was a dark-haired lady in sunglasses and a magenta racing suit. She stood up straight. She radiated energy. She seemed very confident. She reminded me of Mom. These two were a different breed of woman. They weren't average housewives. They both seemed like they were kind of taking on the world. They had some sort of extra strength about them.

But I was noticing more and more that Mom seemed to have lost that spark. Ever since she'd gotten married, she didn't have the same energy.

Now I began wondering more and more why she'd married Fritz, and why she'd moved us in with him. She didn't seem happy around him. And Fritz never seemed happy unless his head was under the hood of one of his cars. And we kids weren't around to annoy him.

ONE WEEKEND, FRITZ FOUND a hairline scrape on his Chevy truck. He decided one of the kids on the block must have hit it with bike handlebars.

Some of us were out riding around the street. Fritz came up the driveway and called us over. His face was red.

"I want each of you, and your friends, to bring your bikes on down to the driveway," he said. "I want to find out which one of you did this."

We were scared enough to obey. One by one, the kids brought their bikes on over.

Fritz took a tape measure and measured the height of the handlebars of each bike.

I knew he was right. One of us probably *had* scratched his truck. We'd been riding up and down the driveway, out in the concrete court and around. Some of the kids had gone near the garage. I hadn't, though.

When it was my bike's turn, the handlebars measured up right at the scratch mark. Fritz stared at me. His hands were on his hips.

Even though I was innocent, I suddenly felt guilty. The other kids relaxed. I could sense their relief.

"No, it wasn't my bike," I said.

I had an idea.

"Look. My grips have caps on them."

I showed Fritz the rubber caps on the end of my handlebars.

"See?"

Fritz glanced at the grips.

"You kids get out of here. Come with me," he said to me.

He led me into the back yard. Mom wasn't home. We were alone.

Fritz shook his head and stared at me. It made me nervous. I looked at him. He was really buff. He worked out on the base. He had a big chest and big arms. His biceps bulged. He knew how strong he was.

I fidgeted. I felt powerless to run away. It was like his strength held me by an invisible force.

The back of his hand swung at me. I saw a flash of red. My knees buckled. I was on the ground. The side of my face smarted. The skin screamed.

Fritz stood over me. His face was calm.

"That's to teach you a lesson about not paying attention, and about lying.

And next time, keep your friends away from the garage."

I felt sick in the pit of my stomach. I felt sick about something else, too. I'd learned a harsh lesson:

It doesn't matter if you're innocent. If you're a suspect in a crime and there's enough information gathered about you, you're going to get your ass in trouble.

I couldn't tell Mom about this. She had enough to worry about. And anyway, I didn't want to disappoint her. She'd been telling Jennifer and me to respect the house and "Fritz's things."

"You can do that for me, can't you?" she'd said.

FRITZ'S PUNISHMENTS STARTED COMING more often. I never knew what would set him off, giving him a chance to slap me or push me down.

"Who left the dishes in the sink?"

"Who left the TV on?"

"You were called in for dinner and now you're late."

This was a whole new world for me. When it had been just the three of us, punishment for Jennifer and me had been predictable and consistent. Mom would talk us through most of our misbehaviors; if my sister or I seriously crossed the line, we'd get one warning. If we crossed the line again — like when I'd roller-skated down two flights of the apartment staircase, hands bouncing on the rails for balance and alarming the neighbors, after having been scolded by Mom that I could crack my head open on the concrete footings — we'd get a spanking.

Even grim-faced, no-nonsense Nana never went further than a spanking.

I began to worry when Mom was away from the house and Fritz was home. I tried even harder to stay out of his way. So did Jennifer.

IN MY OTHER LIFE, outside of home, things were going fine. In school I'd gotten much better at focusing and not being distracted or bored. When my mind wandered, I'd start daydreaming. The teacher wouldn't know I wasn't listening.

I had friends at school, both boys and girls, and was making more friends in the neighborhood, too. One day, a kid, Donny, asked me to come over to his house. It was after I'd gotten home from school. Donny lived up the block, in a nice little house with a swim pool.

His parents weren't home. "Hey, you want to check out something?" Donny said.

He took me upstairs into the bathroom. On a counter was a stack of magazines. They had women smiling on their covers. Women dressed in underwear. I'd never seen anything like them before.

Donny handed me a couple magazines and took a few for himself. We sat on the floor and fingered through the pages.

I was blown away. I already was in love with women. I was used to being around females, so I'd never thought girls had cooties. In pre-school and kindergarten and on into first grade, there always was a girl or two I'd kiss with. It wasn't romantic so much as an act of friendship. Only a few of the other boys in first grade kissed or held hands with girls. Most boys hated girls. Not me. There was always a girl or two hanging around me. At the moment, there was Sarah, a freckle-cheeked girl in my class who had a cute little Dorothy Hamill hairstyle, and wore wooden clogs every now and then — *clack-clack-clack*. We'd kiss sometimes at lunch recess, when I wasn't playing jacket tag or something else.

But these women in the magazines, posing with their smiles or pouts or stares, looked especially kissable. They looked like they wanted to be your friend. They looked right at you from out of the pages. I especially loved the blondes. I already had crushes on two blondes: Stevie Nicks, the singer in the rock band Fleetwood Mac; and Olivia Newton-John, the Australian pop singer and movie actress in *Grease*.

Donny's magazines showed me there were a lot of others like Stevie and Olivia in the world. There were just a ton of these foxes on the loose out there.

I couldn't wait to grow up.

AT HOME, I WAS avoiding Fritz as much as possible. But there was one activity of his I couldn't stay away from. It was when he worked on his cars.

I loved tools. When Mom had her VW Bug at the apartment, I'd help her when she changed the oil or did other minor work. I'd hand her wrenches or screwdrivers and keep her company. Fritz had a giant collection of tools — nice tools. They were arranged in holders on the wall or in tool chests around a workbench. I loved hanging out in the garage watching him work on hotrods.

Even though I'd get my ass whipped by Fritz for this or that, I'd still spend a lot of time around him in the garage as he worked on engines. Often there were other men in there with him, expert mechanics, professionals who later became well known in hotrod circles. Fritz was an asshole and a bully, but if there was one thing that was cool about him it was that he really was a motorhead.

One day, when none of his friends were around, he decided to teach me about tools. He laid a bunch of them in front of me on the workbench.

"All right, I'm going to ask you what these tools are. And for every one of 'em you get right, I'll give you a dollar. And for every one of 'em you get wrong, I'm going to smack you with the tool."

The usual fear welled up inside me. My lips trembled. I wondered if the garage really was a place for me. But I couldn't very well leave. He'd laugh at me, like he did whenever he roughed me up. When he punished me, he treated it like a game, like he'd won something. He enjoyed seeing me cower. That always hurt my pride. It was almost as bad as the pain.

But now he'd challenged me. I had to accept. Whatever urge it was inside me that always kicked in at these moments— whether it was flying up bike ramps or taking a running jump on a mud puddle — it was impossible for me to resist.

My hands were quivering, but I started pointing out and naming tools.

"Crescent wrench."

"Yep," Fritz said.

"Open-end wrench."

Right there, too.

"Ratchet . . . Socket wrench."

So far, so good.

"Channel locks."

He nodded.

Then I got stumped.

He was holding up a wrench of some sort. I made a wild guess.

"Monkey wrench?"

Fritz imitated a buzzer sound, like a TV game show.

"Nine-inch adjustable," he said.

He grabbed my hand and smacked my knuckles with the tool.

It stung like a shock — a white, intense pain — and left a little welt. But the result was that I learned the tool's name. I never forgot it was a 9-inch adjustable wrench.

Every time after that, whenever Fritz decided to teach me the names of tools, I concentrated with intense brainpower. The fear — knowing that a wrong answer would mean instant anguish — sharpened my thinking. There would be no more sheer guessing. I made sure I remembered the names.

It wasn't long before I realized that this ability to concentrate with absolute focus could be summoned whenever I needed it. For example, in school. I could shut out all other distractions and thoughts and memorize information or instructions the teacher was giving.

One day I had a great idea: If I really wanted to avoid getting smacked on the knuckles by Fritz, I could *practice on my own*. I could rehearse the names of the tools when he wasn't home.

I began going into the garage by myself and studying the tools, practicing their names so I wouldn't mess up when he was testing me. Sometimes I'd ask

Mom or one of my friends to come out into the garage with me and quiz me. Mom had no clue what Fritz's punishment was if I was wrong. She just thought he was finally getting involved with me.

My extra effort paid off. I took a few more beatings in the garage, but I ended up learning each and every one of his tools.

Fritz didn't have anything in there that I didn't know what it was. He owed me a lot of dollars. He even paid me once in a while. But it wasn't like I was going to remind him to do it.

CHAPTER FIVE: Sinking, then Swimming

June came. School let out for summer. At night we could get up on the roof of the house and watch movies for free on a screen at the nearby drive-in. Fritz had gone over to the lot when the theater was closed and cut some wires to speakers at a car space. He fixed a wire running to the house, stapled it up the side of the garage and attached it to a speaker. That's how I first saw *Bambi*.

It was great being out of school. The concrete area between the house and guesthouse was perfect for skateboarding or riding our bikes. My friends and I just stayed away from the cars in the garage and driveway. The mercury was soaring, as always in Southern California in the summer, and Jennifer and I kept going in the house for glasses of water. This upset Fritz on his day off. All that opening and closing of the door meant a higher air-conditioning bill, he said.

He brought home a drinking fountain from the base. I guessed he'd taken it from the supply store. He cut brass tubing on the outside of the house, connected a hose and piped up the fountain.

"Now if you guys want a drink, you get a drink from there," he said.

The fountain was a hit with the kids in the neighborhood.

Jennifer and I were playing in the back yard one day when Fritz was home. He came out and yelled at us about not shutting the backyard gate. "I don't want to see it left open again."

A little later he came back outside. The gate was still open. His face flushed. He started cussing.

"You brats need to learn a lesson. Stay right there. I don't want you to move until I get back."

When he returned he had some sort of stick in his hand. It was long with two prongs coming out of one end. He reached out and touched it on my arm.

JOLT!

Electricity ran through my body, up to my eye sockets and down to my toes. It left me trembling. I nearly pissed. My arm felt numb.

Then he zapped Jennifer. She screamed and stood there, shaking.

We didn't know it, but he'd used a cattle prod. All we knew was that we were scared sh*tless.

Now Fritz had become even more intimidating. He enjoyed this power. It made him happy. In fact, the prod became a big joke for him. When we'd walk by in the garage, he'd reach for it just to spook us.

If we weren't fast enough, he'd try to get us with it. Sometimes he would.

It was very funny to him. He'd laugh his high-pitched hyena giggle.

We never told Mom.

THAT SUMMER, FRITZ TOOK us on a camping vacation. We'd stay at KOA campgrounds around California. There was always a big outdoor swim pool. I didn't know how to swim, but I liked to splash around in the shallow end.

One day, Fritz pulled me out of my end of the pool. He carried me over to the edge of the deep end.

"What are you doing?!" I screamed.

"This is how you learn to swim."

I was helpless in his hold. He started swinging me back and forth. I wondered if he was really going to do it, or if he was just torturing me.

"Fritz!" It was Mom's voice.

He flung me forward and let go.

There was a split-second of terror. Then I hit the water with a big splash. I sunk quickly, nothing under my feet, my legs. The water closed above. There was the stifling silence of being underwater, pressure in my nose, ears and eyes.

Suffocation.

Sheer panic.

So this was dying. Everything was going in slow motion . . .

Then I felt bottom. I looked up. There was light high above. I started rising. It felt like an eternity . . . then my head broke surface. I heard the sounds of the world again. People shouting.

I thrashed about, crying, swallowing water, struggling to stay up. For a brief moment I caught a glimpse of Mom at the edge of the pool. She was fighting to get away from Fritz. He was restraining her.

The anger surged through me! He wasn't going to get me like this.

I gained control of myself long enough to think up a plan.

I sucked a big breath and let myself sink to the bottom again. This time, I bounced off hard with my feet, propelling myself upward. When my head rose out of the water, I gasped another breath of air.

I went down again. Pushed up again. This time when I reached top — I flailed my hands in a digging motion.

It worked! I started moving toward the shallow end. My head stayed above the surface.

I dogpaddled to the edge of the pool. I grabbed hold and hung on. I wasn't going to drown after all.

I shook the water out of my eyes, ears and nose. I spit and coughed. I caught my breath. My heart pounded. But in sheer triumph, I realized I'd survived.

What's more, I knew I could do it again. I knew that if I was in the middle of this pool, I could keep myself from going under. My fear of the deep end was gone.

I was in charge. I was confident.

After that, you couldn't get me out of the pool. The rest of the day, I had a blast.

As for Mom, she was furious with Fritz. I was happy about that. He was a sick bastard. I knew that. But I also knew that his meanness was making me stronger. Just like the messed-up way he'd taught me the names of the tools — there was a positive outcome to his tossing me in the water.

What this goon had taught me was that I could survive in a crisis. It gave me confidence. I was getting used to figuring things out very quickly, on the spur of the moment.

I don't want to thank Fritz for anything. But if I had to thank him for something, it was that his sadistic games had forced me to think on my feet.

CHAPTER SIX: Bullies and Lunch

Fritz and Mom were arguing a lot now. There was no more pretending. They didn't like each other.

Jennifer and I stayed away from him. At night we'd usually keep in our rooms. But we'd hear them. Mom no longer seemed just blah. She was downright unhappy.

One evening, when Jennifer and I were playing in my room, we heard Mom scream. We ran into their bedroom. Fritz had her on the ground and was on top of her, smothering her with his body. His hands were at her throat.

Jennifer and I started crying. Fritz turned around. He let Mom go.

She got up, grabbed us and took us into the other room. She hugged us.

"It's all right, it's over. I love you."

"Mom, we want to leave," I said.

"We don't want to live here anymore," Jennifer said.

Whatever Mom and Fritz had liked about each other had worn away. Jennifer and I spent more and more time at Aunt Denise and Uncle Jim's house. Those were two married people who didn't fight.

Nana and Aunt Denise had never liked Fritz. They were now coming to our house sometimes to take Jennifer and me out shopping or to eat, just to get us away from the tension. We already were spending nearly every weekend with

Aunt Denise and Uncle Jim. Nana and Aunt Denise would ask us questions about Fritz. We didn't have any answers except that we didn't like him.

One evening, I heard a commotion in the kitchen. I went in. Fritz had balled a hand into a fist. I couldn't believe he would actually punch Mom. Then he did it, as if it was the perfectly normal thing to do. He socked her in the jaw like she was a man. Her head whipped back.

I rushed in between them. I pushed him away.

He flung me aside. I crashed into a corner. He grabbed her.

She pushed him off.

"I'm sick of this sh*t! I'm going out," he said.

"Jeff, go to your room," Mom said. She was sniveling.

The front door slammed.

I had next to no respect left for this guy, despite his hotrods and handiness with tools.

About all I respected were the ass whippings he gave me.

I quit hanging out in the garage with him.

I pretended as much as possible that he wasn't there. He acted the same toward me. We barely looked at each other.

SECOND GRADE WOULD BE starting up in September. I'd be enrolled in a new school: Highland Elementary. Mom told me I could ride my bicycle to school instead of walking. She bought a lock and chain for me.

I decided to learn to ride my bike with one hand. It was tough getting the balance, but finally I was able to push off and get going straight for a short distance. Then the bike would wobble, and a moment or two later I'd crash. I was scraped and bruised. Jennifer was sitting out there. She couldn't believe how badly I was punishing myself.

"What are you doing? Why don't you just put your other hand on the bike?"

"Next year, Mom said I could ride to school, and I gotta carry my lunch in the other hand."

"You're crazy."

I kept wiping out. But I eventually got the technique down. I didn't give up. I kept at it until I got it solved.

I couldn't help it. It was a challenge.

MY SMALL SIZE BEGAN bringing me trouble in second grade. I was still the littlest kid in my class — smaller even than the girls. That meant that if another kid wasn't fitting in with the others, or if he wanted to show off to a group of friends, I was a natural target.

A boy might walk up and thrust his chest out. "Get out of my way you little chump."

Sometimes it'd be my fault. I was a smartass. I could make fun of someone on a split-second's notice. I could imitate how a kid walked or talked.

If I cut someone down too badly in front of other kids, then I was in for an ass whipping. I had to be careful not to cross that line. I could say or do one or two things, maybe, but then I had to lay off.

Other times I knew I was just being singled out because of my size.

"I don't like your face," a third-grader said.

I'd already learned to think fast on my feet, to talk my way out of trouble. The trick was in finding something that my antagonist could relate to, so he would see I was more like him. If a bully got in my space and I could feel I was an imminent target, I'd start jabbering.

"Yeah, they said that line in *Star Wars*. Remember when Luke Skywalker was in the bar? You saw the movie, right?"

Maybe the bully was wearing a mood ring, one of those plastic pieces that changed color from blue to magenta, supposedly revealing a person's mood. I'd talk about the mood ring — "Looks like you're happy." I'd say whatever I thought could connect with him.

With 90 percent of the bullies, this tactic would work. We'd start talking, and they'd sometimes become my friends.

I began studying people more closely — figuring out their motivations for acting badly. Were they just pissed off in general? What did their faces tell me? The way they were walking?

One day in the cafeteria a big chubby kid, Kenny, was walking around beating on people. He'd punch them in the arm or back. He'd take their food. He did this every lunchtime. He was a lunchroom troublemaker; no one liked him. We called him "Lardo." He was a total slob. His hair fell to his collar and his T-shirt hung out over his jeans.

I'd been watching him for days now. He was bigger than the rest of us in our grade, probably because he'd been held back a year or started late. On the playground he was pretty much just another kid. But something came over him at lunchtime. Every day, he'd make his rounds of the tables. He'd knock food off people's trays or snatch things.

I studied him, and finally zeroed in on the reason for his behavior: He hadn't brought any lunch to school. In fact, he never did. He was jealous of the rest of us. He was angry that we had food and he didn't. I understood that. I also understood that it was just a matter of time before he'd come over to my table.

I always kept my eye on him, and I tried to wolf my food down in case I had to run.

Sure enough, my unlucky day arrived. Here came Lardo. The kids eating around me started getting jumpy.

Then he was standing over me.

Lardo had a lisp. He slurred his speech. Everything about him was sloppy.

"Tho what're we having today?" he asked, in a bully's smartass tone.

My friends got up and scattered. Some moved to a nearby table, to watch from a safe distance. I didn't budge. I was going to deal with this. I'd seen other kids surrender their food without an argument. There was no way Lardo was getting my food, what Mom had packed for me.

It was just Lardo and me now at the big long table. He looked like a big fat predator bird that had found its prey. I turned to my side and faced him, looking him straight in the eyes. I spoke very quietly, so no one else could hear.

"I know you don't have any lunch today, and I know you're mad, right?"

He hadn't expected that. His mouth fell open.

"You're not getting my lunch," I said. "But you can sit over here and I'll share with you, if you call me your friend. But friends of mine don't go around taking lunches from people."

Lardo hesitated. He looked around.

"F*ck you," he said. "I'll just take your lunch."

"You're not getting my lunch."

My voice was calm, which surprised me.

"If you try taking it, then I'm going to be your enemy forever, and all my friends are going to be your enemies, and we'll never stop being your enemies. If you're hungry, I'll share with you — *if* you want to be my friend."

Lardo didn't say anything. He was confused. He was looking out into space. I knew I had him.

Unfortunately, my sarcastic tongue couldn't contain itself. With a smirk, I added:

"Hey, I can see you're a big boy. I know you have to eat a lot to keep going."

Lardo shot me a murderous look. But I could see hurt in his eyes, too. I'd gotten to him.

I kept on eating. He kept on staring.

Then, to my relief, he sat down. I reached into my lunchbox and set some Frito's corn chips in front of him. He popped them into his mouth. He chomped and gulped. He really *was* hungry.

I passed him a half of my sandwich.

He wolfed that down, too.

We'd developed an understanding.

Lardo never bothered me again. In fact, he didn't even show up at our table. My friends reaped the benefit of my standing up to him. They resumed sitting around me, for safety.

I knew, however, that quick thinking didn't work in every situation with bullies. That's one of the lessons of the playground every kid in grade school absorbs. There was that one type you could never win over. You couldn't reason with him. You couldn't negotiate. Words meant nothing to him. All he understood was violence.

If this kind of kid got in your space, you had to get away as quickly as you could because you were in for an ass whipping. Everyone knew who these guys were on the playground. I'd just try to stay away from them the whole school year.

But my analytical skills helped me understand what was wrong with them. I realized they had something bad happening behind the scenes. Their home lives were less than perfect. I could relate. When I saw some kid who never smiled except when he was going around beating on people, kicking balls away, being a complete asshole, I figured that maybe he came from the same kind of household I did.

He had a Fritz in his face all the time.

CHAPTER SEVEN: Oysters, Soccer, Dittos

The beginning of the end of Mom's marriage to Fritz came when she was washing my back in the bathtub one evening. She gasped and pulled away. Then she fingered the bruises, red and purple, dotting my back and buttocks.

These were not the bangs and bumps an active 7-year-old sustained roughhousing. Someone had been using knuckles, or worse, on her son's hide. Mom knew Fritz spanked my sister and me every so often; but she never suspected he was laying it on this hard.

She helped me out of the tub and toweled me off, then hurried out. As I pulled my pajamas on, her voice filled the house. It was shrill, accusing. In lulls, Fritz's voice grumbled, a meek counterpoint.

A door slammed. Mom's rage still carried through the house. She was threatening to leave him if he ever laid a hand on us again.

A couple weeks later, Suzie and George, a couple who were friends of Mom's, came over for lunch. Mom and Fritz had another nasty argument; he slammed her against the wall.

The dirty secret was now public.

Not long after, we packed our belongings and moved in with Nana. Mom searched for an apartment. She filed for divorce.

She worried about Fritz showing up. She warned us he might. But he didn't. We didn't see him again.

THERE WERE REASONS I didn't know about why Mom had stuck with Fritz so long. One was that she'd decided it was a trade-off for her to take his beatings as long as her children were not in danger. She was forfeiting her own comfort for Jennifer's and my sake. She hadn't known he was abusing us, too.

But there was another reason she hadn't mustered her strength, packed us up and split much earlier. She was in chronic pain. Something was seriously wrong with her body again. Whatever it was, it drained her energy.

It was after we'd moved in with Nana that Mom went into surgery at San Bernardino Community Hospital.

Doctors removed a grapefruit-sized cyst with tentacles.

WE FOUND AN APARTMENT. In time, Mom's strength came back. She was smiling and laughing again.

One summer day she asked if we wanted to go swimming and meet one of her new friends. She said his name was Tony and he lived in an apartment complex with a swim pool not far from where Aunt Denise and Uncle Jim lived.

Tony was Italian. He lived with his brother, Paulie, who was a wisecracker, and a buddy named Clayton. These three were clean-cut, clean-shaven, fit men. They were in the Air Force together, stationed at Norton. Tony was a second lieutenant. When Mom introduced us, Jennifer and I saw he was a major improvement over Fritz.

Tony was handsome. He was happy. He was quiet, but he smiled a lot. He cracked jokes. His brother Paulie was even more comical. He teased Jennifer and me non-stop. Mom said they came from a big Italian family back in West Virginia.

That afternoon, Jennifer and I played on inflatable floats in the water. Tony and Paulie splashed us, swam under us. They were used to children.

It was a great time. The adults drank beer or wine spritzers and we kids played in the water, horsed around with Mom's new friends.

She and Tony dated for several months. We liked him. Even Nana liked him.

And then they got married. It was a small ceremony at Nana's house.

We were in for another move. And this time, it was a really big one: to Florida. Tony was going to take air-traffic control training at Tyndall AFB. Mom made it sound exciting. We'd be living right there next to the beach for a year. We'd learn all about sea life, eat seafood.

"We'll be beach bums," Mom said.

It did sound exciting. And it would be my first chance to learn what life was like outside California. The Air Force base was in Panama City, on the Gulf of Mexico.

"It's a great place for kids," Mom said.

WE GOT TO FLORIDA a month later after driving cross-country in a new Volkswagen Scirocco that Tony bought. The car had tinted windows. Jennifer and I flipped off other cars without the drivers knowing. We stayed at campgrounds and motels. We visited Tony's family in West Virginia, in a huge old three-story house. We were welcomed with hospitality, immediately accepted into the clan. These were loud, outgoing Italians. Everything was so different from how life had been with Fritz.

Then we drove to Panama City. It felt like another world! The very air was different — heavy and wet, like you could cut it with a knife. You couldn't get away from sweating. Jennifer and I would be wearing shorts all the time. I decided this was what it was like living in paradise.

The colors in paradise were different, too. Our house on base was so close to the beach that we had a view of the water from Jennifer's window. I was used to Southern California's brown beaches; Florida's were bleached white, with sand dollars and, in season, so many jellyfish washed ashore, they'd practically cover the sand. The water in California was dark-blue, almost black; in Florida it was bluish-green, and always warm, with a calypso breeze. The beaches in California were rocky out in the water and high waves roared in. But the water off Panama City didn't have many big waves. As you waded in from the beach, the ground was flat and the water shallow, and you could walk out a good ways before it suddenly dropped off.

Mom didn't have to work outside the home anymore. She could take care of the house, tend to Jennifer and me. Life was pretty easy living on the base. Tony was in class most of the time during the day, so Mom could spend a lot of time alone with us when we weren't in school, which would be starting soon. We'd go free-diving off the beach. She taught Jennifer and me to fish, casting a line baited with squid.

We were very happy. We were functioning as a family. Mom had a glow about her.

Tony would come home at the end of the day. I didn't call him "dad." I called him by his name. But he was more like a dad than Fritz was, because of the very fact that Tony was human. What Tony mostly was to me was a big brother. Sometimes the two of us walked down to the beach at sunset, digging up oysters with our hands or finding them sticking in the sand like craggy slivers of whitish-gray rock. We'd carry them home in a pail of seawater for a feast. We'd crack the shells open, shucking out the oysters while they were still alive, dip them in Tabasco sauce and eat them fresh.

Seafood was everywhere in Panama City. Mom would take us to Red Lobster restaurants, which were as common, and inexpensive, as McDonald's. We could have steak and lobster for about $3.

Really, it was like we'd moved to paradise.

IT WAS IMPOSSIBLE NOT to make friends on base. There was a horde of Air Force brats. When the new semester for the base school started that September I saw that the newcomers were immediately accepted, because everyone had been new at one time or another. With some of the kids who lived near me, I'd get up early on weekends and go snorkeling and diving in the surf. Low tide extended for a great distance, and we could find strange objects — maybe a diver's watch or knife — plus seashells. We'd hit the beach after school, too. We'd get broom handles and cut them to size, spike one end with a nail, and go spear fishing for crabs and bluefish. I'd bring my catch home and Mom would steam the crab and fish and serve it over rice.

The one good friend I made was an English boy named Alex. Alex's family, the Watkins, lived behind us. His father was in the British military but getting U.S. training. The Watkins had been in Florida a while, and Alex was tanned a deep brown, like most of the other kids, and as I soon would be. Alex was a couple years older but he didn't make much of the age difference. He was polite and proper, raised as a little gentleman.

The Watkins introduced me to teatime. It was the weirdest custom I'd ever seen. This ritual occurred several times during the day at their house. All other activity ceased. We'd sit quietly in an area of the living room and relax. His mother poured tea into delicate cups on saucers and served pastries and black licorice that we dipped in powdered sugar.

I thought teatime was a splendid custom.

THERE WERE COMPETITIVE SPORTS leagues organized on base to keep the children occupied. There were uniforms and practices and serious games. Mom signed me up for a baseball team and a soccer team. I was excited. Small as I was, I was fast and coordinated. I hadn't considered, though, the fright of facing a baseball at the plate.

I was decent enough at catching and throwing, but batting was a whole other matter. The pitchers were mostly 10-year-olds and I felt like I was half their size. They'd wind up and fire. I couldn't help it; I kept backing out of the box. The coaches wouldn't have that. They were hard-ass baseball guys. They told me to get my butt back up to the plate and swing. I was terrified. I dreaded my turn at bat. For the first time in life, I felt out of my element, over my head.

I got one hit the entire season.

Soccer proved a totally different experience.

This was a game that suited me. I took to it right off, like I was born to it. Chase the ball. Get to it first. Boot it hard. It didn't matter that I was short and scrawny. I had speed and balance. I didn't stumble and trip around, dribbling that big ball down the field. All that mattered was controlling the ball. What's more, for once my hyperactive energy was in my favor. I had wind. I could keep on running hard for the ball after the other kids had slowed or stopped and were taking breathers. This game was made for me!

Alex played soccer — "football," he called it — being that he was from England. He showed me some basics. But there was another kid, David, from Africa, whose father was stationed at Tyndall. David had played a lot of "football" back home — and he had skills. On our team he was a forward. He taught me a lot as we practiced, developing passing tactics. He'd fake one way, briefly overrun the ball then dribble past a defender the opposite way. He'd boot the ball through a defender's legs and go around and catch up to it. He'd lead me with the ball and I'd race to it and send it back to him. We could play keep-away, passing the ball back and forth until one of us broke into the clear.

I found I could boot the ball pretty far. The coaches liked that I was a lefty. It made me harder to cover than the other kids. The coaches told me I was a halfback — a position that meant I could stay in the action all the time, racing up and down the turf. Halfbacks play both offense and defense.

We got our uniforms. The day of our first game arrived. I stood out on the pitch. I had butterflies in my belly — all kids do — but there was something else going on inside me. It was a desire to kick some serious ass. It was the same sort of feeling that came over me when I was on a bicycle, facing a ramp the other kids had put up. It was a will to go out and conquer. It was overpowering, consuming. A monster with a life of its own. I couldn't wait for the referee to blow his whistle to get things started.

The match began. The ball rolled into my area. A kid on the other team stopped it with his toe. He started dribbling. I ran up, slid hard and took out his legs as the ball bounced away. I felt like I was at war. *Take no prisoners!* Later, the ball flew high toward me. I got under it. I caught it on my forehead and headed it back downfield. I had the killer mentality. I didn't back off. I'd do whatever it took to win. I was possessed!

Then David scored for us. The parents on our side erupted in cheers. We were ahead. It felt great. We got another goal soon after. We were up 2-0. The other team seemed to be slowing down. The players were discouraged. They looked sad, desperate. I wanted us to pour it on. It was intoxicating. A great, big high. I couldn't get enough.

I got off a few shots on goal myself. We won 5-1. We felt like kings. I loved soccer. I loved winning. The good feeling stayed with me an entire week.

Then we went out the next game and lost. It was our turn to stand there, shaking hands with the other team's players. They were proud. I was angry. I felt humiliated, cheated, deprived of glory. When I got home I didn't change out of my uniform. I immediately started practicing, kicking my soccer ball into a little goal and net set up outside our house. I didn't want to ever lose again.

Mom came outside. "Haven't you had enough soccer for one day?"

"We lost, Mom!"

"You have to be a good loser, Jeff."

I couldn't believe she'd said that. What was she talking about? Who the hell wanted to be a "good loser?" What was the point of being "a good loser?"

It just didn't register.

Mothers, I decided, could be a little crazy.

I kept on practicing.

THIRD GRADE WAS A bit more interesting than first and second had been. There were more subjects. The one that fired up my curiosity was marine biology. The ocean was full of strange plants and animals, thriving in the depths. We were told about sand sharks, how they could swim into the shallow water and bury themselves in the sand. The danger intrigued me. This piece of information was something to make a note on, to use against my sister.

When Jennifer and I were out wading, I'd tell her, "We're in three feet of water. The sharks can be in three feet of water."

The laugh ended up being on me.

Tony's squadron held a party on the beach. Alex and I were goofing off in the water, away from everyone. I stepped on what felt like a soft board. Then it shifted beneath my feet. With a swift movement, it lifted — upending me — and swam away.

Alex and I got out of the water quick. We stayed out the rest of the day.

It wasn't until years later, when I was watching a television special on sharks on the Discovery Channel, that I realized how infested the waters were where I'd played as a kid. Camera crews filming the documentary flew over some of the same beaches I'd been on, and their footage showed all the sharks hanging out there.

Maybe children really have guardian angels.

TONY WAS GENERALLY QUIET. All of us got along just fine. He was easygoing. The only times he got a bit loud was in social situations where there was alcohol. He wasn't a mean drunk; he just got rowdy. He was a partier. He liked his beer. After he got home at night from his classes, he usually had a beer in hand. But he was no slouch. He kept in shape. He was an officer, which meant he had to stay in top condition. He had to pass physical tests every now and then. He ran and trained. He'd head out jogging wearing a tight silver jogging suit, to log the miles in the hot, sticky Florida air. Sometimes I'd smell the beer sweating out of him after he returned.

Tony and Mom were good friends with another married couple on base. The man's name was Jerry. He was a first lieutenant in Tony's squadron. He and his wife, Betty, had no children, but were very friendly toward Jennifer and me. Jerry used to say "tre-mendous" all the time. "The sunset looks tre-mendous!" I picked up on it and started using the word all the time myself. "Oh, man, did you see that jump? It was tre-mendous!" Jerry didn't mind. He had a good sense of humor. That's why he was friends with Tony.

One weekend night our family went to a squadron party on the beach. When it was time to leave, Tony got behind the wheel of our car and I climbed into the backseat. He started the engine. We waited for Mom and Jennifer to join us. Where were they?

Then I heard Mom shout: "Jeff, get your ass out of the car! You're not riding with him!"

I was confused. What was she talking about?

Tony bumped the car into gear. We backed slowly down the hill toward the water. From out the car windows I saw Mom and Jerry and some of the other adults running beside us, trying to get the passenger door open. Tony couldn't seem to find the brake pedal. He began cursing. Finally, he wrenched on the parking brake. The car jolted, throwing us forward in our seats.

Mom opened the passenger door and dragged me out. She was furious with Tony. They had words.

"C'mon!" she said to Jennifer and me.

The three of us left Tony sitting in the car. We caught a ride home with Jerry and Betty. On the way, I fell asleep. When I woke, groggy, I was in Mom's arms. She had carried me out of the car. I realized I was being pushed through an open window of a kitchen.

I began to resist.

"Mom, isn't this breaking the law?"

"No, this is our own house. Tony has the keys."

I got through the window. I went around and opened the front door.

Tony found his way home, somehow.

Neither he nor Mom mentioned the incident again.

ONE DAY IN CLASS, the teacher chose me and another kid to go down to the office with a master copy of a test typed in heavy black ink. We were to make a copy on the "ditto machine."

I was proud to be given this duty. I was now considered one of the smart kids in class. My ability to focus intensely, when I wanted to, had improved to the point where it could be summoned at my command. I absorbed and recalled information like no one's business — when I wasn't daydreaming.

The ditto machine was set up in the broom closet of the office. It was easy enough to operate, once the office lady showed us how. All you did was attach the master copy to the machine's round drum. Then you cranked the handle, and slick sheets of paper whipped fast, one by one, across the roller. The roller was soaked in a sweet but foul fluid that dissolved the ink from the master copy onto the sheets. The sheets came out stained with purple ink. The lines of words were all even, except toward the bottoms of the sheets, where the words grew crooked and faded.

Best of all was the powerful stench — sickening, yet irresistible. When you brought the warm, moist ditto sheets back to the class, the kids couldn't resist holding them up to their noses for hearty sniffs.

I felt important getting to handle the ditto machine. But there was another machine in the office that was far more intriguing: the computer.

Now that was something I yearned to get my hands on! *The computer.* This mysterious invention that seemed straight out of the future — like robots, or deep-space travel. And here it was, at our school.

Before my classmate and I took the ditto sheets back to the classroom, I went over to the computer and checked it out. It was a bulky, box-like apparatus — a one-piece, clunky, light-grayish case holding a monitor screen and keyboard, with two slots in it that were called "disk drives."

Unlike the ditto machine, the computer was off limits. It was too complicated, too expensive, too important for kids to touch.

I just had to find a way to get at it.

The way to get at the computer, I decided, was by talking our teacher into it. So after class I hounded her. So did some of my friends. We all wanted to be shown the computer. We all wanted a chance to see how it worked. Really what we were after was a chance to do something on it ourselves, even if it was just for a second. Then we could say we'd run a computer. It would be better than driving a car.

Finally, after enough begging, our teacher brought me and a few other students down to the office during recess one day to show us the computer. The office lady demonstrated. She clicked it on. It hummed. We grew excited. It took several minutes to "boot up," with a few orange-colored symbols blinking briefly in an upper corner of the black screen, then finally freezing in place.

The office lady typed on the keyboard and on the screen. Orange letters appeared next to the flashing cursor. It was like the void of the screen was outer space and the orange symbols were heavenly bodies being created.

The computer was like a brain, the office lady said. It remembered the information that was typed. It stored it.

This particular computer was used to keep attendance records and the like. When I got my turn, I typed a few sentences: *My name is Jeff. Can you do my homework?* I was so fascinated by it that I wondered why everyone didn't have a computer.

Imagine the work you could do, the information you could record.

After that, whenever our class needed ditto printouts, I always volunteered. It was my chance to get into the office and sneak over to the computer and type words across the screen. There was something magical about this machine. Something that fired up my curiosity to learn how it worked. Something about it that spoke to my 8-year-old mind.

TONY'S TRAINING IN AIR-traffic school was finally completed. Our year in Florida was up. He had a number of options to choose from on where to be stationed. He let Mom pick. She chose the Philippines.

Uncle Jim, Aunt Denise's husband, was an Air Force captain, a flight-crew navigator stationed at Clark Air Force Base in the Philippines. Mom thought it'd be nice to live near her sister.

If Florida had seemed exciting, living across the Pacific Ocean in a foreign country was much more so. It would be a different continent: Asia. It would be *The Orient*. My head filled with exotic images. My family had watched the television miniseries *Shogun*, based on the novel about feudal Japan and its Samurai culture. Like millions of American viewers, I was fascinated by the Orient. The ancient customs. The unwritten laws of honor. The unspoken codes of conduct.

It was 1981. We got vaccinations, and were off on our journey abroad. The trip took two days by plane. There was a layover in Anchorage, Alaska. We shivered in the airport, so used to Florida's balminess. I stared at a Coke machine. "Look, Mom, the decimal point's in the wrong spot." The price was $2.50.

A large stuffed polar bear was on display — immense, white, with giant fangs and claws. It gave me chills.

We flew on to Guam. We tried to sleep as much as possible. When we were finally over the Philippines and making our descent, I saw jungle dotted with little villages. It looked exciting.

We taxied to a landing at Clark AFB. When the plane's front and back doors opened, the outside air hit us like a furnace blast. The heat was so intense it felt like it was sucking the life right out of us. We could barely move. It was stifling.

In slow motion we made our way down the stairs rolled out to the plane on the tarmac. If the air had been humid in Florida, it was absolutely drenching in the Philippines. Sweat poured off us.

Aunt Denise and Uncle Jim were there to meet us. I couldn't wait to get to their house so I could change my clothes.

CHAPTER EIGHT: Close Encounters in the Third World

From that very first night in the Philippines, it was made clear to us by Aunt Denise and Uncle Jim that we were living in a poor, crime-ridden country and we had to watch our backs. This was not America. The next day we sat through an orientation for newcomers at Clark AFB. We were told that the Philippines government was an ally of the United States — indeed, the country was a former U.S. territory — but we were there as guests, and had to obey the local laws as well as the standards of behavior expected of military personnel and their families.

The orientation included an extensive warning about crime. Poverty breeds desperation, and therefore a combination of boldness and wiliness. We were to lock up everything inside our house at night. When we kids were done playing with a toy outside, we were to bring it back inside before taking out another one. In fact, anything not nailed down was an easy target for theft. This was the Third World.

We stayed only a few days on base. Our living arrangements would be off post; there was a yearlong waiting list for living in officer's housing at Clark. The base was outside Angeles City, about 50 miles from the metropolis of Manila. We moved into a tiny house in an Angeles City neighborhood where there were other American families, but we were right there among the local population, too.

The sights, sounds and smells made an immediate impression on me. It wasn't uncommon for raw sewage to flow through the gutters. The concrete work in the streets was terrible: pavement that had been tamped down by wood boards when wet so that it looked as uneven as frosting on a cake. You could ride your bike on it, but you couldn't skateboard or roller-skate.

Filipino guards in blue uniforms, wearing holstered pistols and toting shotguns or submachine guns, patrolled the streets. They wore round, brimmed straw hats or captain's caps to keep the sun off. Their eyes were hidden behind mirrored sunglasses. Toothpicks jutted from their lips, like prison guards out of some movie set in the American South. Our neighborhood would have qualified as a ghetto in the States, but in the Philippines it was the lap of luxury. The guards were professional police, but the politics of the Third World prevailed. We were told that if you needed help they would provide it, *if* they liked you.

Every night, Mom made an extra dinner portion. After our meal, I'd bring this extra plate out to the guard patrolling our street. That was how we ensured he'd watch our house. It also gave me the opportunity to chat with him, learn more about his family, his culture. I was a sponge. I wanted to know as much as possible about the world around me.

Many Filipinos spoke at least some English, and the guard's English was so-so, but we could communicate. I'd picked up some Tagalog since kids learn catch phrases easily. *Manok* means chicken. *Halika* means come here. But I stuck with English with the guards. You didn't joke around with them. They never smiled.

"Where do you live?" I'd ask.

"Three mile from here."

"Do you have children?"

"Two boys, three daughters."

"Have you ever been to America?"

"I go sometime. Have cousin there."

"Have you shot your gun?"

"All right, you go now."

That's always how the conversations ended. The guard would get tired of me. He wasn't about making friends. His job was serious. Or maybe he didn't like Americans.

All we knew was that we had to treat the guard right so that, hopefully, if opportunists were going to try to rip us off, he'd get in their way. We hoped that our bribes of meals were larger than whatever bribes the thieves were giving.

It wasn't hard for a 9-year-old to figure out the economics of poverty. Neediness and desperation hung in the air. Your senses were always on guard against robbery or theft. It was just something you had to live with.

My Aunt Denise and Uncle Jim had been given a new Toyota Celica as a wedding present. They shipped it to the Philippines. But the car had to pass through the unofficial chamber of commerce that thrives on freight ships. On board, members of a crime ring make molds of car keys. About a month after a private car is delivered to its destination in the Philippines, the ship ring's cohorts on land — having been given the car owner's delivery address — show up with a set of duplicated keys and jack the car. In this way my aunt and uncle had their sporty Celica stolen. It was never recovered.

Americans stationed at Clark developed the custom of buying cheap cars in the Philippines and stripping off the hubcaps, spare tire and radio — anything that made the vehicles targets. We called these cars "Clarkmobiles." They were sold along from one serviceman to the next. No one took a Clarkmobile back to the States when a tour was up. My aunt and uncle ended up buying a beat-up Datsun B210 that had been repainted three times.

Despite the immersion in a crime-ridden society, living off-post was fantastic for a kid like me. It was an education at every turn. The tap water off post was undrinkable, so we'd lug 5-gallon jugs to and from the base in our VW Scirocco. We'd shut our eyes and mouths when we showered. There was a 100-watt light bulb in a box on the floor of each closet burning 24 hours a day. The bulb dried out the moisture and kept moths from the clothes.

The sticky, sweltering humidity lasted year-round. I didn't own a pair of pants my whole time in the Philippines. It was T-shirts, shorts, flip-flops. I tanned very dark.

That Halloween I'll never forget. My sister, Mom and I, a couple other American kids and their parents went trick-or-treating at American homes on our block. Before long, a small mob of Filipino kids was trailing us. They knew about the custom.

As soon as the door of a home would open, the Filipinos would rush up, knock us away and take the candy. At the end of the night I had exactly one piece in my bag. It was a harsh lesson not only about the desperation of poverty, but the brazenness it breeds.

The true poverty wasn't on our block, however, but in the barrios. These outlying neighborhoods were a source of cheap labor for us Americans. Through an employment association you could hire house girls, sew girls and yard boys for $5 a month each. But you had to weed through them to find the ones who were capable at their work and didn't steal.

It felt weird, at first, to be living like royalty, with helpers around. I couldn't understand why we needed to pay someone to mow the lawn, sew our clothes, tidy up our house. But I quickly learned: that's how it's done in the Third World. Jobs were coveted by the locals. It was a fair exchange. Mom was a soft touch for our workers. She always gave them extra pay. She sympathized with their circumstances; she'd been on the low end of the economic ladder back in America. Christmastime, she bought them gifts. No employer had ever done this for them. Our family was well liked.

The house girl whom we ended up keeping permanently was a tiny woman in her late forties named Lori. She was our live-in maid five days a week, and she became almost part of our family.

Lori was a skinny woman just a bit taller than I. She was unmarried and had grown children whom she'd see each weekend, returning to her village Friday nights. Lori had a great sense of humor. Filipinos have difficulty pronouncing "f's" and "p's." The Americans had a saying making light of this: "Can you pass me a Fepsi? My dog has please." Jennifer and I would secretly teach Lori cuss words. "Mother-pucker," she'd repeat.

Every couple of weeks, instead of taking Lori to the PX on base for shopping, Mom would give her money to buy food for us at the local open-air market, a 40-minute drive deep into Angeles City. To my delight, Lori got Mom's permission to take me on her shopping trips. What an eye-opener they were! They were my first exposure to commerce on a large scale.

When we'd lived in San Bernardino, Mom had taken Jennifer and me to Tijuana and haggled with the street merchants. But that was a tourist trade in a border town. The market in Angeles City covered 10 acres, and was swarming with people like Mardi Gras. It was where the locals went to shop. And prices were in flux for every deal.

Lori and I would make our way past the stalls, my presence drawing stares. But any notion of the merchants that this maid with a white kid in tow was going to be easy prey for a gouging was quashed in a second when the bartering began. Lori would viciously wrangle over prices. Her voice would rise. She'd grow domineering. She'd pick up a bunch of bananas and quibble over their color, pointing out bruises. She'd always find a flaw. Or she'd claim the prices had been lower the previous week. Whether she actually remembered the price or not, she'd spit out a figure. She'd start low, they'd start high — and the haggling was on. But once she'd settled on a price, that was it. Lori wouldn't budge.

I was fascinated by the psychology of the negotiation. I began noticing physical cues — perspiration on a merchant's forehead, nervous hand movements, a passive posture — that would reveal how far he was willing to bend. Maybe he'd start puffing faster on his cigarette. Lori would keep her eyes fixed on the merchant's face. He'd grow uncomfortable, turn away: a sign she was about to break him, that he was ready to give in.

They'd jabber back and forth in Tagalog. Lori would grind the merchants down, getting her price time and again. I never once saw a merchant get the better of her. Often, she didn't even have to argue. Plenty of shop owners had come to know her well. They'd give her a fair price right off the bat. Deal done.

We'd return home with bags and bags of groceries for the equivalent of $5. Mom would let Lori keep the savings.

The Filipino market was, for me, a glimpse at the world economy in microcosm. Stalls teemed with merchandise of every kind, including stolen goods. Plastic garbage bags full of Nikes and Adidas would be hanging from the stalls, and you could buy a dozen pairs at a time for the equivalent of $2. And then there were the cheap imitations. Asian nations can produce knockoffs like no tomorrow. Fake luxury watches, purses, electronics. Whatever has a market.

I kept hearing Tony's Air Force friends talk about getting "Armani's" specially made. I confused the word with "Aramis" — the brand of soap Mom bought. Who'd want to have *that* made? But I eventually learned that "Armani's" was a line of designer dress suits. Soldiers from Clark would take copies of *Gentleman's Quarterly* magazine down to a Filipino tailor, who would obtain the same kind of fabric and thread of the garment in the photograph and produce a suit so identical it'd even bear an Armani tag, although "Armani's" could be misspelled.

The have-nots — I came to understand — were always looking for an angle. They were clever. They hustled. They knew they could exploit the desires of those who wanted what the rich had but could only afford to imitate the rich.

It was a hungry market.

LORI WAS MY FAMILY'S guide into the real Philippines. When there was a wedding or other celebration in her village, she'd take us. It was a real honor for her, a domestic worker, to escort her American family. Such a thing was hardly heard of. Her hosting us as guests elevated Lori in the esteem of her fellow villagers. It showed she had our trust and affection. It gained her prestige. It made her proud. But she also knew she had to protect us, watching carefully over us when we were there so that no thief would target us.

We never felt uncomfortable with Lori. We were glad to take part in the festivities. We ate the food. Lori said that it was safe as long as we didn't drink the water. We stuck to bottled water, or soda.

Getting to her village was an adventure in itself. We'd ride into the barrios in a Jeepnee, which is an open-backed taxicab, like a Jeep, seating six people. We'd been told at the cultural orientation at Clark AFB that if we ever got in an accident in a Jeepnee or one of the "trikes" — motorcycles with a carrier in back, whipping madly in and out of traffic — that we were to flee the scene. Run to the local post if you could, we were told. The reason was Filipino law. Even though you were just a passenger in a taxi, the driver may blame the accident on you and make you pay damages. But we never did get in an accident, though every driver hauled ass through the teeming streets, honking and rarely slowing until reaching the destination, when we'd holler, "Hey, hey, stop right here," at which he'd screech to a jarring stop.

There were few dull moments in this country. An adventure or bit of drama lurked at every turn. Kids are natural explorers, and my American friends and I ventured beyond our street. In the barrios you'd get hustled by kids for anything. Coins. Balls. Shoes.

"Hey, American, you want to play us?" a kid would call out, noting the soccer ball my friends and I were carrying. Then there'd follow the wager. They'd play us for the ball. Or did we have money?

I understood: Whatever they could convert into cash was going back to their families. I had to be careful. But I didn't let my wariness keep me from mingling with the locals. I knew some of the older Filipino kids carried knives, but my street smarts had been developed to some degree before coming to the Philippines. I'd already lived in a bad part of Southern California. I told myself I wasn't about to let myself get rolled by these punks. I saw through their hustles from the start.

One hustle involved a black-market deal to lure us American kids into back alleys. "Hey, American. Let me show you a gold watch I find. It cheap. It only a dollar." All we American kids had heard the stories as cautionary tales. There was the hustle of feigned friendship. A Filipino kid would start palling around with an American, telling him his name, using all the English he had, then lead the sucker to the remote spot where two more Filipino kids were waiting. They'd beat the American kid's ass and take his money, watch, shirt, shoes.

I'd already been to the market with Lori and I knew the local customs, how to disengage. I'd keep my cool, not act nervous or hurry, and say, "No, I'm not interested, see you later."

But I made a delightful discovery about the psyche of the poor kids in this impoverished country. It was that the urge to play soccer was on an equal footing with the urge to steal. When my friends and I carried my soccer ball out into the nearby streets, it was a magic magnet.

Soccer was the national pastime in the Philippines. The local kids were too poor to have a ball. The first time they crowded around a group of us Americans bouncing my ball, we reached an understanding: If they'd lay off trying to rip us off — looking for a chance to grab our shoes or rough us up and take our money — we could all play, and what's more, I'd bring my ball back again. It was an interesting exercise in diplomacy. And there was an extra reality at play: The soccer ball possessed a power of its own.

This was because a soccer ball was difficult to guard. If the Filipinos stole it from us, someone else in the barrio could very well end up stealing the ball from *them*. Therefore, there'd be no more games. The smartest thing to do, then, was to just safeguard it in my possession so we'd always have it to play with. The Filipinos grasped the stakes. The group of them we ended up playing with protected my ball. I'd show up with the ball and a few American kids, and we'd get a match going. The pitch would be on some abandoned lots between busted-up houses where grass sprang up. It was worse than an inner-city American slum. But it worked. We'd arrange rocks, cardboard boxes or other available objects to mark out the goals. Kids make do.

Of course, the Filipino kids still wanted to play us for money. Hustling was their mentality. They needed to do something to get by. But we American kids didn't accept their bet. If they wanted to play for fun, we said, they could play with us; otherwise we'd just kick the ball around among ourselves. But we did give them little tokens of friendship. When we had a bit of extra money, we'd buy fireworks called watusi. They were like matchsticks that flame and pop when lighted. You could hold them in your hand like popcorn. We'd buy extra watusi or candy and share them with our Filipino soccer friends. And there was another tack we took to interact without hassles. When choosing sides before a game, we'd keep it from being Americans versus Filipinos. We'd mix it up.

The Filipino kids were excellent players. They were rough and aggressive, but they had ball skills. Thanks to them, my own skills improved dramatically.

THE AMERICAN KIDS I chose to hang out with were cool, and nothing like the punks who treated the Filipinos like crap. This was another awakening for me about the dynamics between the world's haves and have-nots. There were plenty of American kids who were spoiled little brats. They adopted a superior, contemptuous attitude toward the locals. They'd boss their house girls around, cuss at them. It embarrassed and disgusted me. I was ashamed of those American kids; I'd say a small percentage of the American families were like that in the Philippines.

But Jennifer and I never treated our Lori that way. Lori was grateful. She told us horror stories she heard from the other house girls when they got together and gossiped. Some of these women had it rough at their American homes. They'd be sexually harassed, or even beaten. The laws didn't protect them. Lori appreciated that she'd caught on with a decent family. Jennifer and I loved her. Mom treated her with respect. Tony was really kind toward her, too.

Tony, by the way, was savoring the Philippines on a different level. He found the country to be a drinker's paradise.

That led to another worldly education for me.

San Miguel beer, a local brew, was very popular in the Philippines. Tony had a taste for it. He liked going to the local bars. And because he had a mischievous streak, sometimes he'd take me along when he and his Air Force buddies went out drinking on weekends.

The custom for Americans on weekends was that the women would go shopping while the men hit the bars. It wasn't illegal in the Philippines to bring a minor into the bars off post. In the barrio, as long as you could get to the bar and had money, you could order a beer. The bar Tony liked best was down the street from our house off post and heavily patronized by Americans.

I remember smelling a weird chemical in the bar, and asked what it was. "Formaldehyde," Tony said. When I asked what formaldehyde was used for, he said it was to preserve corpses so they wouldn't decompose before a funeral. What did that have to do with bars? It turned out the Filipinos used formaldehyde to clean empty bottles.

Sometimes Tony would let me have a sip of his beer, and there'd be a trace of formaldehyde left in it from the bottle being cleaned and reused.

The bars were full of strange things. There were exotic foods, including *baloot* — raw chicken embryos eaten straight out of the shell. I felt like gagging watching bar patrons eat that stuff. But I loved going to the bars. The whole scene fascinated me. I admired the deft, cool skills of the Filipino hustlers at pool and darts, taking the Americans' money. Even Filipino kids not much older than I would fumble around with the cue stick, missing shots, sandbagging the soldiers, then cleaning them out as soon as the stakes were raised.

I developed an admiration for the kid hustlers' competitive prowess, and knew their cunning didn't end at the pool table or dartboard. Their best opportunities were when a GI passed out drunk. That's when they would slink up and slip a wallet out of a pocket. In time, through patient observation, I figured out this game. The kids had an arrangement with the bar owner. They'd pass the wallet's money to the bar owner, and he'd kick them back part of the take. There I was, 9 years old, seeing things a 9-year-old normally doesn't see. And *shouldn't* see.

The deeper you went into the barrios, the grungier the bars became, not to mention wilder and more dangerous. On the outskirts of the barrios it was mellow and safe enough; farther in, the patrons carried knives and guns, and the hustling wasn't just darts and pool. The joints crawled with whores of either gender. Even as little as I was, I was propositioned by girls and boys, some not much older than I. A smile, a rub of a hand, "C'mon, blondie." I'd look amazed and revolted and brush them away. I was getting an education in a hurry.

There was one particularly racy bar that Tony and his Air Force drinking buddies took me to one day. A large rattan basket hung in a corner behind a curtain of beads. It drew my curiosity. I couldn't imagine what it was for. We started shooting darts. I was sipping a bottle of Fanta orange soda (Mom was now letting me drink pop and have candy, in moderation, since my hyperactivity had come somewhat under control); the men had their bottles of beer. On my turn, I'd stand on a barstool, lofting a dart upward. I loved the game. Next to soccer, darts and pool were the national sports in the Philippines. But I couldn't keep my eyes away from the rattan basket.

"What's the basket for?" I finally asked.

"Don't worry about that," Tony said. "That's not for you."

He wouldn't provide any details. But every time we went to that bar after that, I wondered about that basket in the corner.

Then one time when we were in there, I saw a GI give some money to a Filipino girl at the bar. They walked over to the basket and disappeared behind the bead curtain. Two bar workers joined them.

I was excited. Finally I'd see what that thing was for.

Through the beads I could make out activity. The guy eased his pants down. He moved himself under the basket and lay on his back beneath the round opening. The girl undressed and climbed into the basket. The bar workers positioned the basket over the guy. When everything was in place, they spun the basket around.

It was the weirdest damn thing I'd seen in my life.

"You don't need to be looking at that," Tony said. But I was transfixed. My eyes widened.

The girl started moaning and exclaiming loudly.

"Is she OK?" I asked.

Tony just smiled and shook his head.

It was my first glimpse of sex. Even a normal sexual act can warp a kid the first time he witnesses it; but this sordid scene left me with a twisted feeling. I couldn't grasp the appeal of what was going on in the basket.

I never told Mom what I'd seen. I didn't feel like telling *anyone*. I wished

I could forget all about it.

In all, the barrio bars with their hustlers and whores exposed me to the depths that poverty will push people to make a buck. It was an early lesson in reality, how the world works. I discovered a basic truth: Hunger and neediness drive people, including kids not much older than I, to survive any way they can. It was World Economics 101. There wasn't Good and Evil. There were just the haves and have-nots.

I understood there was nothing I could do but deal with it. But this new knowledge sharpened my senses and intuition. I was always alert that I was a target.

It turned out that the only time I had anything stolen from me in the Philippines was when I was actually on base. Some friends and I were playing football on a lawn. I took my shoes off. Some local kids were watching outside the fence. When there was enough distance between them and us, they jumped the fence, sprinted over, grabbed my shoes and took off back over the fence. It was that fast.

I sat there and laughed. I didn't like the shoes, anyway. But then I had a twinge of guilt. I thought to myself: *If you didn't like the shoes, why hadn't you just tossed the shoes to them when you saw them behind the fence?*

That feeling of sympathy revealed to me how much my mentality had changed in the Philippines. Indeed, I'd undergone a total transformation in my view of my family's wealth.

In America we'd been poor. Now, in this country, we were rich. Poor was the status quo in the Third World, and it was real poverty. The kind that was relentless, where crimes of opportunity were also crimes of necessity.

I had it better than I'd thought.

AFTER A YEAR WE moved to a house on base. It felt like living in a standard American community. There no longer was a barrio just down the street. There was no more playing soccer with Filipino kids. The only Filipino children were the half-Filipinos whose American fathers had Filipino wives.

Clark AFB was enormous, and largely secure. If you happened to live toward the middle of the base, you could leave your bike outside your house. But if you lived toward the periphery, you had to be vigilant. The danger was as obvious as the construction of the walls around the base. After the concrete was set, workers stuck bottles poking out the top. After the concrete was dry, the bottles' tops were broken to create jagged deterrents to interlopers. The higher walls, which rose 20 feet, were forbidding, but this glass equivalent of barbed wire didn't work too well on the shorter of the walls. A thief could grind down the glass and climb over.

The Filipino national police posted guards on base and patrolled the walls with the American MPs. There were guard towers. While the base was fairly safe, crime was lurking just beyond the walls.

One of the American kids on base had brought over his Yamaha street bike from the States. Mopeds were highly popular. All the cool high school kids had mopeds at Clark. Tony himself had a Honda Passport. One time at dusk, a group of us younger kids witnessed a fascinating sight.

A ways away from us, four Filipinos came over the fence, attracted by the

Yamaha parked not far away. They quickly descended on the bike, carried it to the fence and hoisted it up and over, where another gaggle of Filipinos was waiting to catch it. The thieves jumped back over the fence and, like a circus act, all four of them mounted the Yamaha and zoomed off. Their shadows receded into the darkness, along with their hoots and hollers.

LORI MOVED WITH US onto the base. And she continued serving as a great guide as we explored all over the country. We took her on vacations. We went to Baguio City in the northern mountains, and Subic Bay in the south, where there was a U.S. Naval base on the Pacific. We traveled all over. We attended a performance of *The Nutcracker* by a premier company in Manila.

Life on the base itself was fun. There are benefits to being a military brat. Days off from school, we kids could spend all day at the base swim pool, part of a big recreational complex. There was a pizzeria with a video arcade. I got hooked on the classics: Space Invaders, Scramble, Phoenix, Missile Command, Galaxian, Asteroids, Donkey Kong, and Galaga. It was a child's paradise.

There was a barbershop in the complex, and Tony took me for my first barber's haircut. Even though we were no longer struggling like we had the first few years of my life, Mom still cut my hair. But I thought going to the barber was neat. I was moving up in the world. Walkmans were becoming popular, and they didn't cost much where we were, being so close to Japan. Tony bought me one. Walkmans, videogames . . . and the movie *E.T. The Extra-Terrestrial.* That was kids' pop culture in 1982. And at age 10, I was right smack in the flow of it.

There was another cultural trend underway: personal computers. They fascinated me. Computers had evolved from the clunky box I'd encountered in the school office in Panama City. At the school at Clark AFB we were sometimes given the option of taking either handwritten tests or tests on the classroom computer. I always chose the computer. Our classroom had a Commodore 64 — a computer and monitor in one casing. Every time I started tapping on that computer's keyboard, it was hard to get me away from it. I discovered that there was a lot more to do on it than just take tests. I wanted to play games, do programming in Basic language. I'd type in commands, trying to figure out how the software worked. I'd spend as much time on the computer as I could get away with. I'd look around, make sure I wasn't being watched, then try to reboot the machine.

Pretty soon, my love of computers was right up there with playing soccer. Well, almost.

THERE WERE THOUSANDS OF kids living at Clark AFB. Youth sports leagues were in force, just as they'd been at Tyndall AFB. The league schedules rotated so that the various sports wouldn't overlap. The kids on the base could play football, then basketball, then baseball, then soccer, instead of having to choose one over another. For me, this was awesome. I got to play all four.

Just like in Panama City, I was highly competitive. In fact, I was ruthless. I had a fierce desire to win. I couldn't help myself. Especially in soccer.

All those barrio games the year before had taught me a lot of tricks. They paid off on the pitch. As competitive as the Clark leagues were, I was put in as a starting halfback on my team. The league had a heavy schedule. Sometimes we'd play doubleheaders on Saturdays. That was fine by me. I couldn't get enough. I had that hyperactive stamina. I felt like I could run forever. But a new experience lay in store for me — something I hadn't imagined.

It was the second game of a Saturday doubleheader. I got control of the ball in close to the goal, nearly on the end line. There is an extra burst of adrenaline that happens when you're in a scoring situation and everything speeds up, like fast forwarding video. I had a chance at the goal, but I had to turn and kick at an angle. I moved in to shoot with my left foot. My knee bent, my foot swung back. A split-second before I kicked, the goalie lunged and swept the ball away. Directly behind the ball was a goal post. My foot smashed into the metal stand and wrapped around it.

There was a jolting impact and shock. The next instant I was writhing on the ground.

It was a pain I'd never felt before. Massive. I knew something was wrong.

I struggled to my feet. My foot and ankle throbbed, shooting pain of agony up my leg. I limped off the field. I had to stay out of the game. It didn't seem real. But there was no way I could get out there in this condition.

After the game, it felt like the longest bike ride of my life. I could only pedal with my right foot. My left leg was on fire. I choked back tears. This was ridiculous! It was taking me forever, pushing with one foot and waiting for the pedal to come around. I'd never make it. I was hurt bad. It was too far to go. In another moment I'd have to stop. I told myself I'd make it just a little farther then I'd get off the bike.

But when I reached a point on the road where I'd promised myself to quit, I found that I wasn't ready to. The pain was terrible, but I entertained a new notion:

What if I didn't quit? What if I just set my mind on making it home?

It was crazy. But I told myself I was going to endure the pain and make it all the way home. Even if it took hours.

I kept pushing the pedal with my right foot. I played a game in my mind, trying to think of anything but the pain. It wasn't easy. Occasionally the left pedal flipped up sharply into my injured instep. The result was excruciating.

The whole thing seemed impossible. I kept on, though. Progress was slow, but I acknowledged that I was covering distance. I told myself I could do this. The only way I'd fail was if I quit. All I had to do was not quit. If I didn't quit, then I'd make it. I decided to stop doubting that I would make it.

I'm going to make it . . . I'm going to make it . . .

Finally I was blocks from my house. And then I was on my street. I coasted up to the curb and climbed off. I let the bike collapse.

I could barely drag myself inside. My leg was awful. My ankle was swollen fat.

"How was your game, Jeff?" Mom asked.

"I need to go to the hospital."

I told her how I'd smashed up my ankle.

She sat me down and got my shoe and sock off. She brought me ice in a plastic baggy and told me the injury couldn't be that serious.

"Just lie down, honey. I'll bring you some aspirin."

I knew she was wrong, but I went to bed anyway. That night, I couldn't sleep. The throbbing pain kept me awake.

In the morning, Mom took me to the emergency room on base. We learned my ankle was broken. The doctor said I'd fractured the growth plate.

I was in a cast, in the humidity of the Philippines, uncomfortable as hell. I knew I'd miss the rest of the soccer season. But Mom told me I had to show up for every game anyway, to help out my team.

I was on crutches for two weeks, unable to put pressure on my bad leg. When I finally was allowed to, I started getting restless. I ditched the crutches and hobbled around like mad, cast be damned. My left leg would be sore at the end of the day, but I just couldn't stay off it. In fact, I started kicking a soccer ball around again — with my right foot, rebounding it off a wall, or passing it around to friends.

I kept at it, and started getting rather good kicking with my right foot. A few months later, after the cast was off and I'd rehabilitated my skinny pale left leg back to normal, I returned to playing soccer — and found I could kick equally strong with either foot. Everyone was amazed, including myself.

From that point on, wherever I played in a soccer league, teams wanted me for a halfback. I was equal with my feet, just as I was with my hands, able to write with left or right, able to kick with left or right.

Breaking my leg was a blessing in disguise.

THERE WAS ONE OTHER bad injury I suffered in the Philippines. It happened when I was running around with my friend Nick.

Nick was a big, energetic kid my age, and even more adventurous than I. He always had a mischievous grin. He was full of the devil. It was natural that we became partners in crime.

Nick introduced me to cigarettes. As bad luck had it, Mom saw us sharing a smoke outside the house. She had the perfect punishment in mind. She and Nick's mother, Jeanie, who was a striking, red-headed Southern belle, sat Nick and me down in front of our friends and made the two of us smoke.

"C'mon, take a deep drag," Mom said. "Let's see how much of a smoker you boys really are."

It wasn't long before we got dizzy and were ready to puke. We were sick the rest of the day. It broke us of the desire to smoke.

Nick, like me, was very interested in anything mechanical. There were air-raid towers on base that had been there since Gen. MacArthur's time. Every day at noon the sirens blasted, signaling lunch. Nick got a notion that rewiring a siren would be a great prank. We'd fix it to go off at a different time. Of course, I was up for that. It meant we'd get to climb a tower, plus deal with the wiring. How could I resist?

We picked out a tower. The wires were exposed about 50 feet up in the air. At the top of the tower was a metal platform, surrounded by a rail, with space for no more than two people to stand. There were two gigantic horns at the top. They'd make you go deaf if you were up there when they went off. So Nick and I figured to climb up early with plenty of time to get down and away before noon.

One morning, we stood at the base of the tower. We were alone. Nick started climbing the rungs. I followed. It was like going up a telephone pole. At the top we found what we were looking for — two wires, a positive and a negative. They were big in my hands, about 2 inches thick. With the fearless immortality of youth, I said, "We're going to do this thing."

I stuck the two wires together. The moment they touched, I was blown backward through the air.

When I opened my eyes, I became aware of sharp points biting into my back. I saw treetops and wondered where I was. I was somewhere very high up in the sky.

Then I focused on Nick's terrified face looming over me.

"I was so scared," he said. "I was getting ready to go home and get my mom."

"Why? What's going on?"

"Man, you've been knocked out for about five minutes."

Nick explained I'd hit the guardrail and landed flat. One arm and a leg had gone over the side but my other arm had hooked around one of the poles. That's what had saved me from going over entirely. The fall would have killed me.

Nick had pulled me back on the platform, wondering if I was dead. He'd seen that I was breathing. Then I'd finally come to.

I sat up with a puzzled expression. The sharp points that had been poking me were from the metal grates.

"Man, when you tried to rewire the air tower you got electrocuted," Nick explained. "That was crazy."

"Really?" I said.

"Yeah, look at your elbows."

They were bright purple. The blood vessels were broken.

Nick helped me up. I smelled burned skin and hair. My lap and legs were soaked. I'd pissed my pants.

"We got to get out of here," Nick said. "These things are about to go off."

"All right," I said. "I just need to catch my breath before I can come down the pole."

It was several minutes before my lungs could hold an inhale.

I was quivering as I rode my bike home. The shock had juiced my system. I just wanted to get home and try to rest.

Mom was alarmed by my condition. I told her I'd fallen off my bike.

"I'm OK. I just want to go to bed."

I woke up the next morning bone-cold dry with the chills. It took me a couple days before I felt normal again.

I LOVED THE PHILIPPINES. I couldn't foresee that my time there would run its course.

Unbeknownst to Jennifer and me, Tony and Mom were having marital problems.

Mom flew back to the States for a friend's funeral. While she was away, with Lori taking care of my sister and me, Tony was gone, too.

He never told us where.

CHAPTER NINE: Turning Japanese

Mom had kept in touch with an Air Force couple she'd befriended in Florida, and who now were living in Japan. That's how we got to spend a summer in that nation — a season that left deep and lasting impressions. In many ways it molded my outlook on life to this day.

The Stevens were a family of three. Gary was an Air Force officer. He and his wife, Gail, had a daughter, Samantha, between Jennifer's and my ages. Gary was stationed in Yokota, the Air Force's only airlift hub in the western Pacific. The wing stationed there had a sword-bearing Samurai in its logo, and called itself the "Samurai Team." Gail told Mom that an English teacher was needed in Karuizawa, one of the towns near the base, in the summer to teach Japanese teenagers and adults. It was a non-paying, volunteer position. We were invited to stay with the Stevens. It was a chance to see more of the world. Tony, of course, would stay behind in the Philippines.

It was immediately apparent how Japan was different from the Philippines. Here was the exotic, advanced civilization I'd expected after seeing *Shogun*! Ancient. Refined. Subtle. Respectful. Honorable. Everything was so clean. And the people, so polite. The Japanese — who had rounder faces and bone-white skin, compared to the brown and shorter Filipinos — didn't stare at us, the foreigners, the way the Filipinos did. The Japanese were courteous. Their society was one laced with palpable pride. There wasn't the undercurrent of deprivation and crime there was in the Philippines. Japan was a developed nation. The people were happier, earnest, confident. It felt to me that the Japanese possessed some inner strength and reserve that seemed quietly powerful. They were in control.

I was surprised that Japanese policemen didn't carry guns.

"How do they bust people?" I asked Gary and Gail.

"Well, here, after the Japanese commit a crime, they're usually so embarrassed, nine out of 10 times they'll turn themselves in," Gary said.

I couldn't believe it. But as time went on, I did.

On one of our first mornings in Yokota, Samantha took me off post to a nearby park. There were quite a few Japanese practicing Tai-Chi. We walked over the stone-laid paths and sat on the ground to one side of the grass, which sparkled with dew. A crisp breeze whispered. Rays from the rising sun slanted through the drop-laden leaves and blossoms of a cherry tree. There was serenity, as if everyone and everything was in a trance. The people. The stones. The trees. The city, itself. A few motorcycles puttered unobtrusively along the streets beyond the park. I was mesmerized, not making a sound, watching the Tai-Chi practitioners' graceful routines. Each had his or her own aura, moving in a self-contained space. Some of the participants were quite elderly. They were the most proficient, using graceful precision. No shakiness. No awkwardness. Clicking into a posture like a perfectly oiled and calibrated machine.

The breaths of the people nearest us were audible — collective inhales and exhales, in through the nose and out through the mouth, slow and extended, in time with the movements. But I could not even detect the breathing of the older practitioners, they were so smooth and effortless.

The Tai-Chi practitioners wore sweat suits or loose-fitting clothes, or even business suits with the jacket removed if their schedule demanded they leave the park immediately for the office. Some were barefoot, some wore shoes. All were joined, unified, by the super-slow motions done as a mass. A newcomer would step into an empty space in a line, see which movement was being performed, and join in, synchronizing with the group's timing. Slow sweeps of hands, sways of torsos, tilts of heads, bends of legs, dips of waists. A silent, gentle dance.

I stood and quietly copied the movements, teaching myself. As the days passed, the beauty of Japan's ancient customs spoke to me of something very beautiful and true. Of some higher plane of existence. I felt a strange peace, as if I was among kindred spirits. A few weeks into our stay, the meaning of this feeling became clearer.

Gail and Gary and an English-speaking guide they hired drove us to see a Samurai warrior exhibition in one of the villages, out in the heartland where Buddhist temples stood and special traditions were kept alive. The contest was a demonstration of ancient battlefield skills. We sat in the seats at a little arena inside a temple. The seats were mostly filled with Japanese.

A pony-tailed man in medieval Samurai leather wraps came tearing down a lane on horseback, spear drawn, toward a row of tiny discs, like washers, hanging by string on trees. *Boom* — he had the first disc on the tip of his spear.

Then *boom, boom, boom*, one after another, he speared the targets.

Horseback archers charged at full gallop down another lane on the opposite side of the arena, facing the seats across from us. One by one the archers rose from their saddles, pressing their knees into the sides of their mounts, turned sideways toward a target and let fly arrows at circled targets. Then each pulled back on the reins and cried out, "hoh — ohhh!" *Poink.* Each arrow nailed the target. Machine-like.

Electricity crackled. Japanese pride filled the arena.

The guide explained that many of these warriors trained their entire lives: living in temples, devoting mind, body and spirit to preserving the traditions, endlessly striving for improvement. They wore the same clothes and used the same weapons as warriors of yore. They were a living museum.

That's when it struck me: Their quest for perfection was the perfect embodiment of the best in the human spirit. They would never achieve perfection. No one can. But they came the closest to perfection I'd ever seen. Their quest was an end in itself.

They never gave up.

Japan, I decided at that moment, and would reconfirm again and again that summer, was a nation bent on maximizing potential. Driven. Disciplined. And devoted to honor: respecting the elderly; taking care of one's parents; watching out for one's neighbors; making one's best effort.

As time went on, I noted how the Japanese took care in even the humblest of acts, such as sweeping a floor. A menial task like that was performed with pleasure. I'd watch a clerk sweeping the street in front of the shop — deliberate, methodical broom strokes, clearing every speck as efficiently as possible, performing a meticulous job in an organized manner. Getting the chore done correctly in a minimal amount of time. Striving for perfection.

THERE WAS ANOTHER FACET of Japan that captivated me. It was the nation's encompassing embrace of technology, as if Japan were leading the world into a brave new future.

That year, 1983, the American rock band Styx released a hit single, *Mr. Roboto*, a science-fiction song about a future with Japanese-made robots. The lyrics included this verse: "My heart is human, my blood is boiling, my brain I.B.M." In the prior year, the movie *Blade Runner* came out. I watched it again and again at Clark AFB. *Blade Runner* depicted a Los Angeles in the year 2019 governed by technology, with mega-corporations, ungodly skyscrapers, and "replicants" — cyborg slaves implanted with human memories. While *Blade Runner* was supposed to depict an ominous world, I was smitten by its vision of a high-tech, ultra-modern civilization. It was a society in which everything was computerized. I saw that not as an ominous development, but a necessary evolutionary step. Science working for humans.

When we visited Tokyo, the giant city's downtown seemed like the set of *Blade Runner*, only without the impoverished masses at street level and the permanent smog hanging above. Everything was clean, orderly, perfected. Skyscrapers. Neon billboards. Gleaming subways. It was a manifestation of the Japanese ethos of perfectionism.

The cleverness of the Japanese mind showed up even in the design of soda containers. You could buy bottles containing clear liquid. You twisted the top, and a capsule in the middle released black syrup that expanded into the liquid, creating the cola mix. That was Japanese innovation: The simple act of opening a soda bottle was entertaining. Then there were the whistle candies — round candies like Life Savers that you blew through. That was the Japanese genius: building extra functions into even common objects. Maximizing usage, conserving resources. It was the opposite of the American disposable society: use it up, throw the container away. I found that Japan was at the forefront of recycling, and of Earth-friendly products. The idea was to do as much as possible with as little as possible, given Japan's dearth of natural resources. Yet the Japanese blended this economy with creativity.

I was smitten by Japanese technology. Television wristwatches were everywhere. There also were "water watches": timepieces powered by battery cells kept charged by dripping a few drops of water over them. I gawked at test motorcycles on the street. There were no handlebars on them; they were operated by hand-control pads. The toy stores were filled with strange new products. There were GoBots: robots that transformed into little cars.

Orderliness and practicality were pervasive. Japan was claustrophobic, overcrowded with space at a premium. The roof of a 50-story corporate building would be fenced in so executives' children could play. There'd be, perhaps, an amusement park with a go-cart track. Some rooftops actually had grass gardens in concrete troughs. (Nature is deeply revered in Japan.) People lived in teeming high-rise apartment houses with no yards. They had to go to the public parks to play. Even the U.S. military base, Yokota, where we were staying in the Stevens' apartment, had high rises. The apartment was in such a building.

Yes, the Japanese conserved, made do with what they had. There was no giving in to excess. It occurred to me that the only fat Japanese person you'd ever see is a sumo wrestler, whose girth is honorable, or a Japanese-American. There was no reason for the Japanese to indulge in junk food or become couch potatoes. They were busy with school, work, social life.

Industrious.

Japanese.

THE 1980S WAS A time when America was going through a Japanese craze, not only purchasing Japanese cars and electronics but eating sushi and tofu, buying shoji screens and studying martial arts. There was even a feeling that Japanese trade and investments were taking over America. But there I was, in Japan itself, at the epicenter of the cultural-technological revolution.

I relished the customs, the orderliness, such as removing your shoes at the entrance to homes. You always made sure you had a clean pair of socks with no holes. I learned to bow Japanese-style, hands at sides, maintaining eye contact. The sense of honor was pervasive. Vending machines sold bottles of sake and beer along with soda pop. Children knew they weren't supposed to buy the alcoholic beverages, so they didn't. I knew such public machines would be impossible in America.

There were sushi bars everywhere, and they didn't stink of fish outside like their American counterparts. Everything was fresh, ocean-smelling, nutritious and healthy. I discovered that I loved sushi. Hibachi bars were everywhere. You picked out raw food from buffets and then either brought it to a hibachi grill or grilled it yourself at your table.

I learned Japanese dining etiquette. One time, after filling my belly, I leaned back, satisfied, leaving the chopsticks stabbed straight up in the food. The maitre d' rushed over. He grabbed the chopsticks and set them beside the bowl. He asked if the meal was not to my liking. Surprised, I told him it was delicious. He explained that leaving chopsticks in the bowl said the food was disgraceful. I apologized for my ignorance and thanked him for telling me the rules. The maitre d' was so pleased, he brought over a complimentary cake. In Japan you are given a chance to save face.

The Japanese were meticulous. They were amazing at keeping their composure. If they were angry with you, you never knew it from their expressions. They maintained an outer, stoic shell. They were professional. They stayed in their role. *Never let 'em see you sweat. Never show pain. Always be polite, even to your enemies.* Everyone seemed to have a winning attitude, like salesmen. It was contagious.

The one exception I saw to the Japanese's stringency was in how parents permitted their children to make mistakes. Yes, adults instilled drive and obedience in their kids; but the Japanese understand that mistakes can be great learning experiences.

Samantha was a tomboy, and we became good friends. She and I would buy fireworks at toy stores. As smitten as I was by the discipline and stoicism of Japan, I was still little Jeff Bowling, with a hyperactive streak. Samantha and I would buy little cheap plastic yellow raincoats and Roman candles, and shoot the candles at each other, the candles bouncing off our raincoats.

One day, we played this game with some Japanese children whose parents knew ours. When the parents saw what was going on, they didn't start shouting at their children. Instead, smiling, they pulled the kids off to the side for a calm conference. They explained to their children the errors of their ways. The children nodded politely.

After that, Samantha and I apologized to their parents, and that was that. The adults saw we weren't disrespectful. They allowed us to continue playing with their children, but in an acceptable game.

THERE SEEMED LITTLE WRONG to me about Japanese society. But one thing I didn't care much for was the secret contempt for foreigners, especially Americans. The same notion of superiority that had driven the Japanese militarists in the 1930s and 1940s toward the conquest of Asia and the Pacific lives on in the darkest recesses of the Japanese psyche. It harbors a detestation of Americans. In the Philippines, our family had driven the route of the Bataan Death March. It revealed to me the depths of hatred. I could not imagine the pain and suffering endured by the POW's on this march.

When we were greeted politely by the people we met in Japan, I was attuned to the possibility of a smirk lurking in the corner of a mouth. Indeed, I saw it many times. There was a saying I heard in Japan, and years later it was expressed in a line in the movie *Black Rain*: "America is only good for music and movies." The Japanese, in contrast, build the electronics that make music and movies possible. That was the Japanese mindset.

I knew that no matter how I identified with the Japanese, how much their culture and history resonated with me, I'd always be an outsider there. A *gaijin*. A foreigner.

Another aspect of Japanese culture I disliked was the hidden agendas, the unspoken rules you had to heed — if you could figure them out. Candor just wasn't part of the culture. A humble smile masked a deceitful intent. If you hired workers — say, someone to do gardening at your house — they quoted you a price. What they didn't mention was the traditional bonus they expected if they finished ahead of schedule. When you found out about the customary extra fee, to save face you'd pay it, and it could be as much as the quoted price.

I watched this happen with a repairman whom Gary and Gail hired. The work was finished ahead of schedule. Gary paid the man a tidy sum. I gawked at the large currency bills.

"I think you overpaid," I told Gary afterward. I knew the denominations of the yen currency from having shopped at candy stores.

"No, no," Gary explained. "It's customary to pay a tip when a job's done and done well and ahead of expectations. It's a bonus."

I never forgot that aspect of doing business with the Japanese, the unspoken but expected payment of a consideration. Just one of the multitude of unwritten laws of that nation. This knowledge served me well, years later, running my own business, when I started negotiating with Japanese clients. I understood that I could be talking with a junior officer, who reported to a senior officer. I'd have to do favors for the junior officer — perhaps offer a paid-for room in a Reno hotel-casino — then also take care of the next guy up the ladder (never knowing who was the actual decision maker) until I finally got to the right person who, hopefully, was interested in the project.

The Japanese never show you all their cards. The good part is, once they're your client, they pay on time, understand you need to make a profit, and cultivate a long-term relationship that includes referrals.

THE ONLY NEGATIVE EXPERIENCE I encountered in Japan was a byproduct of the country's rising wealth and prestige. Some teenagers were rebelling against formal constraints. Punk rock was hugely popular among the youth. But interestingly, teens with purple hair were still polite.

One day, Samantha lent me her father's 10-speed bicycle, and we and three of her Japanese friends rode out to a little farming village a couple hours ride off base. We were in search of a shop that sold a particularly fancy model of a toy pellet gun that friends of hers had bought. Toy guns that were replicas of real guns but shot yellow plastic pellets were extremely popular with Japanese youth then. Magazines were devoted to the different models. Samantha and I found the store and purchased the gun and also some fireworks and candy. We bought a lunch of fish, seaweed, and rice at another store and sat down and ate.

On our ride back, Samantha led us on a shortcut she knew. We ended up in a housing project, obviously lower-income, that was full of Japanese in their teens and early twenties. We had to dismount and walk our bikes through the crowded streets. I felt strange vibes. I sensed hostility. I knew it was a response to our white faces.

"Don't say nothing, just keep walking through," Samantha said.

We made our way slowly. People bumped us, jostled us, shot us dirty looks. It was the first overt rudeness I'd experienced in Japan. The people living in this housing project didn't have the pride, the politeness, I'd gotten used to. It was like I was suddenly in an American city.

We heard yelling behind us.

"Just keep walking," Samantha said.

I turned and looked. Inside an apartment window, three or four stories up, some young Japanese were standing. One of them was shouting at us. He looked like he was college age. Bowl haircut. Sneer. Through the bars on the window he was tossing little glass bottles, vials for perfume or nail polish. The glass was smashing behind us.

I stopped, trying to figure out if this was really happening. He kept yelling, cursing in Japanese.

All of a sudden, my anger just welled up and spilled out.

I shouted at him. It was the first time I'd lost my cool in Japan. I forgot my surroundings, that I was in the midst of a sea of Japanese. Samantha and I could have gotten mauled.

"Come down here!" I screamed.

I wished I knew more Japanese. I felt disgraced — not just by his violence, that it was utterly stupid and uncalled for, but because he wasn't acting like I'd learned a Japanese person was supposed to act. I wanted to rebuke him, make him lose face. He was spitting on his Japanese heritage, this ancient civilization that I had embraced so dearly.

Movement on the street had stopped. The Japanese pedestrians backed away from us, not wanting to get hit by the flying bottles. Their faces looked ashamed, apologetic.

Samantha grabbed me. "C'mon, let's go. You're just going to get us in trouble."

The bottles were landing to the side of us. The jerk had no aim.

We moved on. The bottles stopped coming when we were out of range.

I was shaking with fury. My romantic vision had been shattered. Japan wasn't the ideal society I'd come to believe it to be. I could go to America and get this kind of sh*tty treatment.

Our Japanese friends told Samantha and me not to worry. The jerks in the apartment were just losers. They didn't count.

But Japan now had a little stain on it. I realized it had its share of sorry-ass characters who didn't care.

THE ANCIENT JAPAN WAS somewhat hidden from the average tourist. But Mom, Jennifer and I indulged in the culture as much as possible. We went to Kabuki theater. The act before the play performance was fan dancers who mirrored each other's movements so well it was eerie. It was an art resulting from thousands of years of culture.

I began reading up on Japanese history, the warlords and dynasties in the feudal age. When I learned a little bit, I'd quiz Japanese friends (so many of whom spoke English) about what I'd learned; they were fascinated that I was fascinated by their culture. I wanted to absorb as much as I could. I picked up a tiny bit of the lingo, the polite phrases. I watched Samurai movies endlessly. I didn't need to understand the dialogue. The action told the story. A master would be killed; his disciples would avenge him. Or a woman would be kidnapped; she would be rescued. Swordplay. Hand-to-hand combat. Magic spells enacted in puffs of smoke. Impossible flights through the air.

I marveled how the warriors would get beaten down and yet keep struggling back to their feet — personifying *bushido*, Way of the Warrior. I understood how the Japanese had pulled themselves out of the debacle of World War II and the fallout of the atomic bombs and rebuilt their country. It was about subordinating the individual to the collective effort, acting honorably with thrift and industriousness, working as a team, making do with what you had at hand. The Japanese reached back to the Samurai code of feudal times. In a few short decades, the nation was a modern industrialized power.

I overheard some of the adults on the Air Force base talking about "the sun" and "war." I was interested in warfare, and one day Gary explained to me that they were talking about the author, Sun Tzu, and his book, *The Art of War*. I found a translation of the book in the base library and started reading bits and pieces. *The Art of War* is the oldest military treatise in history, and was originally contained in age-old Chinese scrolls. *The Art of War* teaches strategies for smaller forces to prevail over much larger ones: which way to fight in sunlight, in fog, in wind. Because of my physical size, I was always the underdog, the little guy, so Sun Tzu's philosophy was for me.

Plan beforehand. Defeat your enemy before you even fight the battle.

This was great stuff! I knew it was a guide for life.

I COULD FEEL MYSELF being transformed. I believe the years when we most shape our personalities for adulthood is from pre-adolescence to the mid-teens. There I was, 10 years old. I saw the power of being disciplined: a nation practiced it and — despite lack of territory and natural wealth — was a world economic powerhouse. I saw that I could alter the world around me, so to speak, if I used my mind and spirit.

I picked up the practice of meditation. I had continued going down some mornings to watch the people in the park practicing Tai-Chi. I longed to attain their serenity. I also was impressed by the older men and women sitting around town, perhaps in chairs outside a shop, or in the alleys outside apartment houses, eyes closed, breathing slowly and deeply, barely moving, sometimes with a slight smile on their faces.

When I'd first seen this, I'd thought these people were in an extended state of sleep, just grabbing a sort of sitting-down nap out there in the open. After a while they'd get up and walk away.

"Don't bother them," Samantha told me. "They're meditating."

I eventually learned what "meditating" meant.

In the Buddhist temples that Gail and Gary took us to, I listened to the monks — who were very educated, and spoke English — teaching about meditation. It fired up my interest enough to check out a book on the subject from the base library. I discovered that meditation had nothing to do with a higher power. It had to do with taking a moment for yourself, quieting your mind, getting your energy back. Its benefits were said to be enormous: More calmness, clarity of thinking, sense of wel-being.

I practiced sitting cross-legged, or on my knees with my head down and arms bent before me, eyes closed, thumbs and pinkies touching their opposites. I kept my back straight and inhaled gently through my nose and exhaled through my mouth so softly I couldn't hear my breath. I tried to hear my heartbeat, and imagined I could hear the blood flowing through my veins. I'd mentally move my "chi," my ball of energy, from below my sternum up to my forehead. I became able to meditate for 20 minutes at a time.

Sometimes I'd go out to a hillside and meditate with my eyes open. It slowed everything down inside of me so that I could think clearly. It was an antidote to my hyperactivity. It quieted my mind, focused my thoughts. To this day I still meditate, such as before a business meeting. I've taught my wife how to meditate. If more people did it, we'd have a calmer world.

I learned so much in Japan. I learned how I wanted to live my life. I resolved that in everything I did, I'd give 100 percent effort. Even if I messed something up, I'd do that 100 percent, too — the whole way. I would simply strive for perfection: the unattainable ideal.

THAT SEPTEMBER WE RETURNED to the Philippines. Shortly thereafter, Tony's ugly secret came out:

He had a Filipino girlfriend. He'd gotten her pregnant. He was living with her off base.

This bombshell was quickly followed by a second: With Tony living off base, Mom, Jennifer and I no longer qualified for the officer housing quarters. A written order came for us to vacate.

The impact was staggering. We were stranded. Mom had next to no money to her name. We were stuck with no funds, in a place we couldn't stay. How was Mom going to get us back to the States? She had to get back to America so she could obtain a divorce. And once back, she had to find a job, a home — the works.

It seemed like panic time.

What saved us was Jeanie, my friend Nick's mom. She came up with the perfect plan:

Mom would inform Tony that we would be moving in with him off base until he could come up with the money for us to return to the States.

That did the trick. Tony brought over a $3,000 certified check the next day. He looked anxious. He also looked unhealthy. He'd grown pudgy in the Philippines. His face was puffy, his nose red. He was no longer the quiet, strong, happy guy we'd been fond of.

Even with the $3,000, our future still looked bleak. How were we going to survive back in America? We'd lived so cheaply in the Philippines, where $5 went an incredibly long way. This life of comfort had ended. We were heading back to the American standard, and in that context we were poor all over again.

We did catch one break, though. Nana stretched out her hand to help — the only time she's ever done that financially for Mom. Nana said we should move back to San Bernardino and live with her and she'd support us until Mom found a job and got settled.

Jennifer and I were excited to be going back to the States. But we felt remorse about leaving the Philippines. It had been home for three years. I had made friends. I'd grown up quite a bit. And I was sad about what had happened with Tony. We'd had a good relationship for a long time. We'd been friends.

He'd changed so much from how he'd been in Florida. What had happened? I realized his true character had come out in the Philippines. He'd lost his ambition. He'd let his drinking get the best of him. He'd gotten out of shape. He'd quit running. He'd even failed a few of his officer's exams. I recalled that being a sore subject of discussion between Mom and him. Failing an officer's exam is a big no-no in the military, a career killer. Tony hadn't studied his books. He'd been out screwing around. He'd cheated on Mom.

I had no more respect for him. I was glad we were getting away from him.

I clearly saw now what he was: a quitter. A guy who wanted to lie on the couch and be a nobody.

If there was one really sad thing about leaving, it was saying goodbye to Lori. She had lived with us for three years. She was heartbroken. She badly wanted to come with us.

Our American friends had warned us that it was standard for the Filipino house girl to beg to come along. After arriving in America, she would get established, then leave the family, find a different job, maybe marry an American, and then bring over her children and grandchildren.

Even if we wanted to help Lori, we couldn't afford to take her with us. We couldn't afford the money to sponsor her. What's more, back in the States we'd be just another struggling family, starting all over again at the bottom.

It was a long flight back to California. Fortunately, the government paid for it, since we were still military dependents. Nana picked us up at the airport in Los Angeles. We got off the plane and were shivering.

"What's the matter? It's 70 degrees," Nana said.

We were used to 100 degrees.

One of the first things I wanted was a drink of regular milk. In the Philippines we'd drunk reconstituted milk or my favorite: sour goat's milk with lemon juice in it. It came chilled in small plastic packets. Mom thought it was the most disgusting drink ever made. I'd been able to stomach it. Heck, I'd grown up drinking powdered milk. But now I craved a cold sip of real homogenized cow's milk.

Nana took us to a McDonald's. We ordered burgers and fries. I got a carton of milk, too.

It was nice to drink American milk again.

CHAPTER TEN: Tupperware Truths

Not long after we moved in with Nana, Mom found an assistant's job in the office of a pediatric cardiologist. Mom wasn't interested in wasting time. She was intent on restarting our lives.

Turned out Tony wasn't wasting time, either. We'd been there two weeks when Mom got a surprise phone call. Tony said he was stateside. He'd gone to a lawyer and filed for divorce.

Two weeks later, we moved into one side of a new duplex down the street. We were on a cul-de-sac in a decent neighborhood, and a far cry from the San Bernardino neighborhood I remembered. I settled in quickly. America was home, and I felt comfortable here, safe. In the Philippines, no matter how long we lived there, it was still a foreign country. There was always the undercurrent of poverty, always the potential for danger from just walking down the street. I couldn't just take off whenever I'd wanted and go wherever I'd thought to. I had to watch myself. I was a white American. A target. But now, in California, I was just another kid. I could get on my bike, ride off and explore.

I didn't realize how much I'd missed California. The great big trees: oak, maple and elm, not just the palm, banana or rubber trees as in the Philippines. And the green grass. Clean-smelling air. Warm but not humid weather. Wide streets and evenly paved concrete. Air-conditioned stores.

After the Philippines, everything looked clean and orderly. I could drink water from the tap. I could shower with my mouth open.

I guzzled milk.

I wore long pants.

Every television channel was in English. In the Philippines, about all I'd enjoyed were episodes of *Magnum, P.I.*, which were probably reruns.

You don't appreciate a place until you've had a chance to miss it.

I ENROLLED IN SIXTH GRADE at the nearby elementary school. Jennifer and I were not getting along at all — adolescence hit her hard and she was moody and irritable — so I ended up spending a lot of time after school down the street at Nana's house. Mom didn't get home from work until late in the evening, so Nana would watch me. As always, Nana was stern. She was precise. She liked doing things her way. She was used to living alone. She was a strong woman. She wore pants; I never saw her in a dress. She was not maternal in the least, or affectionate. I don't believe she cared much for kids. To her, kids were just little people.

Nana expected me to mind her and would not put up with any whining. She'd give me an order only once. And she wasn't much on small talk. Since I didn't misbehave around her, we got along great. I got on well with her two housemates, too. These were her black cats: Honey, who had a white nose, and Babe, who had white paws. They were my buddies.

While Nana didn't coddle me, she did give me a chance to earn some money. She had a Toyota pickup. "You wash my truck, I'll give you a buck." That was cool. Jennifer and I didn't get an allowance, so this was my chance for pocket money. With the dollars I made from Nana I could go with my friends to the 7-Eleven. They'd buy candy and Big Gulps, but I'd buy little green bottles of Perrier. I was still avoiding sugar, and the commercials for the mineral water attracted me. I had a taste for it.

Nana was drawing a pension from having worked 20 years as a clerk of some sort in the county district attorney's office. She supplemented her income by selling Tupperware. That meant that when I was being watched at her house and she had a sales call that evening, she'd have to take me along.

I was dubious the first time I accompanied her. How could this stern, poker-faced woman sell *anything*? I knew a person needed enthusiasm, passion, warmth, to sell. But I'd underestimated her. As we drove to the address of the house with the Tupperware party, I was fascinated by her preparation.

Nana got into character. She handed me the Tupperware catalog and brochures and started talking about the products. I leafed through pages and described some of them. Airtight, liquid-tight sets of bowls. Collections of oval and rectangular storage containers. Cooking tools, measuring cups and spoons. Forms for making biscuits and muffins. The lists went on and on.

By the time we arrived at the house full of women, Nana was primed and ready. As soon as we were inside the door, I realized why she'd brought me along. I was meant to be part of the sale. The ploy was meant as an icebreaker, to charm the partygoers. Nana was shrewd!

"Look at this cute little kid!" the women chirped.

"Ah, so you're in sixth grade? And still hanging out with your grandma. How sweet!"

I sat in the corner with a set of Legos I'd brought. But they didn't hold my attention. The dynamics of Tupperware sales captivated me.

Nana started off by writing down each attendee's name. She looked each woman in the eye while shaking the woman's hand and saying her name. "Marie." "Patty." "Wilma." Nana's salesmanship was all about paying attention to details, personalizing the party for each guest, establishing a rapport. She would relate the person's name to something the woman was wearing or how she looked, to memorize that name and use it over and over.

Then Nana swung into her sales. She was an irresistible force — a nicer version of herself. Still a commanding presence, but sweeter. Her order book was already out. She began by explaining "the right way to use Tupperware." She demonstrated "burping the lid." I came to learn that this was a technique most users neglect. After sealing a Tupperware container all the way around, you're supposed to push down on the middle to force out extra air, then lift up part of the lid a little bit and press it down quickly. That forms a tight seal before popping the container in the refrigerator.

In subsequent parties, Nana and I employed a routine. When she demonstrated burping the lid, I'd come up front, pick up a little piece of Tupperware and say, "You've got to *burp* the Tupperware!" The women would laugh. I'd go back to my Legos, but continue watching the party's progress with interest.

Talk about a great way to develop sales skills on the fly! Tupperware parties can't be beat. I studied Nana working the party with her pitches.

"You've got a man that works. He wants his meal. You need this, this and this."

She'd pull out the variously shaped containers, line them up.

"Tupperware," Nana exclaimed, "is perfect for the woman on the go who works outside the home. You cook one meal and you can store leftovers forever."

She emphasized that she practiced what she preached. She'd cook three or four meals on a Saturday and freeze them for thawing and serving during the week.

What Nana was doing was working "relational sales" — relating directly to clients as someone who used the products herself.

"I like to cook," she'd say, "and when I'm making pastries I like to roll this out, and use this and use this and *this*."

She'd pass the different Tupperware sets around, getting them into the customers' hands, letting them look at the products, feel them, subconsciously take ownership.

From my corner of the room, I was absorbing these different approaches. I noted how Nana made her presentation fun. Everyone at the party was having a good time. It was a girl's night out. They sipped their coffee or hot toddies. And then, inevitably, at each optimal moment, Nana would steer the event to the placing of orders.

That was the most exciting part for me. As she jotted down orders, it was absolute proof that her sales job had been successful.

Driving home, I'd ask how many "units" she'd sold. She'd give me a rundown. We always hauled a lot of product to a party. If we returned with an empty trunk, I'd know she'd kicked ass. She'd be in a good mood, too. The kinder, sweeter Nana persona would still be present.

Nana was a great Tupperware saleswoman. In fact, she became so successful in her district that she had a lot of saleswomen underneath her whom she was training. She also sold Mary Kay cosmetics. She did well there, too. Nana really mastered how to move product. I'd listen to her work the phone when she was babysitting me. She was good at "contact management": calling friends and clients for referrals to their friends who might want a house party. Of course, she knew who'd made heavy orders at her Tupperware parties. They were on her marketing list, and she'd mail out promotional products to these people to spur more sales.

Many years later, when I was selling computer hardware and software, I recalled Nana's techniques. Those Tupperware parties had instilled in me the three most important points about selling:

1) You've got to try.

2) You've got to make sure you have a good product.

3) You've got to maintain regular contact: calling premier customers, keeping your marketing list current.

I could never sell anything I didn't believe in myself.

CHAPTER ELEVEN: Back Home and off Again

I hadn't seen Andy Bowling in four years, so I tried contacting him after we'd settled into the duplex. Even though I barely knew him, my thoughts had strayed toward him often during the three years living overseas. I'd see boys with fathers, and that got my imagination working. I considered that there was some blood bond between us — he was, after all, my biological father — and this notion spawned a whole fantasy in my mind about him loving me and caring about me. All that was needed was to close the physical distance between us. We just needed a chance to connect.

As it happened, he was living in a town not far from San Bernardino. He was captain of a firehouse. He was a man of responsibility and status. Mom got the phone number. She called him. She put Jennifer and me on the line. His voice was relaxed, deep, and unconcerned, as if he didn't care about too much. The man explained he was happy we were back in the States now. Unfortunately, he was too busy to see us.

"I'm sorry, kids, my schedule won't permit it."

Mom knew we were disappointed. She kept after him. Finally, one day, he stopped by our duplex.

Andy Bowling was a tall, broad-shouldered, barrel-chested man with short, curly red hair. He was remarried, with a son, a black-haired boy named Jake a few years younger than I. Andy Bowling worked out a visitation schedule with Mom. He would have my sister and me for a day every three weeks. This meant he was actually going to spend some time with us. I was excited! I began thinking that I would have a real dad in my life.

It didn't play out the way I expected.

Andy Bowling was a strange fellow. First, he would only take Jennifer and me out one at a time. That meant my visits with him would be once every six weeks, instead of once every three. He evidently couldn't handle the two of us together. During my turn, he took me shooting pistols and trapshooting, activities we both enjoyed. The next visitation, though, he brought chubby little Jake along. There would be no more one-on-one time with dad.

I tried to overlook his shortcomings. I had matured overseas. I realized each person had good qualities and bad. But I felt cheated. It was simply impossible to get close to this man. He kept my sister and me at an emotional distance. He was friendly without being warm. He cracked jokes without opening up on a deeper emotional level. There were no heart-to-heart talks. There was no discussion of taking trips or seeing each other more often. There was no bonding.

I tried, at first, calling him "dad." But it felt weird and sounded weird. So I backed off and called him by his name, "Andy." He didn't object. He didn't seem to care one way or the other. He kept everything low-key.

Was he just another one of these men who was in and out of our lives, not sticking around? My optimism wilted. But I still didn't give up.

I called him a few times on the phone to chat. He was always too busy to talk. It was frustrating for an 11-year-old!

His wife, Joy, was just the opposite. She was a sweet, plump lady who made Jennifer and me feel comfortable when either of us went to her house. She treated us just as she treated her own son. I liked her. But my anger toward Andy Bowling built and built . . . and finally boiled over one day at his house. I couldn't hold it in any longer. I raised my voice.

"How come you never hang around us? How come you never want to see us? Are we that terrible? Do you hate us or something? You're supposed to be our dad."

"Jeff, you know that's silly," he said, in his even voice. "It's very difficult for me to take time off work. And you also know, I've got my own family to take care of."

I wasn't having it. Something had snapped. Once my anger was unleashed, I couldn't rein it back in. Just like that time on the street in Japan, when that jerk was chucking bottles from the window.

"You've never cared about me or Jennifer! And you don't even care now! We could just be dead and you wouldn't give a damn. You've never even tried to get to know us! Not even once when we were in the Philippines did you bother to call or write or show you care. You don't even love us, and you're our dad."

Joy stepped in.

"You don't know the whole story, Jeff," she said. "Your father didn't want you to go overseas. He went to court to try to block it. He wanted you to stay in America."

She explained that my dad had petitioned the courts to keep us from moving to the Philippines. He'd fought to keep our last names from changing after Mom had married Fritz. I didn't know what was true or not, but I still wasn't impressed.

Wow, he'd fought one time to keep us near him. That was it?

I knew that trying to get close to this man was a lost cause. It would be many years later that I would finally start understanding him. That's when I would learn that he suffered from clinical depression, like my sister. But back then, I just saw a man who coldly refused to reach out to his own son and daughter, his own flesh and blood.

I gave up on him. It wasn't the end of the world. It would have been cool to have had Jake as a little brother to pal around with, but that was now going to be impossible. I wouldn't see my half-brother often enough for us to feel like brothers. That was the way it was, so I got over it.

My dream of having a dad to be close to, this fantasy I'd cooked up in the Philippines, dissolved, just like that.

As it was, after my blowup, I saw Andy Bowling only one more time before we left San Bernardino. It was to say goodbye.

WE DIDN'T STAY LONG in California. Mom was making yet another major change in our lives. Believe it or not, she'd reconnected with Fritz. Or, more truthfully, he'd reconnected with her.

Fritz was stationed now in Montana at Malmstrom AFB. He was on leave vacationing in California, seeing old friends, when he caught wind that Mom was back in town. He called her up.

Nana was not very happy about it. Neither were Jennifer and I.

He stopped by for dinner with us one night at Nana's house. He had the same round face, the same hyena giggle. He was still muscular — in fact, even more than before. But he had mellowed. He was on his best behavior. He and Mom talked casually, as friends.

Nana was abrupt with him. She wasn't buying his act. As for me, I wasn't too alarmed. I knew this dinner was just a visit from someone who'd been part of our lives once. A familiar, if unwelcome, face.

But then he and Mom started dating. And then they decided they were going to make a go of it again. Not tie the knot, but try living together in Montana.

"He's changed," Mom said.

Jennifer and I couldn't talk her out of it. "Let's just stay here," we pleaded. "We just got here."

Nana really laid into Mom about it. Here, she had just gotten divorced. Now she was going to dive into another relationship? And with this abusive asshole, no less?

Mom was determined.

"It's a better life for the kids up there," she said. "Better schools. Less crime. It's a wholesome place to raise a family. And I'm giving him another chance. I'd like to have a man in my life."

Fritz talked up Montana to Jennifer and me. He wore a big grin. He was really laying on the nice-guy attitude.

"Oh, you come up to Montana, it's got snow. It's just beautiful. You can hunt and fish. I'll buy you a motorcycle, too, Jeff."

I considered our situation. Fritz was a nightmare that had come back. But in a way, he wasn't as scary as before. After all, I was bigger now, smarter, than the first time he'd entered our lives. I would not be so helpless. I figured I could stay out of his way and avoid the beatings. But all in all, I was not one bit happy about having to share a roof with this monster again.

I hadn't forgotten about the way he'd demanded the house be neat. Or how he'd taught me the names of his tools. Or how to swim.

Or the cattle prod.

I had no control over the situation, though. I talked on the phone with my Uncle Mark. He was living in Missoula, Montana, with some woman who owned a house up there. He said he loved Montana.

"It's pretty cool living. It gets colder than sh*t, but it's beautiful. And it's old-style. It's like the land time forgot. There are cowboys up here. A handshake and a smile seals the deal. And I'll be close to you guys. I'll come over and visit."

Mom and Fritz said I'd have fun with his nephew, Johnny, who was living with Fritz. He'd be my cousin (if Mom and Fritz got married). He was 15. It'd kind of be like having a brother.

Only a few months after moving back to California, Jennifer and I were pulled out of school. It was September. We were moving to Big Sky Country. To Great Falls, Montana.

I felt like we were moving to the North Pole.

CHAPTER TWELVE: Growth in the Frozen North

Montana didn't turn out to be the North Pole. When we arrived after driving through California, Nevada, Utah and Idaho, it was still sunny late September, cool but not cold. Montana seemed wide open, rugged and beautiful. The sky was deep and blue, streaked with long white clouds. "Big Sky Country," indeed.

We kept driving north, almost to the Canadian border. The town of Great Falls is on the Missouri River. Green, lush grass was growing. But the locals told us we'd only be seeing it for a month or so. After that, they said, the snow would come and we wouldn't see grass again until spring. I didn't believe it.

Great Falls had a small-town feel, even though it was more of a small city than a large town. There was a main street with a few little restaurants, a car wash, an auto-parts store and some other shops. Pickup trucks with antler ornaments and gun racks were parked on the curb. A few of the men walking around wore cowboy hats, but most of them had ball caps with working-man's logos on them. The local fashion for male and female, young and old, seemed to be flannel and blue jeans. I was surprised to see a lot of tennis shoes instead of boots. But everything seemed a few years behind. It was nice.

The people were polite enough, yet kind of weather-beaten and not overly friendly or expressive like city people. They were honest, hard-working, straight-talking folk. They didn't smile much. Living in that part of the country toughened you up, I could tell.

Fritz's house was in the middle of town. He had money, just like in San Bernardino. It was a big, two-story house. The basement had been remodeled with a bar and Fritz's old pool table in it, plus a pinball machine, a jukebox and a big television. There was a laundry room to one side, but the basement was so decked out it didn't even seem like a basement.

There were two bedrooms in the basement. Johnny, Fritz's 15-year-old nephew, had one of them. I was excited about meeting him. Now I'd kind of have a big brother.

Johnny was there when we arrived. He looked tough. He wasn't very tall for a 15-year-old — maybe 5-foot-5 — but he was muscular. His arms, chest and shoulders were those of a guy who lifted weights. He wrestled at the high school. He looked like someone who wasn't messed with. He was real quiet. But he gave us a little smile when we were introduced.

"H-how are you," he said. He had a slight stutter.

His eyes lit up when Mom gave him a small hug.

We'd been told Johnny's mother, Fritz's younger sister, was in the military, but she was a screw-up. She was single and a partier. She couldn't take care of Johnny. He wasn't a priority for her. She hadn't provided him with a stable home. That's how he'd ended up living with his Uncle Fritz.

I had to bunk in Johnny's room until our belongings were unpacked and my room next door was ready. That room was where a weightlifting bench and barbells and dumbbells were set up. Johnny wasn't happy about having to give up that room to me. It had been his private workout room. Now he'd have to pump iron out in a corner of the main room.

His bedroom was cool, a teenager's room. He listened to rock: Def Leppard, Molly Hatchet, Krokus, Rush, Van Halen, Judas Priest, Ozzy Osbourne, Aldo Nova, Quiet Riot. He had black-light posters of rock bands hanging on his wall. Hard rock and heavy metal were big in Montana. That night, as I lay in the top of the bunk bed, he played the loud, crazy guitar music, and told me all about his favorite bands.

"You never heard of Rush?" he asked.

I hadn't heard of many bands yet, including Rush. Johnny put an album on the turntable. I was hooked right from the start — the wicked guitar and drums, the screaming or howling vocals, like an orchestrated earthquake. The music of Rush really moved me. The unremitting and varied drumbeats. The complex extended guitar solos: like a rocket taking off, or a waterfall, or even a whirlpool. The glass-shattering pierces and brilliant cascades of the vocalist: a weird kind of opera. It was the strangest singing I'd ever heard. It blew me away that Rush was a trio, that three people could make so much sound.

Johnny talked about music until I fell asleep that night.

After my room was ready, Johnny and I didn't hang out much. Sometimes he'd horse around with me. He took me and Jennifer sledding on the hills nearby. Later, when the snow had cleared, he took me on the back of his motorcycle. He had a badass KX-80. We'd haul ass on the hills. He even let me take a few spins on my own.

But he had nothing to do with me when his friends were around. And there were times he just closed the world off, sat alone in his room with the door shut. Like my sister did.

Mostly, he just wanted me out of his way.

I WAS ENROLLED FOR sixth grade in Lincoln Elementary School. It seemed a good omen. I always liked Abraham Lincoln; we shared the same birthday.

The morning I was to start at school, I practiced my "new kid" speech. This was one of my least favorite things to do. I'd had to stand up in class and tell about myself a few times before. It was the same routine. I'd begin, "Hi, I'm Jeff Bowling . . ." and my last name would elicit giggles. I'd ignore them. I'd have to win over the crowd and make friends as soon as possible. It was all about fitting in. Survival.

I rehearsed my pitch out loud and reviewed it in my head as Mom drove me to the school. I knew full well the teacher would ask me to introduce myself. When I was called on to get up in front of everybody, I'd touch on high points of my life — the places I'd lived, California, Florida, the Philippines. I'd mention things that related to the other kids' lives: I liked videogames and bicycles. I'd mention my favorite sport: soccer. I'd say all of this in a monotone so that no one would think I was being a show off, trying to stand out or be better than everyone else. I knew that if I sounded too confident, it would be all over for me. My classmates would think I was a total jerk.

When we got to the school, the building reminded me right away of what Uncle Mark told me: Montana was like the land time forgot.

My classroom had a woodstove. The students hung their coats up around it. The stove gave off a warm, homey smell. The wood floor in the classroom creaked when you walked on it, although the hallway had been upgraded to linoleum.

The teacher, Mrs. Prentiss, was a real strict lady. No gentle, coaxing manner about her. She was grim and stern.

"Sit down, shut your mouth and pay attention," she said as students filed in before the morning bell.

Mrs. Prentiss was pioneer stock. I would find out that she'd spent her entire 40 or 50 years in Montana. She wore no makeup, and she was a lady whose manly features would have been improved by makeup. Her black curly hair, gray at the ends, was cut short, almost in a mini-Afro. Her eyes were black as oil. She wore frumpy denim dresses that fell past her knees. Her fingernails were short and unpainted. I bet she'd plucked thousands of chickens with those hands. She was one rough broad. I imagined her home had an outhouse. I guessed she was married to a trapper or someone gnarly like that. Mrs. Prentiss carried a ruler around the classroom.

She told me to stand at her desk until everyone was seated that morning.

"We have a new student," Mrs. Prentiss told the class, her lips tight and unsmiling. She was not excited about having a new student. She didn't feel it necessary to take extra steps to make me feel welcome.

"His name is Jeff Bowling. He's from California. He'll be sitting at the empty desk in this row."

She pointed.

"Now take your seat."

I took my seat.

Mrs. Prentiss, it turned out, was not interested in my past or the places I'd been, not even as an educational lesson for the students. She was not going to call me up to make my speech. I was relieved. I just had to sit in my seat, pay attention to her, and act nonchalant when I knew the other kids were staring at me.

After the Pledge of Allegiance, there was a prayer. That was a new experience for me at school. It really was like we were back in the 1950s.

The students were polite and proper, soft-spoken and reserved. They reminded me a bit of the Japanese. They addressed Mrs. Prentiss as "ma'am." They observed a code of conduct.

That day I witnessed an example of Montana toughness.

Two sixth-graders had a problem about something. One of these boys, whose name was Tommy, was in a different classroom. He was much larger than Ernie, the kid in my classroom, but that didn't matter. They were going to settle it after school. After the final bell rang, we kids quietly and calmly went outside and circled the two antagonists.

There was a fight. Ernie was getting nailed. Tommy was bigger than all of us. He already had muscles; the trace of a mustache showed under his nose. He looked to be much older, as if he'd been held back a grade. Ernie was a small, blond kid. Dark-haired Tommy circled him like a boxer, throwing straight punches and connecting with each one. *Pop. Pop.* It was a ridiculous mismatch. Ernie threw a punch but it went nowhere near Tommy. Ernie was too small to reach him. It was useless. Finally he gave up throwing punches and just tried to keep his hands up.

That, too, was of no use. Tommy was too big, too fast, too strong. Ernie's nose turned bloody. He doubled over from getting socked in the stomach. But he didn't quit. He didn't want to fight, but he had to stay in there. He stood there, taking it.

Suddenly, the bigger kid stopped fighting.

"You've been beat enough," Tommy said.

He walked up and held out his hand. Ernie shook it. Tommy put his arm around the smaller kid, hooked it under an armpit and helped him, limping, walk home.

I'd never seen that sort of discipline. Two kids having it out, settling their differences in what was an accepted way, with the teachers letting it go as normal. These kids weren't rowdy. They minded the teachers, following instructions without a word or look of protest. "Yes, ma'am," to the teacher. "Yes, sir," to the principal. But the kids were plain hardy. Some lived in town and their parents worked at Malmstrom Air Force Base. But a lot of the kids were in ranching families, rising early and doing chores before heading to school.

They were a different breed from what I was used to.

MRS. PRENTISS HANDED BACK the homework I turned in that week marked with red "F's." I was shocked. I wasn't *that* stupid. I couldn't figure out what mistakes she was dinging me for. I asked her.

"The assignments must be turned in in italics," she said, matter-of-factly.

Italics? I didn't know what she was talking about. I was afraid to ask.

I asked Mom what "italics" were. It turned out this was a script I hadn't heard of. There was regular print, cursive, *and* italics. And guess what we had to use for our assignments? Italics.

Lucky for me, Mom was a fine calligrapher. She went to a store and bought me books on writing in italics, and taught me. I basically had to learn how to write all over again.

The rest of the schoolwork was a breeze for me, and winning over friends wasn't too difficult, either. The snow fell heavy and was really high and deep that fall, burying the grass underneath like a memory. Snow can serve as a great equalizer. It helped me quickly bond with my schoolmates.

The students at Lincoln made full use of the snow for recreational purposes. They carved intricate labyrinths of trenches out on the playground. We worked together. You'd bring your feet close together and scrape them on the snow, cutting narrow paths to form the course. We'd make a big maze. Then the chase games were ready to begin. The rules said players had to stay in the paths or jump from one to the next, but forbade breaking a path. The snow was so thick that it preserved our course, and each week we sixth-graders would spruce up the paths and add to them. The most challenging part of the game was the mind work: memorizing how the paths ran. Everyone respected the course. In California, someone would just have come along and busted it up.

After recess, we'd come back inside the school and change out of our boots into the shoes we kept in our lockers. We'd return to the classroom and put our boots by the woodstove to dry. Our pants would be damp, but I got used to the wetness. I got used to hats and gloves, flannel and long underwear.

I loved the snow. I hadn't been in it that much, just at a ski resort at Big Bear, California, and then over one Christmas break we'd spent in Japan. Living in the deep snow in Montana was something else. I sledded with the kids down the street. People traveled on snowmobiles. It seemed like Christmastime lasting five months. A friend of mine and I liked to "hookie bob" to school, grabbing onto the backs of vehicle bumpers and sliding along the packed snow on our feet.

The Montanans were a bit heavier than folk elsewhere. They put on their winter weight. They had to, to survive the season. The cold was bitter, indeed. Later that winter, it got down to 32 degrees below 0 many times, and one severe storm dropped the mercury far below that. If you went outside with wet hair you'd lose pieces of it, frozen and cracking right off. My sister, just walking from our house to school, got frostbite on an ear.

Jennifer liked to stay indoors, anyway.

I HAD COME IN the middle of the year and there were no youth sports in Great Falls to sign up for. No soccer. No football. Snow was coming soon and boys my age were already into hunting.

Our next-door neighbors, the Carvers, owned a ranch. There were two boys, and I became friends with Brian, who was a year younger than I. The other boy, Blair, was Jennifer's age. Brian and his parents were ashamed of Blair. "We don't talk to my brother, he's a freak," Brian told me.

"What's so freaky about him?"

"He's just a freak."

One day when I was hanging out with Brian, I saw Blair coming out the door. He was wearing a black trench coat. His spiky hair was several colors. I smiled.

"Where have you been?" I called out. "You look like you're from California. That's awesome."

Blair invited us up to his bedroom. He was listening to punk and New Wave music — The Clash and The Cure. I hadn't expected to hear that up in Montana.

"You don't think he's weird?" Brian asked.

"No," I said. "There's lots of kids like him in California."

I told the same thing to Brian's dad, Mr. Carver. He was a stoic Montanan.

"There's nothing wrong with Blair," I said. "He's just into what the kids in California are into. The music, the style, everything."

Brian's dad looked almost relieved. It was like a refreshing truth had been revealed. His older son was perplexing. Mr. Carver was a farmer, a simple man. It had humiliated him to have to bring Blair with him to livestock events.

"Blair's normal, trust me," I said.

One weekend that fall, Brian and his dad took me out to the ranch and we got to ride horses. I'd longed for most of my life for a chance to ride horses, and I took to them right away. I figured out how to balance, how to make the animal turn. It was a big ego trip for me. Here I was, a little guy, controlling a great huge beast. But I kept in mind that the horse could buck me off if I wasn't careful. Or he could bolt and I'd be on for the ride, hanging on for dear life. I respected the horse. But I controlled the reins, letting him know who was in charge.

The best part of being out on the ranch was the vast expanse of the country. No airplanes overhead. No cars around. Just prairie, and the sounds of the horses or my own breath. Old-style. The West.

That fall, Mr. Carver drew an elk tag for the region, in the area out by his ranch. The elk in Montana were huge, with 6-point antlers. The herds were so plentiful that you'd see carcasses lying by the side of the road, casualties of pickup trucks. Mr. Carver and Brian invited me to go out scouting for elk. They were glad to have a third person along, since Blair didn't hunt. The three of us stayed over at their ranch, then got up in the morning, mounted up and went riding on the snow-covered prairie and rolling hills.

I felt like a cowboy, even though I wore a baseball cap. We checked for tracks. We stopped and listened for sounds of a herd. Mr. Carver explained it was better to hunt horseback than on foot, because the animal sounds made by your horse helps camouflage your human sounds. I spotted a pair of 2-point deer antlers on the ground, where they'd been shed. I dismounted and retrieved them. I have them to this day.

Montana was giving me a real taste of the great outdoors. I didn't know it, but it was hardening me, too.

CHAPTER THIRTEEN: Hamburger Money

The snow lasted and lasted. It felt like spring would never come, that we'd never see that tall green grass from September again. It wasn't long before I had a brainstorm about making money.

One of my household chores was shoveling the walkway and sidewalk. The snow was heavy and damn hard to clear. There were a lot of elderly people living in our neighborhood. I knew they wouldn't be able to lift a shovel in that stuff. In Florida I'd mowed a few lawns for extra bucks. There wasn't any lawn here in Montana most of the year, so the thing to do, I realized, was shovel snow.

The idea fired me up!

At 8 o'clock one Saturday morning I got up and dressed, borrowed a snow shovel from the house and went around to the doors of the older people in the neighborhood, asking if I could shovel their walks. My price was $5. The man at the first house I solicited said that was a lot of money. I said it was a fair price. The walks were piled 3 or 4 feet high.

He relented. He said this was a new thing — having a kid ask to shovel his walk. His remark made me wonder why no other kids in Great Falls had taken the initiative. An explanation was soon coming.

As soon as I set to the task, I found out that shoveling a walk steep with snow is backbreaking work. I wasn't much taller than the piled-up snow. What had I gotten myself into? Well, it was a challenge, and I wasn't about to back down. What I needed was a system. I told myself I could do this.

I stood for a minute, and developed a plan of attack.

I trudged to the front of the walk and flicked a layer of snow off the top. After all, I was too little to dig in any other way. Then I set in on one area, just one side of the walk, slowly working it and clearing my way down. I scraped bottom. That was a milestone. And then I was actually clearing a path, making progress.

I was careful about the shoveling. I tossed the snow so that it'd spread out evenly next to the walk, instead of forming mountains my customers wouldn't be able to see over. I cut the bank perfectly square, like an artist. I wanted the customers to come out of their house and see a beautiful job. I had enough sense to be a perfectionist. It was like the Japanese, with their deliberate sweeping of a sidewalk outside a store.

I kept toiling away. Gradually the walk was being cleared. I got used to the exertion. I worked slowly but surely, without quitting. I endured. I knew I could summon the willpower, even though nothing would have been sweeter than sitting down. I had my Walkman on, listening to Def Leppard and other music. I patiently plodded on. Instead of thinking about my aching muscles and my fatigue, I focused on all the money I'd get when the job was done.

Five dollars. Five dollars. Five dollars.

The strategy was working! I was just about done. The banks on either side of the walk were straight and even. The pavement, damply dark, was clear almost to the street. I finished up and knocked on the man's door.

He stepped out on the porch. He looked down the walkway and whistled.

The $5 bill gave me a buzz. All the agonizing toil I'd endured evaporated. I wanted more money!

I ended up doing two more houses that first day. *Fifteen bucks!*

There was a gas station-corner store owned by a middle-aged man and his tough Basque wife. She was the first woman I'd ever seen who had a mustache. This couple's store had a big grill for cooking hamburgers. I went in there that Saturday afternoon, exhausted but proud. I felt 6 feet tall, unbeatable. Salt of the earth. A man. When I ordered a cheeseburger, fries and a Coke — the way I wanted it, without asking anybody's permission, and paying my own money for it — a big feeling of liberation surged through me.

I realized this is what I'd worked so hard for: The freedom to go into that store and spend my own money on the food I wanted.

I went out again on Sunday to knock doors and shovel walks. I did it the following Saturday and Sunday. I began to hit my stride. My stamina increased, my muscles strengthened, my mental toughness grew.

My production increased to four walks on Saturday, and four more on Sunday. Weekends became my workdays. I found that I greatly preferred making money to playing with the other kids. I'd get my playing out of the way after school on Friday. First thing Saturday morning, I was out shoveling walks, earning $20 of my very own. I had regular customers. They expected me to knock on their doors. They were glad to see me. Some even smiled.

Making my own money gave me a rush. Going to the mom-and-pop corner store became a ritual. When I'd walk in after hours of shoveling snow, the man would say, "You want a cheeseburger?" and I'd answer, "Yes," and he'd go over to the grill, slap a patty on and begin cooking it. The burger was always delicious. Sometimes the store had buffalo meat and that was tastier still. I was such a common sight in the store on weekends that even the old woman — that tough, no-nonsense Basque lady — began smiling at me, the first time I'd seen her face show any hint of friendliness toward anyone.

I'd take my time with my meal, and sometimes buy a comic book. I'd relax and read, savoring my newfound independence. But I couldn't spend all my earnings on hamburgers or comic books. I was pocketing a lot of cash.

In short time I had more than $100 saved up in my room. This prosperity gave me some leverage in a household situation I found myself in.

JOHNNY WAS A DECENT enough kid, but messed up in the head. He was doing his best to cope with the world as a 15-year-old with no father and a mother who had abandoned him. Because of our age difference, he saw me as just this younger kid getting in his way. Sometimes we'd go sledding, and in clear weather he'd even take me on his dirt bike. But mostly he saw me as a fair target to do with as he wished.

Maybe it was more than just taking advantage of a younger kid. Maybe he was working off some of his frustrations on me. Johnny, as I said, was muscular and wrestled for the high school team. That sucked for me, because he'd practice on me at home before meets. Without warning, he'd pounce on me and lock me in a hold such as "the crab" and keep me in it while he watched television. It was painful. His chin would be pressing down on the back of my neck while his hands were looped around my legs, holding them out so I couldn't move. He wouldn't free me until a commercial came on.

But my wealth from shoveling snow gave me an edge. Johnny, like most teenagers, was hard up for cash. And cash I had. Johnny loved skiing, and a ski pass cost $10. He'd come begging to me. I'd loan him the amount, but tell him I wanted $15 back. I was a little bank charging steep interest. Naturally, Johnny didn't like the terms, but he didn't have any other way of paying for skiing. I made sure Mom and Fritz knew I was loaning Johnny money. That way, he was pressured into paying me back. He'd work odd jobs and get me the money. I was making a nice little profit stream off him.

I wasn't trying to be greedy. I just wanted to have enough money to do what I wanted to do, when I wanted to do it. A hunger had been awakened inside. In fact, from the time I started making money from shoveling snow, I've never lost that appetite.

The taste of wealth hard-earned is addictive, indeed.

CHAPTER FOURTEEN: Finger on the Trigger

Spring came and the snow was finally melting away. Fritz had not been abusive at all toward Jennifer or me. But he and Mom hit a rough spot.

They started arguing regularly. It didn't let up. It became a constant stream of sour words that stretched on for a week.

One Saturday, about 3 in the afternoon, there was a commotion upstairs. I was in my bedroom in the basement. Johnny was out of the house somewhere. I sat up and listened. Mom was screaming and crying. Then I heard thumps like someone getting thrown around. I ran upstairs.

In their bedroom, Fritz had Mom in a headlock, like he was punching her. In an instant I was making for the closet. That's where the pellet gun was. I found it, popped a pellet in the chamber and pumped the air in. I walked up to Fritz and stuck the barrel against his eye.

"You touch my mom again, I'm going to take your eye out! And I'm going to reload and keep shooting!"

Fritz couldn't make a move. He released Mom. She twisted away, sobbing. Then she got hysterical.

"What are you doing with a gun?! What are you doing pointing it at him?! Are you crazy?!"

I screamed back. "I'm the one who just saved your ass! Why are you mad at me?"

Something had snapped. I'd had enough.

"Pack up, we're out of here!" I said. "Let's go!"

It was strange. I was suddenly the one in charge. Some crazy strength and power had taken hold. The earlier abuse from Fritz when I was little, and now this, had unleashed a crazy power. It was like a flood, an irresistible force. There was no fear in me, no hesitation, just action. Maybe there was a physical explanation for this, as well. I'd toughened up in Montana, in the hard frozen country.

I backed away from Fritz, my finger still on the trigger, the barrel pointed at his face. His eyes showed terror. A moment of truth had arrived.

Mom took the gun from me.

I walked back downstairs, staring at Fritz over my shoulder. He made no move to come after me.

THE NEXT DAY, MOM called my Grandpa Herschel, who lived in Reno, Nevada, and made arrangements for us to move down. Grandpa Herschel spoke with Fritz, as well. I think my Uncle Mark called up and talked to him, too.

I don't know what was said, but Fritz stayed out of our way for the next two days. In fact, he helped us move. He rented a moving van, packed us up and drove it down to Reno. We followed him in Mom's car. Just she, Jennifer and I. The three of us alone, again.

CHAPTER FIFTEEN: Grandpa's Side of Life

Grandpa Herschel had been divorced from Nana for years and years, and never really was involved in raising Mom, Aunt Denise and Uncle Mark. Before marrying Nana, Herschel Wilkinson had been a cowboy in California and elsewhere in the West. After he and Nana split, he'd been a wheelin'-dealin' entrepreneur in Las Vegas. Now he co-owned and ran two bars and a couple eateries in Reno. He was a tough old sonofagun whom I barely knew. But we were going to be moving into his house with him and his wife, Fern.

Mom put an optimistic spin on it.

"Your Grandpa has a cool little house on a river. You can go fishing. It will be a lot of fun. It's going to be an adventure."

She was always good about seeing the positive side of things and making it "an adventure." I know now that if she'd allowed herself to wallow in misery, it would have been the beginning of the end. She might've given up on life and just sleepwalked through the rest of it. Too many people do.

Mom's upbeat approach was like a magic pill. Even as down as I was feeling, I managed to muster some excitement about moving to Reno.

We got there quickly. It was April, beginning to get warm.

Even a child grown used to being uprooted, always being the new kid on the block, having a new school to attend, having to make new friends, can grow tired and fed up. He wants to feel settled. He wants to feel comfortable. He wants to be in a place he can call home.

Now, moving to Reno, I was on my ninth living situation. California. Florida. Asia. Montana. Nevada. I was sick of it! When we got to Reno from Great Falls, I saw that Mom had finally tired of it, too.

"This is pretty much it," she said. She vowed we wouldn't be moving again. She promised to find a permanent home so Jennifer and I could stay in the same schools and make real friends.

The three of us were simply worn out from the constant upheavals and dashed dreams of a happy home. It had taken more of a toll than we'd realized. The final scene with Fritz had scarred me. I was still coming to grips with the fact I'd held a gun on the man. My emotions were very raw . . . and here I was, having to wake up in a different place all over again.

We moved into Grandpa's house. It was near the Truckee River in northeast Reno. It was only going to be temporary. Mom was looking for a place for us in Sparks.

There were still a few months left in the school year. Mom took me to enroll in Robert Mitchell Elementary School, in Sparks. As I sat with her in the principal's office, I suddenly felt drained. Weak. Out of strength. I thought about having to walk into a new classroom full of new faces. About making the, "Hi, I'm Jeff" speech. All of a sudden, the strain was too much.

I'd been beaten up inside. I couldn't take any more stress. I just couldn't hold my emotions in anymore.

I burst into tears. I wiped my eyes, but the tears kept rolling down. Mom saw this and started crying, too.

The principal had a look of compassion. He was in his forties, balding, with a kind face.

"There's no rush," he said. His voice was relaxed. "You can stay in here as long as you like."

Mom began to explain. "We've gone through so many schools . . ."

"I understand," he said.

My school transcripts were laid out on his desk.

"I'm looking at his record. That's a lot of schools for a young man his age."

He turned to me. "Go ahead and collect yourself, son. There's no hurry. It'd probably be better if your mom left. That way we can get you ready for class."

His easygoing nature was very calming.

I wiped my face and swallowed.

"OK," I told Mom. "I'm fine. You go ahead."

She got up, gave me a hug and left. The principal sent for a student to escort me to my classroom.

I gathered my composure, choked back the tears. I couldn't be weepy in front of the kids. It's like prison. They see tears, you're done for.

A student came into the office. He was tall, with short blondish-brown hair and large ears. The principal stood up and reached out his hand to me. He shook it firmly.

"Don't worry about it," he said. "It's a little different down here than Montana. But you're going to do just fine."

"I'm Mitch," the student said.

He led me to the classroom. I made it through the day.

IF THERE WAS ANY comfort in our new situation, it was that Mom insisted we weren't going to move again. As soon as she could afford it, she said, we'd move out of Grandpa's house and into a place of our own.

I knew she was good for her word. Mom was always a go-getter. She found a job immediately as a secretary with an international mining company that had an office in Reno. She began saving up for us to get a place of our own.

In the meantime, our living situation wasn't all that bad. There was family around us now. Besides Grandpa Herschel and Grandma Fern, their son, my Uncle Randy, and my free-roaming Uncle Mark dropped by the house from time to time.

The house was about a century old. It had been an old farmhouse. It had stone halfway up the outside, and white-painted wood above, with a gray composition roof. The house sat on a little spread that had been a working ranch by the Truckee River, near Reno's border with Sparks. The basement had a dirt floor. We laid down some carpets and put a bed there for me. There were no windows, and when the light was turned off it was pitch black, even during the day. The walls were insulated with sawdust and newspaper. It was down-home.

So was Grandpa Herschel. Down-home — and downright difficult.

He'd only been a fleeting presence in my life until then. He and his wife — I called her "Grandma Fern" — also owned a winter house near Las Vegas.

When I was very young we'd visited them a few times in Vegas and they'd taken us to the Circus Circus hotel-casino. Grandpa was not a warm, loving person. He was gruff and gnarly, a foul-mouthed, street-smart businessman. He was 6-foot-3, 250 pounds, potbellied but robust, with gray hair slicked back with Dippety Doo gel in a dapper-do from the 1950s. His face matched his unfriendly and intimidating personality. He rarely smiled, but when he did you'd see the gold-rimmed front tooth, like when he laughed his deep rumbling guffaw. He walked a bit bowlegged like the old cowboy he was, swaggering in his Justin boots. He always wore Wranglers instead of Levi's, and often a buttoned-up Western shirt over a white tank top. Sometimes he fancied up with a bolo tie and a Stetson. He smoked filterless Pall Malls or Camels. He reeked of smoking tobacco and Old Spice. He was the real McCoy: an old cowboy businessman. A redneck. And consistently foul-tempered.

From the moment Grandpa Herschel beheld us as we drove up to his property from Montana, he made us feel that we were all right to impose on him for a while, given that we were kin, but that didn't mean he was taking us in with open arms. He sneered at Jennifer, like she didn't look like much to him. Me: I was obviously going to be a scrawny little nuisance.

In time, I found there were things I liked about him. He had a little workshop on his property, and he'd let me come out there with him when he worked on his cars. The reason he liked me to tag along was because I was a source of amusement. He liked to laugh at me. I was just a little sh*t to him. Say, I'd set up a ramp out there, race up it on my bike and wipe out trying to clear the hood of one of the cars he and my uncles were working on.

He wouldn't express concern for my welfare. He wouldn't ask if I was all right.

"You dumb ass!" he'd growl. "Pedal faster next time."

GRANDPA TOOK ME TO weekend swap meets held in the parking lot of the El Rancho drive-in theater in Sparks. He'd barter for engines and transmissions, tools and hardware. He'd beat down the prices with any bullsh*t he could think of. "That's scratched," or, "This don't work," or, "I'm going to have to retrofit this," or, "I saw four of those 10 tables down for f*cking three bucks." His deep voice growled. His large frame swaggered. His was a big, commanding presence. If the vendor wouldn't buckle, Grandpa would stalk off. Either the vendor would call him back and come down in price, or Grandpa would leave for good.

He was a tough negotiator, just like Lori was in the Philippines. The biggest difference between the two was that Lori only bought good stuff. Grandpa Herschel would buy needless crap. Tools or parts he didn't need. Tools or parts that were pure junk. He just loved the art of the sale better than what was for sale.

There was a drinking side to Grandpa, and that went some ways toward explaining why he hadn't been around much for Mom when she was a girl. Someone years before had told me the story about when he and Fern were first married, and had gotten into a bad argument. In a drunken rage, he'd picked up a telephone and smashed her in the face, breaking her jaw and nose and fracturing her front teeth. He could be a real mean bastard when he hit the bottle. Even though he was in his sixties now, I knew I had to watch out for his drunkenness.

Grandpa was hardly a grandfatherly figure toward Jennifer and me. Sometimes he acted like we weren't even around. He was a hard case. But he also was so full of sh*t he couldn't resist promising me things. He was just a talker, a salesman. Mom had warned me about this. Shortly after we'd moved in, she'd taken the opportunity to enlighten me about his bullsh*tting. She told me a story meant as a cautionary tale.

Mom said that when she was a little girl and Grandpa and Nana were divorced, he would tell Mom that he was going to be coming over to the house to visit her. Naturally, she'd be expecting him on the designated day. She'd sit out in the driveway and wait. And wait. He'd never show. She'd be heartbroken. She'd sit out there even after it got dark, sobbing, clinging to a glimmer of hope.

Sure enough, Grandpa threw a promise my way.

He knew I loved motorcycles. I wanted a dirt bike even more than I wanted a computer.

"Yeah, I saw this bike at a swap meet," he told me one day. "I'm buying it for you."

"Awesome!" I said.

Then I remembered Mom's story. I tried to fight away doubts.

Grandpa brought up the dirt bike a couple more times in the following week. "Yeah, that motorcycle is still for sale." He really built me up.

I waited for the next big news: That he had gone over and bought it for me. Or that he wanted me to test it out. But the days passed. Then it was a week.

I finally couldn't wait any longer.

Grandpa was sitting in the living room with a beer in his hand. He was drunk.

"What about my dirt bike, Grandpa? You promised me a dirt bike. You said it. I trust your word."

He looked at me confused. Then he shook his head.

"I never promised you a dirt bike."

HERSCHEL WILKINSON, DURING THE two months we lived at his place, proved himself to be a walking, talking bad example in cowboy boots. He was a real prick.

He constantly put my sister down. "You're never going to amount to sh*t," he'd say to Jennifer, as if she didn't have enough problems as a teenage girl with fragile self-esteem.

He'd cut me down, too — "You stupid little sh*t!" — criticizing something or other. But I didn't give his words any play. *Whatever, old man*, I'd think. I was 12 now, and of late had gotten thick-skinned. I pretty much didn't listen to anyone's opinion anymore. I was doing my own thing, so I was self-protected against his surliness. Mom paid him little mind, too. As for Grandma Fern, she put up with his put-downs because she was kind of oblivious — a ditsy, kind-hearted woman who was off in her own world.

I liked Grandma Fern. She seemed lost in space and time. She still dyed her curly, permed hair red. She'd been a cocktail waitress at the Tropicana in Las Vegas in its golden era, when mobsters were building Sin City into the nation's playground, and movie stars, marquee entertainers and politicians were giving the town its glamorous sheen. Fern had been a real beauty back then, and she waited on all the famous wise guys and Hollywood celebrities, who'd ask for her by name. Frank. Sammy. All of the Rat Pack. She told me stories about the swank, swingin' 1950s that seemed straight out of the classic movies I watched late at night with Grandpa Hershel.

Grandma Fern had met Grandpa in Vegas. She was the perfect mate for him because she was fairly aloof about what was going on around her. She was always sweet, and just got through life day by day without much reflection. She still wore her old dresses from the 1960s. She loved Herschel Wilkinson deep in her heart. But he treated her the way he treated everyone close to him: like garbage.

This is how mean he was. His drinking and smoking eventually put his heart under a surgeon's scalpel four times, but Grandpa kept recovering. Finally, the doctor declared that all that booze Herschel Wilkinson had drunk over the decades had purified his innards. That and his native orneriness were unexpectedly prolonging his life.

"Hell isn't ready for him," the doctor declared.

In a way, I admired Grandpa. He was a salt-o'-the-earth businessman, a charismatic bullsh*t artist with an eighth-grade education and a diploma from the School of Hard Knocks. He'd made a lot of money in the 1970s in various rackets, one of which was making jewelry, another of which was buying old touring buses, such as Greyhounds, then gutting them and turning them into beautiful coaches for high-end customers. He had two sons, Randy and John — from a marriage with a woman named Hazel, before he met Nana. Each son became a master mechanic. The two built dragsters professionally and taught welding at the college level. They customized Grandpa's coaches for country-music stars and other celebrities who needed traveling homes because their business took them on the road. Grandpa made a mint off that.

From there, he went into a new line: managing country artists. One was Johnny Liggett, who was popular in the Vegas area. Grandpa had the negotiating skills and the balls to get things done. He got Johnny Liggett into the recording studio and cut albums. That proved to be one of the stories Grandpa told me that wasn't exaggerated or downright false. He showed me the albums Johnny Liggett autographed for him: "Thank you, Herschel, for managing me."

Grandpa was always looking for a new angle, and when he'd moved to Reno, he and a partner went into the bar and restaurant business. At the time we arrived from Montana, Grandpa helped manage two pizzerias — Pizza Oven I and II — plus two bars: Whiskey River, a sh*t-kickin' country-music nightclub; and Mr. D.'s, a strip joint on Glendale Avenue east of downtown, at the edge of the six-block zone that was the Reno-Sparks Indian Colony.

Grandpa once told me that he single-handedly brought spicy chicken wings to Reno. I more or less believe it, despite him being the source. We'd have the wings on weekends at his house, and I'd watch him cook them. Unfortunately, he never wrote down the recipe before he kicked the bucket. The recipe described the proper mix of spices, herbs and fruit for the sauce. It is nearly impossible to get the ingredients just right. I have yet to taste wings as good as his.

Grandpa also had a barbecue oven made out of a 55-gallon drum cut long ways, with a grate welded on it by my uncles. He was friends with the owner of a local meat company and would get huge spareribs. Some of my best memories are climbing into inner tubes with my Uncle Randy and my Uncle Mark and floating down the Truckee River to the farms on McCarran Boulevard east of Reno. Then we'd drive back to Grandpa's and have a barbecue feast.

Grandpa's wild stories and barbecuing skills didn't make up for all the meanness I had to put up with from him. But it did make living under his roof more bearable.

CHAPTER SIXTEEN: Keeping abreast of Business

Grandpa, being an old cowboy, watched Westerns on TV almost every night. When the weather got warmer that June, I moved upstairs and slept on the couch by the swamp cooler. That subjected me to the nightly cowboy-movie marathon. From it, I developed a big love of movies. Westerns cracked me up: the Indians played by tanned-up white guys speaking in broken speech fragments; the nighttime scenes, such as cattle rustling, where you could see everything as if it were bright as day. For Grandpa, though, the Westerns weren't that far from the reality he'd grown up with in Oklahoma and California. The way he looked and acted and thought — the black-and-white world of the Old West — he would've fit right into a script.

Grandpa also watched old movie classics, and they mesmerized me. My all-time favorite was *To Catch a Thief* with Cary Grant and Grace Kelly. I was smitten by Kelly's assertive style at a time when women were known to keep their place, and her incredible beauty in an era before health clubs and plastic surgery. There was so much panache in the clothing styles and etiquette in that classic-movie era. Polite speech and manners, the entire family dressing for dinner. There was orderliness, dignity, decorum.

Grandpa Herschel, on the other hand, was coarse. He made no pretense of being well mannered. He was shrewd, and he worked in a rough nighttime business, and thrived in it. He lived life the way he saw fit.

Whiskey River was the biggest-grossing honky-tonk Reno had ever known. To run a successful bar in a casino-dominated market was downright impressive. Very few non-casino nightspots survived in Reno beyond two years. When the Reno Rodeo came to town in June, Mom and I volunteered to work it. Grandpa Herschel had connections. I hung out with the rodeo cowboys. Of course, they frequented Whiskey River. It was the place to be. The joint was packed on weekends year-round.

I was always looking to make a buck, so that June, after school let out, Grandpa gave me a job cleaning his bars on weekends before the doors opened. I'd have to mop up the floors, clean the restrooms (which could be harsh), tidy up the bar area. Anything that fell behind the bar was mine, so I could pick up us much as $20 in change and bills dropped by the bartender during the night. Sometimes the work carried on a bit late and it'd be 4 or 5 p.m. and the doors would open to customers. I'd have to rush to finish up. But I did occasionally get glimpses of bar nightlife in full tilt.

Around 10 at night, while Grandpa and I sat on the couch at his house watching old movies, he'd get a call from the manager at one of the bars or restaurants to come down and pick up receipts. They didn't leave money sitting in the tills all night. Grandpa would tuck a pistol in the front of his pants, hidden by his shirt, and take along a big flashlight. I got to go with him on his collection calls, even though I wasn't supposed to be in a bar. Grandpa did things his own way.

Tagging along with him was exciting. Through the smoke and dimly lit crowd he'd shoulder his way in among the mass of patrons, and if someone was too rowdy or wouldn't move out of the way, Grandpa would conk him on the side of the head or back of the neck with the flashlight and just keep on walking toward the office without a glance back. I thought that was hilarious. It was just like in a movie.

When he got into the little office, he'd greet the staff there. And if the money wasn't counted up and ready for him to take, there'd be hell to pay. You didn't mess with Herschel Wilkinson. That's what his partner, Tommy, depended on. Tommy was a dark Italian man who looked like the movie director Martin Scorsese, only taller. He favored dark suits, shirts with wide collars, and gold jewelry. Sometimes he substituted an old-style leather jacket with a big collar. He had real nightlife style, real charisma — drink in one hand, cigarette dangling from his lips. He'd grown up in the Rat Pack era. Naturally, he drove a big Cadillac. He spent every night in a bar or club. He fit into that life. He'd wake up at 9 p.m., then go into one of the bars he owned, kid around with the customers (getting them to spend that much more money), drink until business dropped off. Then he and some friends, maybe taking along a few of the dancers from Mr. D's, would head out to the casinos and gamble until 4 or 5 in the morning. Sometimes Grandpa would join them, but he was getting too old for that kind of partying.

Tommy and Grandpa had a special relationship. They never burned each other. They were too good a business team, perhaps, too valuable to each other. Tommy financed the business ventures, knowing that Grandpa was the key partner — the guy who made it work out there on the floor, keeping the sh*t under wraps. Tommy was the brains and the bank, Herschel the balls and the brawn. Tommy paid the bills, Herschel collected the cash. Tommy gave an order, Herschel saw that it happened. It was symbiotic.

One time when I was accompanying Grandpa on his collection rounds, a brawl broke out in Whiskey River. We were sitting in the joint's business office and saw it on the closed-circuit TV monitors fed by security cameras positioned outside.

"Hang on just a second," Grandpa said.

I stayed in the office, watching from the doorway. He went out on the floor and threw a few people around. This was a man in his sixties!

Grandpa returned to the office. He picked up the hour's till receipts and headed out to go to the next collection stop, Mr. D's Backstage.

The topless bar, Mr. D's, would be another scene that was ridiculous and funny to me: adults drinking and acting stupid. Yes, I was seeing a lot at age 12. It was another course in my education on life.

I even got to attend the auditions at Mr. D's. Grandpa would let me sit there with him on afternoons when prospective dancers came in to be interviewed and show their stuff on stage.

"Now, I'll let you sit here and watch this," he told me, "but if you tell anybody, you're never going to do this again."

As a 12-year-old with hormones beginning to rage, the chance to see grown women gyrate and toss off their tops a few feet away from me was enormously exciting. But the thrill wilted a bit after I saw what most of these women looked like. Mr. D's wasn't a classy place, and the women weren't topnotch talent. Most of them were tough women from the streets.

Others were practically skeletal, victims of some poor lifestyle choice or other. Still, it was a rush for me to see their naked breasts swinging or flopping as the girls pranced and spun around and occasionally did the splits (those who could), somewhat in time to whatever rock music they'd brought on tape.

Before an audition they'd change in Grandpa's office and come out in frilly costumes, red satin bras, spiky heels and the like. Some of the women were freaked when they saw me sitting there next to Grandpa.

"There's a young kid right there!"

"Listen," Grandpa would snarl. "You can't dance in front of this kid, how are you gonna dance in front of those drunk motherf*ckers who'll be in here tonight?"

That would settle the argument. They'd do their routines.

I had to check how I acted while I watched. If I started smiling or smirking, Grandpa would smack me.

"Listen, this isn't f*cking around," he told me once with a scowl. "We're making sure she can work the crowd, get through her songs. She's trying to get hired to make some dough and we're seeing if she's gonna make *us* dough."

I had to maintain the professional integrity of the establishment. I had to sit there with a stone-cold face.

When a dancer's audition was over, Grandpa would turn to me and ask, "Well, did she give you a hard-on?"

"Yeah, she wasn't too bad."

"Yeah, she gave me a hard-on, too."

She'd passed the audition.

A few of the girls were halfway hot. They got me going from the moment they emerged from Grandpa's office in costume. It gave me ideas.

One of the favorites of the Mr. D's crowd was a woman who danced with an albino python. She was top of the line for that place. The standards weren't that high in Mr. D's. The dancers would never be mistaken for models or even escorts, but they helped fill the joint on weekends. The patrons were the dregs of the area. Construction workers who were out of work. Others down on their luck. Unemployed alcoholics from the Indian colony. It was a rough bar. There wouldn't be a weekend night when at least someone wasn't punched, bit or stabbed. Grandpa forbade Grandma Fern from setting foot in Mr. D's. She hung out at Whiskey River.

"Ah, I don't think she's that good-looking, Grandpa," I said about the python lady.

"Well, people around here will like her," he said.

But not just any young woman willing to flash her breasts was hired at Mr. D's. One girl who auditioned got carried away in her fantasy. She danced and grinded around the stage, and after flashing her tits, eased down her panties.

"All right, hold on!" Grandpa shouted, standing up. "Stop dancing!"

She kept right on, though, showing off everything, until he stomped up to the stage, waving his arms. That caught her attention. She froze, staring at him with glazed eyes, head tilted to one side. Obviously doped out.

"Hey, I don't need you showing your pussy to my grandson. Finish the f*cking dancing!"

She finished.

"All right, you're not what we're looking for," he growled. "Get the f*ck out of here."

Grandpa lectured me about the dancers' economics. Many of them were married, he said. That surprised me. Why would a husband let his wife be a titty dancer? Well, drugs had a lot to do with it, Grandpa explained. Their husbands or boyfriends would send the girls out to dance for money, and to sometimes be scandalous off the premises with a customer, then use the money to buy a stash of cocaine or some other drug from a dealer. They'd break up the stash into pieces and then sell them on the street. Then they'd take those profits and buy more drugs for selling on the street.

That was the sales cycle of the underground economy. It intrigued me. I wanted to make money, too, so I reflected on how the drug system worked. I understood that even this illegitimate business model operated by business principles. Initial income was parlayed into an investment that generated cash flow, which in turn was reinvested. It was all logical.

But it also disgusted me. The reality of the husbands and boyfriends pimping the dancers to drum up the investment capital to buy drugs told me that some people would do anything for a buck. It made me flash back to the bar in the Philippines, with the girl in the rattan basket.

I also saw how drugs trapped the dancers in the lifestyle — since they not only worked for drug money, but used drugs themselves. So did their men. These people were not getting ahead. Crime didn't pay for them.

My Grandpa's house rule was that no husbands or boyfriends were allowed in the club when their women were working. And if he caught any of the girls in the bathroom or outside doing or selling drugs, they were fired. Grandpa had to hire strippers, and he understood that strippers came with liabilities. But he wanted to keep his business running as straight as possible.

He didn't need the authorities coming down on him, putting Tommy's liquor license in jeopardy. He didn't need cops busting drug dealers in his club. He didn't need gunplay on or around the premises.

Grandpa made his money from catering to people's vices. He did it honestly, but it was a tricky business.

MY EXPERIENCES AT MR. D's were a graphic lesson in how self-destructive drinking and drugs are. It wasn't pretty.

I'd clean the joint on Sunday mornings. Since Mr. D's was located next to the Indian colony, there might be Indians still passed out at tables when I'd show up at 9 or 10 a.m. One time, three big Indian men were snoozing, heads on arms, at a table.

"Go over there and wake 'em up, get 'em out of here," Grandpa barked at me. He was sitting at a corner table with Moose, the big bartender who, not surprisingly, was an unsavory fellow in his own right.

"Are you kidding me?" I asked.

Grandpa and Moose watched what I was going to do.

Sh*t, a challenge. It wasn't in me to back down.

*All right, f*ck it,* I thought. *I'm going to take whatever these guys are going to give me.*

I walked up to the table, carrying a broom. I stood with my feet pointed away so I could take off running if I had to. I jostled one of the men with the broomstick. He didn't wake up.

Grandpa and Moose were laughing their asses off.

I prodded another man. "Hey, you got to get up."

He lifted his head, blinked, then brought his arm back and swatted angrily. I ducked. The backhand missed me.

That pissed off Grandpa. This fool had swung on his grandson? He got up and stomped over. He stood there, glowering.

"Get him up out of that chair!" Grandpa growled, egging me on.

I choked up on the broomstick like a baseball bat and swung at the back of the drunk's head. *Crack.* That did the trick. He stood up. Grandpa was right there with his flashlight. He whacked the drunk in the ribs, then took hold of him around the arm and neck and threw him out the door.

We rousted the other two, as well.

You didn't mess with Herschel Wilkinson.

GRANDPA KEPT CLOSE TABS on the businesses. He never missed a beat. He said people were about as honest as you'd let them be. That's why you have to keep a close eye on employees.

Sometimes in the mornings that summer when I was at his house, Grandpa took me along when he went around to the bars to check on the previous night's receipts. First we'd have breakfast at a greasy spoon. He'd know everyone in there. Then we'd go to the bars. He'd pull out the roll of receipts that had gone through the cash register and scrutinize the numbers carefully, sitting at a table in the empty place.

"You always got to count your money," he'd say. He'd hand me the receipts to look at.

"Wow, the bar did that much?" I'd say, looking at the bottom line.

"Yeah, that's seventeen hundred, not seventeen thousand. These motherf*ckers are stealing," he'd say.

He'd go behind the bar and measure the volume in the liquor bottles. It taught me about how much liquid went into a shot glass, and how much money a shot of liquor made. The first three or four shots from a bottle make up the cost of the entire bottle, and the rest is pure profit for the bar.

"Courvoisier," Grandpa would say, holding up a bottle of cognac. "That's five dollars a drink. It's halfway full. Where are the goddamn receipts showing the premium drinks?"

He'd nail a bartender just like that. When it came to business, Herschel Wilkinson was anything but stupid. He knew lots of bartenders poured free drinks for friends, females or themselves, or their drug dealers. I saw him have a chat with a bartender one afternoon that ended with Grandpa saying: "If I find out you're taking from me, I'm going to bust your ass. There better be $125 more in the receipts for well drinks when I come back tonight to pick up the cash."

Then he'd phoned Tommy. "Hey, we're a little short on the vodka. I think Freddy's stealing drinks or doing blow."

I learned quickly that many bartenders are dysfunctional. They "circle the bar." That is, they work an eight-hour shift, and when it is done they go from behind the bar to a seat on the other side and start drinking and talking with the new bartender and whoever is sitting there. Then they go home, sleep, wake up, have a sandwich, and go back to work behind the bar again, having spent their previous night's wages at the bar. In other words, they work for nothing.

Yes, Grandpa Herschel made his money from catering to people's vices. He even made money off his employees. But he had to keep a hawk's eye on 'em.

GRANDPA HAD SOME FUN with me at Mr. D's. Sometimes, during a nighttime money-collection round, he'd sit me on the bar, introduce me to the patrons as his grandson, and have me tell jokes. I loved jokes. I remembered the best ones I heard at school. I had a mind for it.

"All right, everybody, shut the f*ck up, my grandson's telling a joke," Grandpa would say.

The patrons would crowd around. There I was, a short, blond kid with an innocent face, feet kicking off the bar, holding my glass of soda. But I loved an audience.

"What do you get when you cross a chicken and a telephone pole?" I'd ask.

I'd look at my audience's eyes, timing my delivery. At moments like these I understood I had the ability to control a crowd, even adults. I had storytelling skills. It didn't hurt living with Grandpa Wilkinson — a world-class bullsh*t artist.

"A 24-foot cock trying to reach out and touch someone!"

That busted up this crowd.

Grandpa had a Queensland healer named Blue. The dog hated people of color. The dog fit in with his master. They were both racist.

Blue was a good guard dog, though. He'd be in the fenced front yard. The house was on Glendale Avenue, across the street and a couple blocks down from Mr. D's. The state's mental ward was across the street and up a ways. That meant a lot of strange characters passed by.

One time a drunk reached over the fence to pet Blue. Grandma Fern came outside and warned him not to reach for the dog. The drunk did anyway, and Blue tore right into his hand.

Grandpa came out of the house growling. "You dumb motherf*cker, we told you not to reach into the yard!"

Then Grandma wrapped the drunk's hand in a handkerchief, and Grandpa gave him a beer and shoved him down the street.

GRANDPA, FOR ALL HIS redneck, crude ways, knew how to make a buck. And he knew how to network his way into influential circles.

He told me about going out to dinner in Reno with the Nevada governor. Naturally, I laughed it off. But then other people confirmed his claim.

It was true. Grandpa was in the Police Constable Association, an organization of which the governor was a member. It turned out they really were friends. In fact, Grandpa had known the governor when the politician was just a young state assemblyman in Las Vegas. So Hershel Wilkinson was capable of telling the truth about some things.

But I never could let my guard down with him, because of the sheer bullsh*t he'd spew. Like his promise to buy me the motorcycle. He had a great gift for not remembering. He'd get drunk and phone up people and cuss them out, then not recall a thing about it the next day.

For all his bargaining savvy and wheelin'-dealin' spirit, Grandpa used to buy a lot of cheap garbage, because it was "a deal." You can judge a mechanic by the tools he carries. He'd buy cheap foreign knockoffs that would break.

Grandpa had a lot of flaws. Still, I learned much from him. He was hardnosed about business, and it paid off for him. He showed me the seamy side of business, and what I saw in the bars cured me of any curiosity to explore the drinking scene when I got older.

I admired how he lived life on his own terms. He never changed his behavior for anyone or kissed anyone's ass. He didn't try to impress anyone. He treated everyone the same. Coarsely. He was always Herschel Wilkinson. Strong and bold. No excuses. No regrets.

He may have been a mean drunk, but he accepted that about himself. He didn't compromise.

It was a lesson, however blunt, about being happy with who you are, with no false fronts. That way of living life is powerful. It's liberating.

It means you can look at yourself in the mirror and not cringe.

CHAPTER SEVENTEEN: Kick, Slap, Stab

Even though I enrolled at Robert Mitchell Elementary with just two months to go to finish sixth grade, I remember the place fondly. Things went well for me in that old brick building from the moment the tall student with the big ears came to get me in the principal's office, to show me around my first day.

"Hey, I'm Mitch. You're going to be in my class. Let me show you around the school real quick and we'll take you back."

Maybe I was due for some good luck. When I got to the classroom, I was in for another surprise. The teacher, Ms. Pepper, introduced me to the class — but didn't force me to make the usual "Hi, I'm Jeff" speech. She seated me and then went right back into her lesson. What a break!

I stole glances around. Some of the kids looked at me, but then went right back to the lesson. Another new face was no big deal to them. The reason, I would come to learn, is that Reno was a transient community. People shuffled in and out all the time. And there were plenty of kids from single-parent households. I fit in.

It turned out that Robert Mitchell was the perfect school for me. A lot of the kids were into soccer. I made friends fast. And I'll never forget Ms. Pepper, even though she was my teacher only those last two months of the school year.

Ms. Pepper was short, a little bit round, with dark hair and a kindly face. She had energy; she was passionate about teaching. She was such a fine teacher that she got me interested in school again. It had been a long while since I'd given a damn. It was obvious she cared very much about each of her students. When I told her about school in Great Falls, I mentioned having to learn italics. She thought teaching italics was very odd. Nobody used italics.

One thing Ms. Pepper did was rekindle my love of books. Once I had been a great reader. When we'd lived in Florida and the Philippines, Mom would take me to the base library and I'd check out books. She even had me read the book, *E. T. The Extra-Terrestrial,* before she'd let me see the movie. But after the Philippines, I hadn't read much. I'd floated along in school in San Bernardino and Great Falls. But now, my appetite for literature was renewed.

After we'd come in from lunch recess, Ms. Pepper would read to us for an hour. She was amazing. She had us spellbound. She'd get into character, dramatize a story, read the dialogue and imitate the various voices. We could close our eyes and simply be carried along, lost in the tale. There was one book about a boy whose family owned a cemetery. The ghosts would come alive during the day and befriend the boy. One was an old ship's captain who told sea tales. Ms. Pepper brought the book to life. Sometimes she'd pause from the narrative and introduce a philosophical or social issue raised by the story. Like how the boy in the story didn't have much around him, but he drew upon his imagination to entertain himself as best he could in his surroundings.

"What would you have done in his situation?" Ms. Pepper asked. "Are there ways we use our imaginations to better our circumstances? What else do we do to escape from the world we're in, into a world of our own?"

I'd never had a teacher do that — seeking opinions from students, asking kids what they made of a story. It was my introduction to critical analysis.

I thought of grim-faced Mrs. Prentiss, walking around with her ruler in Lincoln Elementary up in Great Falls. I wished I'd had Ms. Pepper all year. She took personal time with each student to work on their assignments. She put out a lot of effort. She was fantastic.

It turned out that Ms. Pepper had a son, Ray, who attended a different school but was my age. Ray was also a soccer player, and when I told her I loved soccer, she gave me the information about joining the American Youth Soccer Organization. That was my ticket for making friends.

Everything was falling into place for me in Reno. The stress of uncertainty, of living in different environments and constantly moving, loosened its grip, then let go. I felt that I belonged where I was. I liked my school, the kids I met, the city I now called home.

MOM SIGNED ME UP for the AYSO league. I joined a team. I had a uniform. I had instant friends, including Mitch Dokes and Ray Pepper. Soccer was still my passion. It felt like it'd been forever since I'd booted a ball. But it didn't take me long to scrape the rust off.

There were good players in Reno, but I had an edge in experience, after the Philippines. I could kick the ball from almost midfield to the goal with either foot. I could place the ball in the goal wherever the coach asked. I could slide-tackle. I could arch my back and get extra power on a throw-in. Aside from my forays into Grandpa Herschel's bar establishments, and the things I saw there, I was well immersed in a wholesome childhood once more.

In mid-summer, Mom found a place of our own. It was a duplex out in the newer neighborhoods of Sparks, not far from Reed High School. The duplex was in a complex called Sunrise Villas. We moved out of Grandpa Herschel's house. We were on our own again.

I was very happy. I had my own room. Sunrise Villas had a swim pool. There were plenty of kids in the neighborhood.

A lot of us would be attending Sparks Middle School together that fall.

AFTER ALL THE YEARS of moving around, I really felt like I was finally anchored in one place. That meant I had the freedom to make lasting friendships, not ones that would be cut short because I had to move again.

For me, like most active kids, the friendships I made revolved around sports. And there was plenty of sports activity in Reno and Sparks. There was AYSO. But after the school year started, an unlikely sport — hockey — ended up bonding me with a group of four other boys at Sparks Middle School.

Meadowood Mall was a big shopping center that had opened up a few years before just south of Reno, among ranch pastures. (Today, the mall is practically in the middle of the sprawling city.) When I was in middle school, the mall had an indoor ice rink. There was a local youth league for ice hockey, and two of the kids I knew from soccer were really into hockey.

One of these kids was Derek Kruck. He had moved to Reno from Detroit, where hockey is big. Derek was a sweatpants kind of guy. He always dressed sloppy. He looked sloppy. He slurred and sprayed when he spoke. He wasn't the scholarly type. I'm not sure if he showered very often. I know he rarely combed his sandy-blond hair, or brushed his crooked teeth. He didn't care about that stuff. What he cared about was sports. He was passionate about football, basketball, hockey. He knew all the Detroit teams and players. He was always running his mouth — talking about your momma, and the like — but he couldn't back it up. He was just a smartass punk.

The other kid into hockey was Chris Lummox. He was a short, skinny blond kid — small, but very tough. Even though he was little, he played goalie. His size actually helped him. When he wore all his goalie pads, he was still light enough to move around. He was a nice kid, kind of quiet.

Derek and Chris played ice hockey at the mall. They also lived near me in Sparks. So did two of their close buddies from soccer: John Whalen and Drew Walecka. John had dark black hair and was taller than the rest of us. He was smart and charismatic. He dressed well in Izod polo shirts and spoke well with good grammar and vocabulary. For some mysterious reason, he and Derek, the slob, hit it off and were close friends. Derek didn't smart off to John. John kind of led Derek.

Drew, meanwhile, was the quietest of all of us. He was a shy kid with bleach-blond hair and braces. He never participated in a game unless we invited him in. "Yeah, all right," he'd say. The five of us all went to Sparks Middle School together.

Our great floor-hockey adventure started one day in woodshop. One of us made a wood hockey puck. Back at home after school, the five us started playing a hockey-like game in the street, using our feet instead of sticks to boot around the puck. It was so much fun that it became a morning ritual. At school, before the bell rang to go to class, we'd meet where there was a smooth section of sidewalk sheltered from the wind by the building, which was in the shape of three sides of a rectangle. We'd kick a wood puck around. This little game really bonded us.

One of the activities in P.E. class that semester was floor hockey. Derek and Chris, John and I had P.E. at the same time. We got to talking about how fun floor hockey was, and how great it would be if we started a league at school so we could play floor hockey every day. We organized ourselves into a planning committee of sorts. We wanted to start up an intramural league that could compete in the gym at lunchtime. Students could form teams and compete with the school's equipment. Our first goal was talking to the P.E. teachers — Coach Durant and Coach Wakowski — getting their support. They saw we were serious about our plan. We were enthusiastic. We had initiative.

To our delight, they agreed to let us test out the idea by forming teams in the regular P.E. class.

We did. We gave the league a trial run in class. The other kids were into it. After a few games, floor hockey was all that the students wanted to do in P.E. Within weeks, the teachers were ready to let Derek and Chris, John, Drew and me start up the lunchtime league. But there was a lot of planning to do. We had to arrange to borrow the plastic sticks, pucks and goals from the P.E. classes, and make sure they'd be responsibly taken from storage and returned at the end of each lunch period. We decided to modify the game's rules to keep them simple so beginners would understand them. Then we had to hold a signup and get the kids assembled on teams. The P.E. teachers helped us with signup sheets. The teachers agreed to serve as referees.

The response was overwhelming. Some 60 kids signed up. And that was it: Every lunchtime, the cafeteria was fairly empty; students crowded into the gym to watch the floor-hockey league matches. Some of the teachers took time out from their own lunch hour to come to the gym and supervise the crowd.

The five of us couldn't believe the buzz we'd created. The floor-hockey league was suddenly all the rage at Sparks Middle School. The gym crackled with electricity. As a player, it was a terrific rush to score a goal or make a strong check in front of all the other students. If you scored a goal, after the game they'd be talking about it.

The league was such a hit that it lasted for nearly a month. And it started a tradition at Sparks Middle School. The league was renewed each year for several years after we five founders left. It was our legacy. And it taught each of us the power of organizing.

We understood that the sum of the efforts of our groups' members was larger than what each member could have accomplished individually.

MIDDLE SCHOOL HAD ITS highs, but also its lows. Of course, there were bullies.

Ezra was the worst one who ended up in my hair. He was a racist skinhead constantly professing his ethnic superiority. At 14 or 15, he already had tattoos. That was unheard of in middle school back then. Ezra had gotten bounced out of a grade somewhere along the way, so was repeating eighth grade. He should've been a freshman in high school.

As bad luck had it, Ezra was in my home economics class. He ran his mouth off constantly. He picked on everyone. The teacher moved his seat several times. Finally, he was put right behind me: the smallest kid in class.

I braced for his harassment. It didn't come immediately. It started the second day. A punch on my arm. Then a kick on my seat. I spun my head around.

"Knock it off!"

He laughed, but quit.

I started focusing on the teacher again. It was difficult. I was rattled. Sure enough, here came another jolt under my seat. I turned around. He smirked. I turned back.

Another jolt.

"Knock it off!" I gave him a dirty look.

He stared at me blankly.

The next day he did nothing. Same with the day after. Ezra was leaving me alone. Maybe he'd had his fun with me. I began to relax.

Then the punches and kicks started again. They were infrequent, but that only made them more aggravating. He knew what he was doing. He'd space them out. He knew how to get on someone's nerves. He enjoyed it.

"F*cking knock it off!" I'd say.

He'd wear a puzzled look. He'd act like he hadn't done anything. He'd raise his palms and shrug.

"Stop looking at me," he'd say.

I grew more and more fed up.

One day, after a lull in his psychological torture, I could sense Ezra getting ready to do something. My neck tingled. Sure enough: *smack!* He slapped me on the head.

I had a yellow No. 2 pencil in my right hand. I flipped it into my left hand, twisted around and stabbed the point hard into the back of his hand. The tip sunk in like it was going to impale the hand to the desk.

He was shocked. His eyes grew wide.

"You f*cking stabbed me!"

His face convulsed with pain. He eased the pencil out of his flesh and clutched his bleeding hand.

Suddenly, *he* was the victim.

"F*ck this, I'm telling on you," he said.

My stomach filled with butterflies. Ezra got out of his seat and walked up the aisle to the teacher's desk. She raised her head and listened. He pointed back at me. I waited for her to call out my name and summon me.

But she didn't. She wasn't buying his story. Ezra was a troublemaker. He was always causing friction. Now he was crying wolf.

She sent him to the nurse's office. He left the room without looking back.

I couldn't believe it. I'd gotten away with it! I'd stood up for myself. But I wasn't exactly sure how this equation worked.

I'd committed a vicious violent act upon another student, yet I wasn't getting suspended, or even reprimanded. Ezra hadn't retaliated.

Maybe the reason it had all worked out was that I'd caught him off guard. A quick, bold strike.

Ezra quit picking on me. He wasn't up for messing with a little kid who was crazier than he looked. There were easier victims.

CHAPTER EIGHTEEN: Middle School Confidential

Seventh grade was, all in all, a blast, except for the schoolwork itself. I hated it, but I still managed reasonable grades. I wasn't a straight-A student, but I wasn't a C student, either. History interested me. So did woodshop, working with my hands. My best subject was science. The logic of it appealed to me. But in the lab room we didn't get to use Bunsen burners. The gas was turned off since some dopeheads had sent up ceiling-singeing flames one time too many.

If there was one classroom subject I hated, it was math. Algebra was sheer torture. The teacher went by the book and I couldn't follow his explanations. He didn't go step by step, from theory to principles to practice. He just went right into the formulas and equations. I was lost in a haze. I earned C's and D's. I suffered, thinking I was terrible with numbers.

I scored my greatest academic coup in my language arts class. I wasn't a top student. I loved reading, but I hated grammar. I scored low on writing assignments unless it was creative writing — making up a story. Then I had a chance at a decent grade, even if my punctuation was off. The teacher, Ms. McCoy, was a tough old broad. But at the beginning of the second semester, she said that anyone who managed to get a story published in the newspaper would earn an A for the term.

I couldn't resist taking the challenge. I was all fired up about the issue of school-zone variances. It was a hot topic in the school district. One of my friends lived only a block from me but was zoned for a different school, which kept us apart. I thought it was bull crap. I decided to write an editorial opinion piece about this and send it in to the *Reno Gazette-Journal.*

It was easy for me to get started writing it. I put a lot of emotion into my story: how sad I was that I couldn't go to the same school as my neighbor. How ridiculous it was that we lived in the same neighborhood yet were stuck in separate schools. He had to go to school with a bunch of kids he hadn't grown up with. It made everything harder.

An editor phoned our house. He said the newspaper liked hearing from a younger person. *Boom*, the story was printed, with my name on it as the author.

I clipped the article out, brought it to school and slapped it on Ms. McCoy's desk. "There you go! Where's my A?"

She couldn't believe it. Of all the students to meet the challenge, I was the one who'd done it. I slacked off the rest of the semester. My burst of initiative had earned me a break.

Only one other student in class managed to get a story printed in the newspaper that semester: Kerri, who was smart, blond and beautiful. She was hot and she knew she was hot. She was beginning to fill out. She was one of the most popular girls in school.

What a coincidence, to share an honor with her. But it wasn't the only coincidence we'd share that semester. The second one had nothing to do with schoolwork.

In the harsh, black-and-white world of middle school, certain things could destroy a reputation. One of those things was Kmart. If word got around that you'd shopped at Kmart, you'd be shunned by the rest of the kids. It was a disgrace that would stick with you. Of course, a lot of kids shopped there because the prices were affordable. But they did so with nervous eyes. There is nothing wrong with Kmart, it was just a dumb juvenile thing at that period of time. You could have said Macy's was bad and all the other kids would shun you.

One day, Mom decided to stop at Kmart while we ran errands. I cringed. I'd just have to sit in the car and wait it out while she went in. Of course, she insisted I go in with her. I had no choice.

While we were inside, who should come around a corner of the aisle but Kerri, a member of the in crowd at school. Yes, it was she. Right there in front of me, with her long blond hair. And I was right there in front of her. We turned red from embarrassment.

It was Kerri who thought first. You don't get to be popular without being able to think on your feet. With an urgent hand gesture, she motioned me around the corner.

"Listen," she said in a low voice, "you don't tell anybody you saw me in here, I won't tell anybody I saw you in here!"

I looked at her. "It's a deal!" I said.

We shook hands. And we never told anyone.

Looking back, I should have asked for more.

CHAPTER NINETEEN: The Way the Grass Grows

The summer after seventh grade, I got fired up about earning some extra money and mowing lawns in my neighborhood. I was still cleaning bars for Grandpa Herschel on weekends, staying over at his house, but it wasn't enough money for me, and it was hard work, so I slowly let it dwindle off.

I'd seen enough adult boobs, anyway.

Grandpa took me to a swap meet and we bought a used push mower cheap, without a catcher. I got a rake, and a file to sharpen the blades, and borrowed Mom's hand shears. I was set with gear.

There were other kids out there mowing lawns, and they had gasoline-powered mowers. But I knew there was one niche that was neglected. There were condominiums near our duplex. None of the other kids was knocking doors there, since it didn't look to be enough business in the small, 20-foot-square lawns at the condos. But I saw opportunity: plenty of little patches. They were perfectly suited to my push mower; I didn't want to kill myself on long, sloping lawns.

I decided to charge $5 per lawn — the rate I'd charged for shoveling walkways up in Great Falls. Soon I had customers. It felt great to be out there working on my own again, not for Grandpa or anyone else. Just like when I'd shoveled the walks, I was methodical and meticulous. Some of the homeowners would sit out and watch me as I worked over their square of grass. I'd move like a machine through my work. I'd set the handle, back up, then run and grab the handle and propel the mower forward. A speed routine.

My fingers and palms grew calloused. My cash reserves grew, too. As the money came in, I invested in hand snips to do an even better job. No loose blades would be left. I was a perfectionist. I started getting more customers. That's when I realized I'd have to really be smart about managing my time. If I wanted to keep expanding my business, I'd have to get the production time down to a science.

What I started doing was timing myself. What I was doing was creating what are known in the business world as "efficiency standards." I didn't know that term then, though.

I experimented with different mowing patterns on different-sized lawns to determine the best method. Usually I mowed against the bend; but if the grass was real rough and tall, I'd go with the bend. I paid close attention. I developed techniques for making sure the grass lay down smooth. And, again, I timed myself. I'd rake and bag the clippings, then finish with the hardest part: the post-mowing edging. I didn't have a weed eater yet — I had to save up for one — so I'd get down on my knees with the hand shears. The reason I'd have raked first was so there wouldn't be any mowed grass hiding how straight the lines were on the edges.

After edging, my hands would ache from squeezing the shears. But I'd be done. I'd bring the customer out to the lawn and ask, "Are you happy with it? Is there anything you'd like me to change?"

That customer-service approach was an influence from Mom, who'd always taught me to never do anything unless you are 100 percent committed to it. I found this approach made great business sense: I developed solid customer loyalty. I was the only mower the condo owners would hire. I never got stiffed on payment. What's more, the customers became very trusting of me.

One of my regular condos belonged to two roommates — Tim and Keith — a white man and black man who lived kitty-corner from our duplex. They were hilarious. They may or may not have been gay; people suspected they were. Sometimes on the weekends they'd come outside wearing silk bathrobes. "Be careful around those guys," Mom said. I wasn't worried. They were always nice toward me, and never strange.

Tim and Keith held shirt-and-tie jobs, although I don't know what their occupation was. On weekends they were constantly smoking dope. You could smell it, as well as the incense they burned to conceal the odor. They'd see me and say, "Hey, Jeff, cut our lawn." They'd head out on an errand and pay me in advance. Other clients did, too. They trusted that I'd follow through and do a good job.

Their faith in me meant more to me than money. These people *believed* in me. It was incredibly satisfying. It was a big boost to my self-esteem.

My productivity peaked at 10 lawns a day. Multiplied by both weekend days, that equaled 20 lawns: a weekly income of $100. That was a lot of money for a middle schooler back then!

At this point I started thinking even bigger. I could hire other kids and pay them $2.50 a lawn so I'd have time to play with friends on the weekend. I tried it out, but learned pretty quickly that their standards weren't the same as mine. Some customers said they liked it better when I mowed the lawns because I was more detailed. So I had to go back to mowing everything myself. I realized I couldn't teach kids my age the basics of immaculate lawn mowing. I realized my business would never grow beyond the level I could personally handle.

After summer ended, I transitioned into raking leaves. In this way I had my own spending money throughout the year. I saved it up in my room and spent it on things I wanted — such as clothes and soccer equipment that Mom was hard-pressed to buy. I was practical with my earnings. I needed a soccer ball? I paid for it myself. I needed new shoes? Ditto.

CHAPTER TWENTY: Horseshoes and Hotties

The summer before high school I found a source of income I thought would be better than mowing lawns.

Mom was dating a professional cowboy named Greg. He was a lot older than Mom. He had gray hair and a rough face. He roped on the rodeo circuit. They'd met at Whiskey River. Greg had a friend named Cole who was a horseshoer. Cole was a 6-foot, 300-pound, tobacco-chewing S.O.B. in a cowboy hat. He knew I was looking to make extra money. He offered to teach me how to shod horses.

Cole taught me all I wanted to learn about shoeing horses. He'd pick me up for the day in his pickup and we'd head out to the area ranches. Some of these were actual working ranches, but others were spreads where wealthy people boarded their horses.

"What you do is see how the shoes are wearing," Cole explained. "You study the bottom of the horses' hoofs. You check out the ground around the corral and where the horses are being run to see what they're running on. You look at their shoes and see if the nails are wearing sideways. And you look at the horse, see if he's got a limp or a drag."

Cole showed me how to use the steel, plier-like nail nippers and clippers, the hammers and tongs, and the curved knives with wood handles and short blades.

But it took a long time to get a shoe off and a new one on. You had to go slow. If you made a mistake clipping a hoof, you could make the horse lame.

It was highly skilled work. I watched Cole remove horseshoes, trim hoofs, line up the new shoes, hammer them in. It was work that required care and caution. When you moved around the horse, you always kept a hand on him to let him know where you were. You moved the hand along his back or side and when you reached a leg you moved your hand all the way, gave a tap on the side of the knee to let the horse know you were going to raise the leg up and the horse would have to balance on the other legs, then you tugged the leg and raised it, put it between your legs and leaned into the horse slightly.

Cole let me do the shoeing tasks under his guidance. The work was hot and dirty and tiring, and there was always the danger of one of the big beasts getting nasty or spooked while you were bent over a hoof, trying to remove a horseshoe by twisting the shoe all around to pop up the nails, or trying to drive nails into a hoof.

"If you don't pay attention and watch what you're doing, you could get kicked, bit or stepped on," Cole said.

I found out right away that some horses didn't like to be shod and you had to fight with them and watch out that you weren't kicked. My first week, a horse I was working on got startled. I was going to remove a shoe from a rear leg. As I moved to position myself backward to put its leg between my legs, the horse suddenly kicked back like a reflex. The hoof caught me in the thigh. It was like getting clouted with a piece of heavy metal. It left a nice deep bruise.

Fortunately, horses sense a gentle soul, and I was pretty good with animals.

CHAPTER TWENTY: Horseshoes and Hotties

Cole was rougher — dominating. If a horse wasn't cooperating, he'd walk up and punch him in the head like the horse was a man. Cole also told me how, occasionally, he and the horse's owners or ranch hands would wrestle a horse to the ground, strap him down and nail stakes to hold him. It sounded inhumane. I was glad I never had to see that.

The best benefit of the job was that after I shoed a horse, Cole would let me ride it around a bit, to make sure the shoes sat OK. Some owners, though, didn't want anyone else riding their expensive horse, so I didn't get to ride every time.

It wasn't long before I realized this work wasn't for me. I was working harder than mowing lawns, but earning just a touch more. Cole paid me poorly for all the hours he was having me put in. I considered that I could've been back home being my own boss, and taking videogame breaks in between lawns.

Then there was the girl factor. Some of the horses belonged to rich teenage girls who barrel raced. These girls were hot. Some were even my age. They wore fancy embroidered Western riding tops with the sleeves cut out, and jeans and boots and hats and scarves. But none of them paid me any interest. They wanted nothing to do with me. They barely spoke to me. I was just the little guy shoeing their pricey horses.

After a couple weeks I quit and went back to mowing lawns.

CHAPTER TWENTY-ONE: Freshman Haze

There was one thing I dreaded about the start of high school. I'd heard the horror stories about hazing. Freshmen forced to push pennies down the sidewalk with their noses, and getting duct-taped to flag poles. I was just a little guy. I weighed 98 pounds. I was a ball of nerves. I didn't want to get my ass kicked by guys twice my size.

I got an early taste of the treatment that summer. Tryouts for Reed High's soccer team were held in July, more than a month before school started. All of us incoming freshmen who'd played youth-league soccer seriously had hopes of making the junior varsity. We knew there were a lot of soccer players at Reed, but no one expected that nearly 100 players would show up for tryouts. It was the biggest bunch the school had ever seen. And only 40 would make it on varsity or JV.

It was competitive. We incoming freshmen had to go against incoming seniors. I felt like a boy among men. There were a lot of guys a full foot taller, or more, than my 5 feet 2 inches. And they weighed more than twice my weight. One of the seniors had a full-faced beard. But I was psyched up to succeed. I knew in my heart I'd make the JV cut. I'd never in my life not made a team. I'd just have to crank it up a notch. I liked the odds; I wanted to go up against all of them. I wanted to show them what I could do. I knew I could prove I could make this caliber of a team.

The workouts were intense — skill drills, running, scrimmages. Nonstop. The coaches had to weed out the weak as quickly as possible. They had to cut the group down. I hustled through every drill. I was fast. There were only a handful of players faster than I. I darted in and out. I worked my butt off. I had to.

"Good hustle," a coach would tell me. "Good enthusiasm."

I was showing a lot of heart and spirit.

Some of the older guys talked crap out on the field. One of them was Ron Darby, a lanky, skinny dufus. "You little faggot, you shouldn't even be out here," he told me. Darby was cocky, but a clumsy player. In the two-on-two drills, I dribbled around him and gave the crap back to him. "Ah, look at this little guy — between your legs!" I sent the ball between his legs, caught up to it behind him and continued.

Next round, I beat him with a juke, faking him in the wrong direction. As I went by, I said, "Nice blocking, bitch."

I left some pissed-off guys in my wake. Especially Darby.

When my name was called with a dozen other players who'd made the JV cut on the very first round, I couldn't believe it. I was in. Derek and John had made it, too. We got to sit on the sidelines watching other players struggling to make it on the second cut.

The squad was filled out. Drew got cut. We felt bad for him. But Derek, John and I each proudly received the three uniforms handed out for home and away games and practices. We felt like we'd really accomplished something.

The sophomores and juniors who'd gotten cut were pissed off at the freshmen who'd made it. Darby made it on the second cut. But he was mad that I'd made it before him.

As we left the tryouts, he bumped into me, knocking me down. I looked up. He didn't say a word. He just kept on walking without looking back.

PRACTICES WERE BRUTAL. THE coaches were hard-asses. They wanted to win. You had to obey every instruction, always do your best. Then, after practice, we had to run up Shadow Mountain — a steep hill flanking the fields. The coaches wanted us to get fit in a hurry. Our sides ached as we lurched up Shadow Mountain, panting. It was all we could do to finish after a long, hard, draining workout with two- or three-hour scrimmages. They were so grueling I'd slather Ben Gay sports gel on my feet before tugging my socks on, since my ankles were so sore all the time.

I bought a pedometer at a sporting-goods store to log how many miles I accumulated during practice. I'd subtract half the mileage, figuring it was from movements such as walking or hopping, but the mileage still averaged large numbers.

One day, while I was walking home from practice, Darby drove by in his red Toyota pickup. He slowed. His window was open. He hucked a bunch of eggs at me. One nailed me in the back.

That wasn't the end of it. The next day, he drove by and stopped. He had friends with him. Some had been cut from soccer. They got out. I started running, but they caught me and threw me down into the dirt.

"Punk-ass freshman."

The hazing had begun. I had to watch my back all the time I wasn't on the soccer field.

It was rough out there in practice, too. Brian Knudson was one of the JV goalies. There was a play in front of the goal. Before I could boot the ball he grabbed it, then rolled over on my legs. It was a dirty, dangerous tactic.

It felt like an elephant squashed me. When he finally rolled off, I struggled up to my knees. I felt like crying.

"That was f*cked up," Ricky Smith said.

Ricky was a short, tough guy — a real fighter. He'd been kicked out of more than one school for brawling. He didn't take crap off anyone. He had a reputation. And he didn't dig Knudson's cheap shot.

Ricky stepped in and punched Knudson in the mouth. Knudson went down. He stood up, his mouth torn up and bloody.

I'd never seen such damage from one punch!

Knudson's lips were puffy for the next two weeks. He was teased mercilessly.

Now I knew why nobody messed with Ricky.

I was glad he was on my side. There were some benefits to being small.

Our team's matches started that August, before classes began. High school sports were intense. The coaches played to win. They didn't coddle anyone. If you were good, you started. If you weren't — or if you made a mistake on the field, such as a stupid pass, or didn't put your head over the ball when kicking it and ended up booting it high and short — you sat. The coaches played the percentages. Our JV team was winning every match. We were a formidable side. In fact, we would go undefeated that season.

I wasn't starting, at first, but I was put into every game. And I gave it my all. I was tenacious; I never gave up if the ball was on the other side of the field. I kept running toward the action. Even though I was tiny, my speed kept distance around me so I didn't get elbowed or shoved around. I raced away from opposing jerseys.

Off the field, I didn't have it so easy.

CHAPTER TWENTY-TWO: In the Ditch

The school year started, and already I was on the hazers' list. Just about all freshmen were; but because I'd made the JV squad, and I was so small, I was a priority target.

The very first week at Reed, I discovered that some of the seniors took hazing quite seriously. If you made eye contact with one of them in the halls, you'd get roughed up. You'd get pushed around, shoved up against a locker. I'd already seen freshmen forced to push pennies with their noses. It made me furious. But then I got caught by three seniors one lunch break.

A leg stuck out. I tripped and fell over. Someone picked up my legs. Someone else got my arms behind me in a lock and pushed down on my shoulders, driving my face against the hallway floor. Another senior put a penny in front of me.

"Let's see you push it with your nose, freshman."

I strained my head away. "Push your own f*cking penny!"

I squirmed. There was no way I could get away, but there was no way in hell I was going to crack.

They hadn't expected resistance. Time was on my side. Someone would come along and break it up. A teacher, maybe. Or some other seniors who would say, "That's f*cked up. Let him up."

Finally, one of the hazers slapped the back of my head. Then they let me go.

Now I was even more of a marked man.

A lot of other freshmen gave in to the hazing so they'd be let alone. Especially after the stories started circulating. One freshman had a front tooth knocked out after his head was slammed down on a water faucet. Another had been taken way out of town and left in his underwear with 24 cents: a penny less than bus fare. Another had so much booze poured down his throat out in the parking lot that he ended up in the emergency room with alcohol poisoning.

After a couple weeks, the bullies were all trying to be the first to get little Jeff Bowling to push a penny. Sometimes they'd catch me. "There he is!" But I still didn't give in, no matter how hard they roughed me up.

I fought back. I would not push their f*cking penny.

One time, Ron Darby and two of his friends caught me in the ditch behind the school as I was walking home with Derek and John. Derek took off running, but I was the one targeted. The older guys tossed me down and pushed me around until I was covered in dirt. Then they cracked eggs on me. I was filthy from face to toes, gooey from the eggs. I stank.

John started laughing at me. "You got rolled!"

Just like that, I saw how things were. For whatever reasons, John and Derek had something against me. But my feelings toward them instantly changed.

"Why didn't you help me out?" I screamed at John.

I picked up a rock and whipped it at him. It cracked hard between his shoulder blades.

"Sh*t! What the f*ck did you do that for?"

I glared at him. He got the message.

I left him and walked home through the ditch.

JIMMY MELAY, MY NEXT-door neighbor, tried to look out for me. He would give me rides to school when he could. He was a senior, and respected. But other days I skateboarded to school. Our home was close enough to campus that I didn't take the bus. When I boarded to school, I took the sidewalks along the streets that went to the front of the school. I knew if I took a shortcut through the ditch that ran behind the school, the seniors might catch me there and toss me in the murky, dirty water. So I usually took the long way around. But it meant I'd have to pass seniors waiting out in the parking lot for freshmen to pick on. My best bet was to try to hurry through breakfast and haul ass to school so I could get there early before anyone was outside.

Going home after soccer practice was more grief. There was nothing to do but hope for the best. There were the sophomores and juniors who'd gotten cut and still wanted revenge. And then there was Ron Darby.

Darby truly sucked as a soccer player. I don't know how he'd even made the squad, but I guessed it was because his mother worked in the school office, keeping attendance. He didn't get many minutes during games. Nobody liked him much because he had a negative attitude to go with his lack of skills.

Darby hated me. He'd walk up to me during practice, and without saying a word, bump into me and knock me down. I'd get him back during drills or scrimmage, embarrassing him, faking him out of his cleats. "Not fast enough,"

I'd say.

After practice, I couldn't always get away from him. I'd be walking or skateboarding home, and he'd catch up to me. He'd throw me down and whale on my arms, chest and back.

I'd yell. "Get off me."

He'd rough me up some more.

Darby didn't come from a bad family. His mom was a sweet lady. She didn't have a clue about her son's bullying. It was strange how such a prick could have come from such a nice woman.

I'd get home. Mom would be home from work. She'd see how banged up I was — bruises on my arms and back. This obviously hadn't happened during practice.

She started grilling me. "Who's been beating you up?"

She kept at me for a few days. I saw how upset she was getting. Finally, she drew Darby's name out of me.

"Just don't do anything, Mom, I'm all right," I said. "I can take care of myself."

The next afternoon at soccer practice, we were in the middle of a scrimmage. Out of the corner of my eye I saw Mom standing on the sideline, in her nice work clothes. I wondered why she'd left work early.

She was looking up and down the field. Then she stalked right out onto the grass. She walked right up to Darby and grabbed him by the throat. She started screaming at him.

I couldn't believe it. I froze. This was a nightmare. This was true humiliation.

The scrimmage action stopped as the players shifted their attention to the bizarre scene. They'd never seen anything like this, ever.

It was too much for me. I broke down. The tears just streamed.

The coaches ran out on the field and separated Mom and Darby. The rest of us crowded around. I couldn't look at anyone's face. I wanted to disappear.

Then the asshole tried to take a swing at Mom. I went nuts. I pushed through the crowd and went after him, trying to tackle him, swinging my fists.

The coaches and other players pulled us apart. Finally, they had Darby off the field on one side, Mom and me on the other. It was truly ugly. But it was worst of all for me. I felt like an outsider, now. Whose mother showed up to get involved in a player conflict?

The scrimmage resumed, without Darby and me. The coaches separated us. They talked to Mom, and they talked to Darby, and they talked to me.

I could barely speak. I was still shaking. I couldn't believe this had happened. It was more scarring than a beating.

If there was anything good to come out of it, at least the bullying had come to a head. At the next game, Mom talked to Darby's mom. After that, he left me alone. His family was really all right, except for him. His younger brother was cool; I knew him from youth soccer. But Darby himself was just a goofball.

Maybe it was just a coincidence, but after that confrontation at practice, my beatings at school began dwindling, too. Still, I started to have nightmares about Mom going out there on the field. I wished it had never, ever happened.

Even today, I wish I could blot it from my memory.

CHAPTER TWENTY-THREE: A Lucky Cut

Despite the hazing, I didn't fail any classes. I even earned a few B's. Science, woodshop and P.E. were my favorite classes. I liked English, too. The teacher, Ms. Morgan, was a hottie — a 24-year-old recent graduate of the University of Nevada, Reno. She had blondish-brown hair to her shoulders.

If I'd had teachers who looked like Ms. Morgan in every class, I probably would have had a 4.0. But halfway through the school year, Ms. Morgan got married and moved away, and was replaced by an older woman, Ms. Fehr, who didn't care as much about the class. Nor did we guys care as much about her.

My sister was getting good grades. Jennifer was a good student. She was more or less among the nerds. She'd gone out for cheerleading but, because she was stocky and wasn't popular, had been cut. Too bad, because she was a really good dancer. She'd been a Pop Warner cheerleader before high school. At Reed she was in the band and on the flag team. We didn't have much to do with each other. We'd grown apart so much by now that we barely talked.

We were just two very different people. An introvert and an extrovert. The personalities we'd have as adults were gelling.

One thing I was becoming was a night owl. This probably had started in middle school. I'd get home late either from soccer or from ice hockey, eat dinner, do my homework. Then I'd get in bed and lie awake listening to the *Dr. Demento* syndicated radio show with its comedy songs. Napoleon XIV's *They're Coming to Take Me Away, Ha-Haaa. Gilligan's Island (Stairway)*, by Little Roger & The Goosebumps, which mixed the Led Zeppelin classic with the television theme song. Ogden Edsl's *Dead Puppies*. I'd fall asleep during the show, but the funny thing was, I'd remember the songs and the jokes from hearing them in my sleep. The next day at school I'd tell the songs and jokes. I realized I had an uncanny memory. Somehow it worked while I was asleep, or at least semi-conscious.

There was no time to listen to *Dr. Demento* in high school. I'd stay up until midnight laboring over homework, trying to figure things out. And then I'd have to get up at 6 a.m. to be in class by 7:30 a.m. I'd have six or fewer hours of sleep, and then have to stay focused in my classes. I had lots of energy, but some of the classes were so boring. It was a battle to stay awake.

For the first time in my life, my grades fell below a C average.

There was one bright spot. Reed allowed students to take a "computer literacy" class instead of a foreign language.

I'D NEVER LOST MY interest in computers that had been kindled by exposure to the machines in school in Florida and the Philippines. "Computer Lit" was a general orientation about computers and taught a bit of the Basic programming language. I loved it. Whatever it is that grabbed me about the digital world, the feelings all came back. I could have gladly spent the entire school day fooling around on the keyboard, entering commands, learning the programs.

Computers were growing in popularity for personal use. I was in awe of the personal computers hitting the market. I wanted one so badly, but they cost about $1,700 — way out of my league. But Christmastime, Radio Shack ran television commercials for the TRS-80, a model that had a keyboard and programs and cost $200. There was no monitor. The processing unit was in the white keyboard.

I knew this was how I should spend my savings from mowing lawns: a TRS-80. I had enough money. I went down to Radio Shack and returned with my TRS-80. I hooked a tape recorder by a cable to the keyboard for storing magnetic memory on cassettes. For a monitor, I had an old black-and-white GE brand TV, which I'd found for $5 at a swap meet with Grandpa Herschel.

At home I took what I learned in "Computer Lit" and then read books from the library to teach myself Basic. I started writing programs. When I had the time, I worked for hours at it. To produce graphics in Basic required using a lot of standard keyboard symbols. I'd type in asterisks in different spaces on the screen and with a series of go-to commands send them in motion rolling like waves on a scrolling screen. Simple but clever screensavers.

Next I started mastering basic syntax and commands like Print, Goto, Gosub, Let, and Hline — graphical lines. I designed graphic applications. I was totally absorbed. My friends were playing videogames, trying to master the different levels. But I craved to learn how videogames actually worked.

I'd found a hobby.

I had no premonition it would someday develop beyond that.

I WAS STILL BEING hazed a bit. After all, I was the freshman who hadn't pushed a penny.

But I was due for a triumph after all the ass-whippings I'd taken.

Derek Kruck's older brother, Darrel, was one of the seniors who wanted to break me. Darrel was a big guy, 6 foot tall, 190 pounds. And a real dickhead. He was a poor student, and already a problem drinker. Like his brother, Darrel dressed sloppily. A sweats-and-T-shirt kind of guy. He'd walk the way we used to call "lurpy" — no posture or style — down the halls. He didn't care about anything. About all he was good at was soccer. He'd been goalie on the varsity. He had a lot of potential. But of course, he didn't do anything with it. Like Derek, Darrel just didn't care much about himself. Their house was filthy.

One Tuesday after school I was on my skateboard on the sidewalk along Baring Boulevard, the four-lane arterial that borders the front of the campus. And there in the right lane, shadowing me, was a pickup truck. Darrel was in the passenger seat. The window was open. He was calling names at me. I ignored him and kept on rolling.

There was always a big line of cars leaving the parking lot onto Baring after Reed let out. The cars had to lurch along one by one through a four-way stop. It was a big traffic jam, a big crowd. Darrel decided to put on a show.

He popped open the truck door and jumped onto the sidewalk. I kept skating. I heard footsteps closing in. I could feel him bearing down.

What to do? I couldn't outrace him. I had to think quick.

I kicked my board up, grabbed the trucks in my hands and swung the board upward behind me.

My timing couldn't have been better. The round corner caught Darrel right in the balls. The skateboard felt like a sword in my hands as it hit home.

The next moment he was down on the sidewalk, wailing and writhing in agony. He had an audience, all right. The students in the cars on Baring were all laughing. I raised my board in triumph over my head like a warrior. Then I got back on and beat it the hell out of there.

I heard Darrel was on medication for months, pissing blood. The edge of the skateboard had nearly split one of his testicles in half.

He never screwed with me again.

I made it through ninth grade without getting killed.

CHAPTER TWENTY-FOUR: Small-town Living, and Leaving

That summer, Jennifer moved away. She decided she couldn't live under the same roof with Mom anymore. For the past few years they'd been constantly clashing.

Most of the time when they went at it there was yelling and doors slamming. The issues were infinite. Jennifer wanted to go out on dates, but Mom hadn't met the boys, and said no. Jennifer wanted to take on more hours at work. Mom said it would keep her out too late. Jennifer wanted to cut back on her household chores. Mom said the chores needed to be done.

Half the time I didn't even know what they were fighting about.

Their last big spat was in the kitchen. Jennifer told Mom she had thoughts of killing herself. "I hate life," she said.

Sitting at the table, I was dumbfounded. I'd never heard anyone say such a thing. *How can you hate life? Life is what you make it. You make your own fun. You make your own happiness.*

That was the way I thought. That was the way Mom thought. Any trouble that was thrown at us — we'd put a spin on it and make the situation better. We'd deal with it. We'd get past it.

But any trouble that came Jennifer's way left her troubled. *Life sucks*, she'd think. *Existence is pain and suffering.*

"You have no idea how good you have it," Mom said.

"I want to move out," Jennifer said. "I'm sick of Nevada. I want to move back to California."

"I think that's a great idea," Mom said.

By this time, Uncle Jim and Aunt Denise were living in Vacaville, in Northern California between Sacramento and San Francisco. Jennifer went to live with them and finish her last year of high school.

Our condo was strangely peaceful with her gone. Mom and I had lots of one-on-one time. But it felt funny not having my sister there.

More transitions were on the horizon.

THAT JULY, SOCCER TRYOUTS at Reed went extra well. I was a year older, a year bigger, a year stronger. To my surprise, I made varsity. I was psyched up. Sophomore year was going to be great. I wouldn't have to face freshman hazing. I actually looked forward to school starting.

Then, before I could suit up for our first game, the coaches called me over. They were cutting me. They had no choice. I was ineligible. My grades that second semester of freshman year had been too low. You had to maintain at least a C average.

I had to return my uniforms. I was crushed.

Not long into the school year, Mom broke the news that a guy she'd been dating for a year had proposed.

His name was Garth Pitts, and his family owned a large highway construction company based in Darrington, a small farming town. Mom had met him when his company contracted to build roads out in the desert for the mining company she worked for.

I'd met Garth a few months before, over dinner at a restaurant. The restaurant Mom and Garth had picked out was a coffee shop in Fernley, 30 miles east of Reno. Garth had driven up from Darrington. He seemed all right. He was a tall, husky guy with black hair, mustache and full beard. He wasn't the best-looking man in the world. He looked like a guy who owned a construction company. He wore a flannel shirt and jeans. He had a strong handshake. He was low-key, and spoke in a monotone. He didn't smile. But he was polite. He seemed like a rugged man who was shouldering a lot of responsibilities. He was divorced and raising his two young sons by himself.

After dinner, the three of us walked around the park behind the restaurant. The baseball fields were empty. People were strolling about. We talked casually about this and that. It was nice. Garth was charming, in his reserved manner. His easygoing friendliness, I decided, was what had appealed to Mom. It wasn't his looks. I knew that Mom always did try to give everyone a chance, to look past the surface to what was on the inside. That must have been the case with Garth.

We sat on a bench.

"What do you think of me dating Garth?" Mom asked me.

Garth looked a bit embarrassed. We looked at each other. He was really being put on the spot. But then, I quickly gathered, he wasn't. I could tell from his eyes that he knew the question was going to be asked. He and Mom had planned out this meeting just to win me over.

"I don't know, I guess it's all right," I said.

Garth asked me what I liked to do for fun. I told him I loved soccer. I liked computers, and owned one. I skateboarded a lot. And I really liked dirt bikes.

"I've never been able to afford a bike of my own," I said. "I always borrow a bike from someone."

"Well, I've got a whole bunch of wood on my property," Garth said. "You cut a couple cords of wood, I'll buy you a brand-new dirt bike."

This was a naked ploy. A Grandpa Herschel sales tactic. But who knew? Maybe I could hold this man to his word.

"Cool," I said.

When Mom told me Garth had proposed marriage, I gave her my blessing. I knew she was ready to be married again. What's more, I figured a change would do me good. I was ready to get out of Reno.

"If you want to marry this guy, go ahead. If you want us to move out to Darrington, I could use a break. Let's do it."

What did I have to keep me in Reno? I wasn't sentimental about Reed High, after all the abuse I'd put up with in ninth grade. And since I'd gotten cut from soccer, what else was there for me at that school?

My grades sucked. I didn't have a girlfriend. I was beginning to sprout up now, but still wasn't taller than most of the girls. Except for Drew, I didn't have any super close friends. I hardly ever hung out with Derek, Chris and John anymore. Not since I'd gotten tossed in the ditch.

The more I thought about moving away, the more excited I became. I'd be turning over a new leaf. I'd get to live in a small town again. I still had fond memories of Great Falls. I liked country living.

Darrington was very much out in the country. It was way smaller than Great Falls. It was set amid onion and garlic farms and cattle ranches. Garth was a big man in town. He had a big house. The Pittses had money. Garth's late father had built up the construction company, and Garth and his two brothers had inherited it. I'd be joining a prosperous clan. It would be a new experience.

THERE WAS A BEAUTIFUL little wedding ceremony in a little church in the old Nevada town of Genoa. Some of Mom's friends made it. Nana came. Garth's sons, Kyle and Kody, were there. They were 12 and 9, but seemed much younger. They were shy, scrawny little guys who looked like they'd be more comfortable hiding behind an adult than out causing mischief. I picked them out to be nothing more than spoiled brats.

Mom had already told me there was a reason the boys were so timid. They'd been without a mother for years. Evidently, their mother had some sort of a nervous breakdown and just taken off, leaving Garth to raise the boys alone.

At the wedding I saw how Kyle and Kody really took to Mom. They practically clung to her. They were glad she was going to be their new mother.

Some of Garth's family were at the wedding. His two brothers, Toby and Dwight, were big guys like him. Their wives were outdoorsy ranching women — brown-haired and pretty with suntanned features and nice, athletic figures. The brothers and sisters-in-law were very polite and genuine. Small-town people usually are.

I felt like moving to Darrington, being among these people, would suit me just fine.

GARTH'S HOUSE WAS HUGE. It sat on five acres, part of land that had been in his family for several generations. The large game room was going to be converted into my bedroom. It had a fireplace and 11 windows. Outside there was a giant hot tub. It was quite a jump from my room in the duplex. All of a sudden, I was living on Easy Street. No one was struggling in Garth's family. The brothers lived across town, in big houses themselves. The mother had her own large house — a big place her husband had built — next door to us.

The first night, I had to share Kyle's bedroom. He was a dweeb about it. "These are my toys," he said. "You can't touch them."

He went through the whole room that way. He was just a little brat. So was his brother. I wondered if it would be possible to even hang out with them. They were a lot more interested in Mom, anyway. They seemed more cut out for helping with housework than skateboarding or kicking a soccer ball around.

The next day, we all went over to Garth's mother's house so Mom and I could be introduced. Elly Pitts hadn't attended the wedding.

We found her outside in the garden. She was a plump, white-haired woman in a roomy black dress. She had a sense of importance about her. Kody and Kyle ran up to her. She gave them great big hugs. "This is Karen," Garth said. Elly's face worked into a transparent smile. It was an expression I'd seen a thousand times in phony people.

"This is Jeff," Garth said. "Pleased to meet you," I said. I held out my hand.

She ignored it. She turned around and went into her house.

Mom shot me a look of, "What was that about?"

"Don't worry," Garth said. "She's just an old lady. She'll warm up to you when she gets to know you."

SCHOOL HAD ALREADY BEEN in session for a month, so that Monday I had to enroll and begin at Darrington High. It turned out not to be the best timing.

A dark cloud hung over the school. Mom and I were told in the main office that one of the most popular students had been killed a few days before in a one-car rollover. He'd been driving too fast. The two girls in the car with him — teenagers from out of town — had also been killed.

The principal explained to Mom and me that there'd been an open-casket memorial service for the boy. The church was packed. Almost every student in the high school had attended. Most had grown up with him. He was a Darrington native. They were very depressed.

The principal said it would be perfectly acceptable if I started on a different day, but I said it was OK. I'd start then. Might as well get it over with.

It was the usual routine. A student was sent down to the office to be my guide. His name was Mark Hannigan. He showed me around the building.

As we walked around the halls that morning, I didn't see one happy face. But there was interest in me. New students didn't enroll very often at Darrington High.

Students kept coming up and introducing themselves. It was amazing. It was like I was being immediately accepted, just for being there. They found out I was into sports and skateboarding. They seemed to treat me like I was a cool guy. Maybe it was because my blond hair was a little lighter in front — my bangs teased with Sun-in — and I looked a little different. I was wearing red-and-black Vans. Whatever it was, after I got home that day, I received phone calls from some of the girls at school.

That's a small town for you. Everyone knew the number of the Pitts' residence.

The girls asked what I was doing that weekend. Of course, I had no plans. I was glad to hang out with them. There's something about a rural community. So many of the girls are just really hot. These ones in Darrington weren't up on the latest fashions; they were more into flannel and Wranglers and boots. But they had really nice bodies and fresh, pretty faces.

Later, I thought about it and realized why they'd hit me up. They'd been around the same boys their whole lives. I was a fresh commodity.

The big things for high schoolers to do in Darrington on weekends was cruising and drinking. I ended up joining a group of boys and girls that Friday night. We drove through the tiny downtown. That got old pretty quick, so we drove out into the parking lots and had a few beers. I found out that this was tolerated as long as you didn't drive drunk. There were two sheriff's cruisers, and a pair of deputies usually were parked in a corner lot. They knew most of the kids' parents. The kids would even go over and say hi to the deputies. There was a male deputy and a female deputy. They told us, "If you guys are going to be having beers, just don't drive afterward. Just make sure you watch what you're doing."

After parking and drinking, there were different options available. You could go out "bunny blasting": shooting jackrabbits. The guys had their .22 rifles. If there was a party at someone's house, you could go there and try to hook up.

The whole time I lived in Darrington, I didn't see any drug use. It was just basic, fairly wholesome, small-town fun.

I appreciated my standing as the new kid in town. I knew as long as I didn't act like a jerk, I'd be accepted. It blew me away, though, when the most popular kid in school sought me out and started talking to me.

His name was Mickey Ramos and he was the typical, popular high school kid depicted in the movies. Handsome. Confident. A state wrestling champion. His looks and personality reminded me of "Jake Ryan," the male lead in the teen flick *Sixteen Candles*. His family owned a huge ranch. But he put on no airs. No one did in Darrington.

Some mornings, Mark Hannigan and his brother Mason skateboarded to school with me. Sometimes, Mickey would give me a ride. I couldn't believe my sudden status. What a turnaround from Reed! Here at Darrington I felt welcome, accepted by just about everyone.

There were only two students who gave me bad vibes. One was a ranch boy in cowboy boots. He bumped into me in the halls and told me to watch it.

"Oh, he's a hothead, just stay away from him," Mark Hannigan told me.

The other student who made sure I knew he didn't like me was a large, surly-looking Indian. He shot me dirty looks so that I was sure to get the message.

I decided two bullies wasn't that bad. Not after what I'd been through at Reed.

ON THE HOME FRONT, there was someone I'd have to avoid, too.

Garth's mother did not take a shine to Mom or me. She did not speak warmly to us. Her whole demeanor was gruff. Her body language was aloof. It was like we were unwanted guests taking up her time with her son.

I'd look over at her house when I was outside. She'd be staring out the window at me.

Garth was very close to her. Sometimes he ate breakfast at her place. Sometimes he even had dinner there, just the two of them.

Elly Pitts was my first introduction to one of society's hazards: the bitter old widow with a large bank account, whose greatest purpose and joy in life is treating others like dog crap. She did what she could to satisfy herself. She meddled in her children's lives. She was plain nasty. She didn't even talk nicely about her late husband.

Francis Pitts had been a well-respected man who built up his company from scratch. He was remembered in Darrington, and in the construction industry, for his industriousness and good nature. Garth and his brothers spoke glowingly of their dad.

One day, I tried to break the ice with Elly. "I wish I'd had the chance to have met your husband," I said.

She sneered and walked off.

Another time, I heard her remark to someone, "That old buzzard really left a mess for his sons to clean up when he died."

No one contradicted her. Garth and his brothers were afraid of her. They had reason to be; she shrewdly played them off one against the other. If one fell into her disfavor, his life would be hell. So would his wife's.

Actually, Elly already was mistreating the wives. They weren't of her flesh and blood. They were just competition for her sons' attention.

After a few short weeks, the dynamics of the family situation became crystal clear to Mom and me. There was a reason that Garth's brothers lived across town. They'd listened to their wives. The more distance they could keep from that mean old bitch, the easier their lives were.

Unfortunately for us, Garth had stayed put. His house next door to his mom's suited him fine. His two boys were regulars at their grandma's house. Kody and Kyle were her flesh and blood, so she liked them. Since I was outside the gene pool, I stayed out of her way as much as possible.

Garth himself doted over her. Maybe it was how he kept control of the construction company; she backed her oldest boy. She attended all the board meetings. She was an official member. Whatever the reasons, Garth seemed firmly tied to his mama's apron strings.

Company checks kept Elly Pitts in spending money. She had no reason to be nice to anyone. But Mom didn't give up on her right away. Mom did whatever she could to be polite to this lady — invited Elly to dinner, went shopping for her, was always cordial. But these niceties were wasted. Elly Pitts simply was a vicious old hag. She took pains to make sure we knew we didn't fit in.

Now the mystery surrounding Garth's first wife was becoming clear. Mom told me that the woman had ended up on drugs.

Maybe she'd had been driven crazy, I thought. Or maybe she'd done the sanest thing possible — cut her ties and made her escape.

I BADLY WANTED A dirt bike. With all the open country around Darrington, I could spend hour upon hour riding and exploring. Right after we'd moved into Garth's house after the wedding, he'd told me that if I split the cords of wood stacked outside his house, he'd get me the new bike he'd promised.

There were several cords, but I was up for it. I told him I'd work all fall if I had to, to finish the job.

But the next time I brought up the subject, Garth decided it was too dangerous a job for a kid my size.

"Tell you what," he said. "If you want to come down to the company yard and steam clean the heavy equipment we just bought, I'll give you the old company truck."

He showed me the truck. It was a dirty old Toyota pickup with a couple hundred thousand miles on it, easy.

Still, it was a set of wheels.

I told him I'd do it.

The heavy equipment was three used trucks. Steam cleaning them proved to be a grimy job. But I went out there every weekend, slipped into coveralls and got to work. I cleaned the grease off. I lubed the engines. I got it done. I got all the other equipment — dozers, dump trucks, skip loaders — as they came in.

I got the Toyota!

It was a real mess from all the miles put on it out in the field by company workers. But I was excited. In another year I'd be 16 and able to test for a driver's license. Until then, Garth would let me drive the truck around the construction yard, which was on the back half of the property where we lived.

I set to work on the Toyota with a vengeance. Garth gave me a few bucks for helping out around the company yard. I got a ride down to an auto-parts store in town and bought some accessories. I cleaned out the Toyota, installed new seat covers and rubber floor mats. I got up under the dash and fixed up the stereo system. I washed and waxed the exterior. The truck looked almost new by the time I was done with it. Garth had the clutch repaired.

I was ready to roll!

I stuck to driving it around the property. One day, Mark Hannigan came over after school to check out my new wheels. We started talking about off-roading. That was big out in the country. "Let me show you what my truck can do," I said.

Garth was out of town on business. Elly wasn't home, either. Her Lincoln Continental was gone. It was time to take the Toyota for a little spin.

We drove down through the property, crossed the road and headed out into the fields. I hauled ass. The truck handled well. It had good shock travel and articulation for a stock truck.

I took the Toyota out the next day, too. I didn't know I was being spied on.

Garth's mommy dearest, who kept an eye on everyone, had simply parked her car in the garage.

Naturally, she told on me. Garth took away my keys.

He did whatever his mama told him.

SOCIAL LIFE REVOLVED AROUND the high school. The basketball games were a blast. Mickey invited me to go with him to a game. We climbed up the bleachers to the top rows. There were a bunch of seniors there who played football and wrestled. I was with Mickey, so I was OK. They were mixing room-temperature Dr Pepper and Jim Beam, and passing plastic cups of it around.

It was the best drink I'd ever had. It made the game a lot more exciting. When the buzz hit me, the players running around on the hardwood below — their pounding footsteps and the thumping of the basketball reverberating in the gym — suddenly seemed more important. We all got crazy up there. When a Darrington player sank a basket, stole the ball or was fouled, the loudest stomping and screaming came from our section of the stands.

After the game there was a dance. We all went, still hammered. Practically everyone in school showed up. There was nothing else going on in town. I looked around. The girls were all done up, their hair styled. They were wearing sundresses or Western jeans. There were just hot-looking cowgirls everywhere. But their attitudes were so different from the girls in high school back in Reno. These hotties didn't act stuck-up. You walked up to them and they were friendly. They smiled and said hi. "You wanna dance?" They did. We all did.

There was no room for having an attitude in a small town. Everyone was on an equal footing.

One of the kids in the school actually had a mohawk. His name was Carl. He was probably the only punk rocker at Darrington High. He'd been sitting up with us in the bleachers.

"Hey, you know what slam-dancing is?" Carl asked me.

"Are you kidding me?" I said. "Let's start moshing."

A Sex Pistols song was rocking on the sound system. A few of us started shoving each other around, slamming into each other, knocking each other down and helping each other up.

Then I got jarred and bit down hard on the tip of my tongue. I kept dancing. People were staring. Mark Hannigan came over.

"Goddamn, you've got blood all over your face."

"What are you talking about, we're slam dancing!"

"C'mon," he said. He led me by the arm to the bathroom. He started pulling paper towels out of the dispenser. I looked in the mirror.

Blood was dripping down my chin. My face was a gory mess. Apparently I bit through my tongue.

My buzz was wearing off. My tongue began throbbing.

Mark and I went out to the parking lot and drank a few beers. Then I walked home.

In the morning, I had no hangover. I'd slept it off.

My tongue was pretty sore, though.

AS WINTER APPROACHED, IT snowed hard. Conditions were right for a Darrington tradition: "hood sledding." I had no clue what that was.

"You never ridden on a Volkswagen hood before?" Mark Hannigan asked me.

Here's how hood sledding worked:

You took the hood off a classic VW's front, flipped the hood over, waxed it up and tied the handle to the back of a four-wheel ATV: a "quad." Now you had a curvy sled big enough to hold two people and a bottle of Jack Daniels between them, and the locomotion to go on a whizzing adventure.

The quad would take off through the terraced fields. You'd laugh so hard sliding and bouncing through the snow — the hood launched airborne when it hit a terrace — you'd almost piss your pants.

Jennifer drove all the way from Vacaville to visit Mom and me that December. She drove the Plymouth Aero that Mom had given her after getting married. Mom didn't need the Plymouth anymore. Garth had given her a new Cutlass Sierra.

One night we were sitting by the fireplace in my bedroom with Mark and Mason Hannigan, drinking beers. Mark suddenly piped up:

"Why don't we tie some tractor tubes behind the car and pull them around downtown?"

Why not, indeed?

Mark and I removed the inner tubes from a couple of truck tires lying in the yard, pumped them up and tied them to the bumper of the Plymouth with a 25-foot rope. Then Mason and I sat in the tubes and Jennifer hit the gas. She towed us through downtown Darrington. Mason and I passed beers back and forth. When the Plymouth made turns, our tubes would swerve out wildly and then knock together. It was crazy! We whipped off the road, bounced off trees and ricocheted back into the road again.

On one sharp turn, Mason and I leaned so hard on our tubes that they swung around with tremendous force, spinning the car 180 degrees so that it faced backward. Jennifer screamed. Mason and I laughed our asses off.

There were no cops around at 10 at night. They were home. We were having a blast. Just good wholesome fun like you can't have in a big town.

I pity any kid who never experienced small-town kicks.

MAYBE IT WAS BECAUSE I was happier — or maybe it was because the teachers at Darrington High had half as many students per class as at Reed, and therefore more time to work individually with students who needed extra help — but my grades improved. In class, I paid attention better. I understood more. I did better on the homework and tests. I even had a breakthrough in my least favorite subject: math.

One weekend, struggling over a lengthy trigonometry equation that was filling half a page in my notebook, I had a brainstorm. Instead of following the steps for the problem in the textbook, I decided to write down the answer from the answer key, and work backward from it.

The result was stunning. Working in reverse was all it took. The logic suddenly clicked. I had figured out my own method of learning!

I would use it for the rest of my high school career. And from then on, I realized that I had a different way of absorbing information.

MY GROWTH SPURT CONTINUED. It felt like every morning when I got out of bed I was a bit taller. It was crazy. I stood in front of a mirror and couldn't believe it. I stood next to Mom and it was like she was shrinking. I kept having to buy new pants. By Christmastime, I was 5-foot-10. All of a sudden, I was no longer this small kid. I'd grown about a half-foot in the past few months.

My coordination fell off. I was bumping into things. I felt clumsy and gangly on my skateboard. The kick-flips and Ollies I'd perfected were a struggle now. I had to get used to getting those long legs under me.

My voice was changing. I was coming into my own. Now that I was getting tall, I wanted to get strong, too. Garth had a set of dumbbells and barbells at the house. I wrote out a lifting routine. I decided to be disciplined about my workouts. I hadn't fooled around much with my TRS-80 in Darrington, I was so busy partying and having fun, but I created a program to compute data from my regular workouts with the weights.

I was glad we'd moved to Darrington. It was working out really well. But a thought was nagging at me: This couldn't possibly last.

It was the curse of my life experiences. When had a good situation in my life ever lasted?

Everything was going so well that I had an inkling something was bound to happen.

My inkling was right.

CHAPTER TWENTY-FIVE: A Big Little Man

Garth and Mom were not getting along. Their marital bliss was proving short-lived.

It must have deteriorated very quickly because not long after Christmas, Mom told me she was leaving him.

There were several issues. The one that may have started it all was Elly Pitts. Mom was fed up with her hostility. And Mom was fed up with Garth for not standing up to his mean-spirited mama.

After that, Mom and Garth began disagreeing on everything. She finally accused him of just marrying her to have someone to clean his house and baby-sit his sons. "You just wanted a live-in nanny. Well, that's not me."

Maybe, she said, he wasn't even capable of a real relationship.

After that they slept apart. Mom decided to have the marriage annulled. She made arrangements to move into a girlfriend's apartment in Reno.

"I'm sorry, Jeff. But he isn't the man for me."

I was in a funk. I'd made so many friends, and was having so much fun, I didn't want to leave Darrington.

I had an idea. I asked if I could at least finish out the school year. She agreed.

Garth gave his blessing. "It's all right, Jeff," he said. "No problem. You can stay as long as you want. You can even finish out and graduate from Darrington if you want. You're a good kid. We're still friends."

Maybe he wasn't really a bad guy. Maybe it was just one of those things. He and Mom just weren't right for each other.

But after Mom moved out, Garth's attitude changed toward me. He started ignoring me, almost as if I wasn't really there. He practically stopped speaking to me. He'd take Kody and Kyle out to dinner or somewhere, and leave me behind.

It grew uncomfortable.

Over spring break, Mom picked me up in the Cutlass Sierra that Garth had given her after they were married. We drove to Vacaville to see Jennifer. When we pulled up to the house in Darrington a week later, I noticed my Toyota pickup was missing from where I'd parked it.

Then we noticed that Garth's brother Dwight was sitting in a pickup pulled up against a fence, as if keeping vigil. That was odd. What was Dwight doing there?

Even odder, all the cars were gone from outside the house.

I walked inside. Kody and Kyle were gone. Nobody was home. The place felt strange. I went into my bedroom. My stuff was all boxed up.

It hit me like shellshock.

I was being summarily tossed out of my house.

It was Sunday. How was I going to return to school on Monday? Where was I supposed to stay?

It was obvious: I couldn't go back to school.

What was I going to tell my friends?

I decided to call some of them, break the news so they wouldn't hear some wild rumor.

In a shaky voice, I told Mark Hannigan that Garth had kicked me out of the house.

He was stunned.

I told him I'd call everyone after I got to Reno.

"Reno?" he said.

I called Mickey. My voice had calmed a bit, but was still trembly.

"I can't hang out with you tonight," I said. I explained what had happened.

"You want me to come pick you up? I'll get you out of there."

"No, you don't have to come pick me up," I said. "I just wanted to say goodbye to you."

"Well, I'll come over and say goodbye," he said.

By this time, Mom was wondering why I was inside so long without coming out to say goodbye. She walked in the house and found me by the phone, wiping tears from my eyes.

I told her what had happened.

She immediately walked around to where her chairs and tables had been left. They were packed up, too.

Outside, tires rumbled on the gravel and ground to a halt. We looked out the front window. A U-Haul van was sitting in the driveway. Garth climbed out of the cab and came in the house.

"Load all your sh*t and get the f*ck out," he said.

His face was blank, his voice cold, as if we were nothing more to him than strangers. Not a woman and her son who had lived with him under his roof.

Mom was instantly in tears.

We felt helpless. We felt betrayed.

We were also out of options.

While we'd been inside, someone had gotten into the Cutlass and driven it off. The luggage that had been in the car was stacked in the driveway.

The only way we had out of Darrington was in that U-Haul.

We had to leave right then and there. There wasn't even a chance to withdraw me from school properly.

Elly Pitts was peeking out her window, smiling. Rage welled up in me, then boiled over.

I suddenly felt violent.

Dwight was standing outside his pickup. I walked up to him. "What are you doing here?" I asked, staring up at him. He was about as big as his brother.

"I'm just here in case anything gets out of hand," he said.

"Well, what are *you* going to do?" I snarled.

I was ready to fight anyone!

I walked back into the house and found Garth. I got right up in his face.

"You told me we were friends. You told me I can finish out the year. Then you go and pack my sh*t up. A man's supposed to stand by his word. You know, you're nothing but a f*cking pussy!"

He stood there, arms crossed. He didn't say a word.

I was just getting started. I wanted him to swing at me, grab me, anything.

I'd tear into him.

"You're weak. Your mom's weak. Your brother's weak. The hell with you! We're out of here."

I was shaking. It was more than just this situation. It seemed like all the upheavals I'd had in my life had surfaced suddenly and the emotions had erupted like a volcano.

Garth walked off. He started pulling the boxes out of what had been my bedroom.

Mom and I started loading up the U-Haul. Her anger boiled over, too. She walked back to the house. I ran after her. She was in the kitchen. She slapped Garth. He grabbed her and put her on the ground, holding her.

"Don't f*cking touch her!" I said. He looked at me, and let her go. He wasn't about to mess with me. The look in my eyes was enough.

He picked up the phone and called the sheriff's office as Mom and I carried more of our things out to the U-Haul.

A squad car drove out. A deputy watched as we finished loading up.

Mickey never showed up. Maybe he just wasn't able to come over in time.

The key was in the ignition. Silently, Mom and I pulled out and turned off the property. Garth and Dwight stood in the driveway, watching.

IT WAS AN EMPTY feeling as we drove up the two-lane highway leading to Reno. We were in a bad way. We'd have no car when we got to Reno. We didn't have a place of our own to stay. We had no money. Mom had only just started working again. Everything was in disarray.

I didn't even know if stuff was missing from my belongings. I'm sure Garth and his sissy sons had rooted through everything while I was gone.

"I don't want you getting married again so long as I'm living under your roof," I told Mom.

"I made a mistake, Jeff," she said.

"Well, it was my mistake, too," I said. "I told you to go ahead. I told you that f*cker was all right."

We'd both been fooled.

I soon found out from my friends in Darrington that Garth was covering his ass in town. He started rumors about Mom and me, claiming we'd stolen from him, painting himself out to be a victim.

My friends there knew different, but the adults believed him. After all, he was born and raised there. We were just outsiders.

CHAPTER TWENTY-SIX: Party Man on Campus

I had to re-enroll at Reed High to finish out 10th grade. I was right back where I'd started at the beginning of the school year. Except that everything was different now. I was different. I'd come back from Darrington a changed person. So had Mom.

Garth had killed off something inside her. It was a lingering hope that the right man would show up. She'd resigned herself to singledom. The stable family life, the emotional intimacy she'd sought, had never come her way with the men she'd let into our lives. But there was a silver lining. Mom was now motivated beyond belief. She'd made up her mind to make her own way in the world. She would handle her own affairs from now on. She would buy her first home. She would take charge.

Not long after we'd come back to Reno, and moved in temporarily with Grandpa Herschel and Grandma Fern, Mom bought a used Toyota Corolla and began saving up for a house. She was focused. She borrowed a bit of money from Grandpa and made a down payment on a new modular home in the Oasis Mobile Home Park off Pyramid Highway, in a rural area just north of Sparks.

We were proud of our little doublewide. It was ours. We had a tiny yard on either side and in back. There was a little carport. There was a little back room where I set up my TRS-80 computer and a desk for doing my homework. The place was quiet. We were pretty far out from town. There were a few ranch houses nearby, and a new housing development was under construction. Eventually the area would become a sprawling suburb known as Spanish Springs. The city of Sparks would annex it. But back then it was still very much an unpopulated swath of high desert — a vast sea of sagebrush surrounded by low brown hills. There was no stoplight or even a stop sign on the thoroughfare, Pyramid Highway, which ran out to Pyramid Lake 30 miles away. There was just a flashing yellow beacon warning motorists to use caution. The only store was a mini-mart/gas station.

It was five miles to Reed High, and I had to walk. It took me a while. This meant dragging myself out of bed at 5 a.m. That was a bitch. Here I was, 16, and hadn't even been able to get my driving learner's permit, much less practice for the license test. The long walks were OK, though. They gave me time to think. I had a lot to think about. I was sorting through my life.

I decided that I no longer cared what other people thought about me. They could take me or leave me. This was liberating! I had no desire to try to impress anyone anymore. All that mattered now was how I felt about myself. The fiasco with Garth had given me that. You couldn't rely on other people for your happiness and wellbeing, so why rely on other people for their approval? Their opinions didn't matter. What mattered was being happy in your own skin.

Then I decided that Mom and I were very lucky. We had a roof over our heads. We were taking care of ourselves now, without anyone to interfere with our happiness, push us around, degrade us. What did I have to bitch about? I was alive. I was young. I was healthy. I had a warm place to sleep at night. I had food to fill me. There really was nothing to hold me back from whatever I pursued in life.

I decided that the future looked bright. Sure, I didn't have money to buy a car at the moment. But I would. I was getting around on foot right now — but it was the people who kept on walking to school, kept pushing ahead, kept surviving and not quitting, who were the ones who got anywhere in life. I told myself I was tough. I had endurance. I had perseverance. That meant I'd reach any goal I set for myself.

I decided that my long-term goal was to own my own business. The 6-year-old kid who wore a suit to school on Fridays would end up being a grown man running a company. What kind of company? Something to do with computers, probably. Computers still held me in a spell, just like the first time I'd seen one, as a 9-year-old in the school office in Panama City, Florida.

I decided that my immediate goal would be to save up for a car. I'd have to get a job. What I needed was a car to get around in. A car to take girls out in. I couldn't wait until I had the money for a car. I'd take excellent care of it. I'd change the oil right on schedule. I'd keep it running perfectly. I'd keep it clean. I'd baby it. I'd appreciate it thoroughly. I would never forget what it was like to have to get up at 5 a.m. when it's freezing cold outside, bundle up and trek by foot five miles to school.

FROM THE FIRST DAY I was back at Reed, walking the halls, sitting in class, I realized that the other kids were perceiving me in a new way. I was no longer little Jeff, the smart-mouth kid getting jostled or tripped in the hall, having the skateboard knocked out from under him, being chased and beaten up. I'd shot up in height while I was away. People came up to me, amazed. "Damn, you've gotten so much taller!" I noticed with satisfaction that kids who'd pushed me around before I left were still pretty much the same size. Now they were leaving me alone.

I saw Ron Darby in the halls. He looked away.

I felt like a new person. It was as if I was returning to Reed fresh. My new size, and my nonchalant attitude, had changed my social status. I could feel it. It was in the way I was looked at and spoken to. I was being treated like a normal kid. It was about time! No one was giving me any sh*t. I was being taken seriously. Girls were giving me attention.

The walks to and from school got easier. The weather was getting warmer. The grass and sage were smelling fresh.

THAT SUMMER, MY GROWTH spurt continued. I was now just over 6 feet, tall and skinny.

I started thinking again about soccer. Then I decided that wearing a uniform, putting in all those tiring hours, tying my identity to a team didn't interest me anymore. I'd missed a season. That dream was done with.

Mom wasn't going to move us again, so I resolved that these last two years of high school I'd enjoy myself as much as possible.

I stared junior year with a whimsical attitude. Darrington had turned me into a decent student. I could maintain passing grades without sacrificing my out-of-school hours.

I was just going to work the system.

From the start of the year, I cut classes as much as possible without putting myself at risk of failing. Sometimes I just went out skateboarding. I quickly found myself in a different social echelon: the partiers. But I could hang out with anyone — the stoners, the skaters, the nerds, the jocks. The jocks had a ritual of the "beer break." Between classes, or during class using restroom passes, we'd meet up in the parking lot at someone's car, where there'd be an ice chest in the trunk holding beers. We partied together on weekends, and since the seniors were the biggest partiers, I networked into a group of older friends. Friends with cars. That gave me mobility. There was always someone to swing by and pick me up at my house.

The parties were the breakthrough for me with girls. I'd always been comfortable around girls, cracking jokes, making them laugh. After all, my entire childhood had been spent with a Mom and sister, and a heavy female presence. But there was a difference now when it came to girls at school. I was no longer the short boy with the smart-ass wit — the cute little class clown. I was the tall guy at the parties who was confident and funny.

I was gaining in popularity for good and often mischievous reasons. I was able to mingle with any group comfortably. Even not having a car didn't stop me from asking girls out. They had cars. It worked out fine. I'd just have a friend drop me off at the mall or another meeting spot. I'd catch a ride home later, or take the bus. The girls who lived in Sparks would simply pick me up at my house. They knew me. They knew where I lived. They didn't care I was living in a mobile-home park. Not that I cared what anyone thought, anyway.

Dating was new to me, and I wanted to soak it all up. I wanted to learn about each and every type of girl. So I made it a rule to never get attached to a girl for more than a month. I wanted to keep my options open. Two weeks was average. I wanted to diversify, learn the differences among all the girls. Satisfy my naturally curious mind.

It was tricky keeping a girl from attaching herself to me. They could be possessive. They could be vindictive.

Inexperienced though I was, I came up with a strategy to make it easier to move from one girl to the next. I was loyal while we were going out, but the moment we stopped having fun, I'd tell her that if she wanted to hang out with another guy, no sweat. I'd ease away.

But this attitude, I found, only made some of the girls want to be with me even more. I wasn't pursuing them. I was a challenge. After a couple weeks or so I'd tell the girl, "We've had some good times, but I've got to start studying . . ." or some other excuse about not being able to have the time to hang with her that much. I'd leave it with, "Give me a call some time."

Some would start calling me pretty regularly, but I'd tell Mom, "Please tell her I'm busy, I can't come to the phone." Eventually they'd quit calling.

Some stayed pissed off at me for a long time. But I just kept moving on.

What I came to understand after a few months was that girls aren't really all that different from each other. They each had quirks, but they generally fell into two categories: "low maintenance" and "high maintenance." It didn't matter if they were rich or poor, beautiful or average. Either they were easy to kick it with, or they were drama queens.

Reed was known as a "preppy" school. A lot of students were from wealthy families. There were a lot of stuck-up girls. High-maintenance girls weren't fun to be around. They were pains in the ass, and they cost a lot of money, too. You had to spend on dates and gifts. Even if they were gorgeous, it just wasn't worth it. They were demanding. And they were very critical — especially of other girls. They'd always be snipping about this girl or that who dressed like a "slut" or "whore."

The low-maintenance girls were usually tomboys. I loved tomboy women. They were capable of going out and actually having fun. They weren't the dainty shopper girls like high-maintenance girls. You could play sports with them. They didn't wear a lot of makeup. And I found them attractive without makeup. They had a natural, intrinsic beauty.

The first girl I really fell for was a tomboy. Her name was Jacqueline. She was very sweet. She was tall, dark-haired and athletic. She was the cute girl next door. Even though I was attracted to blondes, it worked for me.

Jacqueline was a freshman — two years behind me. We met in P.E. class. I was always a team captain for volleyball. I always picked her as the first girl on my team. She was a good player. She was tough. She could dig the ball, she could spike. She stood her ground.

"Maybe we should get something to eat sometime," I finally said. "Sure," she said. She'd been waiting months for me to ask her out.

We went with a group of friends to dinner and the movies. Then we started hanging out together. She and I were more like friends than boyfriend and girlfriend. At least, at first.

Jacqueline liked to fish. She liked to hunt. Two of her sisters went to Reed. We all knew each other. Her father had divorced and remarried. The stepmother was a difficult woman. Jacqueline was glad to spend time outside the house, with me.

Jacqueline would come over on a weekend and we'd watch football on television. Mom really liked Jacqueline. Mom liked how Jacqueline was outgoing. Mom liked how good of friends the two of us were.

Jacqueline was the girl I was hanging out with when I finally went to test for my driver's license. Mom drove with me to the Department of Motor Vehicles. I aced the written and driving tests. Driving home that day on Pyramid Highway in the Corolla, I yelled and screamed, I was so jazzed. Now I had my freedom. It was like a ball and chain had been severed from my leg.

Mom let me take the car out that very night. I showered and dressed, climbed into the car, programmed the radio to my favorite stations, then drove over to Jacqueline's house. We went out for burgers then spent the rest of the night just driving around Reno. It was exhilarating.

I could rarely be found at home again after that, whenever I could borrow Mom's car. When it snowed I would get up extra early and drive her to work, since she hated driving in bad weather. Then I'd have the car to myself until picking her up at the end of the day.

I really became a social creature that junior year in high school. And after I got my license, I became an uncaged party animal.

CHAPTER TWENTY-SEVEN: A Bum's Luck

Drew Walecka became my partying buddy.

Drew had been my best friend before I'd left for Darrington. After I got back to Reno, we hung out together again. During my time away, Drew had grown, too. His braces were off and he didn't look as gawky as before. He was maturing.

Drew worked as a bagger at Smith's Food & Drug. One weekend night, I asked if he wanted to go drink beers and cruise around after he got off his shift. He was up for it. We had a blast. We had that indefinable buddy chemistry. We were opposites in many ways. He was quiet, soft-spoken, afraid of people, couldn't talk to girls to save his life. But he and I clicked. We bonded. And after that night, we became almost like brothers.

Drew taught me how to hunt — to shoot better, to track game. He took me out on a weekend to hunt chukar and pheasant, and target shoot jackrabbits.

I taught Drew how to approach girls — to be yourself, but make them laugh. I was good at that. I'd walk up, say something unexpected. I knew how most guys failed miserably. They'd usually use the same approach: "Hey, there's a party. Want to go to the party with us?" It was lame. It rarely worked.

Drew and I were at the mall. It was Friday after school. "Watch this," I said. "This is going to be the most off-the-wall thing you can say to one of these girls.

It's going to be so off the wall, it's going to surprise them, and it'll work."

I walked up to a couple girls. "Hey, what's going on? What are you doing tonight?"

"Well, we heard about this party . . ." one said.

"Party?" I said, acting as if I was surprised. "Well, me and my buddy were thinking about going up to 31 flavors and getting some ice cream and messing around."

They absorbed those words for a second. The invitation was so different from the same things guys had been hitting them with over and over.

"Really?" the one who'd spoken said.

"Yeah, and maybe get some drinks and have a bonfire in the desert and watch the stars. Nothing major."

Her face brightened. "OK!" she chirped.

Another of my favorite approaches, when we were downtown, was to invite girls to get peach Slurpees with us. The 7-Eleven by the university campus sold peach Slurpees. They were delicious. This suggestion would blow the girls away. We'd meet up at the 7-Eleven. After that, I'd invite them to join us at another venue. Drew and I were always focused on what was going on after school. For example, if you did not hear about a party or gathering at the canyon or the pits by Thursday, you were out of the loop.

One of the reasons we were so dialed in was because we could be relied upon to get hold of a keg. We'd actually be put in charge of that task. We had the nerve to do it. That gave us a huge advantage in the under-age crowd. It set us apart.

The big shots at school, the jocks, were just wussies when it came to doing anything daring like that. They might act cocky and tough in a group standing around the halls, or at a party; they might strut around in letterman's jackets. But when it came to taking bold action out in the big wide world, it was too risky for them, and they weren't up to it.

Drew and I were. We thought of ourselves as nonconformists with an attitude. It was our angle.

We stuck our necks out. And we became experts at the art of scoring brew.

YOU HAD TO BE 21 or over to rent a keg from a local bar. But Drew and I figured a system out. We collected the money for a keg from our friends, then staked out a bar and waited for a likely looking adult to happen by. Drew sat in the car, and I worked the parking lot. I was the best shoulder tapper this side of the Mississippi. I had a winning sales approach.

I'd walk up to an older guy, and with a smile say something like, "Do you mind helping us out? We need to rent a keg and we'll make it worth your while." I'd assume his cooperation, and this positive emotion would transfer to the person. I'd give him the rental fee and deposit for the keg and taps, plus another $5 or $10 for his trouble, and he'd do the job for us.

I was rarely turned down. Now and then a family guy who felt uncomfortable about buying beer for minors would decline. I'd just say, "That's cool, man," and wait for another prospect.

Drew's job was to keep an eye out for police cars. But we felt relatively safe. At that time, in the late 1980s, the cops were only slowly becoming more vigilant about watching for underage alcohol purchases.

Drew and I worked the same hustle if we just needed to score beer for ourselves. You didn't want to show up to a party empty-handed. We'd wait outside a 7-Eleven or other convenience store, waiting for the right-looking adult to show up who could make our purchase.

We had a scheme set up to keep ourselves from being ripped off. Drew would stay in the car while I made the pitch. When our buyer went inside, Drew would keep on eye on him, watching for any funny moves, while I'd stand to the side of the store in case the guy tried to run off with our beer and money.

We always got our beer.

One Friday night before a party, we drove up to a little convenience store in Sparks. Next to the store was a public park. Loitering in the park was a flat-out derelict, drunker than a skunk. Almost nobody would approach this barely human figure. I decided he would do as our purchasing agent.

I walked over to him. "How's it going?"

"Good," he slurred. He seemed sort of surprised that someone had approached him. Other than a cop, that is.

Up close, he looked even worse. He reeked of booze and piss and the outdoors. His jeans were soiled with mud and stains. His head was wrapped in the hood of a sweatshirt under a ratty overcoat. He was dark and filthy. I couldn't tell the color of his skin due to all the dirt and grime that was on him. Burn marks covered half his face and neck. He'd obviously had a rough life.

I held out a $20 bill. I pointed to the convenience store and said, "Why don't you go in there and buy us a case of beer, and get yourself a 40-ounce or whatever you want?"

"All right, no problem."

He took the money and staggered off toward the store.

I walked over to Drew's window and gave him the thumbs up.

Drew looked worried. "Are you sure?" he asked. The bum had given him the willies. He was the worst-looking buyer we'd ever hit up. Doubt hung between us.

"We'll just have to keep an eye on this guy," I said.

Through the store windows, we saw the bum trucking an armload of beer up to the counter. A few moments later he was calmly walking out with it in his arms.

"Bring it over here to the truck," I said.

He struggled with the load. He lowered it heavily onto the truck bed.

We were shocked. There were two cases of beer. On top was a brown paper bag. I looked inside the bag. It was a bottle of peppermint schnapps.

"That's mine," the bum said.

"How'd you come out with all that sh*t?" I asked.

He dug in a pocket and handed me the crumpled $20 bill.

"What the f*ck?" I exclaimed. "What just happened?"

He beamed like a hero. He held his arms out and shrugged.

This was really wild. Somehow he'd walked out of the store with a bunch of free booze. The clerk had let him. Or the clerk had made some sort of mistake, or suffered some ridiculous lapse of attention.

"Hey, can I party with you guys?"

"No, we gotta go," I said.

We said goodbye and left him with a six pack of beer and the schnapps.

Drew and I drove off, still mystified. Had the clerk thought the bum had laid the bill on the counter? Or had the clerk just wanted this bottom-of-the-barrel park creature out of the store as quickly as possible?

Maybe it had just been a fluke. Or some grand stroke of drunken luck.

We decided it was just a mystery we'd never be able to unravel for the life of us. But it was beautiful. Three guys getting something over on the system for damn nothing.

CHAPTER TWENTY-EIGHT: Going Mobile, at Last

Drew, myself, and another friend, Bill Johnson, started going out hunting on weekends. Bill was a long-haired headbanger whose family owned a truckstop/casino. He was a good guy. The three-quarter-ton Chevy pickup with cab that Drew's dad let us use was perfect for our hunting trips. We beat the hell out of that truck. We called it "the Hunter's Deluxe."

We started hitting hunting grounds all over the state. I was surprised to see how much of Nevada there was out there. It was one mountain range after another, and between the mountains were bowl-like valleys. Sometimes there'd be nothing but a playa, a dry lakebed, in a valley. We could find ancient seashells left from the age of the great prehistoric ocean. Other times we'd go over a ridge and down a ravine and there'd be a spring, a thick grove of quaking aspens and a meadow.

We had .22 rifles and .12- and .20-gauge shotguns. We not only hunted for upland game birds and took target practice on starlings and jackrabbits, but found Indian petroglyphs and arrowheads. There were ghost towns. There were hot springs. We'd crouch down and see if anything was swimming in the hot-spring water. We'd hold our hands over the steam, then slap the water to see if the temperature was bearable to wade into.

We'd be gone all weekend. Over spring break, instead of going to Lake

Tahoe like the other students at our high school, we'd load up food, water and extra gas cans and be out on a weeklong hunting and camping trip over the mountains that loomed above the school campus. We'd find a spur road and take it far out in the desert, just to see where it went.

It was awesome. It was freedom. I knew it wouldn't last forever.

I REALLY WANTED A vehicle of my own now. I drove Mom's Corolla off and on when I got a chance, but she needed it for work and errands. So I decided to save up for my own car.

Mom was working as a secretary in the Reno field office of a mining company, Hidden Lode Explorations. The company needed someone to do odd jobs. With Mom's help, I was hired at minimum wage. I'd go in after school. The first task they gave me was building up the office's library — cataloguing the books and maps on mining and geology. It was monotonous. But there were more little duties than that, fortunately. Sometimes ore samples would come in. Before the samples were sent to a laboratory, the company's managers would want to have the samples assayed with simple tests. Herb, one of the geologists, was a prickly guy, but for some reason he took a liking to me. He taught me to spray sulfuric acid from a tube onto the split-open rock, watch the acid bubble up and check the rock for signs of precious metal. We'd record the results and mark the sample with a permanent marker. We'd perform other hardening tests — scraping the ore with a penny or piece of iron or other metal — and compare results to a chart to gauge the hardness of the rock. That was interesting. He was an old-school geologist.

I started building up my savings. What I didn't spend on beer or dates, I put toward buying a car. But I wasn't making much headway. If I were going to have something to drive, I'd need even more income. The easiest job to find, outside of fast food, was at a supermarket as a courtesy clerk, the entry-level job. You bagged groceries, helped people out with their bags, stocked shelves when needed, mopped up messes. I got hired at Staley's supermarket. The work was easy enough. And there were a lot of weekend hours. Now I started saving in a hurry. And I started looking around for a set of wheels.

I saw a classified advertisement in the newspaper for a Nissan pickup with a rebuilt engine. Price: $700. I called the phone number. The guy who placed the ad lived in Desert Springs a few miles from me. Drew drove me out there. The guy's house was dilapidated. He was having a hard time. His truck didn't seem to have been taken care of very well, either. I was doubtful how good a mechanic he was. But in my price range, I didn't have much bargaining power.

I wheedled him down to $500 and drove the Nissan home. It was shifting OK but handling a bit weird. I thought: *No problem.* I could rebalance the wheels and fix the drive train. I'd picked up some mechanical know-how from working on cars with my Uncle Randy, Uncle Mark and Grandpa Herschel. What I didn't know I could check out in car manuals. I had my own truck. And this one nobody could take away from me like Garth had done with my Toyota pickup down in Darrington.

I got to work on the truck. The first thing I wanted to do was lower the suspension. I'd bought two inexpensive jack stands. I jacked up the rear axle at both ends. I inched my body feet first under the truck. When I was up to my shoulders, with my head under the bumper, I shifted onto my side.

I wrenched on the bolts to reposition the leaf springs. I disconnected the leaf springs from the axle. My back bumped the spare tire under the truck. There was movement. Suddenly, the jack stands collapsed. The truck came down on me. I was pinned to the ground. The weight was crushing.

It was unreal. It was like an elephant had sat on me. I couldn't move. I strained. With all my strength, I wiggled onto my belly, the weight of the truck moving slightly with me. Then I felt the spare tire crushing my back. It ground my face into the asphalt. Slow-motion torture.

This was it. I was dying.

I felt my heart beating, my lungs heaving. Desperation kicked in. I summoned my strength once more. I tried to push myself up. The truck rose and fell slightly, an impossible force to lift.

I drew in as much breath as I could and screamed. "Help!"

"Hang on! Hang on! I'm getting it!"

The voice was Dick's, the neighbor across the street.

I could do nothing but lie there, trying to remain calm even though I might die. My circulation was being choked. There was nothing I could do about it. My eyes were twitching.

I grew lightheaded.

I began blacking out.

I heard scraping against the ground by my head. It was one of the cheap bumper jacks I'd bought. I felt a shudder in the mass atop me. There was squeaking. Dick had repositioned the jack and was cranking it.

It seemed to take forever. Then I sensed the weight slightly easing off.

Bam! The truck fell on me again.

"I'm sorry!" Dick said. He cranked the jack again. I felt slight breathing room.

Then hands grabbed under my arms. I was being dragged out.

I pushed up onto my hands and knees. I looked up. Dick was catching his breath. He swiped a forearm over his sweaty brow.

"Man, I was watching you work under this thing. When the jack slipped, I hauled ass over here."

I'd been under the truck for two or three minutes. I felt like I'd been squeezed like a tube of toothpaste.

"Sh*t, man," I gasped, "I can't believe that happened." Adrenaline was making me shake all over.

"I'm glad I was there," Dick said. "You could've been squashed to death. Look, you may need to go to the ER."

"No, I'm all right, I'm all right."

But I was far from all right.

I stood up, quivering. I walked toward the house. Dick shouted for Mom to come out.

She came out, holding the cordless phone.

"What the f*ck?" I yelled. "This truck just fell on me, just about killed me!"

Her eyes grew wide. "Jeff, I didn't hear a thing. What happened?"

I sat on the curb. She tried to calm me. She stroked my head and neck.

"He's probably in shock right now," Dick said.

"I'm not in shock! I'm f*cking pissed off!"

For a year after that, I couldn't work under a vehicle. Even today, I'll use drive-up ramps and wheel chocks before I'll get under a vehicle. I'll go nuts being extra safe.

Jack stands? Forget it.

A FEW WEEKS AFTER the near-death experience, my truck stalled during lunch break at school. Jacqueline and I had gone out to eat and were a ways away from campus. We had to walk back. I had the truck towed home.

It turned out that one of the oilers had gotten clogged and frozen the camshaft. That meant I'd have to rebuild the whole top end of the engine. I didn't have the money to cover that. Nor the necessary tools.

Fortunately, Mom was friends with a man who raced cars and owned a garage in town. I had my truck towed there. He and one of his chief mechanics volunteered to help me work on the engine. It was useless, though. As we got deeper into the engine, we found much of it had been destroyed. The previous owner had done a terrible job working on it. It was going to end up costing me $2,000 to repair this $500 truck.

"What should I do?" I asked Mom's friend.

He told me to sign the title over to him and he'd give me $100 for the parts.

An expensive lesson.

I DECIDED TO DOWNSIZE my choice of vehicles to something more affordable. I bought a little mountain bike. Then I saw a classified ad for a "basket case" motorcycle — one that had been in an accident. It was a 1978 Yamaha XS 650. I got one of my neighbors to drive me over to look at it. The mangled bike was laid on a pallet. I bought it for $150.

I took the bike apart. I replaced the bent forks and bashed motor parts and put the machine back together myself. It took me the whole summer, but I got it purring. Now I could get around quickly. What's more, I wouldn't have to pay so much for gas as with the truck.

The only complication was I didn't have a motorcycle classification on my driver's license. I could ride well enough — I'd been riding dirt bikes for years — but the test for motorcycles was ridiculously stringent. No matter how skilled you were, the highway patrol testers could, and often would, find a reason to fail you. Maybe you accelerated too quickly on the little course. Maybe you didn't make obvious enough hand signals. I wasn't keen on taking the test. Besides, I had a very tight schedule. There was school, work and partying. I didn't have time to fool around with bureaucracy.

My lack of a motorcycle designation on my license didn't stop me from riding. I bought insurance for the bike and soon was out zooming around. I'd ride it to school in my leather jacket and boots. The bike and leather seemed to enhance my appeal to the opposite sex. Maybe I *was* a bit of a bad boy.

I had to be careful riding around, though, since I didn't have the motorcycle license. Twice I had to elude members of the law-enforcement community, given my situation.

The first time was on Pyramid Highway one afternoon. A cop's cruiser was coming straight at me, lights flashing. His radar must have picked up my speed. I turned off on a dirt road and took off without looking back. He must have figured I was just out joyriding. He left me alone.

A closer call happened some months later, at night. I liked to ride with the lights off on moonlit nights, going 80 to 100 mph on open stretches. Motorcycles are wired for the headlights to stay on all the time, for safety reasons, so I'd rewired the lighting system so I could shut the lamp off if I wanted. For me, cruising by moonlight was poetic.

On this particular night, my friend Rob was on the back of the bike. As we turned onto the street to Rob's house, a police cruiser was turning out of the street. We passed the cruiser and the officer didn't even seem to see us. We were like an invisible phantom shooting past. Or were we? Had he heard us? Had he suddenly noticed us?

We parked down a ways, turned off the bike and walked to Rob's house. We stayed away from the bike until we were sure the cop wasn't going to come back.

CHAPTER TWENTY-NINE: Mining Computer Time

My part-time job after school at Hidden Lode Explorations was just a way to earn some money. Filing and cataloguing books and periodicals in the library was tedious and dull. Assaying the ore samples was a little better. But mining didn't intrigue me much. I definitely wasn't interested in becoming a geologist.

What I wanted when I was done with school was to go into business — suit, tie, briefcase. The geologists dressed casually. Flannel shirts, jeans, boots. They looked like average guys. About half of them thought of themselves as average guys, and had a sense of humor about it, saying things like, "Geologists have rocks for brains." But the other half thought very highly of themselves, as if their field of expertise placed them among the intellectually elite. Either way, tramping around the outback staring at ridgelines and rock formations wasn't the life for me.

Then an interesting opportunity presented itself at Hidden Lode.

In the late 1980s, more and more businesses were building up their computer capabilities. They wanted their workers switching over completely from typewriters to word processing. They wanted to store data easily and efficiently on hard drives. The digital age was well underway, and there was no stopping it. It was inevitable that every company with more than a few employees that relied on computers would need someone in-house responsible for setting up and maintaining the computer network. Today, companies typically hire an "Information Technology coordinator" (or "director," "manager" or "technician"). But what often happened in the 1980s was that one of the current employees was given the title of Manager of Information Systems: MIS, for short.

One of the mining geologists at Hidden Lode was taken off his regular job and given the newly created MIS position, tasked with setting up and maintaining the office's network. He had to make sure the terminals were connected by cables, like a big loop, and functioned without hitches. His name was Lawrence. He had a tiny bit of experience with computers. He fooled around with one at home. That qualified him as the resident workplace pro, and was enough to earn him the MIS post.

Lawrence had long hair that hung in strands around his bald spot. He was one of those geologists who considered himself brilliant. With enough effort, he could handle the MIS job. The network and programs were very elementary in those days. Computer technicians will smile when I mention Hidden Lode had a basic Novell network — Novell being the company at that time that created the most popular software for operating networks — with Word Perfect (the premier word-processing software at the time) and Lotus 123 to create spreadsheets, charts and graphs. Everything worked in the disk operating system: "DOS." This was before Windows 3.1 was available, with its many fonts and desktop-publishing capabilities. The software being used in typical offices back then had no graphics.

In 1988, this was cutting-edge stuff for the vast majority of computer users. Lawrence was fairly much starting from scratch, learning as he went. Computer terminals with 14-inch, black-and-white monitors were brought into the office and installed at workstations for the entire staff to use. The data from each terminal were being stored on a file server, which was backed up regularly. Lawrence was having a hard time getting up to speed and getting the network set up. I picked up on that right away. He just wasn't getting it. It wasn't intuitive for him, like it was for me with my computer at home.

It was Lawrence's duty to install the software and train the staff to use it. But Mom had been using the software for some time, and whenever there was a question in the office, people would go to her instead of Lawrence.

I smelled opportunity. As always, I yearned to get on a computer and start learning the programs inside and out. At Hidden Lode, I had to wait until a terminal wasn't being used. I'd be cataloguing periodicals and other mining literature in the library, bored stiff, and see a chance across the room to get on an empty computer terminal. Usually there was one off in a corner. I'd wander over, sit down and log on. No security passwords were set up. Anyone could get on. That was the way it usually was with business networks in the late 1980s.

The system would boot up on the terminal. Slowly, I'd wade in, browsing the system. I'd research the help files and manuals, mapping the system out in my mind. I was in heaven. It was like being back in the Philippines, exploring on the Commodore 64, using my own logical, hands-on method of learning a computer system.

I started logging on regularly after my workday was done in the library. The office would be empty. On the command line I'd type in phrases followed by question marks — such as *print queue?* — then a word such as "Escape," and get the hang of the language the program used and the directories structure.

I got hold of a "Que" series book to learn the DOS commands to type on the keyboard. The book was like a Rosetta Stone. I started learning the system's commands. That was the key. The commands are tools — they'll give you enough information to navigate the system.

Whatever it was about computers that grabbed me, I was drawn like a magnet to the mining-company's network. I embraced the concept of a digital electronic world. I watched every movie themed on computers: *Tron, War Games*. It was a love affair. I considered that when I finally did go into business, it would probably have something to do with the computer industry. Maybe it would be writing software. Or working with hardware. Or on networks. I wanted to be a part of this futuristic world. It was where I felt I belonged. It was like I'd been created for it.

Computers were intuitive to me. They made sense to me.

I saw that Lawrence was putting a directory structure together, making directories for data storage. One day I approached him and started talking about the computer system. He hadn't known I'd been getting on it after hours.

"Listen, I have these ideas," I said. "I looked at some of your directory structures. Maybe I could make them more efficient."

He shot me a look of surprise, followed by a smug expression. *What can this dumb kid know?*

I saw I'd get nowhere with such a direct approach. I took it down a level.

"Well, if it's OK with you, can I try creating some screen savers for the terminals? I can do the work on my computer at home."

He thought about that for a moment.

"Well, do you know what you're doing?" Lawrence asked. "Have you designed screen savers before?"

I told him I'd created quite a few at home. It was true. From the bit of Basic I'd learned as a high school freshman, I'd written screen savers on my TRS-80.

"Hmm, well, give it a shot. Let's see what you come up with."

Since my TRS-80 used a tape recorder to store data, instead of a floppy disk drive, I had to print out the screen-saver code on my dot-matrix printer, take it into the office the next afternoon and retype the code on a computer terminal.

The screen savers I created were circles and spheres, boxes and polygons floating or bouncing across the screen, growing larger and smaller, morphing into different shapes. They appeared every 10 minutes on an inactive screen. The constant movement kept the menus from burning into the screens — the characters leaving a shadowy pattern in the glass from the combination of gases and lights inside. That's why screen savers were invented.

Lawrence told me the screen savers were unnecessary. Still, he didn't mind letting me make this little contribution to the workstations. I installed the screen savers on each terminal.

I'd broken the ice. He was warming up to me. I started talking with him more about the office system. I shared some ideas about backing up and archiving data on the disks for the Bernoulli drives that were popular then. In that era, hard drives had extremely limited memory capacity. Even 100-megabyte drives were out of this world. The term "gigabyte" was unheard of.

Lawrence thought backing up and cataloguing data on disks was an excellent idea. We worked together on the project.

I came up with another suggestion. "Maybe we ought to create workstation directories for each person."

He liked that idea, too.

We got it done.

Then I helped him build Macros and shortcuts in programs. That saved workers time when they had to type the same paragraphs for form letters or contracts. Now they could just get the paragraphs with the click of a keyboard button.

Next, I helped Lawrence build print queues to manage printers, and create shared directories around subjects such as "Work in Progress," "Geophysical Data," and so on.

As the weeks went by, Lawrence began relying on me more and more. He'd toil away on the system during the day. I'd come in after school and, when I could break free from the company library, continue our work.

I started setting up security permissions. Only certain workers would be given the passwords to get into certain directories. That puzzled Lawrence. "What are you doing that for?" he asked.

"So other people can't get in where they don't belong," I said. "They could destroy data. They could delete a whole directory. Then you'd have to recover it from backup and it'd be a hassle."

"No, we're not doing that," Lawrence said.

"OK," I said.

I didn't want to rock the boat.

I didn't care that I wasn't getting paid for this side work. Lawrence was the only other person who knew what I was up to. That was fine with me. All I cared about was getting on the computer system. I couldn't afford fancy equipment myself. I'd run my gofer errands for the mining company and organize the library — degrading tasks to my intelligence, but I knew I was paying my dues and couldn't whine about it — and savor the time I could steal from the grunt work to log on and tap away.

I was happy now going into the office at Hidden Lode. I was immersing myself in computer technology. I started learning about BNC cable connectivity. Tim, one of the engineers at Hidden Lode, saw that I was infatuated by computers. He invited me over to his workstation to show me his work on AutoCAD, the computer-aided design software that lets the user draw detailed, accurate models and maps on screen.

Tim had taken AutoCAD training. He was brilliant. He showed me 3D designs he'd created for airplanes to be used for company projects.

That sparked an idea in my mind. I told Tim some friends and I were building a little motorcycle course out in the open terrain where I lived. Sure enough, he helped me plot out the course, complete with terrain relief, on a digitizing table. We printed out copies. I handed the copies out to the guys helping me dig the track and build obstacles. They couldn't believe it. It was so professional.

Computers were just going to make a huge impact throughout society, I could see. It was the same feeling I'd had when I was 8 years old, gawking at the box-like computer in the school office in Panama City, Florida, and wondering why everyone didn't have a computer.

AS THE INEVIBILITY OF high school graduation became ever more a reality as the months passed during my junior year, I fantasized about working in the computer industry. But I knew better. There weren't a lot of jobs in the MIS field. You had to have a four-year college degree to work in MIS, even as a "computer analyst" or some such position. The field was so new that few universities offered computer-science degrees. A mechanical engineering major might steer toward computers. Some companies, such as Microsoft, would take college graduates with almost any major and train them to write software.

A business that needed someone to maintain the system and teach its workers how to use computer programs would hire and train an MIS person. But again, a job candidate needed a four-year college degree. The jobs there weren't going to someone with only a high school diploma. And that's as far as I intended to take my education.

College wasn't for me. Heck, I hated high school. The classes were monotonous. I was anxious to get it all over with. Go on to college and spend another four years in classrooms? The thought repelled me. No way.

As I started eyeing high school graduation a year away, I accepted that I couldn't wait to get out of school. What I'd do was get a full-time job and make money. And if I could somehow manage it, I'd figure out a way to get into a career in computers.

Unfortunately, my hands-on computer training at Hidden Lode came to a sudden halt. Lawrence and I had collaborated on an entire revamping of the storage system. For him, that was enough.

"The systems are getting messed up," he said one day. "It's getting harder for me to manage the network. You've been fooling around too much with them, and that wasn't what you were hired for. You have enough work on your plate, and we need the computers for the people in the office. So, no more computer time for you."

Lawrence was getting overwhelmed. The employees' computer needs were evolving quickly. They wanted more directories, more controls, more terminals, more network printers. He was having a hard time keeping up. He was getting frustrated. He was blaming his problems on me.

I told him that was fine. Actually, it was. I was tired of coming to work at Hidden Lode. What's more, I was tired of seeing so much of Mom. We lived together, and we saw each other at work, and then we drove home together. It was too much for both of us, probably.

I quit Hidden Lode.

IT WAS NOW SUMMER — the summer before my senior year at Reed. I wanted more time for fun. The only hard part was, now I didn't have a source of income. I'd already been fired from Staley's. I'd made a couple bad moves there. Making a flippant comment about a checker's weight was one. She'd complained to management about me. And then there was the accident on the forklift. I'd been helping a stocker, lifting pallets of canned goods. I decided I could maneuver that forklift like an expert. I started going faster, moving in, grabbing pallets with the forks, raising them, backing up and turning, zooming over to the spot. I got cocky. I got moving too fast. I knocked a stack of beverage bottles over. The devastation was a mess of smashed glass and puddles.

I looked around for a new job. I found the perfect one.

Pep Boys, the auto-parts store, hired me. I've always loved cars, so I was in my element. I started behind the counter, stocking parts and retrieving them for customers. The company rotated positions regularly, so I ended up changing tires in the garage, then running the cash register, and finally doing assistant-manager work.

Back then, Pep Boys had a strict code for dress and appearance. You had to be clean-shaven with no sideburns and with hair above the collar. You had to wear polished shoes, a collared shirt the company issued, and polyester pants to protect against battery acid. You had to be polite to customers, and you were trained how to use proper protocol with customers calling in. I liked the professionalism at Pep Boys. It seemed to me it was the corporate way.

August approached. My senior year was getting ready to start. I felt really independent, with my motorcycle and my job at Pep Boys, which I would be continuing after school hours. Senior year, I knew, would be a blast.

But I also knew that I'd have to have some sort of plan for after that. Come spring, it'd be graduation. What would I do?

The picture was unclear.

My sister, Jennifer, is holding me. I was one week old in February 1972, Vacaville, California.

This is Grandpa Herschel and I in San Bernardino, 1973.

This is the aftermath of the famous Gramsie golf swing. I almost lost my left eye in 1975.

This is my sister, Jennifer, and I in my swing, 1972, San Bernardino, California.

Here I am in my "spiffy" suit I used to wear to school on Fridays, 1977.

We were visiting friends in Arizona, and stopped for a break on the side of the road, 1978.

"Ponch" himself, Erik Estrada, was nice enough to give me an autograph. I was a
huge fan of the TV show *CHiPS*, 1978.

My love for motorcycles was in my blood (it has never left), 1979.

My sister and I with a few friends after riding, 1979.

The best fishing trip I had in Oregon. This is where I caught my first fish, 1979.

Disneyland, California, 1979.

I trained my rooster to sit on my shoulder in the
Philippines, 1981.

The first McDonald's in Japan, 1982.

This is the picture that changed my life. It helped launch this book. If I would have quit, this is where the story could have ended. My first time on a jet ski, in Lake Havasu City, Arizona, 1984.

Grandpa Herschel and I in Sparks, Nevada, 1984.

This is me on Wilson in Steamboat Springs, Nevada, 1987.

I was loading the calves in the chute for the next roper, in Doyle, California, 1987.

Jennifer, myself, and Wilson the horse in Red Rock, outside Reno, Nevada, 1987.

My beautiful mom, in Nevada, 1987.

A friend and I at Sand Mountain, Fallon, Nevada, 1989.

My sister, Jennifer, my niece, Brianna, and Mom in Verdi, Nevada, 1992.

Brianna and I right before I went into the Army, Sparks, Nevada, 1992.

Making a free long-distance call while in the field, 1993.

Trying to look like Rambo the best I could, Fort Hood, Texas, 1994.

The first jet ski I owned and rebuilt myself. Belton Lake, Fort Hood, Texas, 1993.

Catching some air on Mount Rose, Nevada, 1996.

Deer hunting on Table Mountain in central Nevada, 1995.

My future wife, Tanya, and I before we were married, 1999.

Jet skiing at Pyramid Lake, Nevada, March 1999.

Taking a vacation in Cozumel, Mexico, getting ready to dive, 2005.

No hands, Lahontan Reservoir, Silver Springs, Nevada, 2006.

My beautiful girls, Taylor and Jessie, Sparks, Nevada, 2007.

Tanya, Jessie, Taylor and I: My family on vacation in Gold Beach, Oregon, 2006.

CHAPTER THIRTY: A Joyride, a Killer

MY BLITHE ATTITUDE THAT senior year of high school started getting me into more and more trouble.

One Friday night I joined the teen-cruising mob downtown. At one point I was sitting in the back of someone's pickup truck, drinking a beer, minding my own business. The cops were on the lookout for teens' misbehavior, seeking ways to curtail cruising in the heart of the casino core. I ended up getting cited for being a minor in possession of alcohol.

I figured this sort of bad luck couldn't happen twice in a row. I was wrong.

The next Friday, I was busted again in the same situation.

The two citations earned me a juvenile probation officer, plus county work crew — picking up litter on the highway shoulders over four weekends with a team of fellow youth miscreants.

Mom was getting fed up with my brushes with the law. She saw how I was treating school as a joke. She saw how arrogant I acted, like nothing could really harm me, like everything could be taken in stride. I was simply thumbing my nose at authority.

She started thinking that the best path to straighten me out was for me to join the Army after graduation. Jennifer already had enlisted. I thought that was a mistake, giving up her freedom for three or four years. But in her letters home she made the service sound like fun. Of all things, she was a military policewoman.

Maybe Mom was right. Maybe I needed an attitude adjustment. A few tickets, and then the probation officer. Deep down, I knew I was going down the wrong path.

Then I thought: Nah. She was overreacting. I hadn't hurt anyone. I'd just been a kid out having fun, and gotten heat from the cops. That was all.

Still, when an Army recruiter visited Reed, I brought home the brochures. And then I started giving the notion of enlisting some serious thought. There was a delayed-entry program that looked appealing. I'd be able to get technical training. I'd have the GI Bill afterward to get schooling, maybe computer courses in college. It sounded sort of appealing. I did have to figure out some plan for after graduation.

Then I considered that if the Army could be good for me, maybe the Air Force would be better. After all, there'd be a greater chance of working on computers. But I realized that candidates for the Air Force had to test very high, and I wasn't prepared to push myself in that direction. Instead, I considered that the Army had more deployable stations in Europe than the other service branches. After living in Asia, I wanted to see Europe. What's more, the delayed-entry program would allow me to postpone going in for two years. That meant I'd be able to do some living first. And if during that time I wanted to opt out of the program, I could.

At school I took the Armed Services Vocational Aptitude Battery, a three-hour standardized test measuring everything from mathematics knowledge and reasoning to vocabulary, reading comprehension, general science, and mechanical and electronics ability. The ASVAB showed that I was high in language and mechanical skills, and medium in math.

I paid a visit to the Army recruitment office. The recruiter made it sound like I'd do great in the service. I finally agreed to sign on the dotted line for the delayed-entry program.

It turned out to be a good thing I did. It bailed me out of yet another scrape with the law.

ONE WEEKEND, A CLEAR winter day, some friends and I were out driving on remote Dog Valley Road, a narrow dirt path in the foothills outside of the tiny town of Verdi, west of Reno near the California line. A bit before sunset, deep in a ravine, we came upon an abandoned Chevrolet Blazer. It had gotten ditched there.

I knew about hotwiring from working on cars with my uncles. I got down under the dash with my pocketknife and started putting wires together until the ignition lights lit up. I knew the trick was to engage the wires but not leave them connected, or the starter would burn up.

Click. Click. The engine fired.

We went off joyriding. I was in the Blazer with a couple guys, and the others were in the car we'd driven in. We headed back through Reno and Sparks.

Around midnight, we were out on Pyramid Highway north of Sparks. The rumbles of our engines were the only sounds. I backed the Blazer down the slope from the pavement onto a dirt road and pointed the truck toward the highway. My friend Troy got out and stood watch, making sure no traffic was coming. At his signal I floored the pedal, rocketed forward up the embankment and jumped both lanes. The Blazer sailed down into the opposite ditch, going about 60 mph. I landed with a powerful, junking jolt.

I climbed out as Troy and the guys in the other car rushed over. The Blazer was done for. Broken axles. Smashed tires. Antifreeze all over the place. We left the wreck and drove off. The guys dropped me at my house, which was nearby.

In the next few hours I couldn't stop thinking about the stereo in the Blazer's dashboard. The wreck was about 500 yards from my home. Finally, I decided to walk back and get it.

Foolish mistake.

Unbeknownst to me, a Washoe County Sheriff's cruiser was parked a ways away, out of sight. A deputy was staking out the scene.

As soon as I got into the Blazer, I heard, "Freeze!" I was bathed in blinding lights. In a moment, a big fat deputy appeared. I thought about opening the door and bolting. I could've outrun him. For some reason, I stayed put.

He walked up and ordered me out.

He stood in front of me, glowering, heavyset in his pickle-green uniform. Pot-bellied and big-jowled.

"Did you steal this car?"

His question annoyed me.

"Yeah, we took it for a joyride. So what?"

He spun me around and shoved me against the Blazer. He slapped the bracelets on, damn near breaking my wrists. Then he yanked me upright and over to the cruiser, opened the back door and shoved me in. Another cruiser pulled up. A deputy got out. He and the fat one conversed for a bit. Dispatcher talk crackled on the police radio. Finally, the fat deputy climbed in behind the wheel, radioed something to the dispatcher, then put the cruiser in gear and we pulled onto the highway.

"Are you taking me to jail?"

"You're going to Wittenberg."

Wittenberg Hall was the juvenile-detention facility near Washoe Medical Center in Reno.

I was dead tired. It was nearly sunrise.

The deputy led me inside the brick building. The handcuffs were removed. I sat at a desk to be booked. A woman took my personal information. Then a guard led me down a corridor. I was forced to strip to my underwear and was put in a cell by myself.

Cold air was blowing through the window opening high on a wall. There was no glass on the window, just wire mesh. I began shaking. As I sat on the wooden bench, my feet pulled up to avoid the cold concrete floor, I knew I'd really f*cked up. All I could do was wait until Mom showed up to get me.

A long time later, it could have been three hours, the cell door swung open and a guard brought in a Latino kid about my age and size. As he entered the cell I felt a sudden chill, like an evil spirit had entered with him.

His T-shirt and underpants were soaked with blood. His eyes were crazy, staring into space. I could tell something really bad had just happened.

The hair stood out on the back of my neck.

He didn't look like a gang-banger. His hair was in a bowl cut. He was a little chubby. He was wearing blue underpants with stitched white ribbing. I thought it was odd that anyone would wear colored underwear. Still, he looked like a normal kid. Yet it was obvious that whatever deep sh*t he'd just been involved in totally dwarfed my charges.

The Latino kid sat on the bench away from me. I wasn't going to say a word until he spoke first. I put my back against the wall and faced him, my legs out in front of me. I figured out a few plans for what I'd do if he suddenly got violent and came at me. I could kick him away, then knock his head hard against the wall. I could scream loud enough so that a guard would come.

I kept my eyes on him. But he stayed passive, lost in space. A half-hour, or what felt like a half-hour, went by in silence. Then he started talking, in a quiet mumble.

His voice was calm. He looked at me when he spoke. He registered that I was a person there in front of him. I realized that the best psychology for me to use to keep him from getting agitated was simply to listen. I'd fulfill the role of being someone he could talk to.

"I can't believe I got busted," he said.

He was coming to grips with whatever had just gone down.

I listened closely. He began muttering about cops and the arrest and his friends. From the jumble of speech, I gathered he'd been in an altercation with some other people and used a knife. I couldn't really follow it all, but I guessed that he'd been on some sort of drugs, freaked out and gotten violent. That seemed plausible. But I wasn't about to ask him for details. I was just going with the flow.

Whenever he paused, I'd nod my head and say, "Uh-huh" or, "Really?"

He continued mumbling.

By now we were both shivering from the cold air coming through the window. We were cradling our knees with our hands, bouncing up and down to keep the blood flowing.

I saw he was slowly coming back down to earth. His eyes blinked. He began warming up to me. His speech became clearer. He was through babbling about whatever he'd done with the knife.

"Man, all these jail cells are always painted blue," he said.

"Yeah," I said. "I think they use baby-blue and yellow because it's supposed to calm you down, mellow you out."

He nodded seriously. "That's good to know." Given the situation we were in, our figuring out the color scheme in the cell was funny. He actually smiled and laughed.

A wave of relief washed through me. I'd done it. I'd talked him down from wherever his mind had been when they'd brought him in.

But I still kept my guard up. I still watched him closely.

Another hour or two passed. Then the window slot on the door slid open. A guard spoke through it. He was addressing my cellmate.

"Your sister made it but your mother didn't."

The words hit me like a thunderclap. The wind rushed out of my lungs. My heartbeat jumped. I could feel the blood drain from my face. My hands grew clammy. I felt like I was about to be shoved off a cliff.

I swallowed hard and struggled to compose myself.

All right, no big deal. This guy ain't in this cell to kill me. He's in enough trouble. Just keep on the even keel. It's been working.

I looked at him. The news from the guard had sent my cellmate back into orbit. We sat in silence for 15 minutes. Then the daze left his eyes. He started talking again. It was the crazy mumbling from before.

I felt like I was on borrowed time. I couldn't wait to get out of there. Finally, the door opened. A guard led me out of the cell. I didn't look back.

AS UPSET AS MOM was with me, she was even angrier at the deputy sheriff for roughing me up. She knew someone in the county district attorney's office. She made a complaint.

Two things worked in my favor in the case. One, the sheriff's deputy using excessive force after I'd been handcuffed. Two, the fact I had already signed up for the Army.

I called my recruiter. He called my probie officer, who decided the Army would straighten me out. The charges against me for grand theft auto were dropped.

But I wasn't out of the woods, yet. My attitude was still bad in school.

CHAPTER THIRTY-ONE: 'Mr. Bowling' Stands up

My English teacher, Ms. Mead, was kind of a difficult woman. At least she was toward me. Drew and I were in the class together. Big mistake. We sat in back, screwing around, not paying attention. Drew's mother was a teacher in the school district and he always got great grades, and was expected to. But I was a bad influence. Ms. Mead finally separated us.

Most of the students in the class were juniors, and they looked up to Drew and me, but we were setting a poor example. We always cracked jokes. I just couldn't resist tormenting that woman.

One Friday, she was critiquing an essay of mine in front of the class. She started picking on some of my conclusions. "And Jeff did . . ." this and this and this. I was very proud of that essay, and her criticisms pissed me off. My resentment boiled over. I had such a big ego that I just reacted. I told her she was full of it.

We started arguing. My voice got louder and louder. So did hers. Finally, she said, "That will be enough, *Jeff!*"

All of a sudden I was on my feet. The words just flew out of my mouth.

"No, bitch. You will address me as Mr. Bowling!"

The students went nuts.

"Holy sh*t," Drew said with a gasp, "you're going to the principal's office."

Ms. Mead's face burned bright red.

"Get out of my class!"

She scribbled out a hallway pass. "You're going to see Ms. Babb."

That was the principal, all right. But I felt like I could defend myself in front of Ms. Babb.

Yeah, I thought, *let's see you make* this *stick.*

I didn't head to the principal's office, though. I went out to the parking lot, got on my motorcycle, rode home.

Drew stopped by after school. "You're in so much trouble."

Yeah, whatever, I thought.

I didn't have a clue how much trouble. Nor did I know how famous that spontaneous comeback I'd spewed at Ms. Mead was becoming at Reed. It had spread around school like wildfire. It was being repeated in the halls, in the classrooms by students in every grade.

When I got to my first-period government class on Monday, Rich, the school security cop, was waiting for me.

"I gotta take you to the office," he said.

Rich was a cool guy. As we walked down the hall, he made light of my line, chuckling over it and calling me, "Mr. Bowling." But he added, "You're in trouble this time. Just keep your mouth shut."

In the principal's office, Mom was sitting, along with a Sparks police officer, my junior-year math teacher, Ms. Fuller, who liked me, and Ms. Mead, who, of course, hated me. The principal, Sabrina Babb, had a serious look on her face. Mom, I could tell, was furious with me.

I knew I was in deep sh*t. Ms. Mead looked very worked up.

"Sit down, Jeff, we're going to get to the bottom of this," Ms. Babb said. She had a gap between her top front teeth, but she was hardly a comical figure at Reed. She was from the authoritarian school of principals.

"He threatened me with death," Ms. Mead said.

"No, I never said anything like that . . ."

"Well, I interpreted it as a threat," she said. "Look at how big you are compared to me . . ."

She went on and on. She was really shook up. She'd had an entire weekend to blow the incident way out of proportion.

"Me, big?" I said. "I'm not big."

I didn't think of myself as big and intimidating.

"Yes, you are big, Jeff . . ." Ms. Fuller said.

Hmm. I guess I still had my little-guy self-image.

"But I can say that this whole thing seems entirely out of character," Ms. Fuller continued.

She was standing up for me. She vouched that I was actually a nice young man, if high-spirited at times. But she also emphasized that I should know that I'd seriously violated the school conduct code.

"Look," I said, turning to Ms. Mead. "I would never hurt you. I'd never do anything like that. You said something that made me mad, and I responded to it."

We went back and forth. She said her whole weekend had been ruined by my conduct. I apologized for that.

I repeated that I wasn't violent.

Then Ms. Babb put in her two cents.

"Well, look at the shirt you're wearing."

I loved themed T-shirts. I even had a Mr. Bubble shirt. But as bad luck had it, on this Monday I was wearing a shirt that read, "Kill 'em all. Let God sort 'em out."

"It's a Marines logo!" I protested.

The Sparks policeman had heard enough. "I don't think I need to be here." He rose and left.

Well, I wasn't going to be arrested for making a physical threat. That was nice. But Ms. Babb was still intent on taking decisive action.

"I tell you what we're going to do," she began.

Ms. Babb said that since Ms. Mead was so upset, it wouldn't be conducive to a healthy educational environment were I allowed to return to her classroom. Therefore, I was being pulled out of her class.

That crushed me. I needed that credit to graduate. Mom knew it, too. She was chagrined.

But it all turned out fine. Ms. Babb announced she would transfer me into a sports-literature class, which was far easier than the English literature class. In sports literature you wrote about sports and stars and the books about them. It was a class for jocks and boneheads. I'd get to write about the National Hockey League, Michael Jordan, Pete Rose and whatnot.

I was happy.

There was more.

"Because you've violated our code for student conduct, Jeff, I am giving you a one-week suspension."

Mom looked disgusted.

"Thanks," she told Ms. Babb, "you just gave him a week's vacation."

Which was true.

During my suspension, I went out to Pyramid Lake every day. I had a good time, just like the week I'd taken off at the beginning of the school year.

I'd also achieved a measure of fame at Reed, and around other schools, even. The line, "No, bitch, you will address me as Mr. Bowling" gave me celebrity status. Students would shout compliments — "Hell, yeah!" — at me in the halls. Even the other faculty members thought it was hilarious.

To this day, my friends from high school still quote that line.

It was just so immature, uncalled for and outrageous that it stuck in memory. Its sheer inanity guaranteed it longevity. I only list it in this book to show how utterly out of control I was.

Your life is your life and you cannot take any of it back — you have to live with it all.

CHAPTER THIRTY-TWO: 'Mr. Bowling' Graduates

The sports-lit class, as easy as its subject matter was, nearly proved my undoing.

As if my experience in Ms. Mead's class hadn't taught me to keep out of trouble and just get the necessary credit for graduation, I started taking advantage of the sports-lit teacher, Ms. Bonds. I couldn't help it. She was a flake. She wasn't there half the time; that is, not mentally. She'd hand out temporary passes to students so they could retrieve a book or something from a locker, and some of the popular kids and I would use these passes to cut the entire period, just head to the parking lot and drink some beers.

Then we started not showing up at all. It was April, with just a little more than a month left until graduation. It was sunny. The last place a senior wanted to be was inside, bored, watching the minutes tick by.

But Ms. Bonds evidently started keeping an accurate attendance roll. As a consequence, I piled up too many absences. I showed up one day to find that I'd gotten bumped from the class. I had 22 academic credits, one more than the minimum for a diploma, but I needed that one last English credit to meet the curriculum requirements.

When I told Mom, she was more than upset. She was outraged. I'd rarely seen her this angry.

"You're graduating, goddammit," she said. "You're taking this much too lightly!"

She was not going to let me flake out on graduating. If I wanted to preserve any kind of healthy relationship with this woman, I'd have to get that last English credit out of the way. And before graduation day.

Time was running short.

I talked to my high school counselor. She told me my best option was taking a correspondence course through Washoe High, the "alternative" school for students who don't do well in traditional classroom settings.

I went down to the Washoe High administrative office. I met with my instructor for the course. He was a pony-tailed hippie type. "You can call me by my first name, Terry," he said. Terry was mellow. Terry was interested in helping me.

He reviewed the course outline. He handed me my assignment packet and scribbled down his home number in case I had any problems. That was it. I grabbed my coursework and went home.

I'd have about six weeks to get through reading three books and writing assignments and reports on them. It was a whole semester's worth of material. But I knew I had to complete it. Mom was stern about this. She wasn't about to let me screw up any more.

"Every day you're going to work in this book," she said.

I chose three titles from a list of books. I tore through the books and the homework. It was easier than I thought it'd be. I realized that I did very well studying on my own, going at my own pace.

Maybe I should've gone the Washoe High route all four years.

Every afternoon I read and wrote, wrote and read. No lectures from teachers. No taking notes. No classroom discussions. No distractions. Just my own steady concentration — absorbing what I needed, when I needed it.

I finished the semester-long course in one month. I earned an A.

This experience with independent study was another revelation for me — just like the breakthrough I'd made in math down in Darrington, when I'd worked through equations backward from the answers. I did great when I was on my own, absorbing information in my own way. It was the same with computers, when I ran through applications and mapped out steps to take me through the entire system. I was my own best teacher.

Suddenly there at the end of 12 years of formal public education, I had confidence that maybe I really was "smart."

I DIDN'T BUY A senior class ring, or get a special senior photo taken for the yearbook, or go to the prom. I didn't like any of that bullsh*t.

Drew and I were the only knuckleheads in the Reed High School Class of 1990 to be buzzed before the ceremony at Lawlor Events Center, the arena on the University of Nevada, Reno campus where all the high schools' commencements were held.

I wore my Oakley sunglasses on stage. Marvin Moss, the distinguished school-district superintendent, was handing out the diplomas. "Take your glasses off, son," he said.

"Nope," I said.

I took my blank sheet, which I was to turn in for the sheepskin, shook his hand and walked off. Mom still has the photo of me in cap and gown and shades. She also has a photo taken of the two of us outside with my glasses off and my eyes red.

Getting school, that unwanted distraction, over and done with was reason for me to celebrate. Now I could get on with my life. I was burning with ambition.

Andy Bowling surprised me. He sent me $1,000 as a graduation present. He'd done the same with Jennifer. He wrote each of us a similar note with the check. He said he'd never been in our lives before, "So here is some money and let's see what you can do with it."

Mom, meanwhile, was turning a page with me, too.

She was burning to have me out of the house. She'd done her job, seeing me through my 18th birthday and high school graduation.

Adulthood had arrived. At least, in theory.

CHAPTER THIRTY-THREE: Trading Time

As the Reed High School Class of 1990 dispersed to college or jobs or the military or just continued in teenage slacker mode, my mind was full of dreaming and scheming. With school over with, through and done, my personal ambition was welling up. I was primed and ready to set the world on fire.

I'd read *The Art of the Deal*, a biography of Donald Trump, and even owned *TRUMP the Game*, a board game in which you bid on and negotiated for pricy properties. I loved the exuberance of the decadent '80s, the *Miami Vice* styles, the go-go attitudes. Michael Milken and junk bonds. Leveraged buyouts. Corporate raids. I never missed an episode of *Lifestyles of the Rich and Famous* on television. I had dollar signs on the brain.

But how was I going to get into the game myself?

My big goal was to make a lot of money. How? Didn't know. Computers? Didn't have enough money to buy a good setup to do designer work. Real estate appealed to me. I'd read a book about speculative investment. But I didn't have money to get started in that, either. Still, I was hungry for an angle, a hustle — something to jump-start me toward wealth.

I wanted money, and I wasn't apologetic about it. As Michael Douglas' character, "Gordon Gecko," in the Oliver Stone movie *Wall Street* said:

"Greed is good."

I agreed with him. I didn't see the line in the way that Stone intended it: as a villainous statement.

But for the moment, I had no clue how to go about it. I was still working full time at Pep Boys. My immediate concern was saving up money to move out of Mom's house.

In the weeks after graduation, she grew more insistent that I had to get a place of my own. That was fine. I'd practically been out of her house for more than a year anyway, after getting my driver's license. I was always on the go, working or out partying, crashing at someone else's place. For me, Mom's house was largely a place to shower, sleep and change clothes.

She had let me be independent. All she'd insisted on was accountability. If we were drinking beers, she said we'd better either do it at home or, if we were out somewhere and too drunk to drive, we'd better call her to pick us up. She'd been a cool Mom while I was finishing school. But now she was ready to push me out of the nest for good.

She contributed to this cause by helping me land an entry-level job with T&A Construction, a mid-size construction company for which a friend of hers, Eric, was a key insulation guy. I'd start at the bottom, hanging Sheetrock and installing insulation. The pay was $10 an hour, $3 an hour higher than Pep Boys. I quit Pep Boys and joined T&A.

I figured it would only be temporary, until I could find something better. I was capable of more.

That belief really hit home after I found out what my coworkers were like.

THE CONSTRUCTION BUSINESS EXPOSED me to a different side of the workforce from the crews at squeaky-clean Staley's and Pep Boys. I discovered that the trades are ridden with drugs and alcohol. It's a hard-living set.

The employee hierarchy of construction became clear to me after a couple weeks.

The workers on the entry level — and that's where I was — do Sheetrock and insulation. Some of them were a few years older than I, some were already in their forties. Moving higher on the food chain, you have the people who do the plumbing, HVAC (heating, ventilation and air conditioning), or framing — a more skilled element, and cleaner living. They had decent clothes, decent rigs, nice tools, and could speak without butchering grammar and using a cuss word in every sentence. At the top of the chain are the finish carpenters.

The skilled workers saw I wasn't a typical Sheetrock hanger. More than once I was asked, "What are you doing working with this bunch of monkeys?"

"It's just temporary. I'm just trying to earn some cash. I don't know what I'm going to do next, go back to school or what."

My job lacked any structure. You could come to work drunk or stoned and no one would notice. It was mindless. It also was dangerous — and not because of the physical labor, but because of the morons I was working among.

Some of the Sheetrockers I worked with were recovering or functioning alcoholics or addicts. This job was their last chance at living productively in society. Plenty of them were still drinking or using drugs, though. They'd come to work drunk or stoned; they needed the buzz to be able to function.

Not all of them were borderline useless, though. One, Willie, was a hard-working guy. I loved working with him. He had long hair like a rock star, and had been a singer in a top local band, but the lifestyle had knocked him down. Too many beers, too many bowls. Run-ins with the law. Jail time. We'd have the stereo going at a job site, playing Queensryche. Willie would bust out the vocals and hit the same notes. "Jet city wo-ooo-man . . ." Willie had a phenomenal voice.

"You need to quit this job and go to L.A. and audition for bands," I'd say. "You got some pipes on you."

Something had made him give up trying in the music biz. Maybe he didn't want to get caught up in the destructive lifestyle all over again.

I had to be careful not to get mixed up in my coworkers' personal business. But it was inevitable that something would happen, especially as I accumulated a small bit of seniority and was given more tasks away from the worksites.

About my fourth month on the job, I used a company pickup truck to drive to California to retrieve supplies from the T&A yard in the Sacramento area. The truck had been used before me by a coworker named Harley. He was a tall, skinny slob of a guy in his mid-thirties. He had red curly hair that he never brushed out. He always stank of cigarettes and various body odors. A word we used in the early 1990s, "lurpy," not only meant gangly and awkward, but could mean creepy and sleazy. That described Harley. I got along with him OK, though. He'd been working for T&A for a few years. He was friends with Bart, the job foreman. Bart told me to ask Harley for the keys to the pickup so I could use it for the supply trip.

I was approaching the California agricultural check station at the state border, where I had to stop and declare whether I was carrying any produce. I happened to glance in the opened ashtray. A little pipe stoked with a bowl of marijuana was sitting in there. That was a cause of instant alarm. Given my string of brushes with the law the last year of high school, and the fact I was driving with out-of-state license plates, I couldn't afford to take any chances were I to be pulled over on this trip. I didn't need to get handcuffed and stuck in a jail cell far from home.

I rolled down the window and tossed the pipe out.

The first thing Harley did after I came back to Reno with the load was check for his forgotten pipe. I got out of the cab. He climbed in.

"Where the f*ck's my dope? Did you smoke my dope?"

"No, I threw it out. I wasn't going to get busted."

His eyes blazed. He jumped out, grabbed me by the front of my shirt and flung me back. He grabbed me again and got in my face.

Some other workers jumped in and pulled him off me.

I was stunned. There I was, 18, getting roughed up by a guy in his mid-thirties. This was a working environment? I'd left the professional, corporate structure of Pep Boys for this crap?

"I'm going to f*cking kill you," Harley said, as he was restrained by two other guys. "If you come to work tomorrow, you're f*cking dead. You better not let me catch you alone."

I knew he was serious. He was bigger than I was. And he was crazy enough to hit me with the hatchet end of the Sheetrock hammer he carried on his tool belt. I didn't want to get the bad end of that.

I had to watch my back from then on. It was an eye-opening lesson about the job-site management style in construction.

If you messed up, you got beat up.

MY EYES AND EARS started opening a lot wider at T&A. These guys were a rough lot — and I mean all of them, from the grunts to the managers. It seemed like everyone was crooked in some way.

I learned from gossip that Bart, the job foreman, got high all the time with Harley. There was more. A lot of the workers were claiming unemployment checks from the state while getting paid under the table in cash. Harley was one of them; he'd go around bragging how he was collecting workman's compensation. In return, guys like him would kick back money to Bart who, by running this little scam, put the entire business in jeopardy of losing its contractor's license, not to mention severe penalties if state inspectors caught wind.

I couldn't believe how asinine it was for a business to take such a risk. It was just a lowlife operation.

Bart and his buddies were suspicious of me. I wasn't like the other drudges at the bottom of the totem pole. I was alert. I was observant. I wasn't sleepwalking around. I wasn't a drinker or stoner. They kept an eye on me. They gave me bad vibes.

I started wondering if I was going to get seriously jacked. I knew that Harley's threat had been sincere. He was going to put me in the hospital if he got the chance.

I asked Mom's friend, Eric, what I should do.

"Just be cool, man," he said. He was wise to the racket going on, but chose to overlook it and do an honest job himself. He ended up being promoted to salesman, and did very well.

I decided what I needed was a job transfer to Sacramento, where T&A had an office. It would be near where my Aunt Denise and Uncle Jim lived. I could stay with them.

Management gave the approval. I moved to California, glad for a change of scenery. But after I got there and reported to the T&A office, I was told there actually wasn't enough work there to take me on.

I had to look for a new job.

It was a blessing in disguise.

AFTER STARTING AT T&A, I'd bought a year-old Toyota MR2 from a Reno dealer. But now that I was between jobs, I had to return it. I couldn't make the payments. One weekend while I was supposed to be returning the MR2 back to the dealer, Drew and I took it to California for one last trip. On our way back through the Sierra I was doing about 100 mph in stretches on Interstate 80. I was going to miss this car!

The MR2 handled as perfectly as ever as I sliced down through the curves of the Truckee River canyon and crossed the Nevada state line. A dozen miles farther, back in Reno, eastbound on McCarran Boulevard, I was going somewhere around 80, or possibly 90, as I reached the rise approaching Virginia

Street, Reno's main drag. Just my luck: A police cruiser was sitting at the left-turn signal of the west-facing lanes at the traffic light at the McCarran-Virginia intersection.

The cop watched as I zoomed past him through the intersection. In my rearview I saw him hit his lights. I knew he was waiting for an opening in eastbound traffic to flip his car around in a U-turn after me.

I braked and pulled onto the shoulder and parked. A couple minutes later, he pulled up behind, lights flashing.

I was expecting him to ask, "Do you know why I pulled you over?" But instead, he walked up to my window, grinning, and said, "Jesus Christ, I had to kick it into 100 miles an hour to catch your ass."

Then he started ripping into me.

"You know, these little cars aren't made to go that fast," and, "I've seen these things go airborne because they flip." And so on.

He asked for my license, registration and proof of insurance.

I handed him my license from my wallet. I rummaged in the glove compartment for the registration and insurance card.

He looked them over and stuck them under the clip on his board.

"We'll talk about these in a moment."

My heart started pounding.

He scribbled out a ticket. "This one's for excessive speed." Then he started on another ticket. He was on a roll. He was putting pen to paper.

"What's this one for?" I asked.

"Careless driving."

"I wasn't careless," I protested. "I was in total control the whole time."

He stopped writing and stared at me.

"Do you realize I could cite you for reckless driving? Do you know what that means? It means your license would be suspended."

He had me in his clutches. He could do with me as he pleased. He knew that. I knew that. And he wasn't through with me.

He was enjoying himself.

He handed back my driver's license. Then he tapped the other documents on his clipboard.

"These aren't valid."

He wrote out a ticket for driving without proper registration. And another for driving without insurance. He wasn't accepting the temporary registration or the temporary insurance card.

I was in deep sh*t.

I took the MR2 back to the dealership.

As for the four tickets, they would come back to haunt me. I got a ride from Drew back to Northern California where I was staying with my aunt and uncle.

MY AUNT AND UNCLE loaned me a car to use. I started job hunting in Sacramento. What I found startled me. Unlike in little Reno, there were a ton of computer jobs. Software analyst. Debugger. Network technician. I knew one of them would be for me. The trouble was, experience was required. I was gifted, but I hadn't officially worked anywhere in the field yet. It was a Catch-22: I needed experience to get a job, but couldn't get experience without a job.

Nevertheless, I persevered, and finally landed a job interview with a small-business owner in his early thirties named Gary Lee, who had a real estate company and a computer company. Mr. Lee was an energetic man of mixed Hawaiian and Chinese ancestry, who spoke in a polished manner with no accent. He was one of the business types you'd run into frequently in the 1980s and early '90s. He lived and breathed the go-go spirit of the age of Donald Trump, Michael Milken and Bill Gates. It was a can-do attitude that wealth was out there for the taking, and if you had the initiative and zeal, the wealth would be yours.

Mr. Lee was hungry for money. His computer company was called The Software Location. It sold software to businesses.

I showed up on a Monday morning at a suite in a nice, modern office building. The cubicles were buzzing with activity; the real estate and software enterprises were under the same roof. Mr. Lee's assistant ushered me into his office. It was tidy and classy, with hardwood tables, chairs and desk. He wore a suit and tie. I felt a wave of gratification after the scruffy environment of T&A.

I glanced out the window. I saw laborers digging a ditch. I felt like I'd made a change in my life. I was landing on the other side of the fence, the side where the players were.

Mr. Lee shook my hand and ushered me to a seat at a table. I recognized him right away for the dynamic entrepreneur he was. A guy with an upbeat attitude, lots of energy. I felt like a kindred spirit. I'd showed up for the interview in a shirt and tie and Dockers.

One of the first questions he asked was whether I did drugs. Cocaine was very popular as a recreational drug. It seemed to go with the money being raked in by young people. Drug abuse was a big concern of employers. I told Mr. Lee I'd gotten into hot water on my previous job because I'd tossed out a coworkers' marijuana pipe.

"I don't do drugs. I'm a hard worker," I said. I added, "I'll make you money."

He loved that response.

After a few more questions, he welcomed me aboard and issued me the icon of the early '90s business world: a pager.

I was ready to go!

Selling for The Software Location was a shirt-and-tie job, commission only. If you didn't sell, you didn't eat. You got 9 percent of a sale — higher if it was for a big package. But it turned out to be a really tough gig.

There were only two salespeople: a guy named Clyde, and I. We sat at our respective workstation cubicles: desk, computer terminal to record leads in and to look up product prices, telephone directory from which to find leads, and phone to make sales calls. We thumbed through the Yellow Pages, making cold calls on businesses, trying to get appointments to show The Software Location's products.

Mr. Lee told me it would take six months to establish a strong enough sales base where I'd be making enough money to live on. I told him that was OK; I was living with family and though I had some bills, I'd do the best I could. I went through the Yellow Pages and created a little database of companies I wanted to hit up. I picked big companies. I wanted big accounts. Lumber, construction, medical, industrial. Companies in these fields all had offices that needed up-to-date, reliable software. I just had to convince them to upgrade. There was no Internet then, so updated software would come out every three to six months.

I did chalk up a few sales my first week. Mr. Lee's wife, a CPA whose office was next to her husband's, was amazed. She liked my spunk. But I found out, very quickly, that I hated cold calling. I could spew my spiel, but it wasn't the kind of work that appealed to me.

"Hi, I'm Jeff Bowling from The Software Location. I was wondering if I could speak with the person in charge of purchasing software for your organization."

If I was told no but that I could leave a message, or if I was told that they didn't take sales calls, I'd say, "Well, do you mind if I drop by a catalog?"

I'd print up little catalogs at work with photos and descriptions of some of the products.

When I made a connection, I'd make a sales visit and talk about the software. Or I'd have the client come to our offices where we had a demo room, and demonstrate the software on a terminal.

New computers were coming out on the market, and the hardware didn't always come with software installed. What's more, new businesses were starting up, so the demand for new software was constant. I just had to hang in there and build up my client base over those first six months.

WordPerfect was the best-selling word-processing software, and a staple of my sales. Then Windows 3.0 came out, and Mr. Lee got the software in stock. He sat at a terminal with Clyde and me plus Marcus, the shop tech. We were wowed. It was a major upgrade over DOS. Windows 3.0 featured desktop icons and great colors, two-dimensional graphics and a wide array of fonts. 3.0 supported multimedia files. It was so unbelievably user friendly — showing the positions on the desktop of directories and windows, folders, drivers and printers — that it was revolutionary.

I sat at the terminal for hours, learning the program.

"This is going to change the entire world!" I said.

With Windows 3.0, anyone could use a computer. I knew that the personal-computer industry was just going to explode. Every household would have a computer or two. I wanted to be a part of it.

But as of yet, I was barely making any money at The Software Location.

THERE WAS ONE PERSON who really inspired me at The Software Location. Looking back, meeting him was probably the most valuable thing I took away from the experience. The person was Damon, the network tech. He changed my way of thinking about computing.

Damon was a computer-network genius. He designed networks before networking was even popular. It blew me away. He was a year older than I, a skateboarder like me. We'd board together after work. He was short, with curly light-brown hair and glasses. He wore stylish clothes from Macy's and drove a new Honda Accord. He had a beautiful girlfriend. He carried a cell phone, still rare back then. He was cocky, but simply brilliant. He was living the way I craved to live.

Damon had a special working relationship with Gary Lee. Before hooking up with Lee, Damon and a partner had started a networking company, MIS Corporation. Then the partner had screwed Damon over, so he'd severed that relationship and partnered with Mr. Lee, offering networking services out of The Software Location, where he had his own office. Damon was making bank doing this. He'd show me the checks he was getting: $1,000 here, $500 there. He was making $3,000 to $4,000 a month — not bad for a 20-year-old with no college education. He'd joke that he had to go out at night and drink beer to kill off some brain cells to balance himself out with everyone else. Unfortunately, the brain cells would grow back the next day, he said. He was very egotistical, but he was riding a wave of success.

What Damon did was open my eyes to the business potential in computing. Any place could sell software, he said, but who could come into a client's worksite and set up the network and security? I started seeing the inside of computers, the engineering. To me, that was the Promised Land, not sales. It's what I wanted to do.

As it happened, a little crisis left over from Reno reared itself at this point, and prompted me to quit at The Software Location and return to my home, Nevada.

CHAPTER THIRTY-FOUR: Nothing in Life Is Free

Mom called me in California to say that police officers had been at her house with a warrant for my arrest.

"What did you do?" she demanded.

I explained about the four tickets in the MR2.

"Well, you missed your court date," she said.

I hadn't checked my mail back home, which was still being delivered to her house.

I mulled this over. There had to be a way out of the crisis. I could just stay in California. But eventually, I knew, I'd have to come back to Nevada.

"Mom, is there a phone number I can call to request a new court date?"

She found the envelope from district court and gave me the number of the clerk's office in the department of the presiding judge.

It took me a couple days of calling, but I finally managed to get through to the judge in his chambers. First, I apologized. Then I explained I'd been working full time and had forgotten the court date. I said that if it would be at all possible to have a new date set, I would travel in from California, even though I would have to make special arrangements because I didn't have my own transportation.

To my relief, the judge told me to show up by 1 o'clock sharp at his chambers, not the courtroom, the following Friday afternoon. But he warned, gruffly, that if I got pulled over on my way in I'd be arrested because of the outstanding warrants.

I promised I'd be there.

Drew drove to California and picked up me and my belongings. I didn't know how this was all going to play out with the judge.

I moved back into Mom's house to get on my feet, and to take care of the legal situation.

On Friday, I went to the judge's chambers at the courthouse downtown. A bailiff was standing there when I arrived at 1 p.m. sharp.

"We've been waiting for you," he said.

With no warning, he grabbed a wrist and began handcuffing my hands behind my back. He led me to a holding area in his office.

"You've got warrants out, so you'll be staying out at Parr until the judge can hear your case," he said.

"Parr" meant Parr Boulevard, where the county jail was.

"Since it's Friday, you're looking at the weekend. The judge can see you on Monday."

I couldn't believe it!

"The judge told me he was going to see me today!"

"He's got a busy schedule."

The bailiff said I could have one phone call. He uncuffed me and let me use the phone in his office. I called Mom and explained I might have to be in jail over the weekend.

"Well, you're 18, you need to deal with this on your own," she said. "Let me know if you need anything, but this is *your* deal."

Her voice was surprisingly calm. And I knew she was right. It was up to me to handle this on my own.

The bailiff cuffed me again. I sat on a bench in his office. A video camera was trained on the seating area. It was uncomfortable with the cuffs behind my back. It was an unnatural position. I leaned back, raised my knees up and slowly worked my legs and hips through my arms so my hands were in front.

In my wallet I had a handcuff key I'd gotten from an Army surplus store. I'd played around with it enough to know what I was doing. I thought about getting my wallet out, pulling out the key with my mouth and picking the lock. But I knew it would be a dumb move. Even if I managed to get out of the courthouse and drive away, fleeing like that would probably mean a lot of jail time. And anyway, I was mindful of the video cam.

I waited two hours. Finally, the judge came into the office to talk with me. He was wearing a regular short-sleeve shirt and blue jeans. He looked like a father in his forties. The bailiff removed my cuffs.

The judge asked if I knew what I'd done wrong. It was like a father talking to his son.

I knew I had to sell him on going easy on me. My goal was to get out of that courthouse by that night and avoid jail.

"Yes, judge, I know what I did wrong. It was my responsibility to check my mail. I was so busy working in California and going to school at the same time that I forgot to have my mail forwarded. But it's entirely my own fault."

The judge seemed satisfied. "Well, OK. I'll give you the benefit of the doubt on that. The fact you showed up now does demonstrate to me that you're capable of keeping your word. But we still need to talk about the tickets."

I explained that I'd returned the MR2 to the dealership. I pulled out the temporary insurance and registration card I'd had when I'd gotten the tickets, and explained that the police officer who'd pulled me over would not accept them.

The judge glanced at the papers. He hummed a bit. Then he peered at me with wrinkled brow.

"I'm willing to be lenient with you. You've had a chance to sit for two hours thinking about your actions. You stayed put in the office. I'll tell you what. We'll write this up as a careless driving, and let you go today."

"Thank God," I said.

I thoroughly enjoyed my freedom that weekend.

CHAPTER THIRTY-FIVE: In the Grip of Workplace Politics

Now that I was back in Reno, I started looking around for a better opportunity. I was hungrier than ever.

I mulled my options and recalled a relationship I had with the owner of a heavy-equipment leasing company. I used to wait on him when he came into Pep Boys for parts. I always took care of him. He liked me.

I called him and asked for a meeting. "I'm into computers, do you need an MIS guy?"

"No, we don't need a guy like that," he said. "We need a service writer."

A service writer is a person who helps out the support manager — writing the service tickets, recording serial numbers off the vehicles, doing the scheduling, making sure customers get their equipment and return it on time, and seeing that parts are ordered.

I applied for the job, was given a management test, and was hired. The company was called Alpine Power & Equipment.

It was decent money: $10 an hour, like I'd made in construction. Plus there were health benefits. I liked the organized work.

Drew and I rented a four-bedroom house north of Reno in an area called Raleigh Heights. It was $800 a month plus utilities — not cheap for two 19-year-olds with menial jobs. We were probably living way above our means, but thought we could swing it.

One night, working late, I went into my personnel file at AP&E and looked at my management test results. They were terrible. Part of the problem was I had no experience. But the results said I had no potential, either. That bothered me. The test was supplied by a professional management firm.

I took the test home and read it over, trying to understand the answers, to see what the company was looking for.

I decided that the test results were right on the money on some questions, but dead wrong on others. One of the questions asked what a manager should do if an employee's sibling called the manager and said there was a family emergency. *Should the manager let the employee leave work?* I'd answered yes. The correct response on this test was no. The manager was supposed to withhold information about the call from the employee until the employee had finished the job at hand, taking care of the employer's needs, and then give the news. (Workplaces have since changed, and my answer would be correct today.)

I realized my chance for advancement at AP&E was limited.

What's more, I was still learning the ropes of working in business — particularly a hard business like construction.

My supervisor, Sherman, was a big guy, 6-foot-5. And a real prick. No one got along with him. A lot of people quit because of him. He was volatile. He was negative. He was always looking for people to mess up so he could come down on them. He liked doing it.

Sherman's chance with me came one day after I'd made a small accounting mistake. I'd undercharged for a backhoe repair. The cashier had caught it when the customer tried to pay. Sherman and I were standing in his office. He was holding a copy of the order, reviewing it silently. His face grew red. He shook his head. Then he brought his hand back and swung at me.

I saw it coming in time to duck. His hand smacked the wall.

Rage surged through me. There was no excuse for him trying to hit me.

"All right, that's the last time you swing at me," I said.

He was unapologetic. He rubbed his hand.

"Well, you f*cked up!" he said. "You're careless!"

He went on and on.

"It's a small paperwork mistake," I said. "I can fix it. I'm not coming here for you to swing on me, you understand?"

I was still learning office politics. A month or so later, I made another error in judgment.

I'd seen one of our drivers on the road around lunchtime. The next morning, drinking coffee in the office, I remarked to Sherman, "Yeah, I saw Bob driving around yesterday."

"Oh yeah?" Sherman said. "When did you see him?"

"Oh, about noon when I was leaving home from lunch."

Sherman checked over the timecards. Bob, it seems, was buffering his hours.

To my chagrin, Sherman called Bob in.

Bob was a mechanic, a big strong guy.

"Jeff says he saw you at noon driving home."

"No, no, no," I said, "I just said that I saw you out and about."

"And you put 5 o'clock on your timecard," Sherman continued. "You're stealing from the company. You should probably be fired for this."

He went on and on.

Bob shot me a cold look.

When Sherman's tirade was over, I followed Bob out of the office.

"Listen," I said, "that isn't the way it went down."

I started apologizing.

"Get the f*ck away from me," Bob said.

Then he grabbed me by the neck and started choking me. None of the guys standing around moved to intervene.

I could barely breathe. I felt like I was passing out. I tried to break his grip. He had powerful hands. I struggled. I elbowed him in the ribs, trying desperately to get him off me.

He let go with one hand and drew it back in a fist. He was ready to drill me.

"Listen to me, let me talk," I stammered, gasping for breath.

He stared at me, then let me go. I felt my neck. It was raw.

"Listen to me, I would never tell on you. All I said was that I went home for lunch and that I saw you. It was an honest mistake. I promise you I did not tell on you. I did not mean to get you in trouble."

I was reasoning with him.

"All right, I understand," he finally said. "But next time you keep your mouth shut. Don't ever f*cking say you saw me again."

"I understand. I apologize. I never should have said a word to Sherman. All he did was use it against me."

It was a harsh lesson about the organizational pecking order.

I saw how it was now.

A subordinate like Bob had no qualms with getting away with what he could on company time.

A guy like Sherman in management looked for anything he could to bust a subordinate's balls and increase his own power.

And a guy like me could easily get caught in the middle. Better to mind my own business.

CHAPTER THIRTY-SIX: Cleaning up in Business, Briefly

I was still gung ho about finding some way to rake in money. It was tough making the monthly rent and utility bills plus living expenses in the house Drew and I were renting.

We were having fun there. We threw parties all the time. There wasn't much furniture: just two Lazy-Boy chairs, a television, stereo and our bedroom furnishings. But our place was perfect for our old friends from Reed to hang out. It was a fun pad. It quickly became a spot on the party circuit. We were popular. And we even found time to play Wiffle ball with the neighborhood kids down the street.

But we knew we were living beyond our means. I wondered what we could do to bring in more income.

One day in the office at Alpine Power & Equipment I came across a contract from a janitorial service. The service was charging $300 a month to clean the office. I couldn't believe it. The janitors were basically just sweeping up and dumping out the garbage.

I saw dollar signs.

I went home and told Drew we were going to start a nighttime janitorial service. "We're going to make some money." Drew was still working as a courtesy clerk at Smith's supermarket. He was game for my proposition.

I came up with the name "Executive Images." I figured we'd be working for executive-type companies, and "images" referred to clean images. We'd keep their professional workspaces up to par. I checked with the Nevada Secretary of State's office, and no one had that business name.

I saw no need for Drew or me to be trained. Janitorial work seemed simple enough. We'd vacuum, sweep up, dust, polish floors, clean windows, toss out the garbage, clean the restrooms — whatever it took.

We found a 24-inch buffer in the classified ads. The owner explained how to operate it with the wax. We borrowed vacuums from our parents, bought brooms and dustpans, sponges, rags and disinfectants, and were about ready for business. I got a business license.

I scanned a few legal books and drew up a standard service contract. What to charge? I called a few cleaning companies, posing as a small-business owner with an 1,800-square-foot office, and had bids faxed to me. I went down to Hidden Lode Explorations and printed out contracts at Mom's computer. Then I started making the rounds of offices where people I knew worked.

I was aggressive in my sales pitch. I wanted the place's cleaning contract. I could undercut the competition's price. What's more, my partner and I would be on call. We could show up with little advance notice if a place needed cleaning right away.

My first contract was with a Vietnamese woman named Sunny who owned a little manicurist salon in Sparks. Mom was a regular there, and told Sunny about my janitorial service. "He's a hard worker," Mom said. Best of all, I charged less than everyone else. Asians love deals. I knew that from living in the Philippines and Japan. I went down to the salon in a suit and tie, looking clean-cut, and negotiated a deal with Sunny. She was a high-strung, domineering little lady with a loud giggle and long nails. She was a tough-minded businesswoman, and added up the dollars and cents. Executive Images would sweep up and buff the floor and polish the mirrors. We'd come in Sunday nights for $100 a month.

"You better do good job!" Sunny said, her eyes flashing under extra-long lashes.

Executive Images was off the ground.

I landed a few more contracts. Most of the work was to be done after hours, when offices were closed. But as our business grew, some contracts called for daytime cleaning. I'd have to call in sick to AP&E to get the janitorial work done. After all, there were only Drew and I. That's how we kept our overhead down.

We began generating an income stream. I made the sales and managed the money, but I was fair with Drew, splitting profits 50-50. He worked as hard as I did, and we were mostly using his Toyota truck to get around to jobs. As we got busier, I began calling in sick more often to AP&E. After a few times, Sherman fired me over the phone.

He was gruff as usual, but I could tell he was happy.

"Y'know, this isn't working out. You're not showing up for work . . . so we're going to let you go."

"All right, fine," I said.

And it really was.

The janitorial business was taking off. I was making my own money. It was awesome being on my own. But it was scary, too. We were living month to month. We'd pay our bills, go out every night to whoever was scheduled, and hope that business kept increasing and that we didn't lose customers. Our business was grossing about $2,000 a month.

Things were going so well that I decided to let go of the safety net I'd had since the second semester of senior year in high school. I contacted my Army recruiter, Sgt. Acorn, to take myself out of the delayed-entry program. It took several phone calls over three weeks before I could even set up an appointment to meet with him. I was told he was out of the office for the day. I was told he was busy but would return my message. I was told he was at lunch. I was told he'd lost my paperwork and would have to send for copies, and would get back to me. And so on. These were tactics to prevent me from opting out.

Finally, I went down to the recruitment center and ambushed him.

He came out of his office as I was sitting in the lobby. He was short and buff, like I remembered him. He was unhappy to see me.

We sat in his office. Sgt. Acorn was pissed off when I announced my decision.

"Hey, we got you out of jail," he said. "We saved your butt from a lot of hot water, more than once. We were counting on you."

He was laying a guilt trip.

I thanked him for all his help, but said I was doing just fine in civilian life.

He started reviewing all the positive points of the program, all the occupations I had to choose from. And my college education would be paid for after I got out. Life would be good. Life would be easy.

He was using pressure tactics. But he wouldn't look me in the face when he spoke.

Finally, I said, "Maybe I'll go in in a couple years."

"No, you ain't ever going in now," he said.

I signed a bunch of forms and stood up to leave.

"Y'know, you're making a big mistake," Sgt. Acorn said. "Your country needs you."

DREW AND I WORKED hard, but managed to have fun, too. A lot of the customers just needed floors vacuumed. The buffing contracts were our favorites. Like Sunny's salon. It took about an hour to clean the place. Unlike some salons, her place didn't smell too bad, despite the chemicals used in permanents and pedicures. Sunny used top hair products such as Paul Mitchell. She also stocked her refrigerator with beer and wine for patrons. We helped ourselves.

After most of our cleaning was done, we'd have ourselves what we called "Buffer Rodeo." We'd gob wax onto the buffer's pad, then I'd sit on the buffer and hold the handle at shoulder level. Drew would stand on a chair and keep the cable off the floor.

"All right," I'd say. "Hit it."

I'd lift my feet up, sit in a crouch atop the buffer, and hit the trigger. The machine would whip around the floor. Drew would swing the cable away so I could keep going. The buffer would buck and jump and spin 360s. I held on, tossed around backward. Like bull riding, the object was to last eight seconds.

We'd be laughing our asses off. It was great being our own bosses.

But we hadn't found out yet about business cycles.

EXECUTIVE IMAGES HIT AN inevitable slow stretch. I didn't have my own car. That meant I had to ride the bus to get around, and schedule all our jobs around Drew's work hours at Smith's.

This made things really tough. After a couple months of struggling, I realized with our limited capital we couldn't ride out the slump. It was time to make some changes. I decided to pull the plug on Executive Images.

I sold our accounts to a competitor, Clean-Queen, and paid off our bills. We'd lasted a year. We'd done a good job for our customers. I chalked it up as good business experience. I'd also gotten a sweet taste of working for myself.

What to do now? Construction again? The notion repelled me.

I started thinking once more about the military. I regretted getting out of the delayed-entry program. I considered that had I gone in right after high school graduation I would have had my four-year commitment more than halfway done. I'd have gotten occupational training, and had savings built up, plus educational credits if I wanted computer courses. My interest in computers had not waned in the least.

I examined my options. I didn't have the capital to be in business for myself. Two years out of school, and I had no trade. I had no savings. I had no interest in, or means of attending, college or vocational school.

I needed to grow up.

SOME GUYS DREW AND I knew were drug dealers. We'd come across them on the party scene. They were selling heroin, cocaine or marijuana, supplied from people in San Francisco. The dealers would send a couple runners to San Fran to pick up the product and drive back over the mountains to Reno.

The few guys we knew selling drugs were taking in thousands of dollars. It was obscene. They were driving brand-new cars, and they were our age. They weren't anything special. They dressed in sweat pants or shorts with T-shirts and athletic shoes. They weren't in shape. In fact, they were sort of overweight and sloppy. In high school they'd just been stoner-types. But now they had hot girlfriends. And they had wads of cash. They sold to high school students, cheerleaders, parents, lawyers, business owners. Their customers were endless. And here, these guys could probably barely add up the cash they took in for the drugs they sold.

The coke dealers asked Drew and me to come in with them. But we didn't do drugs. We didn't believe in them. We saw what they did to people. Ugly scenes.

We went to a few of their parties. The alcohol flowed, the hot bodies were everywhere, the music was cranked up. White lines were being snorted in the kitchen, the dining room, the bathroom, the bedroom. It was a dangerous place to be as an observer. If you weren't doing drugs, you could be suspected of being a narc, or simply look so out of place you'd become a target for violence.

Fortunately, I had a reputation for being a little wild and crazy, so I fit in even though I never partook in the "party favors."

The parties were exciting at first. But then they depressed me. I saw some horrible things. There was a girl in my graduating class who'd been a cheerleader. She was incredibly beautiful and smart. But there she was, out on the lawn during one party, naked, coked up and drunk. Then there were the parties at adults' houses where the parents were addicts and their children were in their bedrooms, doors closed, in bed. I felt terrible for the kids. I'd leave.

One time, I found myself in a room in a dealer's pad — a low-rent apartment near the airport — where some of their customers, ex-convicts, were shooting up heroin between their toes, under their tongues and up in their eye sockets so their probie officers wouldn't detect needle tracks. Keeping these desperate lowlifes hooked up in their addictions was a sorry way to make a living.

And then there was the violence. Drew and I saw someone pull a gun at a party and take a shot at another addict. We saw a stabbing, too. It freaked us out. We didn't want any part of that.

We were really hurting for dough now that we'd sold Executive Images. Bills would be piling up very quickly. But the drug-dealing business just gave us the willies.

The coke dealers we knew ended up coming at us with a proposition. They knew Drew and I were good shots since we went out hunting and target shooting so much. The dealers had prepared a big sale in a room at a small hotel-casino in Reno. They asked Drew and me to act as security for them, packing small-caliber pistols and watching their backs.

This was getting out of hand. I told them we'd hang out and party with them, but we weren't getting into the business end of things. We didn't do that. We didn't want to be in a position to kill anybody for money.

They offered us $2,000 apiece per night.

Drew and I were amazed. That kind of money could keep the wolf from the door for a while. We talked it over among ourselves. We were wavering. But the night before the drug sale, I told Drew, "I've got a bad feeling. We've got to be out of town on this one, man. We can't hang around these guys."

We went out shooting that day in the desert, then went to dinner. When we got home we flipped on the 11 o'clock TV news. There was mention of a big drug bust at a local casino by the Consolidated Narcotics Unit. Drew and I stayed glued to the screen. Sure enough, the story topped the news hour.

There was footage of a team of officers in ball caps and windbreakers surrounding a hotel room, and suspects in handcuffs being led to a van. There were guns drawn, German shepherds barking, the works.

Our drug-dealer friends were heading to prison.

I thought to myself: *That's it. I'm going in the Army.*

To this day I have never even tried a drug unless you count alcohol. I am very proud of this, especially based on my surroundings.

I TOLD DREW I was leaving town to look at colleges in Arizona. I didn't want him being tempted to follow me.

I went to the recruiting office. Sgt. Acorn wasn't there. I signed up for a three-year stint with a different recruiter.

I came to learn later that Sgt. Acorn had gotten one of his female high school recruits pregnant. He no longer worked at the recruiting office. Guess his powers of persuasion backfired on him.

CHAPTER THIRTY-SEVEN: Stripes

It was May 1992 when I went to see the Army recruiter. U.S. military operations had been over for more than a year after ousting Saddam Hussein's troops from Kuwait. There was still a large American military presence in the region, though. Who knew if hostilities would flare up again? I was young and the thought of being sent to the Middle East excited me.

My plan for going in was simple: I wanted to do my time, earn money for studying computers in college, and get out. I wasn't going to be a career military guy. I wasn't going to try to become an officer. I wanted the smallest commitment that offered the biggest benefit. There was a mechanic's position that required a three-year enlistment. It gave full college benefits and full veteran's status.

I signed up. No chance to back out.

NOW THAT I'D COMMITTED, I got myself ready both mentally and physically. I was going to make the most of my enlistment. I started running every day, doing pushups and sit-ups, eating less and cutting back on sodas. I had information about the physical-training requirements. For example, I had to run two miles in 16 minutes. I reached that standard easily at Reno's 4,500-foot altitude.

Jennifer had just finished her enlistment; she'd gotten out early on a hardship tour, after giving birth to her daughter as a single mother. I was now an uncle. Jennifer and her fiancé, who'd gotten out a bit ahead of her, were living in Reno now. Hugo was a large guy — 6-foot-5, with a bodybuilder's physique — and had been in the Army like my sister. They told me what to expect in boot camp. That was invaluable! They told me what I needed to buy before I went in: toiletries, black shoe polish, and so on. They prepped me for basic training.

"It's just a game," Jennifer said. "Go in there and play their game. And don't smart off to the drill sergeants. They're going to get in your face, yell, try to break you."

I studied the recruitment packets for the basic knowledge I'd need. My sister lent me her military books. I pored over them. I memorized ranks, insignias, the Military Phonetic Alphabet, how to salute properly. It was fun. It was like a big Boy Scout club. I studied hard, using memory devices. "Be My Little General." That was a trick for remembering the ranks of generals: brigadier, major, lieutenant, and general. Just like my mind stored up data about computers, it absorbed the information about the military.

In June I got all my testing and physical examinations done. On July 23 I was sworn in at the processing facility in Oakland, California. A group of us five enlistees stood there and were asked to repeat a long speech about sacrificing ourselves for liberty and justice and defending the Constitution. Then we were put on a commercial airliner, seated with another seven recruits, and flown to Fort Jackson, South Carolina.

I looked around at the faces in our group. We were all young guys, in our late teens and early twenties. Just a whole bunch of kids together. A few of us had holes in our jeans and stunk a bit. Some among us looked like f*ckups getting a last chance to make something of themselves in life. I realized I was in that position myself. It was Army or jail for me. And I knew it wasn't going to be jail.

We talked on the flight about all the opportunities in the Army. It turned out about half of us were going in to earn money for college. All of us were eager to travel, to use the Army to see some of the world.

We got to Fort Jackson by bus from the airport about 1 in the morning. It was hot and muggy, reminding me of Panama City.

We all wanted to sleep. But there was no chance of that.

We were hurried off the bus. Sergeants were shouting orders.

We were issued canteens and told to keep them full. We did, filling them up at drinking fountains and sipping from the canteens constantly to keep from dehydrating in the heat. We weren't allowed to sleep those first 24 hours. We were led into larger groups of enlistees and processed through the various stations — big warehouse-looking buildings, noisy with voices yelling and talking. Sergeants herded us like dogs. "All right, let's go. Let's go to the next f*cking one. Are you f*cking paying attention to what I'm telling you?!"

We checked in at one station, stood in line and showed our identification to prove we were who we said we were. At another station we turned over what cash we had and were issued the amounts in travel checks, to prevent cash theft. We had our heads shaved, were issued our uniforms and briefly showed how to wear them, given two vaccination shots in each arm with air guns, handed our boots and other gear.

None of this was free to us, by the way. We had to pay for it out of our paychecks. Again, I knew what to expect.

We were assigned to our basic-training units. We were loaded onto buses that looked like converted cattle cars. When we got to our units we got off the buses, clutching our bags, and were met by noncommissioned officers screaming orders at us, trying to freak us out. They'd grab us by our bags and throw us stumbling across the way. I was ready for this. I took it calmly. It was part of the big process of deindividualizing.

We dumped out our personal items in front of everyone else and the sergeants looked through it all, then bagged up the belongings and tagged them for storage for two months. I had been warned about this drill. The psychological game was in full swing. I hadn't brought any photographs of Kelly, my girlfriend at the time. She had long, straight sandy-blond hair and was beautiful. I didn't want the sergeants talking sh*t. They found some girlfriend photos in recruits' bags and held the pictures up, smirking and saying comments like, "I bet your friends are f*cking your girl right now while you're here." The sergeants found candy in the bags of overweight recruits and harassed them by barking insults like, "You fat f*ck, you think you're going to eat this sh*t here?" Some of the grunts burst into tears.

It was dumb to me, but I understood why the sergeants did this. Their job was to break us down as individuals, then build us back up again as a team. When the sergeants got in my face, I avoided eye contact. They didn't talk any extra sh*t to me. They left me alone.

Then we had to hustle to our unit, and hustle to the barracks. We were exhausted. We were moving like zombies.

MY UNIT WAS A hodgepodge of America. There were only four of us from the West Coast. The rest came from the Midwest, East Coast and South. And there were only six whites; the remaining 30 or so were blacks or Latinos. Only one of us was a college kid: a guy who had a degree in aeronautics. He would be continuing on in Officer Candidate School, but like everyone else had to go through basic training.

My bunk mate, sleeping below me, was a black guy from Georgia. We got along just fine. He had a funny wit. The nice thing was, since we were all being beaten down together, there was no room for racial or social tensions. Once they shaved our heads and handed us uniforms, we all pretty much looked the same. We had to operate as a unit, pull up and succeed together. If one of us f*cked up, we'd all be punished. For the next eight weeks we'd have one common enemy: the sergeants. It was us against the U.S. Army.

We had a class on how to wear our uniforms. Everything in the Army was detailed, meticulous, and methodical. The drill sergeants used the words "surgeon" and "serial killer." That's how precise we had to be. I liked the discipline. I excelled at it. I actually relished inspections.

Basic training was easy enough for me. I had come into the Army in reasonably good shape, and got in condition quickly. What's more, a recruit from Colorado and myself were called "altitude babies" since we'd come from higher altitudes and now were at sea level. We had plenty of stamina. I knocked about two minutes off my time in the two-mile, running it in 12 minutes and change. I liked the obstacle courses. I liked the rifle range, since I'd been hunting so much, although I had to adjust to the M-16 and its open sights. What I disliked most was getting up at 4 in the morning and doing "P.T." — physical training — but I even adapted to the fatigue, and soon was able to rise early and function perfectly well.

There were discomforts, of course. I still cringe thinking about wrestling in the sawdust pits, with the sawdust getting inside my shirt and underwear, sticking to my sweaty skin. And then we'd have to march back, chafing and raw, in the sweltering, bug-infested heat. The pushups and sit-ups were a lot harder than a civilian would think. You had to reel off 40 pushups in a minute, and not every pushup was counted. You had to stare straight ahead and touch your chest on the ground, and if you didn't do it perfectly — or the sergeant wanted to mess with you — you could end up doing four or five pushups and having only one of them count. I was good at sit-ups, but my tailbone was still fractured from a fall while snowboarding. The bone would pop when I came up off my head and shoulders to touch my elbows to my bent knees. I'd twist a bit to the side to avoid the pain, and sometimes I'd get gigged for that. It was tough doing 60 counted sit-ups in a minute. One time I got in No. 60 just in the nick of time before the minute was up, and narrowly avoided failing the P.T. test.

The Army food was bland, except for the breaded veal. Most often, we'd have to choose between fish and chicken, and the chicken was boiled. The best thing to do was mix up the chicken, mashed potatoes and greens, or ham and eggs and grits, and pour Tabasco sauce over everything. You'd get maybe six minutes to eat, so you'd have to wolf it down. Every time after eating, they'd make us run. A lot of guys would double over, puking, but I kept my food in. I'd eaten quickly my whole life, Mom begging me to slow down. Now it was paying off. My digestive system was used to it.

I found to my great satisfaction that the military agreed with me. I was a model soldier. I was getting in rippling shape. I was staying out of trouble.

I felt like I'd made the right choice.

ONE DAY, FIVE OF us were grabbed out of the unit and told we were eligible for a special test. Our M.O.S. — military occupational specialty — was mechanic, and the Army was doing a special training program for mechanics who scored high enough on this test. If we passed, we wouldn't have to take 13 weeks of occupational training following boot camp. We'd be given a four-week A.I.T. — Advanced Individual Training — crash course.

I was excited. I hoped I'd do well on this written test. I'd already rebuilt engines and transmissions. We were brought into a little library. The test was about the basics: engines, rings, tune-ups, and so on. It was easy. I could identify and define O rings, compression rings, flywheels, starters, and the like. I ended up scoring 97 percent. The other four guys from my unit failed.

After my unit graduated from basic training, I stayed behind at Fort Jackson for an additional four weeks. Instead of going on leave like everyone else, I decided to save up my vacation time and go right into the training. I was sticking to my long-range plan, thinking ahead to cashing out my vacation time toward the end of my enlistment so I could leave early.

In A.I.T. I immediately noticed the change in the Army experience after boot camp. The yelling was over. A.I.T. was just intense classroom and hands-on educating. I learned about "PMCS" — Preventive Maintenance Checks and Services — and about trouble-shooting on HMMWV (High Mobility Multipurpose Wheeled Vehicle) and other Army vehicles. I ate this information up. I put to work my note-taking system I'd taught myself while taking the correspondence literature course the last semester of high school. I scribbled down highlights so thoroughly, my hand would cramp. As I sat through lectures and movies (there was very little use of books in the Army), I filled pages of my notebook while the other students took down little. The result: I only missed two test questions the whole month.

I finished as an "honor graduate," a first-ever academic honor for me. The only guy who scored higher than I, as a "distinguished honor graduate," had previously gone through mechanic's school at a vocational institute.

After only 12 weeks in the Army, I already was in my occupational position. It was awesome. I couldn't wait to get to my duty station to see how the rest of the military worked.

CHAPTER THIRTY-EIGHT: Deep in the Heart of Texas

When you enlist in the U.S. Army, you get to choose three places as preferences to be stationed. I chose Germany, Germany again, and Hawaii. I got neither. I was sent to Fort Hood, Texas. I couldn't believe it. Welcome to the Army!

I went immediately, again banking my vacation time. My plan was to work six months before going on leave. I didn't care to go home so soon. I was on an adventure and didn't feel a big need to see my old friends. I was even getting along just fine without female company.

As it happened, I got a letter not long after arriving at Fort Hood from my girlfriend, Kelly, saying she'd gone out with another guy and didn't think long distance was going to work out for us. I called and talked with her. But I wasn't very broken up. I took it in stride. The letters she'd written me every week had begun to grow less sweet and emotional, and shorter and shorter, and finally started closing with, "Well, I'm busy. I gotta run now."

Kelly was only a year out of high school. My idea for her to come live with me off base probably didn't sound that great to her anymore.

I was young, new in the military, with money in my pocket, learning new things. What did I care now about some girl 1,900 miles away?

I'd left that life behind. I called Drew, and told him I'd joined the military instead of going to college in Arizona. That was a shock to him. He had some shocking news for me, too. He'd gotten a high school girl pregnant, and now he was going to live with her and be a daddy.

I was so happy I'd pulled myself out of the Reno party environment, and had taken the big step to making a major change in my life. Even though the Army was no picnic — and Fort Hood no paradise.

Fort Hood is next to the town of Killeen, smack dab in the middle of Texas. On base we called the town, "Kill Me, Texas." It was only 45 minutes, though, from Austin, a town I came to love because of its music scene, art, and nightlife.

Fort Hood is the largest Army post in the nation, with lots of hills, oak trees and lush grass. It's home or workplace to about 40,000 soldiers, employees and their families, and encompasses more than 300 square miles. The huge northern section was where we conducted our training exercises.

I actually liked my posting. I was in Headquarters Company. My platoon sergeant was Tim Kent. He was from Southern California, which was a connection between us two. Sgt. Kent was a big guy — 6-foot-4 — and dark-haired with a toothbrush mustache. When I found out his hobby was hot rods, we hit it off instantly. He took me around base in his 1974 Fleetside Chevy pickup with a long bed. He was glad to have me aboard. He'd seen my A.I.T. test scores. He marveled that I'd scored second out of a class of hundreds.

My rank after Advanced Individual Training was private second class. My sister had already warned me that your rank doesn't say how good you are. The military's all politics, she warned. But I was happy to be a PV2. And

I was happy with my platoon sergeant. Tim Kent appreciated that I was a conscientious mechanic. We serviced the base's motor pool: HMMWVs, Cucv's (which are like modified commercial pickup trucks and Blazers), deuce-in-halfs (big troop-carrier trucks) and wreckers, which were 5-ton trucks with booms hanging off the back for recovering disabled vehicles. The motor pool was a fleet of 150 vehicles in all.

It wasn't likely I'd get shipped overseas since my unit, the 57th Signal Battalion, had just returned three months before from Operation Desert Storm. But my attitude was the same as most new soldiers: I wouldn't mind at all being shipped out. Everyone's job in the Army is as a soldier first; your occupational specialty comes second.

In the barracks I got to see videos and photos of the fighting that had happened in the Gulf. Some of the mechanics had been attached to Army Cavalry or Marine units. There was a photo of a severed head on a post by a road with a sign saying the road had been cleared compliments of a particular Marine unit. There was video footage of oilfields that had been set ablaze by retreating Iraqi troops. And there were pictures of bodies everywhere. You could see in the eyes of these veterans that to them, death was a joke. They made fun of it. It was because they were afraid of it. The images they'd brought home brought the war home to me. But I also felt pumped up and patriotic. We all felt that way.

I didn't start to feel disillusioned about the military until I'd been at Fort Hood a few months.

CHAPTER THIRTY-NINE: Being All They Could Be

Basic training and A.I.T. had been strictly regimented. Everything was down to a science, punctual, to the point, like a well-oiled machine. But now that I was on "permanent party," at my duty station, I saw that regular Army life was just like the real world.

There was alcohol abuse. And there was drug use — soldiers taking methamphetamine on base, and off-duty soldiers doing Ecstasy or LSD at the nightclubs in Austin. They'd buy the drugs in the clubs, put a hit on their tongue and swallow it down with a drink. They got away with it. The urine tests given to soldiers at that time checked only for a few drugs. The soldiers were going right back to the normal f*cked-up lives they'd had before joining the military.

There was theft. The motor pool lost wrenches and other tools. The pawnshops in town were full of Army gear. If you lost a piece of gear — say, night-vision goggles — out in the field during training maneuvers, you'd go to the pawnshops and buy a replacement.

There was blatant disregard for fairness and human dignity. This I would especially find out after a couple bitter tastes of base politics.

There was adultery. Wives of soldiers living off base would come on base when their husbands were out in the field for an extended period, and sleep with single guys in the barracks.

One time, a mechanic who worked with me in the motor pool had a wife who was screwing several guys in the barracks, in a very predatory way, while he was off deployed somewhere. She was banging one of my roommates. I didn't know she was the mechanic's wife. Back at the motor pool, I was talking about a scandalous woman I'd seen making the rounds of the barracks.

"Oh, what'd she look like?" the mechanic asked.

"Blond," I began, and described the rest of her.

Crack! He punched me in the face. Then he was on top of me, trying to choke me out.

"That's my wife, motherf*cker!"

He cooled down, though. Then he apologized.

It was hard on a marriage for a military couple. When a soldier got an order to go, he had to go. To keep a strong marriage, each partner had to be strong. Our commanders sometimes told us, "If we wanted you to have a wife, we'd issue you one."

There were other things that discouraged me about the Army. There was the astounding disorganization. Commanders wouldn't know what the hell was going on, and they'd give directives down to us, and then orders would change in a moment.

My unit was constantly deploying. In an instant we could be sent off to a battle zone. And 10 times during my tour, orders came that had us scrambling out of the barracks at a wee hour, getting our gear together, being issued weapons, standing for roll call. Six of those times we were told it was just an "alert." But four other times we ended up boarding planes and flying to a load-out center in Ontario, California, to be shipped somewhere overseas, probably the Middle East.

On the way to the load-out center there'd be zero discussion about our destination. Our imaginations raced. But each time we ended up being sent back to Fort Hood.

We didn't know if it had all been a drill, a test to see how fast we could load up. We were told it was just another "alert" and had been planned. Maybe we had really been ready to be deployed, but something had called it off. Or maybe some failure had existed in the chain of command.

In any event, it messed with our minds. And I knew that each alert wasted a lot of the money allotted to our brigade, platoon and company.

After a few false alerts, we began taking them in stride, not getting into the proper mental state to kill. That would have been dangerous in the case of a real deployment.

MY LIVING QUARTERS HAD three guys to a room. It was cozy, but livable. But the Air Force, which also had units at Fort Hood, assigned one soldier to the same-size quarters because anything more crowded was below Air Force living standards. That's the difference in service branches.

We three roomies got along adequately. We divided up cleaning duties. Since I had experience buffing floors, it was agreed I'd be in charge of that. I shined our floors to gleam like mirrors.

Everything is in flux in the Army. I ended up having 12 different roommates during my time at Fort Hood. While 10 were fine, a couple were questionable. They illustrated the mix of people you find in the military.

One of these questionable roommates was a guy named Bob. He was a real piece of work. He'd just gotten in under the age cutoff point, which at that time was 34. Bob was one of the people who'd felt they'd failed at life by the time they were in their thirties. They couldn't keep a job, or they'd gotten divorced, or they were alcoholics, so had joined the military. Better than floundering in the real world.

Our unit had its share of guys like Bob. They were lazy. They were untalented. But some of them would get rank quickly because the military thought they were more mature, given their advanced ages. They'd typically stall out at specialist, unable to pass the mental or physical tests to make sergeant.

Bob's background was that he was divorced with a kid to support. He also was screwed up in the head. Bob would drink beer and eat food that belonged to the other roommate or me. He drank a lot to fill the belly in his 6-foot-3-inch frame. He didn't bathe regularly. He was argumentative and would give us a hard time about everything. He was just a pain in the ass. In the middle of the night he'd be awake, jabbering about stuff.

Thankfully, one roommate I had for most of my first year was a guy named Joe Bosco, from Detroit. Joe was happy-go-lucky. He had a Calvin & Hobbes cartoon tattooed on an arm. His chief interests were drinking, smoking, hockey, and girls. He was cool, and he worked hard at his job, "cable dog," laying communication cable. Joe was a loyal roommate. He and I got along great. We trusted each other, and would leave our belongings out without fearing the other would pilfer them.

Joe and I also had an understanding. If one of us brought a girl to the room on a weekend, the other would be cool about it and head out to a movie or something.

There weren't many opportunities to meet girls in the Army, but there was this one brown-haired beauty I had an eye on. She was from somewhere in the South. She was very slender, but well built. The rumor was that she liked to date black men, and wasn't interested in white men.

One day, some of us were sitting outside the barracks, bullsh*tting, and she walked past us by herself.

The black soldiers started saying how hot she was, and that she didn't like "white meat." I challenged them to go talk to her. None wanted to. They teased me that I had no chance.

"I'll bet you 20 bucks that I'll go talk to this girl and she'll go out to dinner with me," I said.

They took me up on it. It sounded like easy money.

I caught up with her.

"Hey, wait a minute. What's your name?"

I introduced myself.

"I'm Sarah," she said. She was kind of quiet and shy, but polite.

"Maybe one time I could take you out for coffee."

She looked me over.

"I don't drink coffee."

"Well, tea."

"I don't drink tea."

"Well, beer. Something. Maybe I could take you out to dinner?"

She looked like she'd heard a million lines before.

"I just saw you talking to your friends over there. I'm sure you bet somebody you could get me to date you."

"No, I just wanted to get to know you. I've seen you for a while and I thought maybe we could go out, get something to eat."

"All right," she said. "We could go out this Friday if you want."

"All right, cool. I'll give you a call at your room Friday. Do you want me to drive?"

I'd bought an old Chevy pickup, and also a jet ski. There was a lake near the fort and I needed some off-base recreation.

"No, I'll drive," she said.

I took Sarah out to a nice dinner. There aren't too many decent spots in Killeen, so we went to a restaurant in a partially upscale hotel.

We had a good time. She was still quiet, demure, but we had some laughs. Then we went and saw a movie.

I didn't make any move that first night. I didn't even put my arm around her.

At the end of the date, as we parked at the base, I turned to her and said, "Thanks. Let me know if you want to go out again."

I could tell my courteous behavior surprised her greatly. She didn't know how to react.

"Uh, OK," she said.

This girl was real different. She seemed on guard. Later, thinking it over, I decided she wasn't used to dating a guy like me. There was a culture gap for her.

But I also wondered how this rather quiet and not very aggressive girl had ended up in the Army. I couldn't picture her getting through basic training, with the harsh yelling from the drill instructors, and the heavy physical training.

In the following days, some of the black guys in the unit — not the ones who were my friends — started giving me grief that she'd gone out with me. I didn't care. I was only interested in dating her that one time. I'd won my $20 bet.

To my surprise, Sarah called me up a few days later and asked me out for the weekend. This time when we went out, she loosened up and was a lot more fun. We went out for drinks, had some laughs.

At the end of the night, she said, "Well, let's go back to your room."

Bosco was in there, but he was passed out, snoring softly. When he got drunk, you couldn't wake him with a sledgehammer.

Sarah, for all her seeming shyness, turned out to be freaky. The quiet girl transformed into a wild animal. It was like Jekyll and Hyde.

Later, I asked, "So what does this mean?"

I considered that it would be cool to have a hot lover right there on base. And Sarah was steaming.

She looked at me strangely. "I kind of got a boyfriend."

My jaw dropped.

"If I'd have known you had a boyfriend, I never would have even talked to you!"

"Yeah, I know," she said. "I figured you're a nice guy and probably wouldn't if you had known."

Her boyfriend, I found out, was a sergeant who was stationed in Korea on a year's tour.

Then I learned that Sarah had been married to a guy in the boyfriend's unit, but while her husband had been stationed out in the field, the boyfriend — the husband's squad leader, in fact — was screwing around with her. Cheating was just her nature.

I ran into her from time to time on base after our date. But I didn't go out with her again. I avoided her. I knew she was trouble.

CHAPTER FORTY: Brush with a Medal

There were a couple lakes in the area, so I got to use my jet ski. I introduced Brad, who was a squad leader in my platoon, to jet skiing, and he went out and bought one. He and I would take off every weekend we could. It was a great escape. No matter what was going on in my life, once I got out there on the water, I'd be fine.

One Saturday, Brad and I were out at Stillhouse Lake. We'd come in from jet skiing and were hanging out on shore. Out on the water, something caught my eye. A man and woman were doing something truly stupid. The guy was driving a Kawasaki X2 jet ski, a small model, towing the woman in an inflated black inner tube. That was idiotic for two reasons. One, the craft wasn't strong enough to pull a tube behind it without wearing too hard on the machine. Two, it was unsafe because two people should've been on the jet ski — one to drive, and one to watch out for danger to the tuber being tugged behind. To make matters even more precarious, the boyfriend wasn't out in the middle of the lake. He was whipping his girlfriend around in the swim area, which was full of bathers and had boats coming in and out from the boat ramps.

Talk about dope on a rope! I kept watching. Sure enough, a bad situation unfolded.

A white-colored pontoon boat started out from a ramp. The pilot was a big fat man. He was swigging a can of beer. The boat approached the area where the jet ski was tugging the tuber. The boyfriend was watching his girlfriend in the tube; he wasn't paying attention to the oncoming craft.

"Hey, watch this," I said to Brad.

The pontoon boat closed in on the tuber. The pilot didn't seem to notice. Then, *boom!* The boat ran over the top of the inner tube.

The woman in the tube was wearing a black bathing suit. We saw her go between the two silver pontoons and hit the head of the motor in back. She flipped underneath the boat.

I watched for her to surface. She didn't. Her boyfriend hadn't even noticed. He kept skiing, maybe thinking the rope had just come loose.

I reacted fast.

"Go get the guy in the boat," I said to Brad. "I'll take care of her."

I didn't even take time to put a lifejacket on. I grabbed my jet ski, pulled it off the beach and threw it into the water. I gunned the engine and got to the spot so quickly I nearly hit the front of her head with the ski.

Her head was bobbing above the surface. She was screaming and sobbing. She was a brunette who looked to be in her thirties. She was barely treading water. Her efforts were feeble. She looked ready to go under.

I maneuvered behind to grab her, and killed the jet-ski engine. I dropped into the water beside her. I held onto the ski platform with one hand and hooked my other arm under her armpits. I hoisted her up until I could get my arm around her chest and then her waist. I got her up on top of me. Without a life jacket I was having trouble treading water. I fought to keep us above the surface. I knew I wouldn't be able to do it for much longer. We were about 60 yards from shore.

I made a decision: I'd have to let go of the jet ski and swim for it. But she was resisting. She was struggling against me. She'd gone hysterical.

"My legs are gone! I know my legs are gone!"

I knew I had to calm her down or we'd never make it.

"I got you. I promise you I won't let you go. Nothing more's going to happen to you. But I need you to quit flipping around. We're going to have to work together to get to shore."

"I can't feel my legs!"

"I'll tell you what. I'll check."

I braced for the worst. My nerves tingled. What if, when I reached down on her body, I felt stubs? I'd have no other choice but to fake it and lie to her so that I could get her to shore and save us.

My hand that was holding her up trembled as it slid down the side of her body. I felt her knees. I inched lower.

Calves . . .

Ankles . . .

Feet.

A wave of relief rushed to my brain.

I shifted the elbow of my arm holding her onto the tray of the jet ski. Thus balanced, with my other arm I hoisted her legs out of the water.

"See, your legs are here."

She nodded and exhaled. She began to relax. She stopped struggling against me.

"All right," I said. "We're going to swim in. I don't want you to do anything but lie on your back and hang tight. I got you. I won't let go."

With one arm around her, I started backstroking toward shore the best I could with my other arm. She was a tall woman, which made the task even harder. Every few yards I'd take a break from stroking, lift her out of the water and propel her behind me, then swim forward, catch her with the other arm and start stroking with a fresh arm.

We slowly made way.

It took about 10 minutes before I finally touched bottom with my feet. Her boyfriend had been far off on the lake when he'd finally noticed that his girlfriend was being helped to shore. He rode in. He killed his jet ski and came over and met me.

"Grab her," I told him, "but don't be too rough with her head or back. Pick her up like you're carrying her into the house, and get her to shore."

He was a big, buff guy. He lifted her up in a cradle hold and carried her to a picnic bench. An ambulance already had been called. The siren wailed in the distance.

My arms and lungs were burning. I stood panting, my feet on solid bottom in the shallow water. But I wasn't through. Brad had gotten on his jet ski and taken off after the pontoon boat, which continued out on the lake after the collision. I looked out and saw that he was out at the pontoon boat now. His jet ski was in the water, bouncing off the boat. Brad was up on the deck, taking on that asshole pilot alone.

Winded and spent though I was, I knew I had to get out there with him.

I turned around in the water and swam out toward my ski, which was floating some 50 yards away. Another jet skier had pulled up to it to keep it from drifting too far.

I climbed onto the ski and zoomed out to the pontoon boat. I got there quickly. I killed the ski engine and clambered aboard.

It was an ugly scene. The pilot was a big fat guy, about 6-foot-3, 300 pounds. And drunk. Brad already had taken the keys from him. I walked up, grabbed the fat guy in a clinch and slammed him down on the deck. I climbed on his back. I got his arms behind him. Brad knelt on his legs. We held him there as his wife and kid watched. The wife was crying.

"I can't believe we hit her," she said. "We were trying to get him to go back, but he didn't want to go back."

I was full of rage. I looked down at his face, which was sideways against the deck. "You're drinking and driving a boat, and you did this in front of your kid? You piece of sh*t!"

Brad and I got him up and sat him in a corner of the boat.

"Move, and we'll beat the sh*t out of you," Brad said.

He stayed put.

I went to the stern and raised up the leg of the outboard motor. The black inner tube was wrapped tightly around the propeller. This had obviously happened when the tube exploded against the blades. That had been a great stroke of luck. It had kept the blades from cutting the woman to death.

With the engine off, the pontoon boat floated in toward the beach and finally bumped against the sand and rocks.

Police were waiting. They took the driver into custody. Brad and I wrote out witness statements. And, as it turned out, not just for the local police. Some of the beachgoers were undercover Army Criminal Investigation Division officers. The CID polices the military, to make sure soldiers aren't breaking the law. One of the CID officers came up and identified himself. He said we had to write a report for the Army, too.

"Why the f*ck didn't you help us apprehend this guy?" I said. "You saw we were out there with this guy bigger than us."

"Well, I can only interfere with the military stuff," he said.

The injured woman now was being tended to by emergency medical technicians from the ambulance. She was doubly lucky in addition to the inner tube having twisted around the propeller blades. Her swimsuit was so tight on her, it had kept her lacerations from bleeding too badly. She'd been sliced open from her sternum to her navel, and on both sides of her crotch area. She had a big knot on her head from the impact with the boat.

She didn't say thank you to me. Her boyfriend, however, did. It turned out he was a high-ranking enlisted man in the tank division on base.

The ambulance took her to the hospital on base. Meanwhile, workers from the boat-rental business were cutting the rubber tube off the propeller blades.

I marveled again at how lucky she'd been. And without my quick reaction, she would have drowned for sure. Her legs had been temporarily paralyzed.

The pilot of the pontoon boat was arrested. But I don't think he got in that much legal trouble. I'm sure he came up with his version of events. The accident had been mostly the jet ski driver's fault for towing a tube in an area he shouldn't have been. But the pontoon boat pilot, too, shouldn't have been drinking and boating.

It turned out he was some government worker. I saw him and his pickup truck on base a few months later.

I had nightmares about the incident off and on. That an accident like that could happen so easily, so quickly, so catastrophically, when you're just out there relaxing and having fun, unnerved me. I'd heard stories about people getting killed on the lake. It seemed stupid to me. I parked my jet ski and didn't go out on it again for nearly a year. And I didn't go back to Stillhouse Lake.

As it happened, I couldn't put the incident behind me right away. Brad recommended me to my squad leader for a commendation. The squad leader recommended me to our platoon sergeant, Tim Kent. The recommendation continued up the chain of command, and to my surprise, one morning not long after, with the platoon in formation, the captain announced that Private Bowling had performed a meritorious act that saved a woman's life. The facts were recounted.

The captain said I was being recommended for the Soldier's Medal.

"What do you think about that, Private Bowling?"

I felt embarrassed. "Well, I don't think I deserve the medal, sir. I think that everybody probably would have done that."

"No, everybody wouldn't have done that."

"Well, I really don't want the medal."

I could hear exclamations of disbelief all around me.

Tim Kent was pissed off.

"Bowling, you need this medal," he told me later. "This specialized medal, people don't have."

"Well, everybody would have done what I did," I said. "If it had been me out there drowning, I would hope that someone would have come out and saved me."

About a week later, I realized how foolish I'd been. Most people turn into bystanders during a crisis, and it had been no different out there on the lake. But I couldn't very well go back to the captain and tell him I'd changed my mind. I'd have had to eat a lot of sh*t, as well as swallow my pride. And back then, I had a sh*t load of young, dumb pride.

One of my big regrets in life is turning down that medal. Someone high up in the president's administration would have pinned the medal on me. It would have been a big to-do, with a ceremony. And I would have had a medal on my uniform that very few have.

CHAPTER FORTY-ONE: A Bad Taste of Bacon

I loved working in the motor pool. Sgt. Kent was a skilled mechanic and appreciated my dedication. I saw how some operational procedures could be improved in how vehicles were serviced, and even though I was this little private guy, I started voicing my opinions.

Sgt. Kent listened to me. He liked my ideas. He started changing some of the rules for turning in service logs and orders. I had a business mentality. I saw how our service schedules could work more efficiently so the various specialists could get their jobs done with less down time. I started training users how to drive and care for the HMMWVs and other vehicles so they wouldn't break down as often.

I increased the motor pool's efficiency to where every vehicle was repaired. Usually it took an entire year to get every vehicle fixed and ready to go. We mechanics began having free time. We'd leave the motor pool and go work out or something. I felt like I was accomplishing a lot. But I knew there were limits. While Sgt. Kent and the other mechanics listened to me in the motor pool, the brass in company headquarters weren't interested in hearing the ideas from a peon grease monkey.

Getting promoted was problematic. Because of Affirmative Action, nonwhites were up for promotion before whites. I'd have to wait until nonwhites of my rank passed their physical-training exams before I'd get a turn. I had to help them pass their tests so I'd get my chance.

There were two guys in my unit who were roadblocks for me. One was overweight, the other was just plain unmotivated. I went to their barracks and hit them up. "You guys know that you're holding my promotion up because you guys can't pass your P.T. test. I'll help you guys pass if you want to."

"Man," the lazy one said, "we don't give a f*ck about that sh*t."

"Well, I give a sh*t," I said. "I want to earn rank. You're the last two dumb f*cks in the unit that haven't been promoted. And I'm behind you."

Every day after that, I ran with them, trying to get their pace up closer to mine. "Pick it up!" I'd yell, pushing them. I knew from my rhythm what my pace was, and where they had to be to hit their mark. All I cared about was getting them to pass their tests so I would have my chance. I told them that they better pass their tests because having failed previous ones meant they were on the verge of being put "on profile," which meant privileges such as leave being revoked. I also told them that when they got more rank, they'd get more money.

But most of all, after they passed they wouldn't have me f*cking with them anymore.

"I'll be on you relentlessly if you don't pass your next test." And I meant it. What was the military going to do — kick me out?

They started running faster, trying harder.

"I can't finish, I can't," one or the other would start whining, as a side ache burned in.

"You sissy," I'd say. "We've only gone a mile. There's one more to go."

They ended up passing their tests, just squeaking by. And I was now in line for a promotion.

Despite the quota system, I couldn't complain about my position. I had it good at the motor pool. Sgt. Kent was a career Army man. He and his wife lived off base. She was pregnant with their second child. As I said before, he built hot rods as a hobby. I'd take my jet ski out to his place to work on it on some weekends. His family kind of adopted me. His wife, Stephanie, was outgoing, a little boisterous at times, and friendly to me. She made me feel at home. The Kents' house was like my family home away from home.

In January, I finally went on leave. I'd spend two weeks back in Reno. The snowfall was heavy that winter and I went skiing and snowboarding with Drew for a whole week. He was happy to hang out with me. It was tough going for him, with his teenage wife and newborn baby girl. He needed to get out of the house. I saw my baby niece, Brianna, who'd been born to my sister, Jennifer, who had married her boyfriend, Hugo. I met up with some girls I'd known before. I went out and partied. It felt like I'd never left.

When it was time to return to Fort Hood, I was really sad. That's when the loneliness of being in the military really hit me. I had two-and-a-half years to go before my discharge.

When I came back to base, I learned there was a huge war-games exercise going on in the desert outside Bakersfield. The battalion colonel needed a mechanic. No one wanted to volunteer for the duty, which meant living out in the desert for 30 days.

I volunteered. I thought it'd help me get some rank. Sgt. Kent was happy. It would make him look good to send someone from our unit. I packed up my gear, and off I went. I already had made a name for myself in the battalion as a decent mechanic. When the colonels sent their vehicles for servicing at the motor pool, they'd demand that Private Bowling be the one to work on it.

My duty in the war games turned out to be more of a challenge than expected. I was put in with a messed-up unit. These guys had a reputation for screwing up everything. They were called the "Delta Dogs" because all the f*ckups were assigned to it. They couldn't do their jobs. They were half-assed about everything. That was their morale.

I was given a wrecker to operate. Soon, I was busy picking up stalled vehicles in the desert, towing them into camp. Then the transfer case on my wrecker went out. It wasn't our unit's echelon to order a part. An echelon above us had to do it. It took several days for a new transfer case to arrive. In the meantime, since I wasn't part of the regular Delta Company, I was assigned to KP duty. I was scrubbing pots and pans from 5 a.m. to 8 p.m. The only benefit was getting to eat as much as I liked.

During my time on KP, I became friends with the mess sergeant in charge of the cooks. Sgt. Campbell was a guy from the Deep South with a strong drawl and his own way of doing things. In the kitchen, he was in total command. Making friends with him was a good move. In the Army, it's said, you make friends with the mechanics, the cooks and the supply clerks, because they take care of you. Most soldiers despise the cooks as lesser beings, but I knew they had a tough job — rising at 2 a.m. to start cooking, then cleaning up all day after that. I respected them.

Before I'd been assigned to KP, I'd done them a good turn. I'd towed in their deuce-and-a-half that had a broken fuel pump, and then went out of my way to replace it. I'd re-primed the engine, getting all the air out of the fuel lines, which was a messy job. They loved me after that. From then on, they'd bring me Frosted Flakes (which usually disappeared early in the morning) and plates of food to my tent so I didn't have to wait in line. My KP duty ended up being very bearable, and the head cook made sure I ate as much as I liked.

Little did I know, I was about to be rescued from the Delta Dogs. It seems the battalion colonel had been calling around, trying to locate me because of my reputation at Fort Hood's motor pool. Finally, he found me, and I was appointed to his command area. He needed me to look at his personal vehicle.

The mechanics in Delta Company were pissed.

"See ya," I said. "No more KP for me."

There were 20 vehicles at the headquarters area, and only a generator mechanic and me to care for them. But I told the battalion colonel that we two mechanics could handle it. Indeed, we kept the whole fleet of 20 vehicles running ourselves. We knew people in supply at Fort Hood whom we could contact by radio. I knew all the signal people manning the secured transmission from working on their vehicles. I'd call Sgt. Kent, too. He'd help us arrange supplies from California bases. We had units dropping off oil and filters — whatever we needed.

The colonel was pleased and impressed. "I don't know if I want to know how you're getting all this sh*t, but everything's running, so f*ck it."

It was kind of a downer turning 21 out there in the desert that February, not being able to go to a bar, but at least I was having fun now. In fact, I ended up getting an Army Achievement Medal for keeping the colonel's fleet going.

One time toward the end of the war games, I called Sgt. Kent to check in. He broke the news that he'd gotten promoted to staff sergeant. I was happy for him. Unfortunately, he said, there already was a staff sergeant in the unit, so he was being transferred to Charlie Company. That meant I wasn't going to be able to work with him anymore.

I wondered who his replacement would be as platoon sergeant.

WHEN I GOT BACK to Fort Hood, I found out that Sgt. Kent's replacement in our company was one Sgt. Bacon.

Sgt. Bacon was from the South and three years older than I. He'd been stationed in Korea and thus had risen more quickly in rank than he should have. His presence was unimpressive. He was about 5-foot-8 and very skinny — a little weasel, just like his personality.

Sgt. Bacon stuttered badly in every sentence: "Go over there and and and . . . check out . . . check out . . . that that . . . vehicle." If you finished a sentence for him, he'd get very pissed. "Don't fin-finish my my sentences!" He was ignorant as sh*t when it came to working on vehicles. In fact, he was plain ignorant about life.

My experience with Sgt. Bacon proved to me that the military was not for everyone. I had to exercise extreme compassion and blinded judgment to cope with him, because his rank dictated his authority over me. But even my concerted efforts to get along with him didn't help.

We clashed. Repeatedly. He immediately began negating all the procedural improvements I'd made in the motor pool. We were back to being inefficient. He couldn't help himself. He was plain dumb, and he didn't care to learn. It was sheer torture for me.

Sgt. Bacon simply was not a mechanic. His judgment on vehicles wasn't accurate. I argued with him. That's how I received my first Article 15 — a general letter of reprimand. It cost me a month's pay and earned me a trip in front of the battalion colonel, Col. Pearl.

Col. Pearl let me off easy. He said he knew me, knew I worked hard. I'd just have to clean up my act, he said.

The mechanics around me saw what hell it was for me in the motor pool, but knew they had to put up with Sgt. Bacon. He'd been assigned to the motor pool for three years. I still had about 26 months left.

I asked my friend, Tim Kent, what to do about Bacon. Sgt. Kent told me I could put in for another unit. The Army did one-to-one switches. If, say, there was a mechanic in Arizona who wanted to switch to Texas, it could be arranged. There was a bulletin-board system at bases. I mailed out requests and found a prospect at Sierra Army Depot in Herlong, California, an hour north of Reno. It seemed perfect. I could move back home.

Wouldn't you know it — the battalion colonel wouldn't hear of it.

I had to go in front of him to request my transfer. Col. Pearl wasn't about to let his best mechanic go. I complained that I couldn't work with the new sergeant. The colonel had to support the man of higher rank, though.

"Sometimes in the military you gotta deal with these type of people, private," he said.

I was really on the outs with Sgt. Bacon now. It grew worse and worse. Finally I just started finishing his sentences for him.

"I don't have time to listen to you all day babbling," I'd say. The politeness was long gone.

Sgt. Bacon, of course, knew he had the upper hand. He actually seemed to relish the tension between us. It gave him a chance to come down on me. He started bragging to others about how he was putting me down. The talk got back to me. I finally had enough of it.

We were off duty. I found him standing outside the barracks with some of his buddies, smoking and joking.

"There go Bowling, sarge."

They were laughing. It was funny to them.

I walked straight up to Bacon.

"Let's just put our rank aside and fight this out," I said. "Let's do this old school. Let's go around back and fight it out. You don't have to write me up."

His friends were watching.

"I could get you fo-for in-in-in-subordination."

"Get me," I said. "Let's go. Let's see how bad you are. You whip my ass, I'll do whatever you say the whole time I'm here."

"This isn't . . . isn't . . . very pro-pro-professional. It's not the-the-the military way."

I got nose to nose with him. "You are weak."

I walked away, leaving him with lost face in front of his pals.

Sgt. Bacon was all show and no go. But he was a weasel. He was waiting for his moment to pull rank and bust me down.

Sgt. Bacon had never been in Texas before, and had no clue about the thick mud. I'd been driving a wrecker around, and was well acquainted with conditions. I knew how easily a vehicle could get stuck.

One day, we got a call at the motor pool from a guy in a HMMWV stuck out in the mud during a training exercise. I fired up the wrecker.

"What are you doing?" Sgt. Bacon asked. "Take the-the Blazer out and tow him out with that."

The Blazer was a CUCV, which weighed half as much as a HMMWV.

"Why?" I asked.

"Well, it's raining out right n-now and I don't wan-want to get the wrecker stuck."

"We're not going to get the wrecker stuck," I said.

The winch was 300 feet long. I wouldn't get the wrecker anywhere near the bog.

"If he's in the mud, you aren't going to get him out with the Blazer," I protested.

Sgt. Bacon wouldn't hear of it. He insisted I take the Blazer.

I grabbed my "shotgun," my navigator, who was a mechanic with the rank of specialist, and loaded up the wrecker. Sgt. Bacon watched.

"OK, fine, go," he said.

I figured he was OK with it.

Sure enough, the HMMWV was in mud up to the top of its tires. There would have been no way to tow it out with the CUCV. We had to winch it out. We hooked it up and darn near broke its axles getting it out.

We had the HMMWV driver, a staff sergeant, climb in our cab and we drove back to the motor pool. We went to the spray point and had the HMMWV hosed off. The staff sergeant checked it for damage. It was fine. He was happy.

When I walked back into the motor pool, Sgt. Bacon was waiting with Staff Sgt. Bard, a borderline human who chewed tobacco so much his teeth were blackened and falling out. It looked like coffee grounds were stuck between his teeth. He was chubby, and I had no clue how he'd gotten his rank or lived this long. He was known to completely lack ambition and personal hygiene.

Sgt. Bard was so obtuse, he'd see me reading *Entrepreneur* magazine and ask, "What are you reading 'opti-manure' for?"

"C'mon, we've got a meeting with the captain," Sgt. Bard said.

I went with him to the captain's office.

At that time, I was up to be promoted from private first class to specialist. In the captain's office, the captain said, "Well, we've got your promotion sitting here for specialist right now, but I'm not going to give it to you."

Why? Because I'd disobeyed orders.

I got mad.

I explained to the captain that the HMMWV had been up to its hubs in mud. Using the wrecker had been the only way to tow it out.

The captain said I'd still disobeyed the sergeant.

I couldn't believe it!

"But his order had been the wrong move. It was the wrong thing to do," I said.

No matter. The military had its own system of logic.

Not only wasn't I getting my promotion, but I was being busted down a rank, the captain said. I'd be a private second class again, earning less pay. And on top of that, I was being docked another month's pay.

I was seething. I was red hot. I could picture in my mind the stupid, grinning face of Sgt. Bacon. And there was Staff Sgt. Bard, beside me, his dumb-as-a-sack-of-hammers face smiling.

"This is criminal, that a mechanically challenged individual like this" — I gestured at Bacon — "can tell a certified mechanic like myself what to do when I have been assigned as the authority in wrecking for the battalion."

"At ease, at ease," the captain said.

He dismissed Bacon and Bard. He tried to talk me down.

"Listen," I said. "I've been driving the wrecker a long time. I've been stationed here at this post. I know the conditions, including the mud. This guy just came here from Korea. He's not even a mechanic; he changed his MOS and was transferred from supply."

It was true. Sgt. Bacon never turned a wrench once when I was there. Sgt. Kent always turned wrenches with us. Bacon didn't know how to. Instead of learning with us, he just ridiculed us.

The captain asked what I wanted to do.

"I got to get the hell out of this unit," I replied.

I went in front of Col. Pearl again to request a transfer.

"Jesus Christ, Jeff, this is the second time."

I told him I knew he wanted me as a mechanic, but I was having a hard time with Bacon.

Sgt. Kent was a couple mechanics short in Charlie Company. He had come to my hearing. Now, he spoke up for me.

"Listen, colonel," he said, "I really need Jeff in Charlie Company, and you can still have your vehicles serviced with us. I will retrain Jeff and get him back to military standards."

Col. Pearl liked Tim. "All right, I'll give you your guy," the colonel said.

Bam. I was transferred to Tim's unit, which was located in the motor pool behind Bacon's. I started doing my own program again.

Bacon was pissed. But Tim outranked him. He went to Bacon and said if he had any problems with me to come to him. "Don't f*ck with Jeff. Don't even talk to him."

I moved into my new barracks. Everything was cool again. Six months later, I was back to private first class, and six months after that I got my specialist rank.

BEFORE I GOT MY transfer to Charlie Company, there was one other messed-up personal situation I had to cope with besides my run-in with Bacon.

Every morning we lined up in platoons for formation. One day, the first sergeant said to our squad sergeant: "Sgt. Smith, you need to take Private

Bowling to CID. They want to question him."

CID, as I said earlier, is the Criminal Investigation Division of the Army. It's composed of investigators who work undercover — wearing different uniforms of different ranks, and sometimes civilian clothes, as situations call for — and do their best to bust people for drugs or other violations. They can pose as just another soldier or officer on base, befriend you, and then, one day, nail you. They're despised. They are essentially what Internal Affairs are to cops.

Sgt. Smith moved to escort me to the CID office on base. The other soldiers in the platoon looked over at me with surprise and pity. I could feel 150 pairs of eyes on me.

I was immediately nervous and confused. *What the heck was this all about?* But just as quickly, I began controlling myself. I drew deep breaths. I considered that I hadn't done anything wrong. No one had told me any secrets that could make me an accomplice to wrongdoing. So there was nothing to be upset about.

Well, no sense getting uptight before I found out what was going on . . .

As Sgt. Smith and I began walking, I got into character. I pictured what lay ahead. I'd have to sit down in an investigation room, and I'd have to present myself as cool, calm and collected, no matter what I was asked. I reminded myself that I hadn't done anything. Therefore, there was nothing to be anxious about.

It would take about 15 minutes to return to the barracks so I could get in my battle-dress uniform (BDU's) and then proceed to the CID office. I would use this time to compose and prepare myself. Whatever charges they'd hit me with, I'd deny. I'd be strong.

"Do you know what this is in regards to?" the sergeant asked me as we walked to the barracks.

"No, do you know what this is in regards to?" I asked.

"No, but we'll find out when we get there," he said.

Sgt. Smith walked me to CID. He waited in the outer office while an investigator led me to an interview room. I considered the irony of the situation. It was lose-lose. Maybe I was being busted for something — although I could not remotely think of what it might be. But if not, if it was just some misunderstanding that had to be cleared up, and I wasn't being busted for something? The fact alone that I'd been in the CID office without facing punishment would cast suspicion on me among the soldiers in the platoon that I was some sort of informant. I'd become an outsider.

Being grilled by CID was also like being in prison. You don't have the right to an attorney. You're questioned, and you're required to answer. No such thing as exercising your rights under the Fifth Amendment. You didn't enjoy those rights in the service.

I was brought into an interview room.

"Do you know why you're here?" the CID officer asked.

"Nope."

"Apparently, some stuff was stolen in Nevada and witnesses have reported you to the police."

"I haven't been home in over a year except in February."

The CID officer picked up a report and began reading off names of three guys I knew back home.

"Do you know these men?"

"Yeah, I went to high school with them."

It turned out that several jet skis had been stolen in California. The guys who'd stolen them were busted at a lake, and when police discovered the jet skis had been stolen, the guys gave the story that they were borrowing the jet skis from *me*, who, they said, had given them permission to use the jet skis while I was in the service. The guys wrote this down in their police statements. Those statements were sent to Reno police, who charged me with the jet skis' theft.

I looked at copies of the statements. It was obvious to me from their messy handwriting and choppy sentences that they were afraid of going to jail, so they'd cooked up the story about me, knowing I was away. One of the guys had gone on and on, really implicating me as claiming the skis were mine; but the other two guys had said very little in their statements, just backing up the basic story line of thinking it was OK to use the skis, though they weren't sure if the skis were Jeff Bowling's.

I was pissed! I read each of the signed signatures, picturing the guys' faces. I resolved to take leave that summer and go back to Reno and handle this with them — especially the one who'd gone out of his way to blame me.

"I don't think you did it," the CID officer said. "I looked at your record and your leave time, and you haven't been absent, ever."

In other words, the date that the skis were stolen back in Reno did not match up with my one military leave. I had been in basic training during the time of the theft.

Now I was relaxed. It was obviously a false report. I wasn't in hot water.

Still, for procedure's sake, he gave me a polygraph test.

He put a heart-rate monitor on me. He fixed electrodes to my temples and my wrists. Narrow tubes ran from the devices to a board on the CID officer's desk. On the board were two styluses that would make marks on graph paper moving slowly over the board. The polygraph machine would measure fluctuations in my heart rate, respiratory rate, blood pressure and sweat gland activity.

The officer began by asking me simple questions to ensure the polygraph was working right and that he could detect a lie by the graph fluctuations.

"What's your mother's maiden name?"

"Wilkinson."

The officer ticked off on the paper where the marks started before the question, and where the marks ended after I answered a question.

"Are you sure that's your Mom's maiden name?"

"Yeah."

The machine measured my response as a lie.

"What's your last name?"

"Bowling."

The polygraph showed that to be incorrect, also. The machine probably wasn't properly calibrated.

The military.

The CID officer proceeded with a host of questions, some whose answers were obvious, and some meant to trip me up about the alleged thefts of the jet skis. In the end, he was satisfied of my innocence. But he asked me to sign a statement against the guys back home who'd lied about me stealing. The military could prosecute them under federal laws that protect soldiers against being falsely accused of crimes.

I decided to myself I couldn't do that without getting the whole story from the guys.

"I don't have any information to give you. I was in basic training at the time. I don't know anything about this."

He told me it was my duty as a soldier to tell him whatever I could.

I told him all I knew was the jet skis weren't mine.

He told me that if the military didn't prosecute the false witnesses, the Reno city attorney would.

That was fine with me. There was nothing I could do to prevent it.

Outside CID, walking back to our unit, I told Sgt. Smith what had gone down in the interview room. I knew he had a big mouth and would spread the word.

Back at the barracks, I told Joe Bosco about the interrogation.

"That's f*cked up, man," he said. "I'd go back and kick their asses."

For the next couple weeks, the other soldiers in the platoon watched me warily. Eventually word got around that it had been an issue from back home, and that I was innocent.

I knew I had to take care of business back home. Telecommunications on base are monitored, and I wanted to keep my business private, so I went off post for lunch one day and got on a payphone outside a Pizza Hut. I called up two of the guys back home and asked, "Is there anything I should know about?"

I explained that I'd been called into a criminal investigation on base about stolen property back in Reno, and I'd read some statements signed by them.

"What the hell is going on?" I demanded.

They explained about getting busted with the stolen jet skis, and about the one guy blabbing his mouth about me.

"I'll tell you what," I said. "This summer I'll be down, and I'll see you guys then and take care of this."

"What do you think we should do?" they asked.

"You should get an attorney because they're going to come after you," I said.

That summer I did go back to Reno. I hit up each of those guys at their homes and confronted them.

The city attorney did harass them for months, too, before dropping charges. They deserved it.

CHAPTER FORTY-TWO: A Reputation Ruined

A sad thing happened while I was in Charlie Company.

There were three mechanics who weren't very good at their work, and who were very disgruntled. Malcontents by nature. One, André was a weird fellow who was trying to get kicked out of the Army by either being gay or pretending he was. He really laid it on, complete with a limp wrist, as if he was mocking the stereotype of gay men. One time he even came to the motor pool in makeup, with his nails glossed. He couldn't correctly say sergeant; he'd pronounce the "g" as a hard consonant.

Another malcontent was a single mom, Annette, who used her baby as an excuse for time off, claiming the child was ill or this or that. She presented a quiet, timid persona. Annette was adept at playing the vulnerable victim. She mentioned one time that she'd just bought furniture and didn't know how she was going to get it home from the store. Some of us guys from the motor pool went on our day off and lugged her tables, chairs and sofa from the store to her house. To our surprise, Annette's boyfriend didn't show up to help out. Also to our surprise, Annette did not even thank us. It was like she'd expected the help all along. Over time, we realized she despised us, for whatever reason. She was a person simmering with anger toward the world. Even the other girls in the unit wouldn't hang out with her, saying, "She's just a bitch!"

The third troublemaker was a guy named Jayson, who was a flat-out sex and drug addict. One time on training maneuvers in the field, we'd had to get a medic over to him because he was complaining that his penis was burning. It was dripping. A tube had to be inserted up it: we called it "getting the silver bullet." He suffered from some STD. I think it was gonorrhea. I wasn't surprised. He and his roommate brought the most vile whores into their rooms. Off duty, Jayson was always smoking a joint or had a glass of gin and juice in his hand. His skin did not radiate a healthy glow.

Charlie Company had a lot more vehicles to service than Headquarters Company. It was a heavy workload, and Sgt. Kent had us on a relentless schedule. The three malcontents didn't appreciate this. They banded together and evidently came up with a scheme. One night after the rest of us had left the motor pool, the three stayed behind and met with Sgt. Kent. A few days later, they started leveling accusations at him, saying he was harassing them. They claimed he was making unprofessional and insensitive comments and even had engaged in lewd contact with Annette.

All this had allegedly taken place the night the three had been alone with Sgt. Kent. They were the only witnesses. There were no counter-witnesses.

Sgt. Kent was called in and quizzed by his commanding officer. Then two of us mechanics who had attended a sensitivity-training workshop were pulled in and questioned.

Had we ever heard Sgt. Kent make suggestive remarks? What about racist remarks? Had we ever seen him slap so-and-so's butt?

I was incensed. In the old Army, if you had a problem with your superior, the unwritten code said you confronted him and talked it out and, if that didn't resolve it, you whipped his ass if you could and made him think your way. But in the new, politically correct Army, with Affirmative Action and sexual-harassment rules in place, a troublemaker could really toy with a superior.

Hearings were set. Sgt. Kent was really shook up. He had 12 years in and wanted to do his 20 to earn his pension and retire. He had a wife and two young children.

I stayed at his house the weekend before the hearings.

"Listen," he said to me, "I'm in a lot of trouble. These guys are making up all these lies and there are no other witnesses since they were the only ones at the motor pool. I don't know what to do."

"I'm your witness, man," I said. "I know how good you are. I know these people are liars."

"I've got a hearing on Friday. I might get busted down in rank. I don't know what to do. And you're right: they're lying."

The hearing was in front of Col. Pearl. I showed up as a character witness to defend the sergeant.

"Now you see the guy before you," I said. " You must remember how Sgt. Kent fixed me."

I played to the colonel's ego, hitting on the fact that he had made the right move in trusting Sgt. Kent with me, transferring me to Charlie Company, after my friction with Sgt. Bacon.

"I know he turned you around," the colonel said.

The three accusers — André, Annette and Jayson — were sitting behind me. I turned and faced them. I addressed them directly.

"Now you three know that these accusations are false, and the only reason you're bringing these accusations against him is because he's making you work, and you don't like it."

They sat there not saying a word.

"This guy's got two kids, a family," I continued. "He's a career person. He's got all these awards. He's been in 12 years. Everybody else likes him. This is entirely wrong what you're doing."

But no one else in the motor pool would speak out on the sergeant's behalf. I couldn't understand why.

As other mechanics were called and questioned by the colonel, they mostly gave simple "yes" and "no" answers. They were playing it straight, not taking sides, not testifying as to the sergeant's good character. *Had they been at the motor pool on the day in question?* Either a simple yes or no. *Did they know anything that would corroborate or counter the allegations?* No. They knew nothing.

Not one of these men or women wanted to get in the middle of this. After all, they didn't know what the outcome would be. They played it straight down the middle.

Just politics.

At the end of the hearings, the three accusers said they were going to bring up even more charges. The colonel felt he had to bring the case to a close, so for expediency he busted Sgt. Kent down a rank to E-5: a demotion from staff sergeant to sergeant. And this proved fatal to Tim Kent's military career.

CHAPTER FORTY-TWO: A Reputation Ruined

The Army had a rule that if you're still at E-5 after 12 years, you were given an automatic out. Sgt. Kent had to take an early retirement. In a few more months he'd be a civilian.

I was sickened. Any small notion I'd entertained of re-enlisting, maybe even making a career in the Army, was dead. Subtracting the three months of leave time (the maximum allowed), I had six months left. I resolved that I'd just do my time and leave.

From then on, I did the minimum amount of work each day, just like everyone else.

AS MY TIME IN grew shorter, the Army tried to tempt me to re-up. I was offered training to become a warrant officer. I was interested in piloting helicopters. There was a warrant officer slot open for a helicopter pilot. A friend of mine was a recruiter, and they get bonuses for keeping people in. He offered to split half his commission with me if I stayed.

I thought it over briefly, and said no way. Serving as a warrant officer meant six more years in.

Then a slot opened up for Officer Candidate School. The captain was going to write me a letter of recommendation. He acted surprised that I turned it down.

"I'm not making any money here," I said. "I'm out of here."

Sgt. Kent and I checked out of the Army about the same time. He looked on the bright side. He'd earned his truck driver's license and had a job waiting for him that would pay twice what he was earning in the military.

I would find out later from Tim Kent, who'd heard about it from a buddy on base long after I was out of the Army, that Annette ended up being charged with dereliction of duty for not showing up for her job. She'd been dishonorably discharged. André and Jayson also had gotten in trouble and been booted out.

WITH SIX MONTHS LEFT before my discharge, I started working up a business plan. I knew what I wanted to do after I got out. I would own and operate a combination jet-ski shop and custom furniture store. I'd work on the jet skis in spring and summer, and in the off-season build furniture.

In my spare time in the barracks I'd done marketing analysis of the Reno area and discovered that a decent jet-ski repair shop was needed. I had a Reno telephone book and had called vendors and suppliers to find out what they needed from jet-ski shops in the area. I'd introduced myself as a businessman who would be starting up my own shop in a half-year and would be seeking their business. I'd also called up the serious jet-ski racers I knew in Reno and asked what they needed and weren't getting from the local shops. I'd found out that the mechanics didn't know how to tune the machines to Northern Nevada's high altitude.

I loved jet skis. I knew I could service them well. And I knew I'd love running my own shop. My plan was to build custom jet skis as well as make modifications and repair what came in the door. I'd do everything from engine work to fiberglass to painting. I'd also sell after-market parts that I made. I was confident. I'd been working on jet skis from the time I was 14. Even when I was in the Army, I'd built custom motors in the barracks for my skis. I knew these machines inside and out.

As for building furniture, I'd worked a bit already in the wood and metal shops on base and made some nice pieces — coffee tables, end tables, entertainment centers. I liked working with my hands. I figured a jet-ski shop is a big warehouse environment. It'd be easy to put the jet skis to one side in winter to do the furniture making.

I'd read some business books and put together a decent, 24-page business plan. I included cash-flow analysis, projections and market research. I'd calculated my budget for marketing, advertising, overhead, and hiring employees (when I reached that point). I used a formula to determine how many tune-ups and repairs I'd have to do each month, and how many after-market products I'd have to sell, to make ends meet.

I printed my business plan out on a computer that belonged to the father of a girl I was dating who lived off base. She ended up complaining, "You're *always* on the computer!"

Finally, it was time for my discharge. I was primed and ready.

I had about $5,000 saved up from the Army — an impressive sum, considering I'd earned only about $900 a month. And I was ready to make a go of it in Reno: the Biggest Little City, where the high desert meets the mountains. Having been away, I appreciated it fully for the first time. It seemed like a perfect place to live, and to prosper.

Oh, I was burning to prosper. I couldn't wait to be, as we said in the military, "back in the world." And to set it on fire. With nothing in my way to stop me.

No restrictions on my time. No limitations. No Sgt. Bacons.

I was so excited to be out of the service that I drove a rented U-Haul, with my old Chevy truck towed behind, 32 hours straight to get home.

CHAPTER FORTY-THREE: In Business, out, Back in

The famous Army recruitment jingle during the era I served wove its way into popular culture, and remains famous in the advertising industry: "Be all that you can be." I was definitely going to be all I could be — but out of the Army.

Actually, I felt a certain sadness leaving the service, because even with all the politics, I'd really liked it. The regimen appealed to my nature. But I knew, too, that there wasn't any money to be made wearing the uniform.

The Army had served its purpose. It had helped me grow up. It had instilled me with confidence that I could excel at whatever I applied myself — physical training, learning weapons and tools, repairing vehicles in the motor pool. And before all that, it had helped me achieve my most pressing goal, the one that had led me to enlist in the first place: getting me out of Reno, and away from the people I'd been around who were causing me trouble.

By the time I got back to Reno, the troublemakers, especially the drug dealers, were either in prison or had split the scene. I knew I'd made the right choice.

The Army had changed me. I was no longer afraid of any kind of challenge. I'd been through a lot, even though I hadn't been sent overseas or to a war zone. I had proved myself as a skilled mechanic, an innovator, a guy who solved problems and got things done and didn't put up with sh*t. The Army had brought out the self-sufficiency in me. I knew that whatever business venture I set out on now, I wouldn't have a fear of failure.

Now that I was out of the service, no artificial barriers stood in my way. I knew that the Army wasn't for me. I knew, when I was in, that I was a cut above most of the enlistees. But I also knew that I couldn't stand out from the pack too much without getting dinged. That would only inspire envy and resentment. So I'd had to watch myself. Instead of running two miles in the P.T. test in 12 or 13 minutes every time, sometimes I'd purposely finish in 14. When I did try my hardest, as in reorganizing the repair-shop procedures in the motor pool, I'd ended up with a dumb-sh*t Sgt. Bacon on my ass.

Now that I was in civilian life, I wouldn't have to worry about such impediments. I could go balls to the wall. I *could* be all that I could be. I could push ahead as I wanted, without limitations. And I had that business plan that I'd prepared six months before my discharge.

Success was up to *me*, and I had supreme confidence. I'd just bear down and get done what had to get done. Even though my financial resources were limited, I didn't worry about running out of money. I knew I could scratch and claw to survive and find a way to build something.

Where would I stay until I found a place of my own? Mom was still working for Hidden Lode Explorations. She had her hands full helping my sister, who was now raising her young daughter, my niece, Brianna. (Jennifer's now ex-husband, Hugo, the bodybuilder, had re-enlisted in the service, unable to make it on the outside.) But Mom offered to let me move in with her until I found a place.

Drew heard about it and offered to let me stay temporarily with him.

He was sharing his house with his teenage girlfriend, Traci, and their infant daughter. They had a little house — one-half of a duplex — with a spare bedroom.

I wasn't there much. I looked around intensely for industrial space for my jet-ski shop. I was searching for a place where it would be easy for customers to load their ski trailers in and out. I found a property on Freeport Boulevard in the industrial section of Sparks. There were 800 square feet of floor space. It would do. I'd signed a 12-month lease — running through the following May — at $500 a month. I was busy around the clock there: fixing the shop up and tending to all the details I needed to take care of before I could open for business.

One night, I heard Drew and Traci arguing. Then he knocked on my bedroom door. "You gotta leave."

Traci was tired of having a boarder. I'd lasted two weeks. It was no use arguing with him. My patience wasn't very thick. I'd spent three years with a succession of roommates in the barracks, and I wasn't up for any drama in my living situation.

I packed up and got out of there and moved directly into my empty shop. It would double as my living quarters until I could get my business flying and afford an apartment. I was prepared to live a spartan existence until then. I'd stretch my $5,000 in savings as far as it could go. I'd work as many hours as I needed to, to make it.

I was still waking up at 4:30 a.m. — on Army time, blinking my eyes and thinking, *Sh*t, I'm late for formation.* In my mind, I was still in the barracks.

Then I'd remember I was out.

I'd get up and get going on my day.

I worked very hard getting my shop ready. I Sheetrocked off an office space in back. My shop would be in front. There was a small upstairs storage space, 6 by 9 feet, above the power box outside. I squeezed a bed in there and covered the opening with a black sheet screwed to the beam that camouflaged the space so, from a distance, it didn't seem there was anything up there at all. I showered using the garden hose in the bay inside the shop. There was a little toilet inside and I built a closet for my clothes. I set up a hot plate and a coffee pot in the bathroom. My bachelor pad/jet-ski shop was coming together.

I named my shop Extreme Dynamics Racing. I bought blue vinyl letters and numbers from a home-supply store and fixed them on the front glass. I drew up an elaborate business card and logo using colored pencils and had a stock of cards printed.

I bought a business license and business insurance. I had accumulated the tools I needed throughout the years of working on jet skis and my motorcycle and cars. To get workbenches, I drove my old Chevy truck around at night in the industrial area, scouting for discarded pallets. I gathered up the best pallets I could find, pulled the boards off and sawed and nailed them into benches.

Two weeks after moving into my space, Extreme Dynamics Racing was ready for business.

ADVERTISING WAS SIMPLE: word of mouth. All my friends who were jet skiers spread the news that "Jeff's got his shop open," and, "You need to bring your skis down; this guy knows how to tune them."

Business began trickling in. The customers paid by cash or check, since I didn't have a cash register. I'd fill out the invoices by hand. I'd take the payment, say, "I'll be right back," go into my office and deposit the money or checks in the little safe I'd bought.

It was a simple operation. Simple and efficient. I got the jobs done, and done right.

Word spread.

My sister had friends with jet skis. They brought me work. A deliveryman with RPS who delivered parts to my business pulled up one day in his truck and said, "Hey, I got a delivery for you." He unloaded his ski from the back. Pretty soon, guys he knew in shipping brought their skis to me, too.

I quickly decided to service street and dirt bikes to supplement my income. I also hit up the Kawasaki and Suzuki, Yamaha and Sea-Doo dealerships and told them I understood they were having a hard time tuning their new jet skis. They could bring them by my shop at night and I'd have them ready by morning. I knew this overflow from the dealerships would only last a little while; their mechanics would surely write down my carburetor settings and not need my services anymore. But it was a great way for me to kick-start my own business. And as summer unfolded, I found myself busy around the clock. I charged $45 an hour: the market rate.

All I was really after was self-sufficiency, to make enough money to support myself, pay the bills, keep the business going, and eventually hire an assistant and move into an apartment. But to reach these goals meant putting in very long hours each and every day and night.

Drew sometimes helped out at the shop. In return, he got his skis repaired and free parts.

To tune the skis I'd load them into my truck at night and drive them to Little Washoe Lake 20 miles away. In the moonlight as late as 1 or 2 a.m., with my truck's headlights illuminating the shallow shoreline so I could keep away from it, I'd be out there tuning the skis and test-riding them. The skis would be ready by 7 a.m. back at my shop for customer pickup. Ultra-efficiency.

The steady stream of business was gratifying, but inevitably began to wear me down. I was a one-man operation. Working seven days a week began to burn me out. Because I had turned a hobby — jet skis — into a business, I began losing my passion for the hobby. I started not liking jet skis. If I did take a day off and took a ski to Pyramid Lake or Lahontan Reservoir for fun, people would bring their skis over to me to have a look. They all knew by now that Jeff was a jet-ski shop owner. That forced me to travel to more distant lakes for privacy.

Business kept flowing steadily throughout the summer and into early fall. By this time, the employees at the dealerships were constantly referring customers to me because the mechanics at the dealerships weren't too capable.

I'd made it through my first four months.

THE BUSINESS PLAN I'D cooked up in the service called for me to switch over to building furniture in the winter. But when the cold weather came, I found an unexpected source of income: People who owned jet skis asked whether I could work on their ATVs.

I figured I could. After all, ATVs, like jet skis, had small engines that I was familiar with from building street bikes and dirt bikes in high school. So they brought in their ATVs, and it worked out fine. What's more, motorcycle owners kept bringing in their machines during the winter. I never did rotate into building furniture.

One lesson in business for me that first year was discovering where the money was to be made. It was in the high-end jobs, the expensive custom skis or bikes. The small repairs to lower-end machines were hard work and ate up time. What's more, being nickel-and-dime jobs, they didn't bring in the high volume of income needed to sustain the business.

But there was a bigger lesson from that year. I grossed $50,000. It was a disappointing figure. I realized that there weren't enough jet skis, street and dirt bikes and ATVs in the Reno area to bring me the kind of income I ultimately craved. The market wasn't big enough even if I captured it all. And frankly, I felt like I had just about captured it all. I'd dominated the market, and it hadn't been enough.

My business insurance sucked up money. The Chevy Blazer I'd bought to replace my truck was a $200-a-month payment. Even if I billed $45 an hour, for 40 hours a week, year-round, and sold all the parts and upgrades, I'd only gross around $120,000.

I realized I couldn't progress. Nor could I hope to swing financing to buy a jet-ski dealership of my own. All the dealerships had been claimed in the market, and even if one were put up for sale, I wouldn't be able to raise the few million dollars to buy it.

CHAPTER FORTY-FOUR: Security Details

I applied for the graveyard shift in security and surveillance at a local hotel-casino, the Saltshaker. I figured I'd work all night at the casino, sleep a couple hours, then get to work in my jet-ski shop the rest of the day. Working casino security seemed a natural job for me since I'd just gotten out of the military. I was used to uniforms, chain of command, carrying out orders. And I was young and strong and in shape. The day after applying at the Saltshaker employment office, I noticed the guy who rented the shop in front of me on Freeport Boulevard was standing in the parking lot, wearing the Saltshaker's security-guard uniform: baby-blue shirt and black pants. I walked up and introduced myself.

His name was Jim. He was a big, nice guy a couple inches shorter than I, and a year younger. It turned out he was using his industrial space for assembling electronic components; it was a branch of his family's business in Utah. It also turned out we had a few things in common. One was a love of motorcycles. Jim's Kawasaki ZX-9 was parked outside.

Jim was working security at the Saltshaker on the swing shift, and working in his shop by day. We'd had the same idea about supplementing our incomes. I told him I'd just applied at the Saltshaker.

"Oh, yeah, I thought I saw you in there interviewing for the job," he said.

Jim did me a favor. He called the head of the security department and asked if I'd been hired.

"You got the job," Jim told me.

I did him a favor next. I said if he ever needed anyone to work on his bike, to let me know.

"Really?" he said. "I can't find anybody in town that's good."

I tuned it up for him. He was elated. It was finally humming right. From then on, I took care of Jim's two street bikes, and his Enduro, doing the monthly service, washing and waxing them. I eventually built him a custom ATV. A friendship blossomed — one that ended up proving important when I went into my next business venture.

THE CASINO SECURITY JOB was pretty much what I'd expected. It only paid $10 an hour, but gave me medical insurance plus a hot meal every shift. It allowed me to cut back on my shop work. My graveyard shift at the casino started at midnight. I'd get off at 8 a.m., open the jet-ski shop at 9 a.m., close it at 5 p.m., nap from 6 to 10:30 p.m., then head back to the security job.

Being a security guard was fairly easy work, just roaming the casino floors and outside the bars and restaurants, making sure everything was on the up and up and no one was causing trouble. Usually, there wasn't any trouble. Maybe an elderly lady needed help getting through the doors and out to her car. We'd keep an eye out for the usual petty casino crimes, such as someone stealing a bucket full of quarters from a player who was transfixed on the action of a slot machine.

Our main concerns were drunks. Alcohol is the fuel that drives the gambling action, and therefore the profits, at a casino. It's what helps wealthy businessmen piss away their fortunes. It's what helps people of average means loosen up and bet over their heads. It's what spurs minimum-wage manual laborers to blow a week's pay in a few impulsive minutes of wagers at the blackjack table. The byproduct of the free casino drinks can be angry drunks. As we security guards walked the floor, drunk gamblers would call out things like, "Toy cop." You had to take a lot of sh*t.

Alcohol affects people differently. Some were depressed. Some were loud and thought everything was funny. Some thought themselves invincible. Belligerent drunks were not pleasant to deal with.

We security guards were trained to understand that an intoxicated adult has the mentality of a child. Getting a call from the control room, we called it "base," to "go over and check out a "1029" (code for a disruptive drunk) meant having to find the inebriated patron and, with a partner, escort him out while remaining polite and professional.

"All right, I understand you had a bad time," or, "You've had enough, it's been a good trip, let's head on out."

First, you'd adapt your personality to cater to the drunk's, so as not to create a bigger disturbance. There was no sense in getting angry at the person, but you had to be cautious because a drunk's behavior can turn on a dime. He might be mouthy, or even merry, one second, and nasty or violent the next.

You'd say whatever you could to get the drunk to stand up off the chair, barstool or lounge couch.

"Show me that you can at least stand up."

The drunk would stagger to his feet.

"We need to escort you out. We'll pay for a cab for you."

"No, I want to eat. Just take me to the coffee shop."

"No, you've already had your chance to go eat. We're escorting you out." Then my voice would lower to a whisper. "We can be polite about this, or you can make a scene and I'll put you in an arm bar, take you out the door."

"Oh, badass security guard. What are *you* going to do? You f*cking pussy, you don't even have a gun."

It was true. All we carried were handcuffs for making citizen's arrests.

When a drunk resisted, one of us guards would hold out a pair of cuffs. "Listen, I'm going to have to arrest you, or we can walk you out and you can call it a night. But if you persist, I'm going to handcuff you and Reno PD is going to pick you up and you're going to jail tonight. I promise you."

The drunk might cooperate at this point. Or he might start spouting obscenities: "F*ck you, you don't have the authority. You ain't going to take me."

"OK, I gave you a warning. Please put your hands behind your back."

At this point, the drunk might take a swing. We couldn't swing back. We could only restrain the jerk. One of us would get the drunk's attention and the other would get behind him, twist one of the drunk's arms into an arm bar, then slap the handcuffs on.

More often, though, we'd just escort a drunk out to a cab, get him inside then say, "OK, goodnight, sir."

If the drunk was a "preferred" casino player, such as a high roller who'd just gotten a little out of hand, we really had to use kid gloves. We carried paper vouchers to give to the cab drivers. The ride was on the house. A lot of the Saltshaker's key players were from Reno itself. The casino catered to a mix of locals and tourists.

The best call of all was a "1010": meaning a fight. Security guards would haul ass over there and get in the middle of the scrap. This was our chance. With all of these guards standing around, obstructing the action from public view, those of us breaking up the fight could throw elbows, knock kneecaps.

But a 1029 was far more common.

Sometimes a 1029 was for a guest of the hotel. In this case, you'd have to escort him or her to the hotel room. We'd help the drunk through the room's door and close it, but we'd never, ever go into the room. That would have been a recipe for disaster. The women were the worst; they had no sense of fair play. They could spit or scratch. They could screech that they were going to sue.

The policy for escorting a drunken female to her room was to do so with the help of a female security guard. The female guard would handle the female drunk. The male guard wouldn't touch her unless the female guard needed help with the struggling woman, such as getting the cuffs on. Helen was a tough old security guard; I'd have her help me with these cases.

Some of the women, particularly those in their thirties or forties, would try to get a young male security guard to join them inside. They had lost their inhibitions and become predatory.

"I want that young security guard guy to come with me and help me get set up in the bed."

I'd make sure our escorting of the woman to her room was captured on camera.

We'd call up to base to follow us with their cameras. "All right," we'd radio up, "we're getting ready to hit the elevator." *Boom*, the control-room operators would have us monitored in the elevator.

"All right, getting out of the elevator, 11th floor," we'd radio up. We'd stay in the elevator until we heard the control-room voice, "OK, got the cameras." Then we'd walk out of the elevator.

We'd reach the hotel door. Helen would get it open, helping the lady use her door card in the slot. The drunken woman would hesitate, swaying a bit, and in a slurred voice ask me, "Oh, you're not coming in the room?"

"No, we can't come into the room, ma'am."

We'd gently push her in and close her door.

I RESOLVED NEVER TO gamble in casinos. I was gambling already in a much bigger game — my jet-ski business. I knew that business always is a gamble; and even if you got successful, and your business grew and you were making bank, it could all be taken away from you in a moment due to some disaster such as a lawsuit. Yes, being in business was enough of a gamble for me. Anyway, the slot machines held no appeal. I saw them just as videogames that cost you money.

But I did marvel at the seductive aspect of casinos. There was a devil-may-care, Frank Sinatra/Dean Martin attitude to the action. Staying out late.

Seeing where the chips fell. Having a Jack and Coke. The air thick with cigarette smoke.

There was even something slightly romantic about the mysterious people pumping quarters into the slot machines. They were like gold panners, seeking their fortune no matter how steep the odds. I knew many were addicted. They were casino-holics. They had a problem. But there they were, chasing after a jackpot.

Then there were the high rollers. There were wealthy gamblers wearing a $30,000 Rolex watch and maybe 10 times that value in other jewelry, pissing away $20,000 a night because they could and because they enjoyed the casino environment. These premium players were immune from getting hauled off by us security guards. We couldn't touch them.

One of the regular high rollers was a prosperous accountant from Los Angeles named Gregory. He'd fly to Reno in his Learjet. Gregory was a short, respectable-looking man who dressed in Versace or Armani and had an attitude of, "Do you know who the f*ck I am?" He knew he had privileges at the Saltshaker.

Gregory liked to shoot craps for high stakes. The dates he took on vacations to the Saltshaker looked to be under 21. Minors weren't allowed to loiter in the casino, much less drink alcohol. But Gregory always brought one of these companions with him. One in particular was his favorite. This boy looked no more than 18, and drank brazenly, cavorting next to his sugar daddy. The security supervisor told us guards never to ask to see his ID. We were to leave Gregory and his little friend alone.

One night around 3 a.m., we got a call from base. Gregory's fairy godson was causing a scene at a craps table that happened to be near a cashier's cage. That was a major no-no. The cage is where the money is taken in and initially counted. We didn't want any trouble in that area. It was a no-disturbance zone, constantly monitored. There had been instances in other casinos where armed robbers had created a diversion, then gotten into the cage and swiftly made off with bundles of money. Grab and dash. A casino's nightmare.

I responded along with the shift supervisor. Gregory's little friend was acting up, talking loud, waving his hands and laughing at the dealers and the other players. He was unbuttoning his dress shirt, half taking it off, and dancing around like he was in a disco. He must have just felt like being at the center of attention, causing a scene. Other gamblers were staring at him. The croupiers were rattled.

"Listen, you gotta calm down," I said.

"My daddy's rich," the petulant boy said. "I can act *any way* I want." He tossed his hair back and sneered at me.

He was wearing tight designer jeans and flat-toed dress shoes. They looked like girl clothes on a boy.

"No you can't, you're bothering the other players," I said.

He stared at me with a look of mock injury, then tossed the contents of his glass at my feet.

In an instant I was towering over him, ready to tear his pretty head off his skinny little neck.

"Slow down, slow down," my supervisor said.

I put my face up an inch from the boy's. "I'll arrest you right now and take you to jail. If you don't calm down, I don't care who your daddy is. We don't mess around in here."

My supervisor moved in and tried to separate us. But I didn't budge.

Gregory dashed around the table to intervene. He was apologetic.

"It's OK, it's OK," he said. He grabbed his little boyfriend by the arm and pulled him back.

The casino shift manager came over. "It's all right, Jeff, just lay off, just back up."

"I'll back up," I said to Gregory, "but you got to keep your little bitch on a leash."

"I'll take care of it," Gregory said.

"He shouldn't even be drinking," I said.

Gregory arched his back, rising to his full 5-foot-5-inch stature in his platform shoes. "I'm a VIP guest and I can bring whatever friends I want," he said with superiority. "But I'll take care of it."

Later on my rounds, I saw the little boyfriend sitting at a slot machine. He was smirking. He flipped me off.

I walked over to him with a grin on my face.

"I get off at 8 if you want to mess with me," I said.

My supervisor dismissed me an hour early that shift.

ONE THING I LIKED about casino work was there were many young people like me with daytime agendas that pushed us to moonlighting in the casino.

There was a beautiful cocktail waitress, Jamie, with auburn hair and an athletic figure. She had worked as a bikini-clad Budweiser Girl for beer promotions, and as a ring-card girl at boxing matches. Jamie worked graveyard at the casino so she could make a little money and have her days free to snowboard. She was a professional boarder. Jamie happened to be friends with Jim, and the three of us started hanging together.

Business slows at Reno casinos after Labor Day and so I got to take nights off here and there from the Saltshaker. That meant I could leave from my shop during the day to have some fun, and make up the tune-ups and repairs at night instead of working security. Jamie, Jim and I ended up taking long backpacking trips in the mountains that winter, carrying our snowboards on our backs, before the ski resorts opened.

Jamie's father, a retired IBM executive, had bought her brother and her a house in Verdi, the town west of Reno in the mountains, right on the California border. The family also owned a cabin farther west at Donner Lake, in the Sierra. Jamie knew the terrain, and we hiked far out to virgin hills. It was great exercise, but instead of carrying a heavy Army rucksack on my back, it was a snowboard and backpack filled with our lunch.

There was no other person around for miles. There was the silence of the snowbound terrain, the rugged beauty of the mountain wilderness. The clouds from our breath, the tracks we made, were the only human marks in this paradise. I had ached for scenery like this when I was in the Army.

Hiking deep into the mountains and boarding down the pristine slopes was true recreation.

I'd sit on top of a slope with Jamie and we'd chat and have a beer. Then we'd board down. Then we'd climb up again. Or we'd check out fish in a melting stream. Or gaze at Donner Lake in the snowfall.

It was so much fun that sometimes I'd also call in sick to the Saltshaker just so I could go snowboarding.

MY FRIENDSHIP WITH JIM was special, too. It rekindled my old passion for computers.

I still couldn't afford one myself, but Jim had an old computer, operated by Windows 3.1, which he used for his business. He upgraded to Windows 95, which had just come out, and was having some driver issues. He let me have a crack at it. I went into the system and started navigating.

The system was organized in a way I understood. I worked out the kinks. In return, Jim let me use his computer to create and print brochures for my business.

The result was that I fell in love with computers all over again. I started spending more and more time on Jim's computer.

Soon I was craving a computer of my own. I paid a visit to Circuit City and checked out an NEC, but the price was $2,000. I couldn't believe it.

Jim told me he was buying a new computer, and would sell me his old one for $500. That worked for me.

Now I had a computer of my own at my shop. I started getting back into the digital universe.

I was entranced again.

CHAPTER FORTY-FIVE: Hot Pursuit

As my one-year anniversary of working security approached, I was considered for a promotion to a supervisor's job. I expected to progress in whatever field I was in, so I was glad enough at the opportunity.

The promotion would mean a $4-an-hour raise. The interview was in the security office, in front of the four department supervisors, including my friend Jim, who'd been promoted a few months before. He'd prepped me about the supervisor's duties, so I felt confident. The supervisors grilled me with scenarios.

"You have a guest who is sick and vomiting, what's the best strategy for handling this?"

"A guest has been stabbed. Where are the medical kits?"

"How would you diffuse an argument between a husband and wife on the casino floor?"

And so on, for an hour.

I nailed the interview. That Sunday, Linda, the head supervisor, called me into the security office and offered me the job. I happily accepted. It would get me off the floor. I figured that it had taken me a year of paying dues.

"Welcome aboard," she said.

I'd start my new position in a week.

When I showed up for my Tuesday-night shift, Linda called me into the office again.

"I have some bad news. We're going to give the job to Bart, instead."

Bart, whom the rest of us called "Grandpa," was a retired L.A. County sheriff's deputy who was working security to supplement his pension and fill in the empty hours. He was good-natured, but a hard drinker. In fact, some of us guards would pull him out of one or another of the casino bars after a shift because he'd get hammered.

Bart didn't really give a damn about the job. This was no secret to Linda. But she figured he had more experience than I, so she'd changed her mind and decided to give him the supervisor's post.

I was disappointed, and angry. Bart had only been working at the casino four months!

I argued with her. Bart hadn't even gone in front of the interview board.

"He's got a lot of police experience," she said.

"You know what?" I said. "You don't promise someone something and then pull it back. That's not professional. I earned this position. On Sunday you told me I had the position. Now it's Tuesday and you tell me I don't have it?"

I gave her my two-week's notice.

She said she was sorry I felt that way, but if that was my decision, so be it.

My last two weeks wouldn't pass without drama.

Early on the following Saturday, at 1 a.m., an hour into my shift, and the casino hopping with late-spring out-of-towners, a middle-aged woman ran up to me out of breath.

"That guy just stole my purse!"

She pointed at a large man heading toward the doors to the parking lot. I started jogging. I caught up with him just before he got outside.

"Hey, sir, excuse me."

His head whipped around.

"F*ck you," he said. He shoved through the first set of glass doors and the second set, leading outside. He took off running.

I picked up my walkie-talkie and radioed to my colleagues in the security vehicle patrolling the lot. Then I charged after him. I had to catch him before he left the casino's property or I wouldn't be allowed to legally pursue him.

He was out ahead of me, running on the sidewalk along Virginia Street toward the movie-theater complex beyond our parking lot. I sprinted and made up ground. He heard my footsteps and veered right, off the sidewalk and into our lot. If he kept going he'd hit the fence separating the casino and theater lots. He suddenly stopped and swung around. We were nearly chest to chest. He was a very big guy.

My radio crackled with the voice of Alex, one of the guards in the vehicle: "Hang tight, just keep him there, I'm almost around the corner."

The purse snatcher shoved me hard in the chest, knocking me back, and took off again, this time across our lot to the west side. Beyond the fence was a street leading to apartment complexes.

"Run after him, I'm right behind you!" Alex radioed.

The security car's headlight beams were flooding us now. The purse snatcher, with me right behind, reached the fence at the west end of the lot. He jumped up, grabbed the steel wire and started climbing. That was my chance. I tackled his legs and pulled him back. Alex jumped out of the security car and grabbed the guy around the torso.

We slammed him on the concrete and pinned him down. I couldn't believe it: He was still holding the purse. We wrestled him over onto his stomach, yanked his arms behind and got the handcuffs on. We patted him down. He didn't have any knives or needles.

I radioed the base dispatch, who radioed the Reno Police Department dispatcher.

A cruiser pulled up 15 minutes later. We had the suspect face down on the pavement, hands cuffed behind his back. He couldn't move. I was using my military training in handling a prisoner of war.

"Jesus Christ, what did you do to this guy?" one of the RPD officers asked.

"This guy just took off running," I said.

The cops loaded him in the back of their cruiser. Alex and I waited by our security vehicle. We had to give our police reports. A few minutes later, one of the police officers came over.

"Holy sh*t, we've got an APB out on this guy. He's wanted for homicide."

It turned out that the all-points bulletin had been posted because the purse snatcher was wanted on suspicion of stabbing another man to death. The cops had been looking for him the past 48 hours.

"Are you f*cking kidding me?" I said. My blood ran cold.

Usually the cops faxed APB reports, with mug shots, to casino security staffs because we saw so many people drift through. It was a great network.

The cops and the casino security guards and surveillance personnel share information. The casinos alert each other about slot cheats and other criminals. But none of us at the Saltshaker had seen this APB.

"You're lucky this motherf*cker didn't stab you," the cop told me.

That cinched it for me. I was glad I was quitting. Putting my life at risk as a rent-a-cop wasn't worth it.

My last day rolled around. Linda, the security manager, called me into her office.

Bart had resigned. He hadn't liked being a supervisor.

"I'd like you to fill the position, Jeff."

I didn't need any time to think it over.

"I'm sorry. It's too late. I'm still leaving."

CHAPTER FORTY-SIX: A Middle Manager

At the time I left the Saltshaker, something really revolutionary was taking shape in the computer world. A new electronic medium was on the rise. Those in the know said it would change the world the way radio, and later television, had. This new medium was the Internet. Here and there, businesses and individuals were hooking up their computers to the Internet via standard telephone lines.

After hearing radio commercials for a local service provider that charged $15 a month for a dial-up account, Jim and I had each signed up. I became active on a CompuServe news group, reading news stories and exchanging typed-in messages with other users on bulletin boards. There wasn't much else on the Internet in 1995. Still, it was clear to me that a magnificent, towering communications wave was rising, though still too distant on the horizon to be detected by most.

I began spending uncountable hours on my computer, in a little hub set up in the back of my jet-ski shop, exploring cyberspace, learning about websites and design. It was a revelation. The vision of a futuristic society that had captivated me in movies such as *Blade Runner* now seemed imminent. I foresaw a brave new virtual world unfolding. This was for me!

I knew that in good time everyone would be hooked up to the Internet.

They'd be doing their everyday work, or watching movies or programs, shopping, studying, surfing websites for fun, communicating by electronic mail instead of by the telephone. I wanted to get in while the frontier was still wide open.

I hooked up Jim's computer and mine with dual analog, 56k-connections. I taught myself HyperText markup Language — "html" — learning the code to create websites. I'd call up a web page and save it on my desktop. I'd open it with the Notepad program. Notepad would reveal the source code. I learned to write code in this hands-on way. Sometimes I'd modify a page, taking out some coding, then hit Refresh and see how the page had changed. I'd discover, for example, that "img" was an image tag. In this way I mastered html. Then I started writing my own pages. It was easy. And I got better and better at it.

I was burning to capitalize on my growing proficiency. What I finally decided to do was to get started with a little side business. I'd charge $25 an hour to set up email systems for small businesses, with my little computer hosting their networks as access points. I started making sales calls to business owners I knew. I told them there was the internal necessity of connecting employees via email to each other and the outside world. Before long, I said, a business wouldn't be able to operate without email any more than it could survive without telephones. In 1995, email was still relatively new to society at large. So using email was a bold concept.

I landed a few clients here and there. There were very few people in town doing what I was doing.

My next step into the cyberspace frontier was to start capitalizing in the arena of websites. I began registering domain names, locking them up for future resale. I registered dollarlotto.com, dollarlotto.net, dollarlotto.org, and so on. It was like staking gold-mining claims in the Old West. As a domain broker, I figured I'd make a bit of a profit on names someone would eventually want. I was way ahead of the curve. So many people weren't even aware of the inevitable e-commerce explosion.

Then I made a move into creating websites for businesses. In my spare time I made the rounds of small retailers and manufacturers: a janitorial supply company; a company that provided wheelchairs, oxygen machines and other medical services; a construction company; and the like. I set up meetings with business owners and attempted to penetrate their lack of interest in having a website by showing them what the Internet could do. They could display their goods and services and all their key information for customers. They could even post job applications on their websites. Of course, I told them, there was the commercial benefit. Customers would someday be shopping online using credit cards. What's more, websites were great indirect advertisements in and of themselves. Before long, I said, businesses without web presences would be at a significant disadvantage to their competitors.

But very few business owners got it. Most of them weren't interested. To them, the idea of having a website — or even the notion of using email — was a joke.

My cyberspace venture was short-lived.

I WAS READY FOR a change. I was tired of the jet-ski shop. I needed to explore new horizons.

I sold Extreme Dynamic Racing's service accounts to another young guy who, like I'd been, was just starting out small with a power-sport business.

I had enough money now to pay off bills and have a little left over to put in the bank. I packed up my tools and my computer and moved into Jim's little two-story apartment. I slept downstairs on the couch.

With a ravenous appetite I sunk my teeth even more into my computer, working on it into the wee hours every night.

I LOOKED AROUND FOR a new job. I checked with the veterans-affairs officer at the state employment office in Reno. His name was John. He was an old Navy guy, a Vietnam vet. He had a receding hairline and some added pounds, but even in his jeans, Western shirt and boots, he still had the strict military attitude. He was to the point. He wanted to get you what you needed. He genuinely cared about helping his fellow vets. He wore a ball cap with his old unit's insignia on it. He was an old salt.

John searched through his files. There was a job as an assistant to a general contractor who built custom homes. Sounded good to me.

I went for an interview and was hired. The contractor, Don Mares, had grown up in the business. He built houses from scratch. He handled it all — plumbing, electrical, tiling. He was really good. He took me on as his only assistant.

I worked hard and he liked me. He paid me what he could: $12 an hour. He was a big-time hunter and would bring elk meat or other game to the site and cook it in a crock pot for our lunch. I liked the job. I liked Don. I was glad I'd switched from working security at the Saltshaker.

Don was different from most contractors. He was a hard-working S.O.B. He'd be at the job site by 6 or 7 a.m. and stay until 5 p.m. Most construction guys would start at 4 or 5 a.m. and knock off at 2:30 p.m. I respected Don. But the work began taking a toll. The loud equipment, the banging of the hammers, the clatter of the nail guns, were causing ringing in my ears at night. I'd wear earplugs on the job, but they didn't help. Fluid was leaking out of my ears at night. I started losing my hearing.

I went to the doctor and was told I really had a problem. My ears were too sensitive for this work.

I told Don I had to quit. He was upset. We were almost done with a house and had another one ready to build. I told him I'd stay on to finish the current project.

"All right," I said, after the house was done. "I can't work on another project with you. I'm dying at night. My health is important."

He still couldn't believe it. He was angry. But there was nothing I could do. I felt bad, like I let him down. He was a great contractor.

I KNEW NOW THAT it was time for me to make some big decisions. Working construction was hard, hard work. It beat me up physically, even without my ear problems. I considered that neither constant work nor security work at the Saltshaker had paid much at all.

I decided I was ready to start using my brain instead of my hands.

I'd look for some sort of managerial job with a company. What business was there in Reno? I didn't want to work in casinos again, so that left the other key industry with plenty of jobs: warehousing and distribution. Nevada tax laws catered to the warehousing industry. The industry was big.

I considered that I knew inventory controls really well, from working for Pep Boys and later in the Army base motor pool. Why not hunt for a job at a distribution facility?

Leverman Corp., a distributor of books and music, software and movies on tape and disk, had one of the largest warehouses in the area, on Vista Boulevard on the eastern edge of Sparks. Leverman was international, a publicly traded company. Its business was taking in shipments from manufacturers and shipping them out to distributors and major retailers. It did a tremendous volume. After all, Reno is positioned right on the doorstep of California, which all by itself is one of the largest economies in the world.

I liked Leverman's organization. Everything was regimented — specific bins for products, specific timetables for intake and delivery — like in the military. I had to interview three times before I was offered a job. I spoke with the first-line supervisor, then the department managers, and finally with the warehouse manager himself. They all liked me, and that I'd served in the military. Leverman's was highly organized. People were hired to make a career with the company.

I was hired at $30,000 a year with full benefits. My position: Ad-mega Floor Supervisor.

If I wanted a tough challenge, this was it!

"Ad-mega" referred to new books, music or movies that had to be shipped out on a special schedule. Publishers and record and movie companies had strict release dates set, all tied into marketing. That meant that the products had to be guarded with tight security as well as not be sent to stores until the authorized dates. The boxes with these items bore stickers with the dates. It was legally forbidden by contract for the product to hit the streets before those dates. Shipping the product out before those dates could get Leverman sued by a manufacturer. Can you imagine a movie studio hitting a distributor with a lawsuit because a video was in stores while the movie was still in theaters? Grim scenario.

Security demanded that if any employee was caught stealing a product — the temptation would be to sell an advance copy of a video or CD — that employee was fired on the spot. Security points with X-ray machines were set up at the entrance.

My job was to make sure all the ad-mega products reached the warehouse on time, were properly stored and then shipped within their narrow timeframe. It was the toughest position in the warehouse and none of the current employees had wanted it. They'd watched one ad-mega supervisor after another fail. Exceptional organizational skills were required. It was extreme multitasking. You had to be Johnny-on-the-Spot. From my first day on the job, I saw what it involved.

The ad-mega supervisory responsibilities afforded little time for "staging" the boxes in stacks for each step in the shipping process, and practically no margin for error. A shipment run could include 500,000 items. Instead of a constant, steady flow of items that reached and left the warehouse, the schedule for the ad-mega products was intermittent. The supervisor had to always be on his toes and absolutely flawless in his organization and execution. His life was dictated by shipments. Getting the product out on schedule was everything — even if you had to be on the job for 24 hours straight. There was no screwing around. The time was *the* time: you had to make it work. We also had management meetings every day at noon, which took me off the floor and away from my job.

The pace of work for the ad-mega supervisor never slacked.

The warehouse managers saw me as a young go-getter full of determination and energy. I fit their bill. I was assigned a crew of 20 floor workers plus two assistants. This was exciting to me. I got to go to work in presentable clothes — nice Dockers or Levi's and a polo shirt. And I got to use my mind now. I was up for the challenge, the pressure. The executive responsibilities.

BESIDES RIDING HERD ON shipments, I had to ride herd on my crew. That meant budgeting employee hours, which was a function of available workers and needed hours. It also meant managing people one on one.

I was younger than most of them — there were just a few teenagers — but I was always ready to get down in the trenches with them, moving boxes. They knew I was just another blue-collar kid who happened to have a white-collar job. If someone was sick or otherwise not up to par because of personal reasons, I'd tell him to clock out and take a sick day or personal day. Then I'd fill in for him on the shift to keep the crew on schedule. But I wouldn't let anyone slack, either. I'd work with them, but not do their work for them. I was fair. If overtime was needed, I'd ask for volunteers.

"Who wants to stay late and earn extra money? I'm not going to pick. I'm going to let *you* decide."

That way I avoided playing favorites. I earned their respect. All I asked of my crew were honesty and hard work. In return, I'd back them up.

If a manager from another division came over and started barking at some of my workers, for whatever reason — maybe saying our lines were moving too slowly — I'd come up to him, in front of everyone, and say, "Wait a minute. If you have a problem with anyone in my crew, you come and talk to *me*."

That went miles toward cementing the loyalty between my crew and me.

If the line was moving too slowly, I'd chip in to get it moving faster.

Leverman was wary of employee theft. Workers passed through security scanners, like at the airport, when they entered or exited. Little metal security stickers were fixed to each box of CDs or videos. But some of the workers stripped the stickers off. Some of the men wore baggy pants with secret pockets sewn in near the crotches, and could walk out with stolen items between their legs.

It worked out. We bonded as a team. There was only one time I had to fire a person for boosting product.

This is how I caught the guy.

Sometimes I'd go out to the swap meet held on weekend days in the lot of the drive-in theater in Sparks — the same swap meet Grandpa Herschel used to frequent — and see if any Leverman merchandise was being peddled. Sure enough, I came upon some CDs. They still had the Leverman sticker on their boxes. I traced the products to the lines that had handled them on a particular day, and isolated potential suspects by figuring out who'd been assigned to that line.

Then I started keeping an eye on the most likely culprits. I returned to the swap meet the following weekend to see if more product from the line was showing up. It was.

I narrowed my surveillance to one worker, Roberto. Finally, one day, I spotted him sticking a CD down his pants.

I went to my supervisor, Wes, and told him about Roberto.

Wes was a long-term Leverman employee — a true-blue company man. He was incensed. He called Roberto into his office with me and shut the door.

Wes stared at Roberto. Roberto stood there with a blank, innocent face.

"I want to see what's in your pants. I can't tell you to pull down your pants, but I know you've got something in your pants."

"No I don't."

"OK. Go sit in that chair over there."

Roberto sat down. A bulge rose over one thigh. It was embarrassing.

"Pull it out of your pants," Wes said.

Roberto did. It was a CD.

"You're fired."

I was pissed at Roberto. There was no reason to steal. Leverman paid $10 an hour as a beginning wage — far more than the minimum wage, or what other warehouses paid at the time. Leverman even covered medical and dental benefits.

By in large, though, my crew was honest and notably efficient. There were times when I rewarded their hustle by buying everyone lunch. I brought in pizzas, on my dime, to the cafeteria. I said we'd have an extra 30 minutes for lunch, then we'd go out and kick ass and save 30 minutes on the floor.

This idea didn't fly with management, though. I was told I had made my crew into favorites on the floor, and the other employees all wanted to come work for me. I argued that I was increasing productivity, but I agreed to stop with the pizza.

It was like the Army. No matter how good an idea you had, your superiors had to buy into it. Someone else above you was always running the show.

My department's people worked hard all the time. They had to. Ad-mega meant pushing all day long when a shipment came in or left. I had to let a few people go who couldn't keep up. This type of work just wasn't for them. It wasn't fair to them or the company.

The other workers liked me well enough. And when one of them — a young Mexican woman — returned from vacation in her homeland, she brought me back a little ceramic bowl as a souvenir. I was surprised and touched.

I got great reviews from management. I did so well that first year, in fact, that after the supervisor of the regular-replenishment department was fired, management decided not to fill the position and, instead, to consolidate that 30-employee department with Ad-mega to see if I could run both.

The extra responsibilities came with a slight salary increase of $5,000 — saving the company $25,000 in salary. That rankled me. I thought that share should have gone to me, too. But I wasn't too disappointed, because I knew my star was rising in the company. Indeed, it was.

Leverman's policy was to promote from within whenever possible. The warehouse managers told me they were recommending me to join the company's training program for vice presidents. It was a two-year program. I was excited. I could be a 25-year-old VP with a big organization.

The future was bright.

CHAPTER FORTY-SEVEN: Watching the 'Net Rise

I liked Leverman. It was a strong company. The warehouse operation was well organized and designed. The work atmosphere was positive. Most of the time I'd work 7 a.m. to 3 or 4 p.m. I was actually having fun. I looked forward to going to work each morning. And my salary was certainly livable for a young, single guy. I relished all the free time I had after work. I had a social life again.

I had moved out of Jim's apartment. He was dating a girl he'd end up marrying. I'd gone out with a fair number of girls myself, and even moved in with some, but the relationships always ended up faltering. Almost every one cheated on me. That was unacceptable to me, given what I'd watched Mom endure with Tony all those years ago. I never cheated on anyone. If I wanted to date someone else, I'd break up with the girlfriend first. I thought that was the honorable thing.

I finally got tired of the revolving door. I couldn't maintain a long-term relationship. I got sick of even the idea of dating. Besides, a different love affair was blooming for me.

Mom was still living in her modular home in Spanish Springs. I moved in to stabilize my situation and save money. I set up my computer in the little back room, and that's where I spent most of my spare time away from Leverman: absorbing applications, learning programming languages and writing programs.

On weekends, I sometimes sat in front of the screen from 8 p.m. to 8 a.m.

Mom started worrying that I had a problem. I was practically glued to the computer screen.

"You're sitting there all night playing games!"

"I'm not. A computer's not for games. I'm learning about development and applications and market structures."

I knew it was no addiction. My old dream of working in the computer industry was ablaze again. I considered that I should start seriously thinking about such a move if a chance arose. I knew that if you do what you love and are really good at it, the money will follow.

What's more, I saw that the talent level in the computer industry wasn't that high. Leverman had an IT team at its corporate headquarters back East. A half-dozen computer engineers showed up to work on the warehouse's systems. Each of our departments had a computer. We supervisors used the terminals for interoffice email, to receive company updates and to monitor workflows.

When the computer engineers showed up, I could tell they didn't know what they were doing. Only one of them seemed knowledgeable. The rest would walk around, asking, "What are your problems?"

There'd be small email issues, such as a sent message showing "error" and not arriving. There'd be small menu issues, such as commands not executing. The computer engineers couldn't fix them. They'd fiddle around, but after they left, problems would remain. I knew if I'd had the access codes to the mainframe, I could have solved these problems myself.

These engineers were in their thirties. They reminded me of Lawrence back at Hidden Lode Explorations. Like him, they were probably recruited from the regular ranks at Leverman and given a bit of training and titles. They were practically useless.

Sometimes I'd tease them, when we were sitting around eating lunch or something. "You guys are too old to be working on computers. This is for the young crew."

"Yeah, yeah, we were working on this when you were in your diapers."

I smelled opportunity. There was a big market for servicing the computer needs of businesses.

As for Leverman's vice-president training program, only a certain number of slots were open each month company-wide, and my application was passed over several months in a row. I began losing hope. Finally, a slot opened up for me. It paid $60,000 to start. The position, however, was in Brazil. I saw photos of the warehouse complex I would be sent to. The facility was surrounded by tall gates topped with serrated wire and policed by guards. I didn't want to live there!

I was told this warehouse was in one of the company's hot distribution areas. I would work a year at the company's headquarters back East, then be sent to Brazil for the second year. It was a term commitment; I'd have to sign a contract committing myself to stay in the program.

That's what rising in the corporate structure required: going where they told you to go and living where they told you to live for as long as they needed or wanted you there. One of the supervisors at the Sparks warehouse told me he'd moved six times in 10 years.

I was disillusioned. I'd moved around enough in my life. I'd put in three years in the Army. I was settled in one spot now. I wasn't about to up and relocate again and again.

I told my bosses I didn't mind traveling, but that I was staying in Reno.

"That's not the way the program works, Jeff."

"I understand."

We left it at that.

I wouldn't sign the contract to join the training program for VPs. And because of that, I no longer was a rising star.

MANAGEMENT STARTED LOADING MORE and more duties on me. The supervisor above me had been a nice guy, but he was under a lot of pressure, too. He had no home life. His job was his life. He began being impossible to work with. Everyone was having a tough time with him.

The company, too, was starting to hit hard times. I felt like the only one in the warehouse paying attention to this. The days were getting easier. Shipments were getting lighter. I figured that this wasn't due to seasonal slowdowns. The real reason? Orders were dropping.

I contemplated the factors why. They seemed clear enough. The main reason was that the Internet was finally taking hold.

E-commerce was on the rise in the latter half of the 1990s. Amazon. com had been founded in 1994. A major cultural change was in full swing in America. More and more consumers were buying merchandise online. In fact, Amazon was using Leverman to ship orders of books and CDs. The Internet was emerging as a new major medium for communication and commerce.

I went to management and said that the company should go online — at least with a website on which customers could log in and track their products' distributions.

My idea was dismissed.

Suddenly, I felt out of step with the economy. Leverman was part of an old guard, not a brave new one. I was on the outside of the digital revolution, instead of in the trenches.

With my growing prowess at html, I'd already begun creating web pages. I knew I was primed for getting in on a fantastic new frontier. I already knew that in good time, all dynamic businesses would need a presence in cyberspace almost as much as they needed their physical facilities. In fact, I anticipated a digital marketplace in the not-very-distant future in which e-commerce websites and home offices would replace brick-and-mortar retail stores and business offices.

I knew that, like an early-bird prospector struck by gold fever, I needed to move quickly now into this virtual wilderness ahead of the hordes.

There were only two computer-network and repair companies in Reno. That meant I could hit the ground running. I put together a business plan. I would have my own network and web-design firm.

Not much later, I quit Leverman.

I was now president and founder of a web-development and computer consulting company: JDB Corporate Developments. It only existed on paper. But it was a beginning.

I was also on the hunt for a regular job until my new venture was off the ground.

CHAPTER FORTY-EIGHT: Blasting off into CYBERWORKS

I knew it would be hard giving up my $35,000-a-year salary at Leverman without having another outside source of income while I launched JDB Corporate Developments. I wanted to get into computers right away, but couldn't find job openings anywhere in town for a computer tech. I paid another visit to John, the veteran-affairs officer at the state employment office. He showed me a posting for computer programmers to work for a billing company that had recently relocated to Reno from California. I figured I'd apply.

The company, NSJ, was a family-owned operation with 15 employees. It was a very simplistic operation. Essentially, it was a mail center whose clients were lawyers working as collection agencies. The lawyers may have bought accounts from collection agencies, or were simply working as collectors themselves. They would have a list of people whose accounts had gone to collections. They would format the list into a database that NSJ provided, then forward the formatted list to NSJ via a bulletin board system. NSJ's computer programmers would pull that list off the bulletin board and drop it into the Visual Basic program, and that was it.

Sheets of paper and address labels, to go to the people getting collected from, would flow out of printers then be loaded into mail sorters.

There are always a lot of people who owe money. NSJ did a large volume of business. A van full of bins with letters would drive off each day to the post office. NSJ seemed very profitable.

The man who owned NSJ with his wife and children was Richard Malkovich. He was a bearded man in his fifties with shifty eyes peering behind wire-frame spectacles. Malkovich was a bit pudgy and reminded me of a smaller version of the Grateful Dead's Jerry Garcia, but clad in a business shirt and tie instead of tie-dye. Malkovich had retired from a San Francisco Bay area bank — perhaps after seeing the profits to be made in servicing the collections industry.

The reason Malkovich needed to hire computer programmers was to integrate the company's database with nationwide databases that contained addresses and phone numbers, which the lawyers would send over the bulletin boards. He needed programmers who knew Visual Basic to write applications to merge the databases into his mailing operation.

I knew nothing about Visual Basic. But if there was one thing I did know, it was how to bone up quickly on a computer program. I downloaded the free trial software from Microsoft and learned the language, writing programs on my computer at home.

I had an advantage in the job-application process. Since I was a military veteran, the state paid the billing company to test me. Malkovich was happy to have me tested. I took the test at the VA office and passed. I was hired. Malkovich welcomed me aboard with a handshake. The grip wasn't very firm, but he was eager to have me there. My status as a vet meant the state would cover half of my wages until my training period with the company passed. Malkovich — I would come to find out — was a big penny-pincher.

When I arrived for my first day on the job, I found two others also had been hired for the programming room. Two of us were vets; the third was a young guy who'd recently graduated in computer science from the University of Nevada, Reno. The programming room was a little space with five desks arranged in a circle and three computer terminals on the desks.

We were introduced to the head programmer, the man who'd written the company's programs. His name was Dwayne, and he was a caricature of the antisocial, arrogant, obese computer geek. He had a hairy, unkempt beard, sweat stains under his armpits, and swigged sodas all day. In his office, he watched *Pinky and the Brain* — the animated television show about two lab rats intent on taking over the world.

It was obvious from the start that Dwayne would provide no assistance to us trio of newbies. Our first week, he waddled into our programming room in the mornings wearing a look of disdain. "I don't like you, so I'm not going to talk to you today," he'd say, then waddle back into his office. If we had a question, he'd say, in his low, corpulent rumble, "You are below my intelligence. I do not speak with you."

Malkovich called us three new programmers into his office and shut the door. He had a secret plan to share: As soon as we were up to speed, he was going to fire Dwayne. That sounded good to me. I was used to the team environment — gathering the group together, divvying up tasks and then moving on out and accomplishing them, like in the military. Dwayne was a liability.

When the three of us were back in the programming room, I decided to take the initiative in getting us started. Our mission: to master the program without Dwayne.

"How about the three of us sit down, let's analyze the program, let's break it down into modules and find out what we have to do," I said. Tony, the other programmer who was a veteran, had experience from the Navy with SCSI interfaces with hardware and software. So we put him on that. Josh, the computer-science graduate, and I went through the application itself, breaking it down into smaller parts.

Within a week we'd outlined a new plan for getting clients' information over the Internet without using cumbersome bulletin boards. It would save us money. Malkovich liked the idea. Josh and I wrote out a program proposal. Everything was falling into place at this new job. Or so I thought. I was working well with the owner. I was integrating my skills into the workplace. I had been with NSJ a month, and everything was going smoothly. I was looking forward to the two-week, deer-hunting trip I'd planned with Drew. I'd told Malkovich about that trip before getting hired on. He'd said it was OK.

When I came back to work after my hunting trip, I was in for a surprise. I went to the building's side door and found my key didn't work. That was odd. Yes, the place was secure, but why had the locks been changed?

I walked around to the main entrance and went into the front waiting room. I explained my problem to the receptionists. "Can you let me in?"

"No, we can't let you in," one of them said.

"How do I get in to go to work?"

"Oh, you don't work here anymore."

A call was made back to someone in the building. Before long, an employee carried out a box of my possessions that had been in the programming room. I was told to leave.

I was stunned.

"Well, what happened?" I asked. "I don't understand."

"We can't tell you anything."

"Well, give me a reason."

"We don't have a reason. We don't have time to talk to you."

I went back to the state-employment office and told John what had happened. He was pissed. He called up NSJ for an explanation.

The explanation was that I had worked "unauthorized overtime."

That was a whopper. How *could* I have worked any overtime? I had been away on a hunting trip for two weeks!

John requested that NSJ send him my time card. It was never sent.

I never did find out what happened. But I have a notion.

Malkovich had a sweet deal going. He could hire as many vets as possible, train them while paying them half of what he would to a normal employee as they went through the "training period," and then let each vet go after he'd been trained and worked a short time. In this way, NSJ could hire new vets at half the wages for a new training period.

John sent no more vets to NSJ.

CHAPTER FORTY-NINE: ABCs of the IT Biz

I still needed to find a day job as I built up JDB Corporate Developments. I had a handful of clients by now, but there was no way I could support myself yet on JDB alone. I religiously scoured local want ads and called companies I'd worked with before to see if they had MIS positions.

An ad from the ABC computer company caught my eye. ABC needed a web developer and a network technician. I believed I could handle either job. The company was a startup with four employees and had been in business 10 months. ABC built computer systems, retailed hardware and software and set up and maintained networks for clients. It was, in effect, providing turnkey computer service. If a business needed to ramp up its computer capabilities, all it had to do was call ABC and it would be outfitted with computers and software, have the computers set up and the network kept running.

It struck me as a great new field. Catching on with ABC would be a great opportunity. I would learn the ropes and — if the time came that I wanted to leave the company — I would be able to strike out on my own.

ABC was located out on the edge of Sparks, in a large office complex in the industrial section. I was impressed by the large glass walls, plush carpets, expensive furniture. I didn't know at the time that the offices were sublet from a larger corporation, a situation that gave ABC an image of being larger than it was.

I was excited to interview. I did well.

The owner, Randy Reyes, was impressed that already I was designing websites for my few JDB clients. He wanted to offer me the job of web developer. Randy was a heavyset man in his late thirties who had started selling computers after working for a city parks department. Later, he'd worked at a computer store that also provided technical support. Then he'd decided to strike out on his own.

The pay was $10 an hour. That didn't tickle me, but I smelled opportunity. If I could get in the door, I'd grow with the company and hone my skills. Randy talked in a slow, somewhat dopey voice, but I figured he had a mind for computers and business.

He asked me to bring along my web-development clients from JDB. I turned thumb's-down on that. I said I'd finish out those projects, but to be fair to the company I wouldn't take on any new clients of my own. It was agreed that I'd wrap up my current projects, then join the company. And so I did.

IT WAS A GOOD fit from the start. I loved the work. My first duty was designing a corporate website for ABC itself. ABC was an aggressive little company that had a range of clients: a small downtown Reno casino, a public water-treatment facility, and so on. I not only designed websites and got them up for clients, but started interacting more frequently with clients, answering their questions, fielding their requests.

ABC was a computer lover's dream. I loved the access to the latest software and high-end systems I couldn't afford myself. ABC ordered the best, so we employees could learn them. I was immersing myself in cutting-edge technology. New Pentium processors. The first SDRAM of memory. The first flat-panel monitors. It was a digital candy store. Whenever the UPS deliveryman dropped off boxes, we techies would rush to open them and see what came in.

Four months into my job, I was at the company Christmas party in the office complex decked with holiday trimmings. Randy came up to me.

"Jeff, we're hiring a new web designer."

My jaw dropped. "Does this mean I'm fired?"

He smiled. "No, no, we want to promote you and have you start going over to the systems side of the business."

Technical support? That didn't sound good to me. I loved building websites. Tech-support was dead end.

"But I like web development," I said.

"The guy we're bringing in has a computer-science degree," Randy said. "He has more programming experience. But don't worry. You're going to kind of be his boss, and interact with him and our clients."

The next week, I started working on systems and networks. Tech support wasn't too bad. I grew to like it. I set up systems for clients and responded to problems: printer issues, network issues, monitor issues, workstations down, servers down. They usually weren't hard to solve, although they could take some time, methodically working through the systems, analyzing if there was a problem with the hardware, or a bug in the software. Maybe they'd installed applications that had taken down the protocols and services, and the applications would have to be uninstalled. Maybe someone had tried to print out a file that was too big for the printer's memory to handle. There were thousands of scenarios. I'd trace back what programs were last working before the system went down. It was forensic work.

I liked the deference that clients paid to me when I made a call. I'd show up in a collared shirt and jeans, carrying my little gray toolkit with precision screwdrivers and pliers. I'd be treated like royalty. "Do you need coffee? Do you need a sandwich? It's lunchtime, can we get you a burger?" Their fate was in my hands. Yes, sometimes it took a while to find a solution, going online to research particularly tricky problems. But it was extremely satisfying after the system came back online and I walked away, mission accomplished. It felt awesome.

My tech-support role lasted six months. Meanwhile, ABC's business continued to grow. More employees were added. I was given another promotion.

RANDY MADE ME ABC'S sales manager. This position, too, proved to my liking.

I could talk about the latest hardware and software, and the networks a business would need to survive in the marketplace. I was hitting the road all over the county, meeting with company owners or executives and IT managers, getting new accounts, discussing solutions to clients' needs. I had my own soft-sell pitch, rooted in concern for the client's needs.

"These are our certifications. Let's talk about exactly what you are looking for, and I'll get you the exact solution you need."

This approach worked because it was straightforward and honest. I believed in the products and services — just like Nana had believed in Tupperware. I racked up success after success. An Indian reservation. Two major printing companies that had set up plants in Nevada. A slot-machine manufacturer. Accounts each worth $100,000-plus a year. I grew more confident each time, and that only contributed to my success. My closing rate was about 97 percent. I relished the work. I was a hyperactive promoter of technology from the computer world.

Then I came up with an idea for a service support contract.

Here's how it would work.

The owner of, say, a ski glove-making business would call and say, "Our systems are down. We need help."

I'd go in, do an analysis, find the problem and fix it. Then I'd report on their software. "Your accounting package is out of date. You need to upgrade that." I'd have a laundry list of other updates. Then I'd sit down with the owner and make a proposal:

"Instead of spending money to get up to speed, why not sign up for a support contract with us? I'll come out each month and service you. And when you have a problem, just call us, and we won't bill you. We'd just consider the call as part of the support contract."

ABC would have the first IT support contracts in town. But Randy wasn't hot on the idea.

"We're not going to make money doing this."

"Sure we will," I said.

I showed him a basic formula I'd worked out that covered ABC's overhead expenses by 20 percent and allowed us to hire another technician or engineer.

I researched legal documents and state financial law to the degree that I could write out the first draft of a service contract. Randy agreed to try it out. He had the company attorney polish the contract.

I was proved right. The service contracts made the company money.

AT THIS POINT I was totally immersed in computers. I was working 18 hours a day for ABC, seven days a week. I was in love with my work. I was bringing $70,000 to $100,000 a month in sales to the company. I sold so much that our support staff couldn't keep up with me. I'd have to come in on the weekends to help get product out and networks installed.

When I wasn't selling or backing up the support staff, I kept increasing my skills, getting sales and technical certifications from software and hardware manufacturers. I was soaking up computer expertise like a sponge.

One day Randy, his wife, Elaine, who was the company controller, and one of the head engineers, Jake, came into my office.

"Jeff," Randy said, "we like what you're doing and we'd like to make you a partner of the firm. We see you're in here on the weekends. You're in here all the time. We know you have our best interests at heart."

My computer passion, my thirst for constant knowledge, was paying off dividends. Partner? I was most definitely intrigued.

"Send me over the paperwork," I said. "I'll take a look at it."

Jake was also being offered a partnership. He was only 23. Jake wasn't the best engineer. He didn't have the obsessive mentality. But he could bear down long enough to figure problems out. His weaknesses were his ego and his age.

He was making good money, and enjoying recreational drugs and party girls. He could be arrogant with clients. He also didn't push himself to learn all the new software and systems coming out. Still, he and I got along well.

It took six months for Randy and Elaine to get the partnership paperwork to Jake and me. By the time the partnership contracts arrived, I'd been promoted again: to vice president of sales and marketing. ABC now had 20 employees and a second location, in the Silicon Valley, where it built systems and serviced a large client that developed high-tech media products.

The engineers and technicians were productive. But we saw the owners begin to coast on the success. Randy and Elaine were spending less time on site. They were taking vacations and letting us managers run the show. I didn't mind. I was 26 now, earning, with my sales commissions, $60,000 a year. If I became a partner, the dividends from company profits would push my income to $100,000.

I considered that wasn't too bad for a guy with only a high school diploma.

My life was pretty simple: Work hard, keep mastering my computer and sales skills. My outside needs were few. I had moved back into Drew's little house. He and I were best of friends again. He'd married Traci, but divorced her. That was a great emotional relief to Drew, but brought him financial hardship. Even working two jobs, he was hard-pressed. He was in debt. He had to pay child support. The divorce decree had heavily favored her, a young single mother. Drew had to cover her car payments.

I'd made him a deal. I'd cover his monthly child-support payment so that he could climb out of debt. I was content with my tiny, 7-by-10-foot bedroom.

I'd get off work late, and Drew and I would head out to a bar for a bit. It was like our freewheeling days when we had the janitorial service, except that we didn't party hard anymore. We weren't out scamming chicks. This is because there was only one woman in my life now, a girl named Tanya. What spare time I had for dating, I spent with her.

The rest of the time, I was an IT junkie. One who expected to own a piece of an IT company, ABC, very soon.

THE ABC PARTNERSHIP OFFER wasn't what I'd expected.

I met with the company attorney and accountant to review the papers. I was dismayed. Randy must have thought I'd never been in business before. The terms were one-sided. It was 20 pages of horse pucky. I was being offered 5 percent of the business. There were stock options in the deal, but they couldn't be exercised for 10 years and would go away if I quit or was fired during that period. The dividend payout schedule was similarly set up to keep me roped in.

Jake was unsure about signing the papers, too. "What do you think about this?" he said.

"I think it's sh*t," I said.

Jake had his father's attorney look the papers over. The attorney agreed with me.

Jake and I were settled on the issue. We told Randy that we each wanted at least 10 to 15 percent of the business. We showed him that we directly contributed to 80 percent of the last few years' growth. He said we could keep negotiating. He was certain we'd come to terms. He smiled broadly. His slow voice was full of warmth.

"Right now, guys, I consider each of you partners. We don't have to wait until you sign on the dotted line."

That was an expression of confidence, indeed. Unfortunately, that's all it turned out to be.

Instead of joining the inner circle of decision-making, Jake and I found ourselves learning of key moves after the fact.

Randy went out and hired another salesperson for the Silicon Valley office. Then he hired an operations manager for Reno. We didn't need an operations manager in Reno. Things were running smoothly. We didn't need another layer of management. What rankled me even more was that Randy paid this new guy a higher salary than the engineer's or mine.

When the year's end came, there were no dividends paid out to us "partners." Instead, Randy and Elaine dipped into profits and bought themselves a fishing boat.

I found I had little influence on Randy's thinking anymore. Success had gone to his head. Where he'd listened to my input on marketing and strategy in the past, he was now turning a deaf ear.

I kept up on the developments in the computer industry. I was in the trenches, selling, and I was online and subscribing to trade publications, learning all about the newest software and the direction the industry was heading.

Where it was heading seemed clear as day. There was a big neon billboard called the Internet that was flashing in every computer-user's face now. "eBay!"

"Amazon!" Software companies were making massive investments in Internet technology. Oracle announced that every one of its new software products was Internet compatible. The shift of commerce into cyberspace was in full swing.

I told Randy that the Internet and networking were shaping into the big revenue generators for ABC and all the other turnkey businesses in the country. But he disagreed. "No, no, hardware sales," he insisted.

"In a few years, hardware's going to be given away," I argued. "The money will be made on networking, security, services. Things you cannot purchase without talent."

"Nah, I'm not interested."

It was maddening! How could he be so blind? Was it the age issue rearing its head again? Was it that he couldn't believe someone 15 years younger than he could have market vision?

I'd been with ABC three years now. The company had grown. So had the owner's head.

I was disgusted. I was just an employee to Randy now. Just a minion to bring in the dough and support his high-flying lifestyle.

I never wanted to be someone else's monkey. At the end of the year it was time to collect bonuses and dividends. I was advised that during our record-breaking year, sales reached an all-time high. But there would be no bonuses or dividends that year because the owners needed money to purchase an RV. So they took all the partners' money and bonuses without letting us know, and spent it.

My loyalty to ABC suddenly evaporated. *Poof.* Right there and then.

"You know what? This isn't working out. I'm giving you my two-weeks' notice," I told Randy.

He was calm.

"Well," he said, slowly, "I figured you were going to do that pretty soon."

"You know, it didn't have to end like this," I said. "If you had offered me a better partnership deal and did not steal my money, you could've kept me here."

It was true. He could have. Had he only let me run more, I would have made the company a lot more money. Then, in time, I would've bought him out.

"So what are you going to do now?" he asked.

"I don't know. But there's tons of companies that want me to work for them."

And there were.

Clients of ABC wanted me to come aboard as their IT guy, or as a salesman, or as a business manager. They'd seen how hard I worked, how driven I was, how much business I brought in to ABC.

I had options.

CHAPTER FIFTY: In the Company of Nuts

I mulled over my options. One was obvious. I could immediately start up a turnkey business to compete against ABC. I could launch very quickly. I could go out and hit up the clients I'd brought in to ABC, and tell them I could continue to offer them the service they were accustomed to. These clients were not off limits to me; Randy was so foolish, he hadn't had any of us employees sign non-compete agreements.

But I didn't pursue this avenue. It wasn't honorable. I remembered the stories Randy had told us at ABC. When he'd been working at a computer store, Digitage, and had decided to start his own business, he'd gone around to the clients he serviced and told them that Digitage didn't want them as customers anymore and that it was OK for him to pick them up. "I don't want you guys left without service," he'd told them.

Randy was proud about that bit of subterfuge. "Business is business," he'd said.

I never wanted to stoop to such sliminess.

One company that wanted to hire me was a family-owned maker of repair kits for hardware. Nutmender, Inc., had a little factory that produced kits that contained tools for fixing loose, stripped or broken screws, nuts, bolts, washers and other hardware. The kits were especially useful to motor-vehicle owners, and Nutmender had carved out a wonderful little niche in the automotive after-market.

I did a bit of research and found that Nutmender made one of the best repair kits on the market. The father who'd built the business was retiring, and his twin sons, Pete and Pat, wanted to bring in a general manager to run things. I'd jet skied with them; they'd been customers at my jet-ski shop. We were friends. They were fun to hang out with. The GM position they offered me paid $120,000 — a salary plus bonus.

It seemed like a good move. I accepted. I knew I could bring fresh ideas and energy to Nutmender. The operation was, frankly, underperforming. The company was a tenth the size of its nearest competitor. Fortunately, Nutmender's product was far superior.

Nutmender was decent size, with 40 employees. "We're grossing $5 million a year," Pat said, proudly.

I wasn't impressed.

"You've been in business 20 years and you're only grossing $5 million a year?" I said. "ABC is doing that and it's only been in business four years."

I knew Nutmender could do better — much better.

Pete and Pat's father, Perry, had suffered a mild stroke and was retiring after 20 years, which is why Nutmender needed a GM. Pete and Pat had the titles of "president" and "production manager," but they weren't prepared to run the place by themselves. The twins wanted a hands-on manager who would report to them.

I was eager to start.

I WANTED TO LEAVE ABC on good terms. Justin, a cousin of my girlfriend, Tanya, had computer-sales experience. He was unhappy in his current job for an electronics corporation in Arizona, building components. He wanted to come back to Nevada. I figured I could train him to replace me. It'd do a favor for a relative of Tanya's, to boot.

I talked him up to Randy. Justin didn't have much money, so I paid for his plane ticket. I told him to wear a suit and tie. I briefed him on the company. I counseled him on what to mention in his cover letter and résumé: his computer experience, his time in the Navy.

He passed the first job interview. Randy had him show up a second time. I paid for Justin's airfare again. It was agreed that ABC would hire him to replace me as a salesman. I'd train him over my final two weeks, introduce him to all my clients before I left. So I did.

There was still a matter of about thousands of dollars in commissions I had coming to me. ABC's policy was that a commission wasn't paid until the client paid on the invoice. I was worried that Randy would try to stiff me.

I sat down with him and Elaine, the controller, with a spreadsheet I'd prepared, showing the accounts I'd brought in that I was still owed commissions on. "When an invoice is paid, send me my commission check and I'll mark it off on the spreadsheet," I said.

When I left, I was given a check for $2,000 for commissions. Randy assured me that I'd get my remaining commissions as invoices were paid.

The commission checks from ABC were still not showing up. I called Justin and inquired whether certain clients had paid. He said they had.

I called Randy. I was still cordial with him. I'd even just bought a new computer system from ABC, to show I was a good sport. He told me to be patient about the commission checks.

I never did get the money. I could have gone to court, but considered that after attorney and other legal fees and lost time, it wouldn't have been worth it. Out of the money due me, I might have seen $5,000.

I'd gained the confidence of running a multimillion-dollar corporation. But the big lesson I took away from this period was that trust in business is not always assured. Maybe if a relationship lasted many years it justified trust, but I was dubious.

I'd been with ABC three years, helped the company grow, helped the owner make money. And Randy was still only too glad to not pay me what he owed. I was no longer working for him, so he was perfectly content to screw me.

FROM THE START, I found that Nutmender was a very ingrown operation, in need of fresh blood and ideas.

The place was just running off the toolkit the old man had invented all those years ago. The front-desk receptionist had been with the company since day one. Harriet was already in her sixties, years before, when she'd started at Nutmender. Now she was hard as a fossil. A fossil with an attitude. She acted as if *she* owned half the company.

Pete and Pat introduced us. "This is Jeff, our new general manager."

"Oh, now *he's* my boss?" she snarled.

Harriet was obviously having difficulty adapting to Perry retiring.

I spent the first week getting a feel for the place by working in each section — the different stations on the assembly line, shipping, even janitorial. I wanted to understand the entire operation. I frequently had a bilingual employee with me to translate. Most of the workers only spoke Spanish.

One thing I had to change right away was how I'd decorated my office. I'd hung the framed certificates from my computer career on the wall. Pete stopped in and told me I had to take them down. His dad, who still came in once a day, had seen the awards on my wall and been offended.

"He says they make it look like you own the place."

I took the certificates down. I replaced them with prints of abstract paintings and nature scenes from a picture gallery.

It didn't take me long to see why Nutmender was only grossing $5 million a year. On the floor, the products were being assembled by hand. There was no automation. It was crazy. Not only was the operation inefficient, it was vulnerable. The entire assembly line was at the mercy of the employees. Sometimes production came to a halt if a worker called in sick or showed up late.

I called a meeting with Pete and Pat in my office. They were wearing shorts and T-shirts. They liked to play a lot, jet skiing or four-wheeling or driving their sports cars with expensive stereos. When they were in their offices at work, they'd often be playing on their computers, or watching videos on their TVs. They were frequently away from the plant. They acted as if coming to my meeting was an imposition. Their body language said it all: They slouched, their eyes wandered.

"We've got to spend a little money to automate the line," I said.

The brothers gave me funny looks.

"We can't do that," Pete said.

"Yes you can," I said. "If you automate the processes, we can at the very least triple production after we've tooled up."

I ticked off the list of jobs being performed by hand. Workers were standing at shop tables, each working on one tool, or one machine — a drill, press or lathe.

"You guys haven't invested any time in tooling or automation," I said.

"That stuff costs too much," Pat said.

"You have to look at it in the right way," I said. "Let me prepare some comparative analyses for you on the cost to tool up. We can take out business loans, receivable loans against what's going out. It's possible."

It was agreed I should put together some analyses. I got started on them right away.

I made phone calls and surfed the Internet for prices on machines. I called the bank where the company did business. After a week I had figures prepared.

I met with Pete and Pat again. I handed them copies of spreadsheets.

They flipped through the pages. I started explaining various figures.

"Don't talk to us like we're stupid," Pete said. "We understand these numbers."

Pat nodded.

"The main point is," I said, "we could be selling 500 to 1,000 kits a month, instead of 50 to 100. We wouldn't be stuck with all these back orders. We'd be making and moving a lot more product. We could be grossing 15 to

20 million annually if we just tool up and spend around a million. Your bank is willing to loan that to us based off the receivables and the proposal I presented to them."

"No, we can't do that," Pete said.

Pat nodded.

My face must have shown disbelief. Were these guys *children*?

"You're going to spend two-and-a-half million dollars to make 15. *And* you're going to reallocate half your employees to other areas in the plant."

I knew that the employees' hold on the production line would be broken if there were fewer of them. At the moment, each employee was trained on only three tools, instead of all of them. That meant that if a disgruntled or irresponsible employee didn't show up, half the operation could grind to a halt. What's more, the employees worked only as fast as they wanted to. That was another reason production output was below where it should have been.

One Monday, a lathe operator didn't shown up. It was 7:30 a.m., a half-hour after the shift began.

"Where is this guy?" I asked one of the two floor managers.

"I think he went to Mexico on the weekend."

"Do we have a phone number to call this guy?"

"No, we don't have a number."

I couldn't believe it. About all the company had on file about its employees were their addresses. No phone numbers. No work visa numbers. No driver's license numbers. No employee work histories.

I told Pete and Pat that we needed to train someone else on the lathe and fire this guy.

"No, Humberto has been with us for seven years," Pete said. "We're not letting you fire him."

Pat nodded.

I knew now that I'd made a mistake in signing on with them. But I couldn't help myself. I had other ideas to share.

So I continued, despite my better judgment. I called another meeting.

"Nutmender knows how to make its product, old-fashioned though the operation is. But we fall short in marketing and selling the product."

I noted that the extent of the advertising was a few ads in trade publications. There was no strong distribution strategy. The logistics in shipping were backward. We needed an up-to-date database to track orders and deliveries. We needed a conveyor belt and bin receptacles to move packages from one end of the shipping area to the other.

The knowledge I'd gained working at Leverman and ABC had taught me a lot about how a business should be run.

Pete and Pat weren't receptive to any of my input.

We had reached an impasse. I saw Nutmender as being broken. They saw it as not being broken, and therefore not in need of any fixing.

I understood why. They were drawing their six-figure salaries, which supported their lifestyles. They didn't want to toy with the financials. They didn't want to risk losing their playful lives. They were afraid.

It was the father who had built the business. The sons, who had barely made it out of high school and probably couldn't have found decent jobs outside of the family business, regarded Nutmender as their personal cash cow. They were spoiled. They just didn't have much business sense to speak of.

Well, at least I was making a good income. Except that there was a hurdle to getting paid. That hurdle was Harriet. In addition to running the front desk, Harriet was in charge of cutting checks.

My first check hadn't shown up. I asked Harriet about it.

"I don't know why we're paying you," she said, sourly. "You haven't done anything here. The company's the same as it's always been."

I called Perry. He told Harriet to pay me. She wasn't happy about it.

I asked Perry if I could discipline Harriet.

"No, this lady has been with me from the start," he said. "Let me talk to her."

Her attitude toward me didn't change.

This company was in dire need of a shakeup, from one end to the other. But I was a GM with no power to act as a GM.

AT THIS TIME, ONE of the big three U.S. automakers was interested in acquiring Nutmender, to add to the automaker's tool division. Discussions had been going on for a couple years. Nutmender provided tool kits to the automaker, which sold them as options with some of its models.

Perry's retirement seemed like a good time for the automaker to get serious. Two representatives from the automaker's industrial plant flew out to Reno to meet with Pete and Pat and tour Nutmender's facility. I had the machines stripped of their tools so the reps couldn't glean any trade secrets. We brought the reps in on a Saturday.

Even with the place idle, the reps saw the same flaws in the operation that I did.

The five of us went out to dinner at a casino steakhouse. They said they were interested in seeing if Nutmender could boost production. If so, the numbers would be right and their company would be very interested in buying Nutmender. The market potential for the tool kit was vast.

Pete and Pat said they'd looked at the operation and decided it was most efficient just the way it was.

I was confused. Here, the automaker was preparing to offer $20 million. Pete and Pat weren't interested in getting the company in shape to attract that offer.

"It's not a real offer," Pete told me later. "They're just bullsh*tting us, trying to get inside our operation, see how we do things, so they can end up copying us."

Pat nodded.

The automaker reps took me to dinner. "Do you think you can turn this company around and sell it to us?"

"No, I'm just an employee," I said. "Why don't you invest in them, let them tool up and get bigger, and you'd have a percentage of the company, and eventually buy the family out?"

"That's a good idea," one of the reps said.

I met with Pete and Pat. I told them they should try to get the automaker to invest in Nutmender, so there'd be capital with which to automate the plant.

"No, that's not a good idea," Pete said.

Pat nodded.

I'd reached the end of my rope.

I called for a meeting in my office. Pete and Pat arranged to come down in the morning, before a fishing trip.

I got straight to the point. "You guys aren't letting me do anything. You hired me in here to manage this place so you guys could take more time off. You're not letting me make one decision. Your inventory's out of control. Your finances are out of control."

"When are you leaving?" Pete asked.

"Right now if you want me to."

"Fine," Pat said. "We were going to call our dad and ask if we could fire you anyway today."

I'd lasted three months.

I grabbed the little photograph I had of Tanya on my desk and put it in my pocket.

I walked out of there at 1 p.m. with one determined conviction:

That's it. I'm going into the computer business for myself. Right this very moment! At 2 p.m. April 23, 1999.

My Chevy Blazer had been rear-ended the week before, and was in the shop being painted. It was supposed to be ready for pickup that day. I'd already turned in my rental car. I called the shop. The Blazer wasn't ready. It was still being worked on.

I walked the five blocks to the office of Hidden Lode Explorations, where Mom was still working.

"I just quit my job," I said.

She looked at me with surprise. And suspicion. This was the second big-salaried job I'd quit in four months.

"Are you crazy? You were making more than any of us."

"It ain't the money."

"What are you going to do?"

"I'm starting a business on my own. I need to borrow your car keys. I'm going out to get a cell phone and a business license."

"Seriously?"

I was.

I made the rounds immediately. I filled out an application for a business license at the city of Sparks clerk's office. I would name my company CYBERWORKS. It was a calculated choice. I'd searched on the Internet and knew there were many companies with that name around the world. That was good camouflage. The folks at ABC wouldn't be able to figure out for a while that CYBERWORKS was owned by me. As soon as word spread around Reno that a new computer-services company was in town, they would check out the name and decide the newcomer was part of a large chain. They wouldn't guess it was Jeff Bowling's one-man operation. At most, they'd believe I was a CYBERWORKS employee.

I drove back to Hidden Lode. Mom helped me complete the forms for articles of incorporation, which I overnighted to the Secretary of State's office.

I bought a cell phone at AirTouch Cellular.

By 5:30 p.m. I started calling potential clients, leaving messages that I was in the computer business, and the number they could call to reach me.

CHAPTER FIFTY-ONE: By the Seat of My Briefs

I knew I could pull this venture off. I'd earned a decent wage with bonuses in my three months at Nutmender. After paying off my bills and Blazer, I had about $7,000 in savings as a safety net.

I decided that to get going I'd take on whatever business I could. ABC charged $65 an hour for technical services and $85 an hour for engineering services. I was certified to provide both. I decided to charge $10 an hour less than ABC's rates.

Drew brought me a client right away. His employer, an extrusions plant, was a client of ABC, but management was unhappy with ABC's service since I'd left. My cell phone rang the very day Drew told his bosses I had my own company. I took the high road.

"I'm not advocating you leaving the old place I used to work at," I said.

But evidently the dissatisfaction with ABC was incurable. I had my anchor client.

More customers followed. A shipping-supply company whose owner I knew from buying boxes from him for Nutmender. Then CQT, a large ad agency in town that also had gotten fed up with ABC's service. CQT handled the extrusion company's advertising. Through that connection, the ad people found out I'd left ABC and was on my own. The office manager got hold of me right away. Now I had two large clients and a small one. A wave of relief rushed through me.

I billed out $15,000 that first month. I set up and hosted networks. I ran my business from my little bedroom in the house I shared with Drew. I had three computers already set up and networked, hooked up to an Internet connection. It would get so hot in the room, with a server and two other systems running, I'd have to strip to my underwear.

I didn't mind. I was busy building a business, handling everything. I forwarded my landline to my cell phone. I printed out invoices and mailed them myself. I logged jobs in and out. I had little time to rest.

Word of mouth spread quicker than I'd expected. Evidently I'd had a loyal client following at ABC, and these clients had grown dissatisfied with my former employer. I prided myself on service, reliability and honesty. That put me way ahead of the place I'd left.

ABC had gotten increasingly pricy, and did not follow through on deadlines. Lying, unfortunately, happens to be big in the computer industry. Clients are sold hardware and software they really don't need because they aren't knowledgeable enough to know they don't need it. It's how some computer companies make money. But I've always found that practice dishonorable. Clients are also given snow jobs about when a job can be completed. I didn't go that route. I was upfront. "Yes, I can get the product by that date." Or, "We should expect 10 working days before the software will be delivered, so I'll do the best I can." And I did do the best I could. When a job was waiting, I'd show up and get it done. I would work as late into the night or following morning as needed.

I'd research which hardware went with which software, which best served clients' needs, which manufacturer offered the best warranty, which product had the best shelf life. I'd customize workstations for each client. An industrial client needed a system to perform data processing and word processing, spreadsheets and email — no graphics or other fancy applications. No problem. I built a simple workstation with a Pentium 300 computer with 512 MB of memory, mouse, keyboard and printer, and a standard 15-inch monitor. I installed the Windows NT 4.0, and a dial-up modem for the Internet. DSL wasn't in widespread use back then.

I drew a lot of satisfaction, and confidence, from building and deploying systems that stayed up and running. A happy customer was the best kind of advertising.

My cell phone kept ringing and ringing.

During the second month, one of my bankers referred a real-estate firm needing 35 systems, two servers and a network. It was a good contract. And it led to another big contract with one of that firm's clients. I set up a network for its California, Oregon and Reno offices.

By the end of the third month I had $70,000 in the bank.

It was ironic. I'd figured at the start on getting two or three clients with regular servicing, so I could work three or four days a week, pay my bills, save up for a house, and spend the rest of my work time on software research and development, coming up with applications I could patent and sell around the world. That was where the big money lay. I didn't want to be bound by servicing clients around the clock.

But all of a sudden I was too busy to devote any time to R&D. I'd filled up the living room and garage of Drew's house with computers for the systems I was building and installing for clients. UPS was making shipments to the home like nuts. The deliveryman laughed about it.

"You need an office," he said.

He was right. I knew that I needed to rent an office and hire employees.

IN THE FOURTH MONTH after starting CYBERWORKS, I opened an office in a little 800-square-foot space in Sparks and hired another cousin of my girlfriend, Tanya, to work in web development for me, so I could focus more on networks and security.

Three months later I had a staff of six. We offered turnkey service: handling any computer-related need a customer had, from buying hardware and software, to installing it, setting up a network, training staff how to use the equipment, servicing the equipment (available 24-7), designing websites, hosting the websites and networks.

It fit my competitive personality. Whatever the game, I will use every tool in my arsenal to win. I will go all out.

By now, ABC was trying to find out as much about CYBERWORKS' growing business as possible. There were incidents of someone "port scanning" our network — sending network probes to our computer ports to look for weaknesses and try to crack into our system. The intrusion-detection system I'd put on our network logged the probes and the Internet provider addresses of the sender. I looked up the IP address. It was ABC's.

I knew Randy was used to hiring people on the sly to dig up information, which he'd pay for. When I worked for ABC, I'd see a stranger go into his office. Then, in the afternoon, Randy would come to me and say, "I found out so-and-so needs a bid on some systems." I suspected that Randy not only was paying informants for business leads, but paying people in companies' purchasing departments to buy from ABC. He used spies, and he paid kickbacks. That's the way he did business.

I was in the CYBERWORKS office about 1 o'clock one night, catching up on paperwork, when I heard rustling in the alley where I parked my Blazer. It sounded like a person. I grabbed my .22 pistol and went outside.

I turned around the corner into the alley. Someone was hunched over the top of the trash receptacle, 30 feet away.

"What the hell are you doing?!" I shouted.

The person took off running in the darkness. All I could see was his back.

The lid of the receptacle was flipped open. I looked inside. Sheets showing the source codes we were using to create websites were stacked up in one side of the receptacle.

The next day I made sure that all the employees adhered to policy and shredded all documents before throwing them away.

Sometimes I'd see ABC employees driving by my office in daylight, checking it out. One day, an IT administrator for one of the state agencies that ABC serviced sauntered into my business. His name was Jeremy. We knew each other. I'd sold software to his agency when I was at ABC, and then I'd set him up personally with some hardware and software, too. Like a lot of IT guys, he moonlighted as an IT "consultant."

Jeremy was a short, sloppy fellow who was always running his mouth, always asking questions. Just a chatterbox and busybody. He could be annoying, but he was harmless enough.

"Hey, what's going on, man?" I said. "You need some computer parts?"

I figured he'd defected from using ABC as a supplier and was coming over to CYBERWORKS.

"No, I want to talk to you about a few things," Jeremy said.

"Well, come into my office and sit down."

I brought my service manager into the office. I figured we were going to be discussing a new account.

"Oh," Jeremy said, "I just want you to know that Randy asked me to come over here and spy on you. He wants me to report back to him."

I did a double take. Was he serious?

Jeremy was.

I was appalled.

I lost my temper.

"First of all, you're a state employee," I said. "Why would you get yourself mixed up in this?"

"Well, I don't want to get in the middle of this —"

"Well, you are in the middle of this now," I said. "Second of all, I'm not going to tell you anything. I cannot believe that you came over here and said this to me right now. You can go back and tell Randy he needs to do his own legwork, and that I'm going to beat him in the marketplace legally and on my own."

Some time after that, a letter arrived in the mail from Randy, cc'd to his attorney. Randy was too cheap to have his attorney draft the letter. I've kept it to this day. It accused me of stealing ABC's clients and of badmouthing his company, and reminded me I'd never been a partner in the business. He threatened to sue me based on clients he thought I was going to take.

I'd had it!

It so happened that I had a service call at CQT, the big ad agency. Jeremy's wife, coincidentally, was a media buyer at the agency. I usually small-talked with her when I was there, but this time I avoided her.

Ted, the chief operating officer, with whom I was on friendly terms, noticed that I was ignoring her. "You don't want talk to the girls, today?" he asked.

"No. That woman's husband just came by my place and tried to spy on me to report back to my old boss at ABC."

Ted saw the angry look on my face. He was a sensitive guy. He admired how I was getting my business up and running so quickly.

"Why don't you come in and tell me what's going on," he said.

I followed him into his office. He closed the door.

I told him about Randy's letter.

"You don't have to deal with that," Ted said. "I'm going to refer you to our firm's attorney, David Castle. This guy is topnotch."

Ted explained how CQT had been threatened with a lawsuit by a board-game manufacturer. CQT had created a casino advertisement using a game board similar to that of the manufacturer's famous game. David Castle had kept the case out of court and all the ad agency had paid was Castle's legal fees.

"This guy is good," Ted said. "You need to talk to him."

Ted got on the phone right then and called up Castle's office. He got the lawyer on the phone. "David, I'm sending you over a new client. He needs some help. It's a simple job if you wouldn't mind taking it."

Later that day, David Castle called my office and asked to see a copy of Randy's letter. I faxed it over.

Two hours later, Castle faxed me a copy of the letter he'd written to Randy. Castle referred to himself as CYBERWORKS' general counsel. The letter said that ABC had no grounds for legal action against me, and that I was entitled to any clients I could find, since there had been no non-compete agreement between us. Randy, indeed, had been unbelievably foolish not to have had his employees sign NDA's or covenant to compete. Furthermore we were not seeking ABC's clients; they were calling us after firing ABC.

Then came the kicker. The letter informed Randy that I was suing *him* for libel, slander and harassment.

Castle had a constable deliver the letter, requiring Randy to sign for it.

It worked. Word got back to me from Jake, who still worked for ABC, that Randy had sh*t his pants.

"You guys are going a little too far," Jake said. "He was only trying to scare you. You didn't have to do that."

"Listen," I said, "we're in business. This isn't a f*cking game. The attorneys are dealing with it. Don't talk to me."

I hung up.

Randy settled with me out of court. He didn't pay me off, but he did agree that ABC's people were not to talk with my company's people, interact with us, or come anywhere near our place of business.

I heard from Justin, Tanya's cousin, that Randy had called an emergency staff meeting and told everyone they were not even to mention the word CYBERWORKS in conversations with clients.

Castle had done his job. He only charged me $900, since I was a small business. It was money well spent.

THE WORKLOAD AT CYBERWORKS swelled. I knew I had to be careful and not take on more than we could handle. I knew it would be wrong, and ultimately damaging to my business, to take on a job we couldn't get to. ABC had fallen into that trap, and it had boomeranged by costing them clients who grew disgruntled at having promised goods or services delayed for weeks. My reputation was everything. CYBERWORKS would grow slow and solid.

I prided myself on professionalism, of taking care of clients' needs, of saving them money over what they would have been charged by gouge-happy firms. I wouldn't sell services they didn't need, or use the scare tactics rife in the IT field, such as saying a client needed special firewalls and security safeguards "because you're wide open on the Internet, everybody can crack into your system and steal data, and you're vulnerable to all the viruses." I never jabbered about "Y2K" and the need to upgrade. I'd sell hardware at only 1 percent over cost — just enough profit to fill out the paperwork. That alone set me apart from competitors; CYBERWORKS could bid a job lower. Also, I recommended clients buy quality hardware that wouldn't break down. And I didn't insist they buy it through CYBERWORKS. They could buy it from whatever source they wanted. What I *was* charging for was the actual work we did: our expertise in installing software, setting up networks and maintaining the systems with technical support. I'd tell each new prospect: "Shop around. Get quotes." I never tried to hard-sell a job. I knew we gave the best, and the most reasonably priced, service. Because of this, business was relentless. We were so cramped in our little office that I rented a storage facility for our inventory.

About this time, six months into CYBERWORKS' existence, I experienced a moment of rapture.

Ted, the COO of CQT, needed me to analyze the computer system at the ad agency's Las Vegas office. We flew down together. He bought the tickets. We sat in first class with our drinks. I leaned back, glanced behind me at the rows and rows of passengers, and realized there were no passengers in front of me.

Suddenly, I was beaming, practically laughing.

"What are you smiling about?" Ted asked.

"Oh, nothing," I said.

But I thought to myself: *Damn, I've made it. I did it. I've gotten the business I always wanted off the ground. And less than a year after the launch, it's soaring. I'm finally on top of my game. I have faithful employees managing accounts. I'm on a plane with a big client. I don't have bill collectors coming after me. This is great!*

It was an unbelievable high. And every time this heady feeling has come over me since, I've thought back to that plane trip. To that first realization that I had conquered a big life goal.

Now I wanted to see how large CYBERWORKS could get.

I landed more accounts in Las Vegas. Ted arranged to let us use office space in CQT's facility in Vegas in exchange for servicing CQT's system. It worked out fine. I stationed an employee there and flew down a couple times a week to help out. CYBERWORKS landed accounts in Salt Lake City, as well.

I discovered that many of our clients had high-end systems and web servers, but they'd crash because their power would go out. The supply wasn't reliable. That was a major headache for clients, because their operations would grind to a halt.

I hit upon the idea of expanding CYBERWORKS' services to include co-location. We'd host clients' systems at our facility and manage them for a monthly fee.

I figured out how many amps each circuit needed, budgeted over that and bought battery arrays to double capacity and give 40 minutes of backup. In our tiny data room we set up ISDN lines and T-1 circuits and began housing servers. Every rack had a server; there were about 50 in all.

Our business was literally humming.

We expanded co-location to the Las Vegas area and leased space in the suburb of Henderson.

We placed so many orders for circuits that word got around the communications industry that the little startup CYBERWORKS was growing like a weed.

A YEAR INTO BUSINESS, a man called up out of the blue and said, "I'm interested in talking to you about your business. I'm a business broker and

I represent some people who are interested in buying your firm."

I suspected it was another of Randy's ploys.

"We're not interested in selling," I said.

"Well, this is a big telecommunications firm. They have the money. I can't tell you who they are right now, but if you're interested in talking further with me and sending me over some financials, we can go from there."

He left me his name and phone number. He was in San Francisco.

I had my lawyer check him out. The business broker was legit.

I called him up. I asked who the buyer was. He told me to keep it secret because he could get in a lot of trouble for divulging that information. The suitor was T.D., a foreign-owned telephone company. T.D. wanted as many U.S. telecommunication and management-service companies as it could acquire, because Federal Communications Commission regulations were making it hard for T.D. to get the licensing to sell its services and telco circuits.

The offer was $1 million. I thought long and hard about it. But I decided that $1 million, that fast in the game, was just too cheap a price. I was going well.

I said thank you, but no thank you.

My confidence in my business was sky high. Success was intoxicating. It was like tequila. I felt unbeatable.

I was "bootstrapping," not funding the company through business loans or by selling off shares. CYBERWORKS was growing quickly, and eating up an enormous amount of cash that first year to keep it growing. Still, I had made enough profits to buy myself a nice little house. That had been one of my goals.

I'd finally made it.

CHAPTER FIFTY-TWO: Lunch with Starling

As the new millennium approached, a strange investor's mania gripped the business world. Dotcoms were rising from out of nowhere. Their values were over-inflated and very few of them had soluble business plans. It was as if "Internet" was some magic word that opened the purse strings of venture capitalists.

All that these hyped-up startups were doing was selling merchandise of one sort or another over the Internet. All they were, were cleverly marketed — but ultimately senseless — business ideas concocted by groups of MBAs who could write business plans, and who knew investors with money to supply the venture capital. These young MBAs were quite capable of raising millions of dollars and paying themselves huge salaries with generous stock options. Their companies' stock prices were going through the roof. The bubble expanded so large, so fast, that I knew it had to deflate or burst. It could not sustain itself at this volume.

Dotcom business was flooding into CYBERWORKS. We were getting orders from dotcoms everywhere to set up websites and security. Arranging e-commerce alone was bringing in $100,000 a month. At this point, it was nuts.

CYBERWORKS had been in business two years and I was well on my way to becoming very successful, but I was scared. Something didn't feel right. It gave me a flashback to the 1980s, and the overexuberance of the junk-bond craze. I sensed the carpet was going to get yanked out from beneath all of us in the IT trade. This boom time was too good, too long, too easy. I was pessimistic. I'd worked so hard for so many years for peanuts, that I couldn't make myself believe that success like this could last.

I thought about junk bonds — all that paper wealth that didn't really exist. Overexuberance. Overspending. Venture capitalists tossing billions around. How could a dotcom business issue an initial public offering and raise $100 million without even having a real product to make and sell? For entrepreneurs starting up businesses, it seemed that getting their hands on the IPO money was the game. That was all it was about. Get the money — and you're done.

In Reno, there was a prime example of an archetypal dotcom startup. This business sold batteries of every kind. If you were hard put to find a specific battery for a laptop computer, camera or whatnot, you could call up the toll-free telephone number and order what you needed from this catalog business. Its owner, Ben Starling, a Stanford MBA graduate, had carved out a nice little niche. He had a great business idea. However, not surprisingly, Starling decided to join the dotcom mania. He had connections to people in the financial world.

He renamed his battery company with a smart-sounding, three-letter phrase — "iDo" — issued an IPO and raised millions. He presented himself as a high-tech guru helping turn Reno into the next Silicon Valley. The

Truckee Meadows would become "Silicon Meadows." He moved his company into a vacant building that already had been set up by its previous occupant, StorageTek (which designed and made high-capacity data-storage devices), as a cutting-edge, employee-friendly workplace with wide-open spaces, artsy wire fences instead of walls, spiral staircases and even fire poles to descend from one floor to the next. iDo touted this environment as perfect for stimulating employee creativity and productivity. The workplace resembled a playground, complete with basketball courts, ping-pong tables, and lounge areas in tiki huts for employees to use at lunch or after work.

It all made for sexy business stories: Look at this dynamic startup headed by a young, visionary executive, a captain of industry in this new go-go economy. Starling joined the board of an economic booster organization, Tech Alliance, and was quoted constantly in the local newspaper's business section. But the only thing actually high-tech about iDo was that it had an Internet presence and, yes, sold batteries and other accessories.

iDo was a client of CYBERWORKS. iDo's development people had struck a contract with us. I had never met Starling, but CYBERWORKS had a solid board of directors by now, and one of the directors, a banker named Rick Chamberlain, told me I needed to go to lunch with Starling. "We think you two could do some great stuff together," Rick said. He, like so many leaders in the business community, was high on Starling. He set up a lunch meeting for Starling and me.

I was interested in meeting this guy. We talked on the phone. "Have you been to Tres Faux Nez?" Starling asked. Of course I had. I'd grown up in Reno.

Tres Faux Nez was a cramped little upstairs coffeehouse near downtown, with an obligatory funky inner décor and a menu that tended toward the vegetarian and pretentious.

I was on time and waited outside at the bottom of the stairs. At six minutes after noon, Starling pulled into the lot in a BMW convertible. I recognized him from photos in the newspaper. All the yuppies milling around the parking lot and staircase hailed him with, "Hey, Ben!"

Starling climbed out of his Beemer like a celebrity greeting fans. He was thirtysomething, about 6-foot-5, and obviously used to commanding the center of attention. He was wearing the standard techie garb — Oxford shirt and Dockers — just like me. He finally looked over and saw me waiting. He walked up.

"Jeff? Hi, I'm Ben Starling. Glad to meet you."

We shook hands. Then he proceeded to hobnob with his admirers.

"I'll get a table," I said. I walked up the stairs and into the coffeehouse. Fifteen minutes later, Starling joined me.

I ordered my ice tea and Cobb salad. He had a Perrier and a slice of quiche.

"I'm not sure what you've read, but let me tell you a bit about myself," Starling began.

He launched into a polished spiel that touched on his hardscrabble childhood and how his mother was his inspiration. As he spoke, he didn't look me directly in the eye. The lines were rehearsed, practiced. "My Mom used to buy rundown houses and we'd live in them and fix them up and flip them for a profit, and that's how we got by . . ."

It was a standard, poor-kid-made-good story. Yet, somehow, despite his supposed disadvantaged background, Starling had managed to attend a prestigious university back East, earn an engineering degree, and then get an MBA from Stanford. School of hard knocks, indeed. I had met a few of his friends from back East at a dinner party and they told me he came from an exceptionally well-off family. They bought everything for him. I think the hardship story just worked better with the public. Eventually the whole town found out he was full of B.S. So did the Securities & Exchange Commission, which went after him and a few of his officers.

Starling's pitch took me back to my days with Grandpa Herschel, mingling with all the bullsh*t artists in his world — hustlers who'd spew concise résumés about the famous people they'd worked for and the colleges they'd attended.

Starling told me he was starting a venture-capital company. "Chamberlain told me I should take a look at you and maybe invest in you."

"Ben, you don't have enough money to invest in us," I said.

He looked startled.

I kept eating my Cobb salad. I'd done my homework. iDo was publicly traded and I'd read about the loans the company had secured. I'd asked around about Starling, too. I never went into a meeting blind.

Now that I'd met Starling in person, I put two and two together. A conman with Stanford connections to venture capitalists. A small, successful company he could pass off as high-tech. A board of directors with a few prominent names that would help him take the company public as a dotcom. Still, he'd only been able to raise $60 million. Dotcoms were raising $100 million to $300 million.

Starling rattled on. He asked me a lot of questions about CYBERWORKS. He began jotting in a little notebook, oblivious to the fact I was just giving him surface information about the tech work we did.

Starling switched subjects and started asking questions about new networking standards that hadn't even come out on the market yet. They were just buzzwords. Evidently, Starling was considering investing in someone who was developing wireless technology.

"Yeah, they're great," I said. "Go ahead and invest in that."

He didn't know anything about technology. Maybe he didn't even know that much about business.

What he *did* know was how to sell bullsh*t. He could tell a story. All he was, was a pitchman.

Toward the end of our lunch, he started dishing out advice about how to improve *my* business. "You need to include your board of directors more."

Our lunch ended. "All right, Ben, it was a pleasure to meet you," I said. "I got to take off. I got another meeting."

I stood, thanked him politely for lunch and left.

What a joke, I thought, as I drove back to the office.

I knew the day would come when iDo wouldn't be able to pay its bills.

There were hundreds of such façade-driven dotcoms bubbling up everywhere. I saw the bottom dropping out imminently. I told my key employee, Brennan, that I had a bad feeling about the economy. "I think everything's going to crash down on us," I said. "We need to slow down now and start building up for this."

The time seemed right to me to retrench, to focus on solid clients who would still be with us tomorrow. Another reason to cut back had to do with my personal life. I wanted to keep from overextending myself.

I didn't like having to travel to Vegas and Salt Lake to handle problems personally when a service rep couldn't find a solution. I was tired of frequent miles, sick of sleeping in hotel rooms. It had long since ceased being exciting. Because I'd mastered, out of necessity, a wide set of skills, it was difficult finding employees who could replace me on the road. I'd need to hire three or four of them to cover the work I'd been doing myself: selling, setting up and monitoring networks, routing, switching, handling telecommunications. What's more, new hires wanted $60,000 to $70,000 a year, plus benefits. I couldn't justify the expense. It was cheaper to do it all myself. But now I was burned out.

A larger company in Vegas had offered to buy my out-of-town accounts. I accepted.

Just like that, CYBERWORKS was downsizing. And then I made another decision: to change the company name. We had our market share now and could afford to have our own identity. I wanted a name we could trademark so that no one else could have it.

One of our web designers and I put our heads together and came up with the name TELXAR. It was pronounced TEL-zahr, and the name was entirely made up. It had a telecommunications feel to it, and a futuristic, outer-space feel. It was original. It resonated.

TELXAR!

There was one other major change facing me in life at this point.

I was getting ready to marry Tanya, my girlfriend of three years.

CHAPTER FIFTY-THREE: The Better Half

When I was at ABC, I was working so hard, putting in so many hours, working seven days a week almost nonstop and honing my skills, that I had no social life. My sister was beginning to worry about me; I hadn't had a girlfriend in two years.

Jennifer was in the dental-assistant program at Truckee Meadows Community College. One day in class she was chatting with a younger student who mentioned she liked jet skiing and volleyball. Something clicked in Jennifer's mind. "Are you dating anyone right now?" she asked.

"No," the younger girl said.

"You ought to hook up with my brother," Jennifer said. "He's your age and he's real successful, and he loves to jet ski."

"Really?" the other girl, whose name was Tanya, said. "Let me see a picture of him."

Jennifer pulled out a photo of me from her wallet. It was my Army boot-camp photo. I was shaved bald. I looked horrible.

Jennifer told me about the conversation, and that the girl had looked at my military photo and said, "Oh, he's cute."

I laughed. "Wow, she's got low standards."

Jennifer told me that this Tanya was very nice, very beautiful, very smart, jet skied, and was very outgoing. "You two ought to hook up. I think you'll like her."

I shrugged it off. But Jennifer kept reminding me about Tanya over the next couple weeks. I was too busy working to put much interest into it.

"Listen," I finally told my sister, "I don't have time for this."

"No, no, you got to meet this girl."

Around this time, ABC signed me up for a management seminar. It was held in the conference center at a Reno hotel-casino over one entire weekend. It was ludicrous. Workshops ran all day long and you had to stay on the property overnight. There were exercises in projecting your voice, unmasking your true feelings and emotions, getting in touch with the real you, and so on. I'd been through similar training routines in the military. This was a waste of time.

I checked my cell phone voicemail on Friday evening and there were messages from Jennifer pestering me about calling Tanya. *Whatever*, I thought. I called Jennifer back and said, "All right, I'll call her." She gave me Tanya's number.

I punched the numbers on my cell and a girl answered. She had a real deep voice. A deep female voice worried me, because it might be coming from a big girl, and big girls aren't my type. But there is nothing wrong with a big girl.

Oh Christ, I thought, *it's probably one of my sister's friends. Someone desperate enough to find my bald military photo attractive.*

I told this Tanya hello, and explained I was Jennifer's brother. Tanya was nice about that. Jennifer had obviously been hounding her, too. Well, now that

I'd called, I had to follow through and set up a date. I figured that a bad blind date was in the offing. I'd never been on a blind date, but a horror story was shaping up. Yet I'd committed myself, and I was a gentleman, so I said, "Listen, I have this management seminar. But maybe Sunday evening you'd like to go out for a beer and dinner, or something like that."

"Cool," she said, "let me know."

"I'll give you a call," I said.

I called back Jennifer to say I'd asked Tanya out.

"What does she look like again?" I asked.

"Blond hair. Tall."

"Now, she sounded pretty manly. Is she big?"

"No, she's not big!"

Jennifer started giggling.

"She sounds big," I said.

Jennifer was now laughing so hard she could barely speak.

"I *promise* you she's not big."

"Bullsh*t," I said, remembering how mean my sister could be. You never erase bad memories from childhood.

Jennifer kept laughing.

Well, she could play her little prank on me. I'd called up this Tanya. I was committed.

The management seminar continued in its ridiculous fashion with psychological exercises. We were encouraged to let our emotions flow. Some attendees got right into it. They were screaming out their long pent-up frustrations. They were sobbing about baggage left over from childhood. Around me, people were crying, confessing about how they'd been misunderstood and abused this way or that. A full-blown pity wagon.

"Why weren't you around, daddy?" one of my colleagues at ABC whimpered.

The group leader told me I needed to get into the spirit of the workshop and learn to express myself.

"I've never had a problem expressing myself," I said. "I'm comfortable with me. I'm a team player."

I decided I'd better get with the program if I were to earn the certificate for passing the weekend seminar. So I went on an improvised rant just like everyone else — venting my emotions, screaming swear words at my colleagues, and castigating the workshop.

"You losers, this class sucks! You're all mental!"

I overdid it. I yelled so much that I lost my voice.

The seminar wrapped up Sunday afternoon. I called Tanya's number. Her Mom answered. To my horror, I found I could barely push the air out of my mouth. My vocal cords were thrashed. My voice was cracking like I was going through puberty.

"I apologize for my voice, ma'am," I said. "I just got out of a management seminar and we'd had to yell. Really, I'm not 14, I'm old enough to take your daughter out."

She laughed.

"I wanted to know if Tanya is there and if I'd be allowed to take her out to dinner tonight." I was always very formal with parents.

Her Mom said Tanya would call me back.

She did, and I explained again about my voice. "I lost my voice, I'm very sorry I sound this way. But I'd still like to take you out to dinner tonight."

She laughed. She said she'd be ready when I came.

Then I started panicking. How could I carry on a conversation with my voice in this condition? It would be embarrassing.

I called Jennifer and pleaded with her.

"You're going to have to go on this date with me," I said. "I can barely talk."

"No way," she said. "I'm enjoying this. You're going to mess this up."

"No I won't," I said.

My mind raced. I figured we'd go somewhere on the date where we didn't have to talk so much. Maybe a movie.

I WENT HOME, SHOWERED, changed, then drove over to the address in Spanish Springs. *Please don't be big*, I thought. I considered that maybe her voice had sounded husky because the reception on my cell phone in the casino was bad.

Either way, I had to go through with it, so I began getting into character, just like a salesman. I'd be professional. *No matter what this girl looks like at the door, don't freak out. Be polite, be a gentleman, and show her a great time.*

The address was in an upscale neighborhood. The yard was neatly landscaped. Good vibes.

I rang the bell and braced myself. I forced a smile on my face.

The girl who answered the door was tall. She had long blond hair with bangs, a pretty face — and a nice athletic figure. I nearly sighed with relief.

"Hi, Jeff," she said in that deep voice, "I'm Tanya."

We shook hands.

"Why don't you come in and meet some of my family?"

I was nervous. Her mother and both her grandmothers were sitting in the living room. I apologized again for my voice.

They thought it was funny that my voice was cracking.

Tanya was wearing jeans, a sweatshirt and Doc Marten boots. She looked very cute. *Score one for Jennifer*, I thought. This could shape up to be a fun evening.

I took her to Applebee's. We ordered good-size meals. We talked a bit about ourselves. Her last name was Hannigan.

"Hannigan?" I said. "That name sounds familiar. I used to live in Darrington."

"Really?" she said. "Do you know my cousins Mark and Mason?"

"Get out of here!" I said.

They'd been my two best friends the year I'd lived in that small town.

"Do you know my Uncle William?" she asked. "He's a judge now."

I hadn't known that. Mark and Mason's father had been a firefighter when I'd lived there.

What a small world.

We went to see *Something About Mary* after dinner. I figured we'd laugh through the whole movie and I wouldn't have to talk.

I brought her home. I politely walked her to the door. "Thanks, it was awesome," I said. "Would you mind if I called you sometime to go out again?"

"Sure," she said.

I called her the next day and said I had some time in my schedule that evening and wondered if she'd like to go out to dinner again. She accepted.

We had fun again.

Each day after that I had a reason to call her: for breakfast, lunch or dinner. It must have been chemistry. It was so weird. We just really clicked.

Why wasn't she going out with anyone else? I found out she was a lot like me: headstrong, opinionated, sure of her goals and determined to pursue them. And she didn't take crap from anyone.

I kept things pretty formal still. I hadn't even kissed her yet. We were just getting to know one another.

When Friday rolled around, I showed up at Tanya's house and said, "I'm not going take you out unless I can meet your dad tonight. It's not right that I haven't met him yet."

Her dad, a senior partner in a large CPA firm, hadn't been around when I'd showed up. But I knew no father wants his daughter going out with a knucklehead. I wanted to present myself well.

Tanya showed me in. And who should be there along with Tanya's two younger sisters and her parents, but her Uncle William.

"Hey, Jeff, what's going on?" he said.

Tanya's family was shocked.

"You know Jeff?"

"Yeah, he used to play with Mark and Mason when he was this big."

That broke the ice. Tanya's father, Don, said, "It's a pleasure to meet you." I was in.

Tanya later told me that her father and uncle usually were rough on the boyfriends.

We went out to dinner, had champagne. In the truck afterward I said, "Would you mind if I kissed you?"

"No, not at all," she said.

We agreed that starting from then, we'd be exclusively dating.

We liked each other. We were actually friends. This was no typical young boyfriend-girlfriend coupling that is all about the physical and not the relationship. We didn't jump right into the romantic part.

This was new for me. Tanya was so different from the girlfriends I'd had. I thought about it, and realized they'd been pushovers. Tanya, on the other hand, was a dominating personality. She was so high-caliber that I didn't want to mess this thing up.

My sister thought it was awesome. "Just don't forget, when you guys get married, who set you up."

"We ain't getting married," I said. "We're just hanging out, having a good old time."

But we saw each other every day for the next six months. Tanya's parents used to make fun of us for this. Out of curiosity, I itemized my meals and calculated that I'd spent about $7,000 going out with Tanya. It was an expensive courtship. She'd offer to pay for meals, but I wouldn't let her. She was working part-time at her dad's office while going to school, and didn't have that much money.

Tanya was so refreshing. She was serious about life. She was very focused on her goals. I wasn't her No. 1 priority. Finishing her schooling was. She wasn't the sort of person to wait on me hand and foot. She had her own life. And she was so blatantly honest about everything. She was polite and ladylike, but she had her own opinions and wasn't shy about sharing them. She'd grown up with solid values. She had self-esteem. She saw no reason to hide behind lies or play games. She was a winner.

She also was game to try all kinds of things, with that tomboy quality I liked so much in the opposite sex. She had no trouble hanging out with the guys if I wanted to go out bowling with them and have a few beers. She loved sports. She knew more about the NFL than I did. She knew the players, the rules, the strategies. My friends were amazed. "Where did you find this girl?" Tanya was easily at home in a sports bar with beers and a basket of buffalo wings. She fit right in. My other girlfriends would have freaked out spending hours in a sports bar watching a game on the big screen.

Tanya and I jet skied together. She was a good athlete. She'd played softball and volleyball in high school. She'd even been asked by the University of Nevada, Reno volleyball coach to walk on to the team. But she didn't like the coach, who'd been her coach in high school before getting hired at UNR, so she'd passed on the opportunity.

She was that strong-minded.

IT WAS FORTUNATE WE didn't know each other's ages at the start. Two months went by before we exchanged that information.

"By the way, how old are you?" I asked one day.

"Twenty-one."

"Twenty-one?!"

"Well, how old are *you*?" Tanya asked.

"Twenty-six."

She was surprised.

"If I'd have known your age I probably wouldn't have dated you. I thought you were around 21 or 22."

"Well, mentality-wise, I'm around 16."

We agreed it was lucky we'd been in the dark, because we'd have blown a good thing at the start. For my part, I was tired of young, dumb girls, and wouldn't have agreed to go out with a 21-year-old. And Tanya, for her part, was tired of older men who were too slow and inactive and didn't want to go out and do anything. She'd dumped her previous boyfriend because of that.

December was approaching. This was the time of year I'd break up with whomever I was going out with so I wouldn't have to be with her and her family over the holidays. But this year was different. I took Jennifer with me as I went shopping at jewelry stores. We found a two-tone gold Italian bracelet that would fit Tanya's petite wrists.

I told Tanya that I was used to spending Christmas with my Mom, sister and niece — just a small get-together. "I don't want you to get me anything for Christmas," I said. "I'll probably get you something small, nothing major.

But I'm going to be busy with my family and I'm not going to have too much time."

I didn't relish the thought of having to be with Tanya's giant family at Christmas. She had aunts and uncles and cousins and grandparents. Such a large gathering would make me very nervous. I wasn't used to it.

As fate went, on Christmas morning Tanya called and asked me to her family's Christmas dinner. Mom told me I should go. I was nervous! Now I had to meet 50 people.

When I showed up, a large table was decked out. It was quite a party. I was relieved that I already knew her parents and sisters well enough, and her Uncle William and cousins Mark and Mason, of course. But I'd be on display in front of a lot of strangers.

I got in the mental zone. When the food was served, I took small portions and finished quickly. That way I was able to talk with people without having them watch me eat.

After dinner, I told Tanya I'd brought her little present. She'd gotten me something, too. So had her parents. Tanya's mother really liked to shop.

Patti, the middle sister, was the hyperactive one in the family. "What'd he get you, what'd he get you?" she asked excitedly. Her antics drew a crowd, including Tanya's parents.

Just what I didn't want!

I opened my gifts first. Tanya had bought me a movie CD. Her mom had gotten me a shirt. I felt bad I hadn't bought her parents anything.

Tanya unwrapped her box. I knew if she pulled something cheap out, I was done for. I was immeasurably relieved I'd put some effort into choosing the present.

Her face turned bright red. She held the bracelet up. "It's beautiful," she said.

"It's no big deal," I said. "I just thought this would look nice on you."

"Let me see, let me see," Patti said.

For the rest of the evening, Tanya showed off her bracelet, holding it up for her relatives to admire. I got through the dinner.

I realized that from this point forth, in her family's eyes, she and I were a serious couple.

IT WAS SPRING NOW. Patti was playing softball for Illinois State University. Her team had games in Arizona, and Tanya was preparing to fly down to watch her sister play. The night before Tanya was to leave, we went out to dinner. Then she drove me back to my office in her truck.

We talked a bit, and then she turned to me and told me she loved me.

I sat there for a second. She looked at me, waiting for me to say something.

The words came out of my mouth: "I love you, too."

I'd said that to a girl maybe once in my life. This time was different, because I meant it. It was refreshing to say those words — and mean them. Our relationship was honest. Obviously, we'd just confirmed to each other how serious it was.

Being with Tanya was a fresh start for me. Whatever girls I'd dated in the past, their names and faces were suddenly fading from memory. They didn't matter anymore. Tanya was everything to me now. She was The One.

As we got closer to the one-year anniversary of dating, I asked how she felt about marriage and kids. Tanya said she wanted to be married with a family someday, but only after she was established in her career.

It was clear we could have a future together. Of course, we had to keep from breaking up, though.

Inevitably, there were the arguments that tested our affection. Tanya is Irish, like me, and has a temper about herself. The one big argument that threatened a breakup occurred after I'd installed a new stereo system in my Blazer.

Tanya asked me to hand her the remote control to change the radio station. She might as well have asked to borrow my razor or to have me put on a dress. I'm a man who is into his tools and electronics. They are not to be shared.

"You're not changing anything," I said.

She got mad at me.

I got mad at her.

She didn't talk to me for the rest of the date.

That night, she wouldn't return my calls.

This non-communication lasted the rest of the week.

I grew really worried. I realized that this great thing we had going might be over. All because of that one disagreement.

I couldn't believe it!

That weekend, I went out dirt biking, raising hell.

Sunday, I finally got her on her cell. "Where are you?" I asked.

"I'm in Sacramento," she said. She'd gone out of town with her family.

"Why aren't you returning my calls? This is bullsh*t."

"I'm pissed off at you."

"When you come home, I want to talk about it," I said.

The next night I went to her house. We finally talked. We hugged. The old feelings were still there.

"Listen, I thought it was over," I said.

"I did, too," she said.

"This is stupid," I said. "It's a remote control!"

We went out to my truck.

"Here, you want to work the remote control?" I asked. "Here, here's the remote control."

"No, I don't want to work it now."

"Here we go again!"

Then I calmed down.

"OK, stop!" I said.

I sat her in the truck and put the device in her hand. "Work the remote," I said. "That's all it is. It's immaterial. Just work the remote."

I explained that when I was little, stuff was tough to come by for Mom, Jennifer and me. I didn't usually share anything. My childhood hadn't been like hers, growing up in her upper-middle-class family, with a two-parent household and leisure money. That was why I'd been so possessive of the remote control.

"Here, please take it now," I said.

Reluctantly, she did.

The crisis was over.

She chose a lightweight chick-music station.

TANYA AND I HAD gone out of town together on a few trips to Northern California. We'd visited the wine country, and we'd had a blast learning about grapes and vineyards, and visiting the magnificent estates and sampling the offerings at the wineries.

But now I wanted us to take a real vacation far away. By this time I'd started TELXAR. I'd been working incredibly hard. I needed a break. I thought about taking five days off. I proposed going to Cancun, Mexico, for five days. Tanya loved the idea. The farthest away she'd ever been was Hawaii.

I called her mother and explained I was taking their daughter out of the country for a few days. Our plane was leaving at midnight Friday. Would it be possible for us to go out to dinner on Friday and then later on catch a ride from them to the airport?

Her mother agreed.

Then I dropped a bombshell.

"Maude," I said, "some things have come up with Tanya and me. And I think it's best if you, Don and I talk."

She was freaked out. That's what I'd intended. I'm sure she thought I'd gotten her daughter pregnant.

"I don't want you to tell Tanya," I continued. "I'd like to tell you two after dinner, in private."

Our dinner at the restaurant went by fast. Maude and Don wolfed their food down. I was secretly enjoying it.

"Tanya," I said after dinner, "I've got to drive home and pack up and see a few friends and take care of some stuff. I'll meet you back at your house."

Her father said, "Yeah, I have to stop by work and take care of a few things."

"I'll go with you," Maude said to her husband.

Tanya took off in her car back to her house. She had no clue that her parents and I had planned a meeting. I drove to Don's office. He was sitting behind his big desk. Maude was sitting to his side. I took a seat across from them.

"So," Don said, leaning back, his hands behind his head. "What do you want to talk about?"

"Well," I said, "I've been dating your daughter for two years now. As you know, we're in love. I'm a pretty proper guy. We're not going to Cancun for a vacation. I'm asking you for your permission to marry your daughter. I'm taking her to Cancun to propose to her."

Maude erupted in excitement and relief. "Oh my God!" she said, "I'm glad this is what it was about."

"You're serious?" Don asked.

"I'm dead serious," I said. "I have the engagement ring right here in my pocket."

Maude begged to see it.

A friend of mine worked for a diamond wholesaler in Texas. Through him I'd been able to get a deal on a beautiful stone. I'd designed the ring and setting on computer on AutoCAD, and taken the design to Jim, a man I knew who worked at a jewelry store in Reno, and who made amazing custom jewelry.

I didn't want Maude to feel strange about the ring, so I gave an explanation before producing the box.

"The ring might be more than you guys gave each other when you were engaged, but Tanya means a lot to me and the ring symbolizes it. I had it custom built — it is a one-of-a-kind ring."

In fact, I'd saved up 12 months for the ring and paid in cash.

I produced the box and took the ring out.

Their eyes grew large.

"You should have gotten something smaller and saved for a house," Don, the accountant, said.

"You could say it's nice if you want, Don," I said.

"Oh, it's nice. But it's too much ring."

Maude was turning it over and over in her hand.

"I've been married 28 years and I don't have something like *this*," she said.

"I built this ring from my heart, for the person I'm going to call my wife," I said. "I don't care what anyone else thinks. I don't want this ring to be a problem."

"Well, I have no problem with you marrying my daughter," Don said. "Congratulations. But, you know Tanya can be difficult. She has a temper and an attitude."

Maude chimed in. "You know she can be a pain in the butt sometimes."

"I know that," I said. "I can be the same way. I'll take the good with the bad."

Maude had tears in her eyes.

That night, back at their house, Tanya couldn't understand why her Mom seemed so happy.

Maude drove us to the airport.

Waiting for our flight, Tanya put her head down on her bag and shut her eyes. She looked so innocent. We were from such different backgrounds. She didn't have a clue that people can steal your luggage right out of the airport. While waiting to change planes in Dallas, I stayed alert. I had my legs positioned around the bags, watching everything. I didn't close my eyes until we were in our plane seats and my arm was looped through my bag.

We flew nonstop to Cancun and arrived in the late afternoon.

Tanya was awake now, and hungry. When she's hungry, she can be a bear.

I wanted to get to the beach, lie out in the sun, have margaritas.

"Let's get some food first!" she roared.

"Let's just go out to the beach and videotape the sunset," I said. "See how beautiful everything is."

Maude had asked me to videotape the proposal. I didn't see how that was possible. But I was going to try.

Out on the beach, with the surf and the sunset, Tanya was being a petulant little butt, still whining about being hungry.

"I want to play a game with you," I said. "Indulge me. I want you to close your eyes and I want to say a few things to you and get your reaction."

"Oh, yeah, I'm going to close my eyes and you're going to throw me in the ocean," she said.

"I promise you I won't," I said. "The beach is beautiful."

And it was. The sun was setting right behind her. It was perfect.

Tanya shut her eyes. I pulled the video camera out. She didn't know it.

"We've been going together a long time," I said.

"Yeah, hurry up, hurry up," she said.

"Will you shut up, I've prepared something I want to say to you and you're messing it up! I've been memorizing this."

Her eyes were still closed. She wore a snotty look. She was tapping her foot impatiently.

I told her how much I cared about her, and that I loved her.

"You know, we didn't come to Cancun for a vacation," I said.

"What?" she said. Her foot stopped tapping.

"I came here to Cancun because I want to ask you to be my wife."

I slipped the ring on her finger. I was still videotaping her.

She opened her eyes and held the ring up, staring at it. Her mouth fell open.

Her eyes watered, but she wouldn't let her tears fall.

"So, will you marry me?" I said. She said yes.

Her emotions just flowed except for crying. All on tape. It was beautiful.

Our mood was romantic for the rest of the vacation.

We had a private cabana on the beach at the hotel. We put the ring in the safe every night. One day, Tanya wore it outside the hotel district. When I noticed that, I said, "Are you crazy? They'll cut your finger off for it. This is not the States."

"Well, I wouldn't give it to them," she said.

"No, you give it to them," I said. "We have insurance. But you don't wear the ring out here."

I had her spin the ring upside-down with the stone in her hand. When we got to the bus stop, I took it away and put it in my pocket.

I kept it in the hotel safe after that. "You can wear the ring once we get on the airplane," I said.

The moment we were on board back to Reno, she slipped it on with delight.

I STARTED PREPARING FOR married life. I was living in the modest 1,500-square-foot house Tanya and I bought on a half-acre in Spanish Springs, nine months before we were married. Spanish Springs was the fast-growing area in the desert hills north of Sparks. Tanya continued living with her parents; she was unwilling to move in with me until we were married. She finished her dental assistant's degree and got a job, just as she'd planned.

I started feeling nervous. Some of our friends had gotten married. Tanya and I had gone to their weddings. The reality struck me. I intended to get married just once in my life. That threshold was straight ahead of me now. The permanence of what I was heading into began to wear on me. The tension had me in its grip.

We'd set a date: July 14, 2001. Tanya's parents were planning a large wedding. They wouldn't let us chip in anything. The ceremony would be at Wingfield Springs, the upscale golf-course community in Sparks. Three hundred guests were invited to the ceremony.

The bachelor and bachelorette parties took place on the Saturday night a full week before the wedding, instead of the night before. That was to ensure that if anyone got too out of hand, he or she could still make it to the wedding. The bachelor's party was mellow. I'd partied enough in my life. I got my friends together and said, "Listen, let's go out to a restaurant and have a fancy steak dinner, then go to the pool hall afterward, have a few beers and play pool all night." They were surprised there'd be no strippers on the itinerary. "Been there, done that," I said.

It worked out fine. I got home, actually sober, by 1 a.m. I called Tanya. She and her bachelorettes were still out on the town.

It turned out that they stayed out until 4 a.m. The girls got Tanya drunk. Then it was decided that they'd all hit a topless club, since none of them had been inside one before. Tanya was in for a surprise: a lot of the dancers are sex neutral, as I like to put it. That means they do not really have a preference. They are open. Naturally, they really liked dancing for a beautiful woman such as Tanya. In fact, some of them got aggressive. Tanya is 100 percent straight, and their come-ons made her very uncomfortable and eventually angry. As drunk as she was, she was offended. She was riled by what she saw as women deliberately subjecting themselves to sexist exploitation in front of men. It was more graphic than she'd expected.

We talked about that later. I told her about working at my grandfather's topless bar when I was 12, and explained that it's really the women who are in control in the clubs, using their bodies to exploit the men. "Trust me," I said. "They get off knowing they're getting the guy off and that they're getting his money." Tanya understood now. But she didn't want to go in one of those clubs any time soon.

"Those girls were all over me!" she said.

"You are very beautiful, what did you expect?" I said.

The day after the bachelor and bachelorette parties, we had to meet with the caterer to discuss food for the wedding reception. Maude picked me up at my house in her new Toyota Avalon. Tanya looked ill, as if she was fighting a battle with nausea she was ready to lose at any moment.

I couldn't resist. "Are you sure you don't want a greasy pork chop in a dirty ashtray?" I asked.

"Mom, I don't feel good," she moaned.

"Don't you puke in my car."

"I think I'm going to be sick!"

"Hurry, Jeff, grab something from the back!" Maude pleaded.

All I could find were street maps in a zip-lock baggy. I flipped them out and passed the baggy up to Tanya. Not a moment too soon.

Vegetable soup.

We were on Rock Boulevard, a main thoroughfare in Sparks. Maude braked at the stoplight. Tanya had an audience of passing motorists as she poked her head out the passenger door and was sick again.

We reached the caterer's store. An array of food samples was laid out for our selection for the reception menu.

"Great, we're ready to try all of these," I said, not missing a beat. "Do you have any exotic hors d'oeuvres?"

I munched away happily, frequently walking up to Tanya with my mouth open, stuffed with delicacies.

She vomited again on the way home. She spent the rest of the day in bed, head pounding, stomach suffering, hating the thought of topless bars and alcohol and wise-ass fiancés.

Now it was the day before the wedding. After the rehearsal, the wedding party went out to a little Chinese restaurant. We drank a form of boilermakers, pouring a shot glass of hot sake into an ice-cold glass of Tsingtao beer and slamming it. This was a moment when I could have tied one on, drinking myself courage before the big plunge the next morning. But I didn't. I stopped at two of these bonsai bombers.

When I woke up the next morning, I was strangely calm. It amazed me. I'd thought I'd be nervous, anxious, maybe even a little frightened.

I phoned Maude and said I wanted to take a spin on my dirt bike. She was horrified. "You're going to risk getting injured on this most important of days?"

"No, I'm going to go out and ride, do about 100 miles an hour, take my hands off the bars, then I'll come to the wedding," I said. "I got to get that one last blast out of my system."

Poor Maude. She wasn't in the mood for kidding.

I was as ready as I'd ever be. I'd attended to every detail.

The day before, I'd called a friend and arranged for him to follow me in Tanya's car while I checked into our hotel for Tanya and me to spend our wedding night. The Adventure Inn in Reno had all kinds of themed rooms. I know it sounds tacky, but so many people recommended it that we felt we could not go wrong. It was a great experience. The Irish Castle Room seemed a good fit. I'd booked us a room for a night and left Tanya's car there. I told my friend to keep the destination secret. No way did I want Tanya's family finding out, so they could pull their pranks on us. I'd heard about when Tanya's parents got married. The relatives got in the room beforehand, cranked the thermostat to high, put Saran Wrap over the bed sheet and covered it with powdered sugar, and even flipped the mattresses around so the box springs faced up. I decided to keep our lodging secret even from Tanya, in case she got to drinking at the reception and spilled the beans.

Her Uncle William, the judge, officiated at the civil ceremony. The reception was in the big ballroom at the Kerak Shrine Temple, in Sparks. I felt almost like a stranger at my own wedding. Tanya's parents had gone all out. The wedding cake had seven layers, with waterfalls cascading in different colors. I started feeling worried, as if something bad was about to transpire. I'd never had it so good in my life. It seemed like a dream. Too good to be true. When was the roof going to cave in?

But nothing bad happened. It all went off without a hitch. The party was fabulous. The guests had a great time, drinking, dancing. Many knew each other. Drew was my best man; we found out that his cousin's mother is married to Tanya's Uncle William. The reception had the feel of a huge family reunion on Tanya's side. On my side, I had two tables of guests, mostly friends who knew me when I was growing up.

We took care not to start any serious partying until after the older guests had left. That's when the party shifted into high gear. The DJ cranked up the music. I told the members of the wedding party that if they weren't drinking, dancing and having a good time, there was something wrong.

I got on the microphone. "I'll match shots of Cuervo Gold with anyone who'll come up to the bar and congratulate me," I said. Cuervo is my drink. I found out in the Army that I have a strange tolerance for this tequila.

I had three gallon jugs of Cuervo Gold brought to the bar. There were many challengers, even the bartenders.

I kept doing shots and drinking out of the bottle. I didn't want the party to end.

The staff kicked us out at midnight.

Married life had begun.

CHAPTER FIFTY-FOUR: An Untimely Programmer

Since I had extra cash to spend after selling the Vegas operation, and since space was unbearably tight in the Sparks office now for my company renamed TELXAR, I found a larger facility in a new, high-end business park in south Reno.

The business park was on one of the new glistening, wide boulevards winding off a newly constructed freeway ramp in the fast-growing area where ranchland was being paved over and converted to residential subdivisions or commercial space. The business park would accommodate the tide of newcomers, including business startups, washing over the Sierra to the Truckee Meadows from overcrowded, overtaxed California. All the dotcoms in the South Meadows were our clients.

There would be room in our new suite for a spacious data center in back, a large shop area, a conference room, staff offices and a big office for me. It felt great. But then, a few weeks before we were to move in, the dotcom bubble burst.

I now had reservations about making the move, even though we'd signed a lease. I consoled myself that we had enough clients to meet the higher overhead.

So TELXAR moved from Sparks to Reno.

MY GOAL NOW WAS to balance our client portfolio with more industrial clients and fewer dotcoms. With the dotcom bubble deflating, business was slowing down. As the e-commerce companies dropped off as customers, I filled the gap with more manufacturers. This was possible since TELXAR was willing to provide tech support any hour of the day. We'd send engineers, including myself, out on a plane to reach the worksite in the wee hours, if needed. Because of this, we began picking up manufacturing clients whose operations needed service at 2 or 3 a.m., since they couldn't afford to shut down during daytime hours.

I knew we'd weather the slowdown. Still, it forced me to lay off some of my web developers. It disappointed me; we'd put together a great team. I made sure to let them know more than a month before Christmas, and I kept them on until New Year's so their holidays wouldn't be ruined. I gave them bonuses and promised good referrals.

I was happy that each of them found jobs elsewhere.

DISCIPLINARY PROBLEMS AROSE WITH some other employees, primarily programmers, who can be difficult, as I'd already learned.

Some programmers live in a world that exists beyond ours. A programmer's world is like a science-fiction environment that the programmer controls and is the sole ruler of. It's an alternate realm in which the programmer god works with codes and creates programs and makes things come alive. This digital universe is more real to programmers than the external universe. To them, the external universe is just an intrusion — a necessary evil to contend with until the programmers can return to the environment they want to be in: enrapt in computer codes. To work with a programmer, you must understand this.

I did understand it. Countless times over the years, I'd become entranced in marathon sessions in front of my computer screen, learning and writing codes. But I'd snapped out of that trance and transported back to Planet Earth the moment I'd logged off.

Heath was the best programmer I had. Indeed, he was the best I've ever worked with. He'd started with me a year after I'd opened CYBERWORKS, as the third employee I'd hired. He'd left a job with Verio, the big Internet-services company, and moved to Reno to escape California's high cost of living and congestion. Heath was a rail-thin, chain-smoking guy in glasses, shy and introverted, and whip-smart with computer languages. He knew a great many of them: C, Perl, Visual Basic, JavaScript, html. He could program in Flash and create graphics in Photoshop. It was so rare to find a front-end programmer, designing graphics, who also could do the backend work of writing the code.

From the first day he joined us, Heath kicked ass. Everything I asked for in a website, he delivered to a tee — the shapes, the colors, the source code. If only his time-management skills had equaled his talent.

Three months into his job, Heath started showing up at 10 a.m. instead of 8 a.m., the hour when clients began calling. I didn't understand at first, but finally gathered that Heath was staying up all night long, writing codes, learning more languages. It's the same thing I did. The difference was, I could function on two or three hours of sleep, if need be. Heath needed to sleep in.

He'd show up, unshowered, his hair mussed. Word got around how he'd driven away from a gas pump with the hose still in his car's tank hole, tearing the hose off. His mind was just endlessly whirring with computer codes.

"Heath," I finally said, "how about we change your hours so that you come in at 10 o'clock, but then you work until 7?"

"No, I got to get home at a decent hour," he said. Though he was in his early twenties, he was married with two children.

"You've got to be fair to the company," I said. "If you come in late, you've got to work your eight-hour shift."

"What if I came in at 10 and worked until 5?"

"Heath, you can't do that."

He said 8 a.m. was fine. He fell in line, for a time. Then he fell out of line. His periodic tardiness became chronic again, and persisted for six months.

I had to take decisive action. I called him into my office again.

"Heath, I will let you come in at noon if you want. Just give me eight hours. That's all I ask."

He began showing up at 8 a.m. again. But he couldn't sustain it for long.

I sat down with Steve, my branch manager. We determined that of the 238 non-vacation workdays in the past 12 months, Heath had worked fewer than eight hours on approximately 90 percent of the days.

I called Heath into my office once more. I hated to do it, because we were swamped with work. I had two programmers working to meet our orders.

"Heath, you're the best programmer I've ever worked with, period," I began. "I don't want to lose you. But I have these standards in my head set for the way I run a business, and it has to work this way.

"It's not fair to the team. Everybody sees you're coming in at 10 and leaving at 5 or 6, but you're getting paid for eight hours. We're going to give you 30 days to clean up. It's been a year now. If you're late one time during these days, I'm going to have to let you go."

"All right, no problem," he said.

He was late not only once, but every single day.

"Heath," I said, "I'm going to have to let you go, and it kills me. I've given you so many chances. I just can't have you coming in here not working eight hours, not working your shift."

"All right, I understand," he said.

He found a job as a network administrator for a company that manufactured steel covers and other pre-cast construction materials. His programming talent was wasted there, but the hours were right. As long as he kept the network going, he could come in whenever he wanted.

OUR STAFF SHRANK FURTHER, to four. We made due during the post-9-11 recession. We had to weather a hit of about $500,000 in bad debt from dotcom clients who'd gone bust — either before the terrorist attacks or in the immediate aftermath.

I sat down and figured out a cash-flow model that would sustain us. I decided that service contracts were the way to go, and determined how many contracts, equal to how many billable hours, would keep TELXAR going. I shifted our policy of taking on new business. We now were only interested in service contracts, not in one-time hourly billings. We would commit our services only to clients who committed to us. Service contracts would be for a minimum of 12 months.

I analyzed the productivity of the employees. Steve, the branch manager, was squandering hours every day playing videogames and otherwise goofing off. He had gotten too comfortable. He had grown lazy. I didn't want to hurt his feelings, so I told him we just didn't have enough business coming in, and I had to let him go. Of course this was not true. He was lazy and sat in his office playing golf videogames and not helping the rest of the team hustling up business. He worked himself out of a job.

As 2003 rolled around, business began picking up again, thanks to our growing clientele of manufacturers. I considered that our business had swung toward the first clients I'd had when starting CYBERWORKS: manufacturers.

Maybe I should have just niched with these folk, instead of expanding to serve the ill-fated dotcoms.

CHAPTER FIFTY-FIVE: Service to the Stars

Venture-capital firms had begun looking at TELXAR as a good prospect. They'd caught wind of us from the Silicon Valley and San Francisco Bay area dotcoms they'd been involved in who used our services. My answer to the VC folks was always the same: We were interested in raising money, but not by giving up 20 percent of our company.

But the VCs were interested in us for our services, too. They wanted to hire us to set up the computer systems for the software and other tech companies they were incubating. The VCs didn't want these startups wasting money. The VCs also wanted us to analyze the companies' new technology products to ensure they were worth investing in. I loved that. It was research and development, what I yearned to get into.

One venture capitalist, Ted Ruff, lived on the Nevada side of Lake Tahoe, which is a haven for multimillionaire entrepreneurs who can choose where they live. Nevada has no state income tax, and that has been a lure for the wealthy since the 1930s. What's more, Lake Tahoe is one of the most beautiful places on the globe. I drove up to Tahoe from Reno to look at a software application that Ted Ruff was considering backing. He lived in a beautiful castle-like home in Incline Village, with a view of the lake.

The wealthy fraternize with the wealthy, no matter how it is they have gained their wealth. Money is money. And once you have it, you're guaranteed entry into a certain social circle. That circle intersects with other circles, with placement determined by net value. Ruff was in a very exclusive circle. During our visit, he told me he had a number of associates who couldn't use the regular Internet service providers because they were celebrities and couldn't trust the security of the networks. They needed to know their email was safe, their websites secure against sabotage.

Would I be interested in servicing them?

It sounded right up my alley. By now I was very experienced at hacking, which is a term the media have misrepresented. "Hacking" refers to the act of working away at a computer program, figuring it out or tweaking it. "Cracking," in contrast, is illegal. It refers to the act of breaking into a system. My skills had developed to the point where I could help protect systems from past experiences. I could provide high-end systems with the sort of security support that wasn't easily found.

"Sure," I told Ruff. "But I'll do it as long as they are prepared to sign a contract to preserve the secrecy of our working relationship. I don't want to risk word leaking out from their end that we were providing their security, and then us ending up getting blamed for breaching that secrecy."

"No, you can believe they won't spread the word," the venture capitalist said. "They'll tell their friends, but they won't tell anybody else that they're working with you. And believe me, you'll have to sign a lengthy agreement that protects them against you violating their secrecy."

And so I went after my first celebrity account: a movie star who was a neighbor of Ruff's at Tahoe.

I KNEW THE ACTOR'S work. He'd co-starred in a string of action movies, some of them big box-office hits, in the 1980s. He was still working, and had probably appeared in at least 50 flicks. He'd invested well, so he could afford a mansion at the lake.

I called the office of the actor's business manager. I got a call back. The manager briefly outlined the services needed, but said he'd have to send over a legal disclaimer for my lawyer to look at and for me to sign before we talked any further. I agreed.

The contract required strict anonymity, and threatened financial penalties if I breached the terms. There were a lot of stipulations. For example, I had to come in plain clothes and an unmarked car. No one but the client and his people would know why I was there.

A week later, I drove up in a rented Chevy SUV and stopped at the electric security gate outside the entrance to the driveway. I was surprised that the gate was right there just off the boulevard that ran along the lake. The guard booth was behind this gate, instead of the normal position outside. Two security guards were there, waiting for me. It was the appointed time.

The electric gate rolled open. I poked my head out the car window and introduced myself as Jeff from TELXAR, and gave the name of the business manager whom I was to meet.

The head guard checked his clipboard.

"All right, we see you on the list. Pull forward and stop your vehicle."

The second guard climbed in the passenger side and we drove up the long, curving driveway to the house and parked.

We got out. He patted me down real quick. I thought that was funny; they should have had me get out of the vehicle back at the gate and checked me for weapons there. What's more, he didn't even look inside my tool bag.

The business manager came out and escorted me into the house.

The computer problem was simple enough to fix. It just had to do with a network-security issue in making purchases with the client's credit card. I tested the issue when I was done, then reviewed it with the business manager.

I gave him a few pointers. "Now, when you're on the Internet and you want to look for (this, this and this), be careful about (this, that and that)."

The actor came into the room briefly. He was talking with someone on a cordless phone. He looked a bit older and rougher than his appearance on screen. He was wearing a simple sweater and slacks.

"Jeff, I'd like to introduce you," the manager said.

I stood up, looked the actor in the eye, and said, "It's a pleasure to meet you, sir."

The actor smiled and returned to his call. He walked out.

The business manager said he'd explain the points to the client.

"If he has any problems, feel free to call me. And thank you very much," I said.

"Send me the bill. We'll take care of it," the manager said.

I walked out, got in the rented SUV, told the security guards, "All right,

I'll see you guys later," and drove off.

I'd been professional. That's what I was hired for. Not to gawk. Not to pitch a movie script. Not to ask for the guy's autograph.

The actor was happy with my work. He ended up referring me to friends. *Bam.* Just like that, my celebrity clientele mushroomed. It is a quirk of that social class: If one celebrity has a new toy or service, everyone else in the circle wants it, too.

The celebrity grapevine carried the word about TELXAR's services. It kept me on the go. All over Lake Tahoe. Arizona. Palm Springs. Hollywood. Visiting the palaces of the rich and famous. I couldn't afford to have anyone else in the company go on these calls. I couldn't risk any breach in the anonymity. I could've ended up sued for a small fortune.

Rarely would I meet directly with a celeb. I'd usually meet with the business manager, agent or security guard at an office or restaurant, then drive to the residence together. Often, I'd never even see the celeb. At the residence I'd set up the client's computer with secure Internet access and applications that were maintained on secure servers at one of TELXAR's co-location sites. I'd also be on call to repair whatever hardware needed servicing. If a celeb's computer breaks down, it can't just be brought to a regular computer-chain outlet's service department. Data could be taken off the hard drive, chunks of a person's private life. Each celeb client was assigned a security number. If a computer problem developed, I could be called at the office or on a toll-free line routed to my cell phone, and determine the account by the number. No names were used.

I did meet my fair share of famous faces. On the trip to the site I'd get into character, put my nervousness in check. Some of these people were very down to earth; others had their heads stuck in the clouds. I knew I had to go with the flow. Be polite. They lived on a different planet from the rest of us.

"Hello, Mr./Ms. so-and-so, I'm Jeff with TELXAR, so-and-so told me about you, I'm here to take care of your email." Sometimes the celeb would tell me to call him or her by the first name. Otherwise I'd remain formal. And I never, ever, asked for an autograph.

Some of the celebs were so security conscious, they wanted their children's Internet service protected, too. After all, their children had to go to school with bodyguards to shield them from the paparazzi. I learned very quickly that it takes a very strong person to be able to handle living in a fishbowl of fame. It made me appreciate my privacy even more. The celebs, in turn, appreciated that I didn't name-drop clients. They knew I would maintain their privacy.

TELXAR SOON HAD A growing client list of entertainers and agents, politicians and CEOs. The economy was still sluggish, and this market niche of network security was helping the company zip along. I considered that the niche might prove to be short-lived but in the meantime, it was bringing in revenue.

I didn't envy celebrities' fame. I value my privacy. Fortunately, in the computer industry, there are few people camping out on your lawn for autographs. Unless you're someone like Bill Gates or Steve Jobs, you're fairly safe. The most attention I'll ever get from a fan is a client saying, "Hey, Jeff, I appreciate that software package you wrote. I've been using it for five years. It's great."

The undesirability of the celebrity lifestyle was driven home to me one afternoon sitting in a trendy café in West Los Angeles with a Hollywood agent, who was meeting me to discuss my servicing his client, a star in film and music.

The hostess greeted the agent with a fawning, "Hello, Mr. White! Thanks for coming back to us! Where would you like to sit? Your usual table?"

"Yes, thank you."

We were led to the patio. Like me, he preferred a side table, where it's more private and you're not in full view where other diners can watch you eat. We sat, inhaling emissions from the traffic crawling past. I glanced at the menu. It was true L.A. chic: None of the entrées looked mouth-watering and filling. Tuna in fresh saltwater with seaweed wrap. And so on.

A waiter came to get our drink orders. The agent ordered a Perrier.

"Perrier?" I said. "I thought you were upscale."

"What are *you* having?" he asked.

"If you want a definitive bottled water, you order a San Pellegrino, with a lime wedge. You can taste the difference. I like both the waters. I choose to drink either one by occasion and availability."

He laughed. "For a guy from Nevada, you sure know a lot about fancy water."

That broke the ice. We hit it off. We small-talked. But before long, we began getting interrupted. Actors and actresses, both the established and those obviously trying to gain traction in the biz, would approach the table to say hello. An actress-model type with an impressively displayed front end (standard issue in Hollywood) sauntered up and nasally purred, "Oh, Mr. White, how are you doing?" It seemed exaggerated, just like in the movies.

Occasionally, a car horn would beep from out in the inching traffic and the driver would call out the agent's name and wave. The agent would raise a hand and flash a frozen smile.

"Don't you get tired of that?" I asked.

"You kind of grow into the environment," he said. "You gotta, to be successful here."

The restaurant was filling up. Celebrities whose faces I recognized from the movies or television were being seated at middle tables.

"Oh, they got the bad tables," I said.

"No, not in Hollywood," the agent said. "They sit in the middle so that everybody can see them and watch them."

It was all part of the game, he explained. They needed the visibility. They needed to stay on the industry radar.

"I could never be a celebrity," I said. "I don't envy them."

"I don't, either," he said. "They're like children, constantly needing attention and approval. They have a f*cked-up life and people don't realize that. To keep working, they have to stay in the public eye. And when they have kids, their kids end up in the *Enquirer*. There's absolutely no anonymity. It's the business we're in. If someone writes a bad article about you, you have to be able to laugh it off and remind yourself that you're beautiful and great. You have to have tough, tough skin, and be extremely shallow and vain, to survive in this business."

Image was paramount. It was practically everything. Talent seemed to run a distant second. It was only the very biggest stars who could afford not to play the game.

ONE ACTRESS HAD WORKED very hard to earn a part in a big movie, to re-energize her career. Now she was filming on location, and had brought her family with her. She was having a printer-driver issue on her laptop. She actually left a message herself on my cell phone. I flew down and drove out to the set. When you have a large service contract, you go wherever the client needs you.

I felt a bit uncomfortable since I'd worked directly with her business manager and had only met the actress once.

I met her in her trailer. It was during a break in filming.

I fixed the problem in two minutes. It was very minor — kind of a waste of a trip. I could have walked her through it over the phone.

"I really appreciate you flying out and taking care of this. I know it's a ridiculous request," she said.

"No, don't worry about it," I said. "This is what you pay me for."

She was very thankful. She started small-talking with me, on a personal level. That surprised me.

She asked if I was married. I said yes. Tanya and I had tied the knot a couple months before.

I normally wouldn't have dreamed of discussing non-computer business, but I said, "I wanted to tell you congratulations for this role. I thought you'd be good in it. I actually read the book when I was younger."

She was blown away. I could tell by her face she didn't think computer engineers even picked up novels.

She seemed moved. "Thank you very much. That was very sweet. Coming from someone who's not in the industry, appreciating art, that really means a lot."

That made my day. For that one instant, she was not a star, but a regular human being communicating directly with me, on a personal level.

That was so rare with my celebrity clients.

NOT EVERY SECURITY-CONSCIOUS client was worth taking on. More than a few celebs were intolerable.

There was a professional football star. We'll call him Leon. He was friends with a client of mine who had a vacation home at Tahoe. Leon was borrowing the house for the summer. He was staying there with his family as well as his entourage.

When I showed up, Ferraris and other pricy wheels lined the driveway. Inside, it was like a gangsta-rap video. There were 20 or 30 of Leon's homeboys partying, pimped out with bling, the stereo blasting with the bass thumping like a minor earthquake, voices shouting above the din, skunk clouds of chronic forming from giant joints.

I was out of place. A clean-cut, Oxford-and-Dockers, white computer technician. Faces grinned at me. I was a big joke.

I had to announce myself and go through a handful of people before I was finally passed on to Leon. "Hi, I'm with TELXAR. I'm here to look at the computer. I was told to ask for Leon."

I was finally led to a room where Leon was sprawled on a giant leather sofa, watching a movie on a big-screen TV.

"Hey, yo, wazzup man?" he said.

"Hello, sir, I'm here to take a look at the computer."

Leon brought me into the office where a workstation was set up. I got to work on it. It was just a matter of fixing access to the Internet so the computer could connect. I opened a few windows, checked out the preferences, made corrections.

Homeboys poked their heads into the room. There were comments. "Look at this motherf*cker. He's a brainiac on that computer."

"White boy looks like he knows that sh*t."

I finished up super quick.

"Goddamn, man!" Leon said. "I got computers at home I can't get fixed. You need to talk to me so we can hook up."

"Well, usually I work through the business manager," I said. "So have your manager call me. I cannot guarantee I will have time. I have a full case load right now." I gave him a card.

Indeed, the agent called a week later.

"I'm just not available now," I said. "I'm really too busy to take him on."

"Really? We can cover your rates."

"It's not about that," I said. "I'm overloaded right now. Plus, I'm phasing out individual clients."

"What am I supposed to tell Leon?"

"Tell him that I apologize. I'm so busy right now that I lack the logistics and ability to be able to service him in his other locations."

In truth, I was turned off after the first visit. Sports superstars can be more Hollywood than Hollywood stars.

And, anyway, the celeb accounts were getting out of hand. I had about 20 of them now, and it was almost more than I could handle while still keeping TELXAR moving ahead for the major accounts with the big companies.

But working for the stars had served its purpose. It had kept my company afloat in very stormy waters.

I ended up retaining a handful of the celebs as I focused on landing business from industrial giants.

CHAPTER FIFTY-SIX: Adieu to a Dotcom

The office suite in south Reno was too small for us now. I wanted to move TELXAR out. I also was upset with the landlord.

Rodney Sutton was from Southern California and had an attitude of coming to Nevada and milking the place for all he could. It was the opposite of the Nevada way of doing business by which people forge long-term trusting relationships as befits a small business community.

My first inkling of Sutton's greed had come when the building shell was being prepared for us to move in. I had to bring in a lot of fiber-optic, CAT-5, and power cables that would be run throughout the facility before the walls were to be Sheetrocked. The cable would run through the walls and to different connection points within the facility. Over a weekend, my employees and I laid the cable out in conduit where it would go. That way, after the walls were built, it'd be simple to hook the cable up.

I went in on Monday to check the status of the construction. The Sheetrockers were busy putting up the walls. Then I saw, at the back of the warehouse, a shocking sight. The cable — all $20,000 of it — had been piled in the back of the warehouse. I hurried over. I couldn't believe it. And even worse, the cable had been sliced into large pieces.

"Who cut all this cable?!" My voice roared at the top of my lungs, and echoed.

The workers stopped.

"You realize how much money this cable is?"

The foreman spoke up. "Well, it was in the way."

"It was in conduit!" I screamed. "You had no right to cut this cable. Everything was run the way it was supposed to."

The dope-smoking Sheetrockers hadn't wanted to work around the conduit laid out while they hung their Sheetrock. By watching them, I could see they were barely able to stand. The office reeked of pot and alcohol.

I called Rodney Sutton and told him to get down to the site as quickly as possible. I was pissed. "This is a deal-breaker!" I said.

Sutton already was in Reno. He came by the next day. He was dressed like an urban cowboy, in a Chaps shirt, jeans and $1,000 alligator-skin boots. His eyes grew wide at the sight of the piled up cable.

"They didn't cut it," he said.

"Yes they did."

"Well, how do you know they cut it?"

"I talked to the foreman."

Sutton didn't miss a beat.

"Well, I talked to him, too. He said they didn't cut it. He said someone came in and said the cable wasn't run to code and cut it up and piled it."

Sutton said all this with a straight face.

"Rodney, you're full of sh*t," I said. "They cut everything. They even cut the power cables. Why would someone cut power cables?"

Sutton finally agreed to pay to have the power recabled and granted me seven months off my lease.

The landlord-tenant friction continued. Sutton kept raising the CAM — common-area maintenance — fees above the agreed-upon rate. Our initial lease called for monthly rent of $1,600 and CAM fees of $300 a year. Now we were paying $2,000 a month with $700 in CAM fees. But that wasn't all. Our lease contract gave us the first right of refusal on both sides of the property, in case we needed to expand. Sutton put new tenants on either side without letting us exercise our option.

I told him that I was forced to move my growing company, even though it would cost me $100,000 to relocate. I also pointed out all the upgrades I'd made with the building's security system and power supply. That was $40,000 out of my pocket.

He told me I couldn't get out of the lease. Not true, I said; *he'd* broken it.

Sutton finally agreed to let me out of the lease. He must have figured I was small potatoes to him. He'd already bought hundreds of acres of Reno ranchland at bargain prices and was busy building even more business parks and residential subdivisions.

I resolved to move back to the industrial section of Sparks — something that was true-blue Nevada, not newcomer money. And that wasn't all. I was tired of the grind, just taking on every client and being treated as any other tech-support company. Now that TELXAR was specializing in enterprise services — meaning, serving large businesses, the biggest players in the market, with huge operations and integrated computer networks to connect the companies' many divisions and departments — I wanted to work solely with the mid-size to large, enterprise clients.

And I wanted clients who appreciated TELXAR for what we do.

AT THIS POINT, OUR list of clients had reached about 1,500, including in Canada, Europe, Australia and Japan. Our trademarked motto was, "Empowering the digital revolution!" We still provided turnkey service and kept our work in-house. In addition to the high-end, security-conscious celebrities I'd gotten as clients, we had telecom companies, Internet service providers, property-management firms, a broad array of retailers, construction companies, and more. We developed and hosted websites. We provided co-location services for the companies needing highly reliable networks, and didn't buy space in another company's data center and call it our own. We sold hardware for workstations, servers and routers. We wrote custom software, and didn't outsource the code writing. For clients who had 20 or more personal computers, we provided 24-hour service — keeping an edge on competitors who couldn't handle jobs outside normal workday hours. We charged flat instead of hourly rates for service calls. We made sure our phones could be answered 24-7.

I divested my business of all the pains in the ass, including the clients whose people would cuss at our engineers when they arrived. I kept the clients who treated us with respect — the same respect we gave them. Our company rule was that employees would always maintain politeness with clients, no matter how ugly a client became. Let the client be the bad guy. If the relationship was strained, I'd end it.

iDo fit into the bad-guy category.

IDO HAD BEEN WITH us a year when it hit its inevitable downward spiral with the rest of the shaky dotcoms. iDo's stock price plummeted so far that the company was at risk of being delisted by its exchange. There were massive layoffs. There was a big management shakeup. Sure enough, the company fell behind in paying our invoices.

It was mid-July. I'd just gotten married the previous Friday and was enjoying a vacation at Lahontan Reservoir with our friends. It was Tuesday, and Tanya and I were set to fly to Tahiti for two weeks, for our delayed honeymoon, later that day. Steve, my righthand man, called me on my cell phone. I was needed back at our office in Reno for an emergency meeting with iDo's executives, he said.

I had trouble maintaining my composure. I told Steve to relay to the iDo people that I was not clean-shaven, hadn't showered in two days due to the fact I was camping out at the lake with family. I was wearing a T-shirt and boarder shorts, and I'd be there.

I told Tanya, and she was quite a bit more than pissed.

I told her that she might as well come into town with me. So we had lunch in Reno, then drove to TELXAR. Tanya was still steaming. She sat in my office while I went into the conference room to wait for the dotcom people to arrive.

It was iDo's newly installed IT director who showed up. I didn't like him from the start. He was wearing a T-shirt and jeans. His attitude was aggressive. He told me that his company had just fired its team of web developers, the people TELXAR had worked closely with. The new IT director had a stack of our bills in front of him.

"We want to see the data center," he said. "We want to see what we're paying for. We want to lock all these people out."

I listened to him then calmly responded.

"First of all, you're not on my security contact list," I said. "Under contract I cannot speak with you unless your CEO emails or calls me to say you're the one for us to deal with."

We have very strict rules and security guidelines in place to protect our clients. Procedures had to be followed.

The IT director picked up his cell phone and called the CEO, Ben Starling. Starling spoke with me and confirmed that all the web developers had been terminated.

The IT director started reviewing our invoices. His lack of technical knowledge revealed itself very quickly, and made me wonder how he'd gotten the position. Whose ass had he kissed? What favors had he done someone?

"What is this item?" he asked.

"That's a power backup unit," I said.

"Why do we need them?"

"It keeps your equipment up if the power goes out."

"Show me. Let me see what it looks like."

I took him back to the racks where we had iDo's servers and showed him the backup units.

The IT director continued through the invoices, trying to nickel and dime me, getting me to discount charges.

I was being very patient despite the circumstances. I politely responded.

"Listen," I said. "These are the prices. This is what it is. Twenty-four hours a day we're at your beck and call. We've updated your routers at 2 in the morning. And we were the ones who found all the security issues with your site." I told him about our discovery that customers' credit-card numbers had been left unprotected for three years, accessible to any Internet browser. TELXAR had discreetly fixed it, then notified the development team of the repaired issue.

"I'm not willing to discount our labor for you," I said.

"Well, we can get this somewhere else," he said.

"Have you realized that we're the only co-location facility in Northern Nevada? Good luck!"

"We can find a place in California."

"Fine. Let me know when you're ready and I'll shut your servers down."

The IT director started accusing us of mismanaging the dotcom's equipment, of causing the network to be down too often.

I begged to differ. Their equipment and software had suffered almost no downtime since we'd been servicing them. Steve was so irate I had to physically hold my arm between him and the IT director.

"You just fired all your web developers," I said. "Who's going to code your sites now? We're the only ones who know how the sites work."

The meeting ended.

I called iDo's chief financial officer and told him what I'd told the IT director: We weren't going to reduce our prices. The prices were fair. Even though we had his company over a barrel — since we were the ones who'd worked with iDo's development team, helping it code websites — we weren't charging higher-than-normal rates. In fact we were 40 percent cheaper than the closest competitor.

The CFO still wanted to negotiate. His company was paying us $1,700 a month to host its servers, but an Arizona company was only going to charge $100.

I'd heard enough.

"Go for it," I said. "Friday, come pick your equipment up. I want you out of my facility."

It took iDo's workers all day to remove the racks of equipment.

The company ended up getting delisted from the stock exchange, then acquired by another company. iDo closed its Reno headquarters and moved elsewhere.

Its bright young CEO with the Stanford MBA started a venture-capital company. A press release I read about Ben Starling described him as a "serial entrepreneur."

Eventually, the Securities & Exchange Commission went after Starling and iDo's former CFO and its senior vice president of sales, alleging the trio had fraudulently overstated the company's revenues by millions of dollars.

CHAPTER FIFTY-SEVEN: Marks of Success

One night as I prepared to leave TELXAR, I had a flashback. As usual, I'd been the last one in the workplace, catching up on paperwork. I shut my office door, turned off all the lights. In the darkness, I loved to watch the blinking LEDs of the servers, like a little constellation. I marveled at the tiered black racks in the data center, holding secured servers for systems of some of our clients. Business was literally humming. It still gave me a charge to behold those servers working away.

Then suddenly, I was transported back to seven years before — to a humbler scene.

There I was, working in a pair of underpants in my tiny bedroom in the house I shared with my close friend, Drew. I was sweating; the room was almost as hot as a dry sauna from the workings of three computers, hosting servers for the handful of clients I had for my seat-of-the-pants, startup business, CYBERWORKS.

This fledgling venture had started spontaneously, like a microcosmic big bang, the very day I'd quit a job managing a manufacturing plant. I'd walked out, bought a cell phone, paid for a business license, and started making cold calls to small businesses. *April 23, 1999.*

Now it was seven years later. I had a lot more to my name than a cell phone and a Chevrolet Blazer with 120,000 miles on it.

I left the TELXAR offices and drove home in my new Chevy Silverado through the suburban sprawl of Sparks. I pulled up to my house. The lights were on; my young wife was inside, caring for our two young daughters, Taylor and Jessie. The RV was parked in the driveway. My workshop was around back, with the tools I used to work on my jet skis, trucks and cars. I had more toys than I needed. And I had assets. Savings, investments, a real-estate investment firm I have since sold.

Wow, I'd thought. *I've made it.*

And then, a reflexive jolt:

I need to sell some of this stuff! I'd rather have cash in the bank . . .

You can't escape your past, no matter how far you've come. Inside me would always be a 6-year-old boy, sitting in a dinky apartment, drinking powdered milk because the fresh kind was too expensive.

This little panic attack passed. But not the lingering notion that all my material blessings could be taken away, in a flash, by any of the number of disasters that can befall a business owner.

AS I WRITE THIS, my company is seven years old, and I've managed to retain majority ownership.

How successful is TELXAR?

To measure success in pure dollar terms is pretty shortsighted. A better mark is whether the company is making enough money to sustain itself without outside investors. It is. TELXAR was built on a solid foundation because my philosophy was to grow only through profits. Recently I've pondered taking on investment capital. That's the reality of reaching a certain size. TELXAR can't continue entering new markets without new capital.

A second mark of success, equally as important as the first, is whether the company provides great products or services to its clients. TELXAR does. I'm a perfectionist by nature. When I bid on an account, I'll factor in enough hours for our team to do a 100 percent perfect job. We offer quick response, 24 hours a day. We outhustle the big, clumsy firms. That means we can get underbid by some companies. But I know that these companies will end up doing such an insufficient job, rushing through everything, that the client will likely call us up later and bring us in to fix the mess the first contractor created. TELXAR gets it right the first time. This saves the client money over the long run. We're very proud of that.

A third mark of success is whether the company is making enough money to provide my family a decent lifestyle with a house and cars, and pay off all our bills. It is.

I don't go in for flaunting wealth. I don't wear a lot of jewelry. I have my Seiko watch: functional, with the date and time, but not gaudy or pretentious. I wear a silver necklace because I bought it in Cancun, Mexico, when I proposed to my wife. That's what the necklace symbolizes. My gold wedding ring is custom-made and designed with ocean waves to remind me of rocky and smooth times in a relationship, and also represents my love of the water. Again, no diamond-studded rings for me.

I just don't see value in ostentation. How useful is a Ferrari? Consider the outrageous expense of insuring such a luxury vehicle. I like driving fast cars, but if I want to race a Ferrari I'll go to a track and rent one. My old lifted Chevy Blazer suits me fine. It's reliable, it represents me, and I love Chevy products. It's practical. Same with our house. Tanya and I and our two daughters live in a small house. It meets our needs. There's our bedroom, the girls' bedrooms, a living room, two baths and a kitchen. There's a workshop I've built in back. There's a back yard that doesn't take me hours to mow and trim. The house is livable and doesn't need a housekeeper to keep tidy.

If I splurge on anything, it's the RV, my jet skis, the two dirt bikes, and the quad I bought for Tanya. But these are recreational toys, not symbols of status. And as for the RV, it will eventually serve a business purpose, allowing me to travel in comfort to each of my business locations without flying and staying in hotels.

BUT THERE'S A FOURTH measure of a company's success: how strongly it can run by itself, with the employees I've hired, so that I can enjoy time away to enjoy my success. After all, time is our most precious resource, a commodity you can't buy.

That fourth mark of success is the hardest to achieve. This is because it's always more difficult finding decent people to work for you than it is drumming up more business. By decent, I mean people who come to work motivated to do well, whom I can train to run the business the way I want it run, and who can perform vital functions so that I don't have to perform them myself.

As I write this chapter, we have clients worldwide. We've written an application that helps automate our entire business.

We're valuable to our clients and our clients are very valuable to us. Even though I'm the CEO of TELXAR, I'm always swamped with work. But this is work that I love. I have been fighting, hustling, and dreaming to be at this point. It's hard to resist expanding the business. I've met my life's goals set in my teen years: to own a profitable business, get married, own a house and have children.

Since I'm goal-oriented, I've set some new goals.

I'd like TELXAR to have close to 100 employees in 25 offices nationwide, and make a big dent in the Information Technology market. I'd like to go after the midsize to enterprise, $330 billion IT market. I'd like to shake up the whole industry. The IT industry can be run a lot cleaner and more efficiently than it is.

I know I can't remain the brain and heart of TELXAR. The company must be set up to keep going without me, or any specific CEO. A viable corporation can't be structured around one person. I'm not worried about taking care of my family. Savings, investments and insurance will do that. My motivation for preserving TELXAR is because it's needed in the world. I want to grow it as big as I can. If either of my two daughters wants to run the company when she's grown, she'll have the opportunity. Same with my niece. But even if none of them does, I want the company to continue on. I want TELXAR to outlive me.

THERE ARE OTHER CHALLENGES for me.

Ideas continually pop into my head. I jot them down. I estimate I've come up with about 1,000 ideas for inventions so far. I have hired a large international law firm to start patenting these ideas. The creative flow is so relentless that, ironically, I've created a software package to manage my ideas. I've thought about developing this package for sale to inventors. I've written a program that helps inventors log in their ideas and track their development. Another entrepreneurial idea I have is to form a company to market my inventions.

Yet another of my dreams is to raise enough money to start an incubator park in Reno where entrepreneurs and inventors could develop startup businesses from their innovative ideas. And that's related to still *another* idea for priming the computer industry: hiring a grant writer to raise industry money to build a training center for young students talented in computers, so they can enter the IT workforce with real-world skills. It would be a technical school to teach students not only about working on computers, but also how to handle clients professionally and be valuable, productive employees.

Every young employee I've hired at TELXAR has had to be retrained. There's so much I want to see instilled in new employees, including work ethic and a good attitude. How to work harder and smarter. It's senseless to have job descriptions so narrow that one person is charged with placing orders, and another is responsible for adding printers. A well-trained employee can wear many hats. America's gotten so lazy! My competitors could be so much more efficient with fewer employees if those employees were properly trained to begin with.

I love working with young minds. TELXAR sponsors a program for high schoolers. When school counselors come across students proficient on computers, TELXAR will donate workstations and software to the school to nurture their talent. One of my young employees, Stuart, came out of this mentoring program. My employees are far better trained and productive than their counterparts at our competitors. That's why TELXAR does more business even though we have a smaller labor force.

My ultimate mission in life is to develop products that people can use. I see so much inferior software and hardware on the market that I want to provide better goods. I'm an innovator, a creator. I like to make stuff that enhances the way we live. I'm not after profit or fame, really. I just wish to be respected by my peers, to be recognized for contributing to the field.

My biggest regret is that there are only 24 hours in the day. So often I hate turning in to bed at night, knowing there's so much more I yearn to have gotten done. It's no wonder I'm an insomniac.

The best analogy I can apply to my drive to produce is I'm like a kid who's having so much fun playing outside, he keeps on going even after it grows dark and he's late for dinner. He only goes home because everyone else has finally left.

IF I HADN'T FOUNDED TELXAR, I'd be a CEO of some other outfit. Running a company is all I ever wanted to do, ever since I was a first-grader dressing up in a suit and carrying a briefcase to school on Fridays. I love business. I love making things happen. I love coming to work. I love interacting with people. I love helping clients out and saving them money. TELXAR is one of the most respected IT firms on the West Coast.

My wife often asks me, "Why do you work so hard?" I tell her it's because the deprivations of childhood are a powerful motivator. It's because I remember what it's like to not have milk in the refrigerator. To not share toys with other kids because if a toy got broken, I'd be in trouble. To move from one living situation to the next. And, when I got out of the Army, to live in the back of a shop and shower with a garden hose.

I never want to go back to those hardships. It's always better to control your world than be controlled by it.

My background has left me with shortcomings. I don't trust many people, given the constant upheaval in my life during my formative years. I'm always suspicious of someone trying to work an angle, to take advantage of my business or me, to try for that sweet taste of getting one over on someone else, which is part of human nature.

Mom always said it takes years to build trust with someone — and one second to break it. It's the absolute truth! So many people lack character nowadays. It's like the truth ain't in 'em.

I'm always appreciative of business, because the moment you grow smug or cocky, you're heading for a fall. I watched that happen not too long ago with a former employee who liked to show up an hour or two late to meetings with my clients just as a mind game to impress upon the clients how important he was. Such arrogance is too rampant in the IT industry.

I keep my mind focused on the elements of success: honesty, openness, hard work, taking care of the client's needs. Core business values.

Humility and dedication are the keys. Not dumb pride.

I'M SO GOAL-DRIVEN that my greatest satisfaction in life is achieving a goal. It's a real high. There are so many times when each and every one of us falls short, that when I reach a goal it makes up for all the frustrating and disappointing times. The sense of accomplishment is invigorating and exhilarating: the stuff of life! It's a feeling that can't be bought. And it spurs me on to setting my next goal.

One of the best feelings I've had was when TELXAR was really beginning to make money for the first time, sustaining itself, and I flew to Las Vegas with a client, the COO of an ad agency, to work on the system at his agency's Vegas office. I felt buoyant, undefeatable. *Wow,* I thought, *it hasn't even been a year yet, and I have a successful business, I have faithful employees managing accounts, I'm on a plane with a big client, I don't have bill collectors coming after me. This is great!*

As I considered how far my company had come in such a short time, my face broke out in a giant grin. And I wore that grin for the entire one-hour flight.

It was simple euphoria. And I've found that this high only comes from reaching a hard-strived-for goal.

That's what most people don't ever understand. You can get high on drugs, indulge in other addictions, seek thrills. But the euphoria that fills you up from head to toe when you realize you've reached a summit after an arduous climb — especially if you've failed on previous attempts — is unequaled.

Accomplishing something that few dare to do, such as building a business from scratch, and then realizing one day that it's become strong, thriving, growing, fulfilling your every wish — it's like a genie that's popped out of the bottle and granted your wish.

Over and over in business since then, when TELXAR has reached an objective, I've experienced deep satisfaction. I live for it.

I know that this is a trait that large corporations look for in high-end executives: goal-oriented achievers who are all too happy to toil into the wee hours, night after night, until a goal is met. Hard drivers who don't look at work as work, but as a journey.

It may sound funny, but I don't mind facing new problems. To me, they're opportunities to find solutions. When problems surface, it means you're breaking fresh ground in the business, restructuring, reorienting, moving forward. Not stagnating, not succumbing to the status quo. I like problems because I like to see how to solve them. And I'm committed to staying on a problem until I've found a solution for it.

Maybe I'm a stress junkie, but I've always performed well in periods of crisis. I like pressure.

That's why I'm in business. You see: If you never quit you'll never fail!

CONCLUSION

The opportunities we have to achieve in this world are astounding, limited only by our minds. This is true for each and every one of us. Sometimes I'm amazed by what I've been able to do just by daring to do so.

My philosophy of life is to live it. Not to analyze it, or try to understand why we're here, or search for some great truth, some grand destiny, some purpose tied to a higher being.

Why are we here? It seems pretty plain and self-evident to me. Look around. There's one answer: To live.

It's to be the best person you can be, live as long as you can, then you're done. We each have such a short time on this planet, and it's such a beautiful planet with such a wide array of things to do on it, that you should pursue your passions to your heart's desire. I define a "passion" as something you don't have to do, but want to do, because it defines part of you. The opportunities to pursue your passion are really only limited by your mind.

What you *shouldn't* do is waste your mind and time in contemplation, angst, despair.

I'm successful today because I determined that in my life I'd become successful. I didn't have a road map, but I kept pushing forward until something clicked. That something happened to be my computer company. Every day,

I'm ensuring my ongoing success because I'm working at it.

Life is a constant process. Nothing is guaranteed. You do the best you can to prepare, and to continue achieving and growing. I could get hit by a car tomorrow, but I've made sure my family is protected financially. I could get sued and have my business taken away from me. But if that were to happen, I'd just pick myself up and start a new business.

To me, that's what life should be about. Always fighting. And never quitting.

IN THE LAST ANALYSIS, I've written this book — as I mentioned in the author's note — to inspire readers, especially entrepreneurs, to take a chance on life.

I'm not like some writers, who hope to change at least *one* person's life. I'm a businessman. I'd like to change *thousands* of lives. Especially the lives of people with ambition who feel stuck in an unhappy job that wastes their talent, their time, their spirit, their soul.

If you're in this category, then I hope you've enjoyed reading this book. And I hope you'll do one more thing after finishing this last page:

Take some time off, perhaps a weekend, go somewhere quiet, and think about what you really want to do in life. Plan out intelligently the steps that will get you there. Then, as soon as it's feasible, get out of your current career and go do what you were meant to do!

I've met enough millionaires who are completely unspectacular. They just worked hard. A few didn't even do that; they just were in the right place at the right time. One guy I know, worth $80 million, can barely tie his shoes.

Most of life's hurdles are not put there by others, they are put there by ourselves. I believe in myself and you should believe in yourself. You can do it. You just have to believe and execute.

Always remember: If you never quit, you'll never fail!